Chopin in Paris

The Life and Times of the Romantic Composer

TAD SZULC

A LISA DREW BOOK

SCRIBNER

A LISA DREW BOOK/SCRIBNER
1230 Avenue of the Americas
New York, NY 10020

Set in Adobe Garamond

DESIGNED BY ERICH HOBBING

Manufactured in the United States of America

1   3   5   7   9   10   8   6   4   2

Library of Congress Cataloging-in-Publication Data
Szulc, Tad.
Chopin in Paris : the life and times of the romantic composer / Tad Szulc.
p.   cm.
"A Lisa Drew book."
Includes bibliographical references and index.
1. Chopin, Frédéric, 1810–1849. 2. Composers—Biography. I. Title.
ML410.C54S895   1998
786.2´092—dc21   97-36402
[B]
CIP

ISBN 0-684-82458-2

This book is in memory
of my grandfather
BERNARD BARUCH,
a Warsaw amateur pianist

Contents

Preface

FRYDERYK CHOPIN EXPRESSED everything he had to say to the world through his music, according to one of the most eminent performers of his works, and this unquestionably is true. The depth and the breadth of his creation is extraordinary, from love to furious anger, from joy to endless sadness and melancholy, from tenderness to pride and defiance. Its beauty and enchantment are supreme. Unpredictability and mystery are, of course, part of art, and his compositions are rich in them and ever surprising to the listener. He was, by contemporary accounts, one of the greatest and most innovative pianists of the nineteenth century. And, finally, he was a splendid teacher.

Chopin's music was admired, analyzed, applauded, compared, critiqued, criticized, described, discussed, dissected, examined, and judged to an exhaustive extent even before he died at the age of thirty-nine a century and half ago, and the fascination has continued ever since. Timeless, it arouses, bewitches, caresses, and charms today as it did at its first hearing.

What Chopin's music says *about* him (and whether it does so at all) is an impossible and probably idle philosophical, psychological, and aesthetic question. Few specific compositions, if any, seem to reflect his mood or the state of his health at the particular moment of creation—add to that the fact that often we have no exact dates for the completion of a given work and only know that sometimes years elapsed between the start and finish of a composition. Some of the merrier, upbeat mazurkas and polonaises, for example, were conceived when he was believed to be quite ill and/or depressed—while sad, wistful nocturnes and ballades were written when he was thought to be well and at his amusing and playful best. Then there are études and préludes, in the same cycle, wholly distinct from others in mood.

A private individual, Chopin was the least helpful in unveiling the mysteries of creation—or the mysteries with which he chose to surround himself. Who, then, was Fryderyk Chopin?

My fascination with this man of genius provided the overwhelming reason for writing this book. I wanted to present in an entirely new light—often in his own words and words of those close to him—this immensely complex man, his time, joys, frustrations and tragedies, hopes and defeats, illusions and hallucinations, and the frightening physical and mental suffering he bore.

That Chopin was a genius, that he was both part of the breakthrough Romantic movement in the arts and a romantic figure in his own right—he was loved by a succession of extraordinary women, first and foremost George Sand—and that he regarded himself as an ardent Polish patriot when his homeland was under brutal foreign occupation, have long been the stuff of the Chopin legend. In a literal sense, it was all true. It was also true that he had displayed astonishing courage, discipline, and willpower—as well as a very special brand of quiet, self-deprecating humor—in fighting to the very end the terrible illness that destroyed him.

Uncounted millions of words in Polish, French, English, and many other languages were written about Chopin in newspapers, magazines, books, and encyclopedias of the day, and memoirs and letters from as early as the 1830s, when he first set foot, barely twenty-one years old, in Paris, determined to conquer. More than a century and half later, however, he remains an elusive personage.

I have always felt that the human dimension was missing, that I could not really understand the man. So, rather than embark on a standard birth-to-death biography, I decided to concentrate on the eighteen years Chopin lived in France, or nearly half his life, because this was both musically and personally his richest (and would prove most mature) period, when he lived side by side with the most remarkable creative men and women of the century. It offered a unique cast of magnificent characters—the people Chopin had befriended, those with whom he had associated professionally. And I believe that the artistic, personal, and political closeness of his circle (never replicated anywhere else to the best of my knowledge) played a crucial role in fashioning the quality and scope of culture of that era in Europe: Sand, Balzac, Hugo, Lamartine, Delacroix, and Heine; Franchomme, Liszt, Berlioz, Schumann, Mendelssohn, Bellini, and Rossini—as well as the Rothschild bankers. They were all among Chopin's friends and acquaintances; even Karl Marx was on the periphery. And *Chopin in Paris* represents an effort to grasp that human dimension.

To command a sense of Paris in Chopin's time, I visited the eight locations where he had lived between 1831 and 1849. With the exception of one location on the Chaussée d'Antin and the house in Chaillot, they remain exactly as they were in his day; Paris does not change very much. Square d'Orléans, where he lived the longest, looks today just as it did in the 1840s, to judge from contemporary sketches and drawings. The building on place Vendôme, where he died, is unchanged (though the address now faces the Ritz, opposite). *Le grand siècle de Paris* by André Castelot, *La curieuse aventure des boulevards extérieurs* by Jean Valmy-Baysse, *Listening in Paris* by James H. Johnson, and *The Love Affair as a Work of Art* by Dan Hofstadter added to my knowledge of Parisian life and culture at the time. About Nohant, which I visited during my research in France, I found *Chopin chez George Sand à Nohant—Chronique de sept étés* by Sylvie Delaigue-Moins to be immensely helpful. Nohant, two hundred miles south of Paris, was Sand's country home.

I went to Żelazowa Wola near Warsaw, Chopin's birthplace, and to the monastery of Valldemosa in Majorca, where Chopin and Sand spent five horrid months, years before I conceived the idea of writing the composer's biography. But the images remained clear in my memory. Chopin's Warsaw (partly rebuilt after World War II) is basically unchanged in appearance although the Saxon Palace is gone. Vienna is still Vienna. In London, two out of the three buildings where Chopin lived are still very much there.

This is therefore the story of Chopin and his friends (and enemies) and contemporaries. It is *not* a study of Chopin's music because I am neither a musician nor a musicologist—and because his music has received the distinguished attention of generations of outstanding composers, performers, and critics, from Liszt, Schumann, and Berlioz to Wilhelm von Lenz, Frederick Niecks, Bronisław Edward Sydow, Alfred Cortot, Arthur Hedley, Jim Samson, Jean-Jacques Eigeldinger, Charles

Rosen, Krystyna Kobylańska, Mieczysław Tomaszewski, Tadeusz Zieliński, and Hanna Wróblewska-Straus. Their works have made it possible for me to place Chopin and his life in the context of his music. I have, of course, learned much from all the above.

Chopin's life ran on parallel and frequently overlapping tracks: his music, his physical and mental health, his personal relationships with his family, his relationships with women (most notably George Sand) and friends—and his sense of Polishness and patriotism. I have found it more judicious to abstain from categorical judgments concerning, for example, blame in the Chopin-Sand rupture; some earlier biographers have chosen to take sides. Admirably, Sand's best biographer, André Maurois, allows history to tell the story, a fine precedent. Enough written material exists to let readers reach their own conclusions over this emotionally charged relationship.

Notwithstanding the huge volume of work concerned with Chopin, I found surprisingly few of the more thorough biographical studies satisfactory or effective in terms of conveying Chopin's personality lucidly. Perhaps the most important, useful, and insightful are Niecks's biography, first published in London in 1902, and Zieliński's biography, published in Warsaw in 1993. Chopin's first biographer, Marceli Antoni Szulc (sadly, no relation), published his work in Poznań, Poland, in 1873. Both Niecks and Szulc had the advantage of having known or corresponded with people who were Chopin's friends or acquaintances.

Under the circumstances, my reliance—and my entire voyage of discovery into Chopin's time—was on his own correspondence with his family in Poland; the surviving (but very limited) correspondence between him and Sand; Chopin's correspondence with men and women friends, acquaintances, publishers, bankers, tradesmen, and "unknown addressees"; Sand's correspondence with her own family and a vast array of friends and acquaintances; and, very importantly, correspondence between third parties about Chopin and/or Sand.

Equally important were memoirs and journals, starting with Sand's massive four-volume *Story of My Life* (there are autobiographical and Chopin-related clues as well in many of her novels, such as *Lucrezia Floriani*), Chopin's twenty-four-page diary confined to the early 1830s, and memoirs by those well acquainted with him. Outstanding among them are the diaries of Eugeniusz Skrodzki, a Warsaw family friend, the diaries of Józefa Kościelska, the sister of Maria Wodzińska whom

Chopin had come close to marrying, and who was present during the courtship period; the diaries by Chopin's childhood friend Józef Brzowski, a musician who saw him often during the formative years in Paris; and the diaries by Klementyna Tańska Hoffman, a refugee from war-torn Warsaw who became an articulate chronicler of Polish emigrés in Paris. *Chopin, Pianist and Teacher, as Seen by His Pupils,* assembled by Eigeldinger, is a priceless collection of reminiscences by Chopin's students, describing him, his moods, and his teaching methods and style.

Delacroix's *Journal* provides insights into Chopin's thinking on art, philosophy, and even science. As close friends, the two men held lengthy discussions on these themes over more than a decade of frequent get-togethers.

Chopin and Sand's correspondence presents, however, a tantalizing problem: It is grievously incomplete. In his case, approximately four hundred letters and notes (some one-liners) have been preserved out of a total that may have exceeded one thousand—although he professed to detest letter writing. The most revealing thoughts, moods, and impressions are found in Chopin's letters to his parents and sisters (and later their husbands and children) in Warsaw. Many of them are extremely long and they offer, among other things, colorful reportage on life around him in France (and earlier in Vienna), acute social and political critique, and dollops of society gossip.

But only forty-seven of them, over the eighteen-year period, have survived. There are no letters home, for example, for the years 1826, 1827, 1833, 1834, and between 1837 and 1843 (the high point of his life with Sand); for 1832, 1835, 1836, 1846, and 1849 (the year of his death), there is only one letter extant for each of these years, and only two letters from 1848 have survived. Krystyna Kobylańska, the leading authority on the Chopin correspondence, points out that it can be deduced from Chopin's father's letters that the composer must have written at least twenty more letters than we know. By the same token, no letters to Chopin from his family, who were fanatic letter writers, exist for 1830, 1838–1840, 1843, 1846, and 1847. Reading the existing letters, one becomes painfully aware of the enormous gaps in the available materials, compounding the difficulties in trying to reconstruct Chopin's life.

Most of his letters home were burned on September 19, 1863, when in retaliation for a bomb attempt on the life of Warsaw's Russian governor, Count Berg, Russian troops set fire to the midtown Zamoyski Palace in front of which the attack had occurred. Izabela and Antoni Barciński, Chopin's sister and brother-in-law, who occupied an apartment in the palace, had inherited Fryderyk's letters home after the elder Chopins died, and most of the correspondence they kept went up in flames along with portraits of Chopin, the furniture, and other belongings. Antoni Jędrzejewicz, one of Chopin's nephews, wrote that it was "a miracle" that any letters at all were saved. Most of the family letters to Chopin, sent to Warsaw after his death by Jane Stirling, his Scottish "official widow," must have perished in a similar fashion.

Out of an estimated four hundred letters exchanged between Chopin and George Sand, twenty-three from him and nine from her have survived. We have, however, their farewell letters, sealing the breakup in 1847. Ludwika Jędrzejewicz, Chopin's older sister, who was at his bedside when he died, is believed to have taken most of Sand's letters to Poland, leaving them (for unclear reasons) with friends at a provincial estate. Alexandre Dumas *fils,* the novelist and a friend of Sand, had subsequently visited that estate and was given the letters (also for reasons that are unclear). He turned them over to George Sand, who burned them. Twenty-one letters from Chopin to Solange Dudevant Clésinger, Sand's daughter, and seven from her to the composer have been preserved.

Fortunately preserved are most of Chopin's numerous letters to Wojciech Grzymała and Julian Fontana, his close Polish friends in Paris, and they are essential in understanding how he lived and operated during his years in France—as are Sand's letters to Grzymała.

Put together, all these letters, memoirs, and other materials have made it possible to reconstruct, at least to some degree, Chopin's personae and his environment. Many of the letters, especially the chatty ones, create the illusion that one is listening to casual, gossipy conversations—sometimes I had the impression I was interviewing Fryderyk, George, and the others. Given such a mind-set, it was frustrating not to be able to ask follow-up questions, to learn more, to challenge and clarify. Such are reporters' and biographers' dreams.

It should be noted that the bulk of the extant materials is in Polish and French; most of it has not previously been translated into English or other languages, except for excerpts from some of the correspondence. The two-volume edition of Chopin's correspondence, assembled and edited by Sydow, consists of letters written in Polish and French (with translations from French into Polish, the collection having been aimed at Polish audiences). Niecks has translated into English some relevant passages of Chopin's and others' letters and a few diary entries. As far as I know, none of the Polish diaries have been translated in extenso.

This explains why I have decided not to include chapter notes in this book: All the sources are identified in the text, in addition to the listing above of the most outstanding Chopin scholars and the bibliography.

Why did I become interested in Chopin as a subject for biography, after a lifetime of political and political-biographical writing? The short answer, of course, is that, in my opinion, no adequate Chopin biography exists in any language, and that I felt that, at the approach of the 150th anniversary of his death (October 1999), the time had come to make a new attempt. I hope to have done it justice.

But there are a few very personal reasons as well. My paternal grandfather was an amateur pianist and a Chopin worshiper, and as a child in Warsaw, I certainly heard a great deal of Chopin's music—music that has remained embedded in my subconscious mind. I also had the privilege of knowing, most pleasantly, Artur Rubinstein, the greatest performer of Chopin in our time, as a family friend, and heard him play both in person and on record. And a personal note: My wife and I spent our honeymoon listening for hours to the music of Chopin played by a dear old friend in the library of a great mansion in Mount Kisco, New York. In retrospect, perhaps I was fated to make this attempt at bringing Chopin back to life.

Prelude

LATE IN THE AFTERNOON of the last Tuesday of September, 1831, Fryderyk Franciszek Chopin, just six months past his twenty-first birthday, entered the great city of Paris, determined to conquer it—and quietly prepared to die there long before reaching old age. Both prophecies would be fulfilled.

Along with fifteen fellow passengers, Chopin arrived in an impossibly overcrowded public stagecoach from Strasbourg on the final leg of his exhausting two-week journey from Stuttgart in Germany where he had first experienced—and described—the choking sensation of being a "living corpse."

Slim and pale, five feet seven inches tall, almost feminine in his blue-eyed, blond delicacy, Fryderyk Chopin was born in a village near Warsaw in 1810, the Polish son of a Frenchman who had settled in Poland. Now, in turn, Chopin, the genius musician, was bringing Poland to France, yet remaining unassailably Polish until the moment his breathing ceased.

Two months before he left his native Warsaw on November 2, 1830, for Vienna, Germany, and Paris, "Frycek" (the diminutive of Fryderyk used among family and friends) wrote his closest friend: "I think that I am leaving to forget forever about home; I think that I'm leaving to die—and how unpleasant it must be to die elsewhere, not where one had lived."

He was a Polish patriot to his bones and the divinely inspired romantic poet of Polish music. He had composed his first polonaise when he was seven years old and his first two mazurkas at fifteen. Strangely, how-

ever, Chopin never returned—by deliberate and unexplained choice—
to his homeland.

Fittingly, one of Chopin's first impressions of Paris was a touch of Poland,
a bizarre but nevertheless welcoming sign: The diligence, pulled by two
huge Hanoverian horses, reached the hilltop village of St. Maur as the setting sun's red rays illuminated Paris, presenting the composer's avid eyes
with a stunning spectacle. He was seeing, after all, the "capital of the world,"
bisected by the Seine and, beyond it, the Left Bank hill of Montparnasse.
Ten minutes later, the stagecoach entered the Porte de St. Martin, one of
the gateways to Paris, still a walled city. Peering out of the small side window on his right, Chopin could discern a square structure covered with colorful posters. It was the Theater of the Porte de St. Martin, and the
performance announced for that evening was *La vieillesse de Stanislas* ("The
Old Age of Stanislas"), a preposterously lachrymose epic on Polish themes.

Chopin might not have realized it as he reached Paris, but France
in the autumn of 1831 was seized with an enormous outpouring of pro-
Polish sentiment. Early in September, Warsaw had been captured by the
besieging Russian armies, and it marked the end of the heroic though
dreadfully ill-directed nine-month national uprising against the czar
who had ruled Poland as king since the Congress of Vienna (1815) and
the close of the Napoleonic era in Europe. Poland had not existed as a
sovereign nation since the final decade of the previous century, when it
had been partitioned by Russia, Prussia, and Austria, and its rebel cause
fervently supported by most Frenchmen.

The failure of the supposedly liberal French constitutional monarchy,
in power since the revolution of July 1830, to come to the aid of the
uprising had led to massive pro-Polish riots in Paris. A week or so before
Chopin's arrival, a demonstration in sympathy with Poland had been
held at the Porte de St. Martin Theater. It was triggered by the news of
the fall of Warsaw on September 8, and the cynical announcement by
the French foreign minister at the Chamber of Deputies that "Order
Now Reigns in Warsaw."

France was not alone in turning its back on the Poles. In Rome, Pope
Gregory XVI condemned them in an encyclical letter, describing these
freedom fighters as "certain intriguers and spreaders of lies, who under
the pretense of religion in this unhappy age, are raising their heads
against the power of princes." With papal power challenged by simultaneous rebellions across Italy, Gregory XVI regarded all European upris-

ings, starting with Poland, as an imminent peril to the established order. Austria, naturally, took the side of its Russian allies. Chopin, in Vienna when the Warsaw revolt broke out, found himself virtually ostracized overnight along with fellow Poles there.

Although Chopin had left Warsaw a year earlier, convinced that his musical career could prosper only in Western Europe and most notably in Paris, the national uprising and its ultimate collapse were unquestionably among the reasons—if not excuses—for his decision never to set foot in Poland again. He had departed Vienna for Paris via Germany on July 20, 1831, when a triumph of the rebellion still seemed possible, and it does not follow that even in the absence of revolutionary turmoil (even with a patriotic victory) Chopin would ever have gone home. He had already made his decision.

While maintaining extremely warm, loving ties with his parents and two sisters in Warsaw, Frycek preferred under all circumstances to create his private "Little Poland" in Paris.

As it happened, word of Warsaw's conquest by the czarist armies had caught him in Stuttgart, where he had stopped for a few days en route from Vienna to Paris, and he did react with a paroxysm of fury and despair that he recorded in his diary. This outburst is believed to have inspired his extraordinary Étude in C minor, which subsequently became famous as the "Revolutionary" Étude. It was actually completed in Paris late in 1831 or 1832, contrary to myth, and published in 1833. And it was Ferenc Liszt who first called it "Revolutionary," having himself composed the first movement of his "Revolutionary" Symphony in 1830 in honor of that year's Paris revolution.

Because Chopin wrote and compulsively rewrote, fine-tuned, and chiseled (his word) all his works, sometimes over months or even years from the conception, and because most of the original manuscripts carry no dates, it is impossible to determine precisely when and where he had first conceived and begun to compose the "Revolutionary" Étude— or, for that matter, the exact time any of his creations were born. Moreover, he very seldom wrote or spoke of compositions in progress.

Although the idea of the "Revolutionary" Étude may well have been nurtured that sleepless night in Stuttgart, it must have taken a good while to mature. But Chopin is not known to have ever discouraged the myth that this great two-and-a-half-minute study was set down at the peak of his emotional trauma at Warsaw's surrender. Even before that catastrophe, in 1829 or 1830, he wrote the Polonaise in G minor, his first dramatic-heroic polonaise, but it was not published until seventy-seven years after his death—forty years after composition. It is in fact unknown to most contemporary pianists.* Chopin was totally capricious about the time of publication of his works, withholding a surprising number of them altogether during his life, perhaps enjoying in some cases the mystery surrounding his creativity.

In any event, at no time did Chopin contemplate rushing back to Warsaw to be with his family in the aftermath of the national disaster. After a few more days in Stuttgart, he went on to Strasbourg and Paris to build a new existence—and to make a place for himself under the sun of the world's artistic capital and within the constellation of its resident talent in music, literature, painting, and sculpture. Chopin wrote later from Paris that it was "in Stuttgart, where the news about the fall of Warsaw reached me, that I decided fully to go to that other world."

None of Chopin's surviving letters to family and friends during and after the uprising (with few exceptions) mention it or its consequences. All of them are devoted almost entirely to descriptions of Vienna and other cities where he spent time after Warsaw, the name-dropping of celebrities he had met and been entertained by, complaints about not attaining recognition soon enough, accounts of the first successes, and requests for money addressed to his father.

In a monologue-like letter from Vienna to a young physician friend a month after the uprising broke out, Chopin wrote that "if it were not that it could be a burden for my father now, I would return immediately . . . I damn the moment of my departure." But there is nothing in the preserved family correspondence to indicate that Chopin's father had encouraged him to come back to fight the Russians—as his closest friend and traveling companion, Tytus Woyciechowski, had done instantly. In a letter to the family four weeks after the start of the rebellion, Fryderyk actually sent regards to Tytus and demanded that he write him, "for God's love."

By the same token, there is no evidence that his father had urged Fryderyk *not* to return. The only hint to that effect appears in the memoirs of the writer Eugeniusz Skrodzski, who was eight years old at the time and knew Chopin only slightly. In his diary, published over fifty years

---

*See the reproduction of the sheet music for the Polonaise in the photo insert.

after the fact, Skrodzski wrote that "the last thing . . . I remember about Chopin was a letter written to his parents shortly after the November 1830 events in Warsaw, with candent desire to return to the country. . . . Panicked by this noble intention, Mister Nicolas succeeded in persuading his son that he could better serve the motherland in the field of arts than by wielding a rifle with too weak a hand." This is not very credible mainly because there would have been no time for such an exchange of letters to affect Chopin's decision. Mail was slow in the days of stagecoaches, especially during a war. So much, then, for this myth.

It is entirely plausible that, given his fragile health, Chopin would not have made much of a soldier and that he accomplished more for Poland by staying away and composing stirring patriotic songs and music. Three of his songs were chanted by the rebels during the uprising. Yet Chopin could not resist affectation.

In a letter to a physician friend, he announced on a note of self-pity—after explaining that he did not wish to become a burden to his father—that "all the dinners, evenings, concerts, dances that I have had up to my ears bore me: I feel so sad, somber . . . I must dress, do my hair, shoe my feet; in a salon, I pretend to be calm, but returning home, I thunder at the piano." And on New Year's Day, 1831, Chopin exclaimed at the end of a missive about his social life in Vienna, "You are going to war—do come back as a colonel. . . . Why can't I be with you, why can't I be a drummer boy!" (In the same letter, Chopin described at length the establishment of a sausage shop by a Frenchman who had fled the July revolution in Paris, remarking that some Viennese "are angry that a French rebel was allowed to open a store with hams when they have enough swine in their own country.")

It was already dark when the stagecoach made its way through the narrow, muddy streets of Paris to the terminal of the Strasbourg-Paris line on rue des Messageries in the Poissonnière district of the city. The coachman shouted, "Terminus!" and the bone-tired passengers poured out of the diligence (France had gained its first railroad the year before, but it only went from Paris to nearby St. Germain).

Chopin brushed off the dust from his tight-fitting black frock coat and approached a clerk at the terminal office to inquire in Polish-accented French about a place to spend the night. He knew only a few people in Paris slightly, and the two letters of introduction he carried from Warsaw and Vienna could not be delivered so late at night. The clerk had recommended an inn on rue de la Cité Bergère, five blocks to the south, and Chopin, weighed down by a large satchel and a case with his musical manuscripts, marched off toward the hostelry, elbowing his way through the evening crowds and among the carriages in the gas-lit streets.

He would stay for nearly two months in his small room at the Cité Bergère inn. The process of reinventing himself as Frédéric Chopin, the virtuoso darling of Paris salons and genius composer of the exploding Romantic Age, was now underway. So, too, the unfolding of his destiny as a poignantly tragic figure of loneliness and lovelessness, surrounded by friends and admirers, beset by relentlessly devastating physical illness and ever-deepening psychological suffering.

Andante
1810—1837

Chapter 1

FRYDERYK CHOPIN WAS BORN a genius, but he was blessed as well by the environment in which he grew and developed. And the most crucial elements were his devoted and very wise family, the French-Polish background, and the quality of general and musical education he received at home in Warsaw. He was exposed to music from the earliest childhood, responding to it naturally, enthusiastically, and indeed astonishingly.

Frycek came into the world on March 1, 1810, in the melancholy village of Żelazowa Wola on the Utrata River, some twenty miles west of Warsaw, the second child of a transplanted French tutor who played the violin and the flute. His mother was a "poor relation" cousin of a Polish small nobility clan, who played the piano and sang in a pleasant soprano voice. Chopin's unusual family background was a prime example of the historical closeness of Franco-Polish ties on all levels; it made it much easier for him to feel reasonably at ease (if not at home) in Paris when the time came. Perhaps it was predestined that Chopin would wind up in France forever while maintaining his emotional links to Poland, Polish music and literature, and all people and things Polish.

According to existing records, Nicolas Chopin was born on April 15, 1771, in the village of Marainville in Lorraine in northeastern France. *His* father was François Chopin (the name had been spelled occasionally as Chappen or Chapin), a wheelwright and owner of a small vineyard who also served as county commissioner. Lorraine had been awarded as a lifetime principality by Louis XV in 1738 to Stanisław Leszczyński, his father-in-law, after he had been dethroned as king of Poland. Maria

Leszczyńska was the queen of France at that point, and large numbers of Poles settled in Lorraine along with their exiled sovereign (the Stanisław Academy, a lyceum, exists to this day in Nancy, the capital of Lorraine). Lorraine reverted to France at Stanisław's death in 1766, five years before Nicolas was born.

The village of Marainville had belonged to the vast estates of Count Charles-Joseph de Rutant, Leszczyński's chamberlain, but it was sold in 1780, when François Chopin was nine, to the Polish Count Michał Pac. As this complicated story unfolded, Count Pac brought his own administrator from Poland, one Jan Adam Weydlich. Soon Weydlich and his wife became acquainted with François Chopin, the wheelwright, and took an instant liking to his son, Nicolas. Seven years later, Count Pac sold the estates, including Marainville and three other villages, and the Weydlichs returned to Poland.

For reasons that remain obscure, they invited the sixteen-year-old Nicolas to accompany them, promising to help him settle in Poland. For equally unknown reasons, Nicolas agreed to go. In the words of a Polish historian, he left in 1787, two years before the French Revolution, "taking with him his violin, his flute and a few books by Voltaire." Nicolas never returned to France, just as his son, Fryderyk, would never return to Poland. Under this curious reversal of attitudes, the father would always write his son in French from Warsaw and Fryderyk would respond in Polish from Paris (Fryderyk was four when his French grandfather died; he never met any member of his French family).

Once in Poland, Nicolas Chopin found work as a bookkeeper at a French-owned snuff factory in Warsaw. When the factory went out of business, he was hired as a tutor for the four children of Countess Ewa Łączyńska, the widow of an officer killed in an anti-Russian uprising after the second Partition of Poland in 1793, at her estate in Czerniewo. Nicolas, who began to regard himself as a Pole, changed his first name to the Polish "Mikołaj" and volunteered for service in the Warsaw National Guard in the course of that uprising, attaining the rank of captain. He was among the defenders of Praga, the town across the Vistula River from Warsaw, and survived miraculously the final assault on the capital by the armies of General Aleksandr Suworow, the most famous Russian commander. An identical scenario would be repeated thirty-eight years later, climaxing the 1830–1831 uprising that Mikołaj watched from his Warsaw home and Fryderyk from his Vienna and Stuttgart self-exile.

Superbly educated and multilingual, Mikołaj Chopin was an ideal tutor for Countess Łączyńska's family. He must have been quite surprised some years later when Maria, the youngest daughter and his best pupil, became the mistress of Napoleon Bonaparte as Madame Walewska. It was still another French connection for the Chopins, and, years later, her son, Alexander Walewski, would enter Fryderyk's social life in Paris.

In the meantime, Countess Łączyńska agreed to allow her friend, the recently divorced Countess Ludwika Skarbek, to let Mikołaj become the tutor of her five children—but especially of her ten-year-old son Fryderyk—at the relatively modest estate at Żelazowa Wola. Arriving there in 1802, Mikołaj met the Skarbeks' orphan cousin and godchild Justyna Krzyżanowska, who at the young age of twenty was the administrator of the estate. They saw each other every day, shared meals, talked, and made music together. In what must have been a situation of mutual liking and respect rather than love at first sight, Mikołaj decided after four years to ask for her hand in marriage. They were wed in 1806; he was thirty-five, she was twenty-four. Countess Skarbek assigned a small one-story structure on the Żelazowa Wola estate to serve as their home.

Six months after the Chopin wedding, Napoleon and his armies entered Warsaw, crowning the great campaign against Austrian, Prussian, and Russian forces. He occupied Vienna, defeating Austrian and Russian armies at Austerlitz, then smashed the Prussians at Jena and took Berlin. In Warsaw, where the Prussians had replaced the Russians as occupiers at the outset of the century, the French emperor was greeted as a savior. Polish regiments had been fighting alongside the French for years to win the restoration of a sovereign Poland. It was during his 1806 stay in Warsaw that Napoleon met seventeen-year-old Maria Walewska, the wife of Anastazy Walewski, sweeping her off her feet.

Poles, however, were disappointed. Under the Tilsit Treaty he had signed with the Russians and the Prussians in 1807, Napoleon formed a small duchy of Warsaw, instead of making all Poland an independent state again. Friedrich August, the king of Saxony and an ally of Napoleon, was named the duchy's ruler.

The Skarbeks and the Chopins had fled Żelazowa Wola for Warsaw because of seesaw battles in the surrounding countryside, and the couple's first child, Ludwika (named after Countess Skarbek), was born in April 1807. The following year, all of them returned to the estate, and Fryderyk Franciszek Chopin came into the world at the Żelazowa Wola house in March 1810. He was named Fryderyk after young Skarbek and Franciszek after François, his French paternal grandfather.

Mikołaj Chopin decided, however, that there was not much future for him as tutor at Żelazowa Wola, and, seven months after Fryderyk's birth, moved the family to Warsaw for good. He had accepted a position as "Collaborator" at the Warsaw Lyceum—this made him a part-time teacher at the boys' school—and the Chopins went to live in apartments at the Saxon Palace in the Saxon Gardens where the lyceum was located. Two more daughters were born to them: Justyna Izabela in July 1811 and Emilia in November 1812.

In 1815, the Congress of Vienna, redrawing the map of Europe and creating the "Holy Alliance" of "Kings against the People," as the pact became widely known, resolved the Polish problem by inventing the "autonomous" kingdom of Poland under the tutelage of Czar Alexander I of Russia, who was crowned King of Poland. The Vienna Congress had followed Napoleon's 1812 retreat from Moscow and his ultimate defeat and deportation to St. Helena. The Bourbon dynasty was restored in France under Louis XVIII.

Though the new kingdom was smaller than the duchy of Warsaw and real power was vested in Archduke Konstanty, the czar's brother (married to a Polish noblewoman), who was named commander-in-chief of the Polish army and lived in Warsaw's Belweder Palace, most Poles seemed to accept the latest status quo. Czar Alexander was believed to have liberal tendencies, at least by St. Petersburg standards, and leaders of the Polish aristocracy rallied behind him in the hope that, sooner or later, the nation would regain full independence. In fact, one of the czar's advisers in establishing the kingdom was the greatly respected Prince Adam Czartoryski; years later, in Paris, the exiled prince would emerge as a protector of the self-exiled Fryderyk Chopin.

Meanwhile, Fryderyk's father was among those who enthusiastically greeted the new order in Warsaw. A conservative man who deplored the French Revolution, distrusted Napoleon, and applauded the Bourbons' return to the throne in his native country, Mikołaj Chopin favored the kind of tranquillity and progress brought by the creation of the kingdom. Neither he nor his Polish friends seemed particularly disturbed by the knowledge that Archduke Konstanty had the inclinations and behavior of a tyrant and martinet who often blew up in uncontrolled rages, hitting and drastically punishing subordinates—and independent-minded citizens—who incurred his displeasure. The archduke was accepted as the leader of Warsaw polite society and invitations to the Belweder were eagerly sought. Young Russian officers courted young Polish ladies.

By then, Mikołaj Chopin was prospering. He was accepted as a Pole (and to this day many people spell Chopin as "Szopen" because in Polish the sound of "sh" is written as "sz" and "e" sounds like the "i" in French). And he was given the title of full professor of French language and literature at the Warsaw Lyceum and professor at the army's Artillery and Engineers' Cadets School. His revenues improved further when the Chopins established an expensive home for student boarders from wealthy out-of-town families who attended the lyceum at their Saxon Palace apartments. In 1817, the lyceum was moved to Kazimierz Palace on midtown Krakowskie Przedmieście Boulevard because the archduke had decided to take over all of the Saxon Gardens for military parades, his preferred pastime. The Chopins received even ampler quarters at the new location, expanding their home for lyceum boarders.

Warsaw under the kingdom was as sophisticated and music-conscious as any city in Eastern Europe, at least when it came to its increasingly rich aristocratic and bourgeois elites. With a population of one hundred thousand inhabitants, Warsaw enjoyed a rich diet of opera presented at the National Theater and concerts at three concert halls, churches, and private homes. Every "decent home" had a piano and at least one person in the household who could play it, according to an article in a Leipzig publication, and there were several piano factories in the city.

And Warsaw had twenty literary periodicals—new trends, including Romanticism, were discussed in their pages—and a music weekly. Such was the demand for sheet music by Polish and foreign composers that nine music stores were in business; the most important belonged to Antoni Brzezina, who also was a music publisher. Famous international performers, from the violin virtuoso Niccolò Paganini to the singer Angelica Catalani, came to Warsaw to appear before highly knowledgeable audiences. Among Polish artists, the favorite was the pianist Maria Szymanowska. Fryderyk heard them all.

And, naturally, there was a piano at the Chopins' apartments. Justyna played it alone or to accompany Mikołaj when he picked up his violin or flute. Soon, she began teaching piano to her daughter Ludwika as

Frycek, then three or four years old, listened with rapture (legend has it that as a baby he wept uncontrollably at the sound of music). Before long, his mother started teaching him, too, but Fryderyk mastered the instrument so rapidly that before he turned six, he could play every melody he had ever heard, and began to improvise. He had essentially learned the piano by himself, including harmonizing melodies with simple chords, but his parents concluded that henceforth he should be taught music seriously and systematically.

Wojciech Żywny's greatest contribution to the history of music was that he recognized that he was in the presence of genius and did not attempt to improve on it. Instead, he simply guided and helped it. Żywny was a sixty-year-old florid, snuff-redolent violinist and music teacher from the Czech lands, hired by the Chopins to instruct six-year-old Fryderyk in composition and harmony. He never tried to change the boy's unusual and intricate piano fingering.

His other contribution was that from the start he acquainted Fryderyk with the music of Johann Sebastian Bach, made him love it and be inspired by it. Afterwards Chopin would play a Bach fugue as a daily exercise—and a soul-saving religious obeisance. When Chopin went to Majorca for the disastrous 1838–1839 autumn–winter stay, the only music he carried with him were the two books of Bach's *Well-Tempered Keyboard*. It was there that he completed his cycle of twenty-four Préludes, unquestionably inspired by Bach's own forty-eight preludes and fugues, and probably meant as an homage.

The préludes of Opus 28, jewel-like "fragments" or miniatures (some less than a minute long), are among Chopin's most sublime works, described by the great German composer Robert Schumann as an "intimate diary." Employing all twenty-four major and minor key signatures and exploiting their characteristic colors, the Préludes Opus 28 enhance Chopin's skill as an innovator. In the words of the Polish music historian Tadeusz A. Zieliński, the préludes offer "an immense fan of emotions, psychic states, moods and their subtle variations."

The Bach influence may explain, as some historians believe, why Chopin seemed to be more in tune with Baroque masters (Handel was among them, too) than with his Romantic era contemporaries, although he clearly belonged to the Romantic generation. To some musicologists, Chopin became a bridge between two epochs—where Ludwig van Beethoven had left off at his death (when Fryderyk was seventeen). Bach, of course, was also the model for Wolfgang Amadeus Mozart and Beethoven, looming as an ancestor of the Romantics.

Fryderyk's first creations were the two polonaises composed in 1817, when he was seven, and transcribed by his father. They illustrate how he transmuted the traditional, slow eighteenth-century Polish court dance— the elegant polonaise—into startling bravura passages. Chopin had obviously heard the very popular Polish airs played by his mother and pianist friends, and drew on them for his compositions, enriching them with new gestures and exploring their dramatic potential formally. Later, as historians have observed, Chopin transformed the courtly dance into heroism and even "brutal" violence.

The Polonaise in G minor was published in Warsaw in November 1817—his first published piece—and it was instantly hailed as a major work of art. The respected periodical *Warsaw Diary* informed its readers in January 1818 that "the composer of this dance, an eight-year-old youth, is . . . a true musical genius." It was the first time the word "genius" was applied to Chopin publicly and, inevitably, he began to be compared as a prodigy and talent to Mozart (who died in 1791). Actually, Mozart was five when he composed his first piece, and the comparisons were meaningless as they so often are. Chopin idolized Mozart, but he had no particular desire to be a "new Mozart." He wanted to be Chopin. Until at least 1926, Chopin scholars and pianists were entirely unaware of the existence of the Polonaise in G minor, except for the mention in the Warsaw newspaper, because the original 1817 edition had vanished. Zdzisław Jachimecki, a Polish musicologist, found it shortly after the First World War in a four-volume collection of piano music, printed in Warsaw between 1816 and 1830, and published it in 1926. But, even then, few musicians seemed to notice it. The first (1817) edition was in the possession of the two Ciechomska sisters—Chopin's grandnieces—but it entered the public domain only in 1959, when it was presented as a gift from a new owner to the Fryderyk Chopin Society in Warsaw. The only other copy of this edition is at the Katowice Academy of Music. The Polonaise in G minor was reprinted in 1990 by the Chopin Society and a Japanese publishing partner, but, again, it failed to attract attention. Eugene Istomin, a leading American Chopin performer, who saw and played it for the first time in 1997, believes that "a straight line" connects this child's polonaise to his future compositions.

The first part is "melancholy, pathetic," but the second part—the trio—is "courtly, gay dance music . . . for *petites demoiselles.*" Istomin suspects, however, that in transcribing the work, Chopin's father committed an error in the first part, creating a dissonance by marking a passage F-sharp instead of G-sharp. Fryderyk's second polonaise, in B-flat major, also composed in 1817, has disappeared altogether. Both polonaises are now listed in Krystyna Kobylańska's 1977 catalogue, considered the most authoritative and complete listing of Chopin's works.

Without missing a beat, Fryderyk made his public debut as a pianist in February 1818, a month after the *Warsaw Diary's* plaudits and a week before his eighth birthday. The occasion was a charity concert in the ballroom of the Blue Palace (also known as the Radziwiłł Palace, after the Polish royal family that built it), owned by Prince Stanisław Zamoyski. His brother-in-law, Prince Adam Czartoryski, lived at the Blue Palace as well, and it was there that Chopin met him for the first time, beginning a lifetime acquaintanceship.

At the concert, Chopin played a piano work by the Czech composer Adalbert Gyrowetz. He must have made a fine impression (although Warsaw newspapers published no reviews) because henceforth he became the darling of the aristocratic society, constantly invited to perform at the homes of the greatest noble families. He was a charming child with exquisite manners, always saying the right thing and smiling modestly, but there is no record of Frycek's reaction to this first concert, except for an often-repeated anecdote of uncertain origin that when his mother asked what the audience had liked best about his appearance, he replied, "My English collar" (the lace collar he wore with his velvet suit).

Chopin's fame spread so rapidly that soon he was commanded to play for Archduke Konstanty and his family at Belweder Palace. The archduke may have been a "bloody satrap," in the words of Polish chroniclers, but he was a music lover and he, too, became an admirer of the boy. Fryderyk not only was invited to Belweder repeatedly, but he composed a military march for the piano for Konstanty, who had it scored for full brass band to be played at army parades.

When Empress Maria Feodorova, the mother of Emperor Alexander and Archduke Konstanty, visited Warsaw in 1818, she listened to Chopin at a performance at the lyceum and he presented her with two new polonaises of his own composition. During Czar Alexander's stay in Warsaw in April 1825, shortly before his death, Fryderyk was chosen to perform for him on an "eolomelodykon" (also called "choralion"), a quickly forgotten contraption combining the features of a piano and an organ designed by a Polish professor-mechanic. For this, the czar gave Chopin a diamond ring. When he was nine years old, the great Italian singer Angelica Catalani, mesmerized by his playing, had given him a gold watch.

The question does inevitably arise as to why Fryderyk's parents allowed him to play for imperial Russian occupiers and to be feted by them, especially the hated archduke, considering the anti-Russian sentiment of many Poles. Mikołaj Chopin himself had fought against the Russians in the 1794 uprising. The best answer is that, most likely, Mikołaj—essentially a man of the status quo—did not wish to antagonize the rulers. At the same time, access to the Russian court in Warsaw promised to enhance Fryderyk's career. It certainly helped with the Polish aristocracy, which had accepted the kingdom of Poland as a reality, and these friendships could serve him well in the future. In any event, Fryderyk learned early in life the importance of top-level friendships and patronage.

There is no reason to believe, however, that Chopin's father—unlike Leopold Mozart in relation to *his* son—had made any effort to force Frycek into a premature musical career, certainly not pushing him into profitable concert tours. Wiser, more relaxed, and perhaps more loving, Mikołaj preferred to let nature take its course, being helpful when required by circumstances. He may have understood that such pressure could be psychologically damaging to the boy prodigy whom he knew to be highly emotional and sensitive. Nor did Mikołaj have any family financial interest at heart: Frycek played for nothing in the Warsaw salons. In this sense, Chopin grew up free of pressure at home—whatever tension did build up for him at the time was self-imposed.

As far as is known, Chopin performed only seven times in public in Poland over an eleven-year period—until his first journey to Vienna in mid-1829. This does not include, of course, scores of appearances at Belweder or private residences of which no record has been kept, or his Sunday organ playing at a Warsaw church when he was fifteen. Inasmuch as he would make it plain in Paris that he actually *detested* playing before concert hall audiences—he performed only when it was absolutely necessary for his career or immediate income, summing a lifetime total of thirty concerts—the unanswered question is whether this phobia dated back to childhood performances, and, if so, what

explains it? He was, after all, the *least* publicly heard among the important pianists of his time, though greatly desired.

In letters, some of them very long and chatty, written by Chopin in
Warsaw to his two best friends, who lived on rural estates, there are only
passing references to music he was composing and just a few to his
public concerts. Perhaps this is because many of the letters may have been
lost (as have others) or, simply, because Fryderyk did not enjoy playing
before large audiences—"people I don't know," as he put it many years
later—and therefore he did not care to discuss it with his friends.

From the very beginning, Chopin was much more at ease at small gath-
erings, for psychological or purely musical reasons. In the words of
Ryszard Przybylski, a leading Chopin scholar, Fryderyk's "playing, with its
discriminatory sensitivity of touch," was best suited to "initiates in society drawing-rooms." A more brutal conclusion might indicate that
Chopin, who in many ways was an elitist (not to say a snob), only felt comfortable at the piano when surrounded by his social equals and friends.

More devoted to assuring a fine education for his son, in general culture
as well as in music, than to pushing him into a prodigy career, Mikołaj
Chopin decided in 1822, when Fryderyk was twelve, to place him in the
hands of Józef Elsner, a fifty-two-year-old Silesian German, who was a
highly regarded composer, scholar, director of the newly established
Warsaw Conservatory—and a personal friend. Himself a teacher,
Mikołaj had concluded that the time was ripe for Frycek to study music,
and especially composition, on a higher level. Żywny, the Czech, had
reached the limit of his teaching abilities, but he would remain a close
friend of the family. Just before he ended their lessons, Frycek had dedicated a polonaise to him on his saint's day.

At the same time, however, Fryderyk was expected to pursue his regular studies at the lyceum. Before he was sixteen, he would acquire a
working knowledge of French (which his father spoke at home along
with Polish), German, and Italian. The latter had a special importance for
him as the "language of music" in which score notations are made. He
learned Latin as part of the normal Polish school curriculum. He became
familiar with European literature. His teenage letters to his friends, pep-
pered with French, German, Italian, and Latin words and phrases and
with literary allusions—as well as with very crude and funny observations—show how cultured Chopin was even in adolescence.

Fryderyk studied with Elsner for three years, concentrating on counterpoint which, he reported to a friend, he did at the rate of six hours weekly. But it was a priceless investment in his future. Counterpoint is a plural melody—a melody added to another melody in a piece or a combination of forms—and its mastery opens limitless vistas to a work. As Charles Rosen, a music scholar and himself a pianist, has written, "Chopin was the greatest master of counterpoint since Mozart."

Musicologist Jon Newsom observes that "good harmonic voice-leading is the art of counterpoint," harmony and counterpoint being "intimately a part of the other." He adds that "one of the wonderful and mysterious things about music is the fact that a succession of pitches can suggest the horizontal movement, or movement in time, like a glowing ember floating across a dark field or the night sky. The human mind can integrate the complex of separate pitches that make a musical event into a continuous fabric, of which, somewhat crudely speaking, harmony is the warp and counterpoint the weft." Newsom believes that it was "Chopin's extraordinary sensitivity to the sonority of the piano together with his equally fine ear for melodic and harmonic relationships that enabled him to make his innovation effective, for he could perform daring harmonic feats and make them sound musically coherent."

When Fryderyk turned sixteen, Mikołaj Chopin decided that his son was ready for the next serious step in his education. Rather than have him complete the last year of the lyceum, he enrolled him in the three-year course at the Central Music School—part of the Warsaw Conservatory—also headed by Elsner. Frycek went on composing while studying at the school, producing at least two rondos for the piano, a trio, a mazurka, a sonata and a funeral march (not the famous one, which came much later). All was going superbly.

Chapter 2

ON APRIL 10, 1827, tragedy struck the Chopin family. Emilia, the youngest daughter, died of tuberculosis at the age of fourteen. A month earlier, Fryderyk described her illness in the midst of an otherwise amusing and chatty letter to a friend: "She caught a cough, started spitting blood . . . all that time she would not eat anything; she turned so pale that one could not recognize her, and only now she is beginning to be herself again."

But there is no mention of Emilia's death in any of the surviving Chopin correspondence. Beethoven died the same year, and it was once held that the classical period in music ended with Beethoven. Fryderyk must have read about the passing of Beethoven in a Warsaw newspaper, but he never mentioned it, either. The thought of death always both frightened and fascinated him.

Chopin himself is believed to have died of tuberculosis although there are no existing medical records and there is too little precise information in his own letters and in his friends' correspondence about him to provide solid evidence. But no modern medical authority disputes the finding by Dr. Jean B. Cruveilhier, who performed the autopsy on Chopin, that the composer had suffered from lung tuberculosis for thirty years (reported in a letter to George Sand from a mutual friend).

Dr. Czesław Sielużycki, a Chopin scholar and laryngologist, has emphasized in a study published in Poland in 1983 that, quite possibly, both Emilia and Fryderyk may have suffered from a "pretubercular" condition. Dr. Jean-Claude Davila, a French pulmonary specialist, remarked in his 1995 doctoral dissertation at the University of Toulouse on Chopin's health that Fryderyk was "contaminated very early by the Koch bacillus" at a time when tuberculosis was widespread in Poland, accounting for one death in every one hundred. It had not yet been defined as a contagious disease. Actually, the bacillus of tuberculosis would be isolated only in 1882 by the German bacteriologist Dr. Robert Koch, but there is no question that the illness, then known as pulmonary consumption or phthisis, was tuberculosis. The stethoscope, the instrument for listening to sounds inside the body, had been invented by a French doctor in 1819, and was not yet available in Poland. Cough and pallor were the main basis for diagnosis.

Both youngsters had gone in 1826 for cures at the southwestern health resort of Dusznik to drink "metal" waters and goat's milk (prescribed at the time for lung ailments), and to receive "inhalations" of vapor. Dr. Sielużycki has suggested that Emilia succumbed to the malady while "the condition of Chopin improved decidedly . . . in the spring of the next year, when a small lung inflammation healed by itself." Two years later, in 1828, Chopin was rushed for a cure to the Sannik resort (where he began composing a trio for piano, violin, and cello).

Dr. Sielużycki has concluded that from childhood Fryderyk's health had always been most delicate, if not worse, and that this may have led in time to the reappearance of tuberculosis to which he evidently was susceptible. Fryderyk's first recorded reference to illness appeared in a typically jocular letter to a friend just before he turned sixteen. He reported that he was in bed, under covers, with a headache already lasting four days and his neck glands swollen, and that the doctor had told him that he suffered from a "catarrhal affliction."

From childhood, Dr. Sielużycki has written, Chopin was "predisposed" to rheumatic diseases, gastric troubles, severe headaches, and "rotting teeth." He was often short of breath and sweating, and he was a "poorly eating child." He complained about "acidity" in his stomach and was on varying diets at home and during rural vacations (he was not allowed, for example, to eat peasant rye bread, which he adored). At health spas where his parents sent him in his teens, Fryderyk drank mineral waters, bathed in oak bark solutions, and consumed infusions of acorns ("one day, I drank seven cups"). He was given wine diluted in water in a beer mug to "build up his blood." He took "pills" for appetite.

Chopin was kept at home during inclement weather, studied at home until he was thirteen, and was not permitted to play soccer or *palant* (a Polish homegrown version of baseball). When he went ice-skating at the age of sixteen, he fell, injured his head, and was carried home "almost unconscious" to be treated by a surgeon. That same winter, Fryderyk came down with a "catarrhal fever" in his throat, high fever, headache, and the swelling of neck glands. Leeches were planted on his throat to bring down the swelling. In the spring, when he turned seventeen, Chopin suffered from "fatigue," an increased "nervous and emotional anxiety," low-grade fever, cough, and headaches, which made him miss lyceum lessons and prevented him from receiving his graduating diploma (some modern physicians suspect that Fryderyk may have been afflicted with mononucleosis). At the Dusznik spa, where he spent several weeks in August and September 1826, Chopin was forbidden to climb "high mountains," walking over hillocks quite unwillingly and often "on all fours." He also developed a "fear of open spaces," a phobia that never left him. However, his letters home showed that he was in excellent humor, joking and commenting amusingly on his surroundings. Back in Warsaw, doctors ordered him to be in bed by nine o'clock in the evening ("all the teas, evenings, and balls went down the drain," he wrote to a friend, "and I drink emetics and fatten myself on oatmeal").

Though his gradually worsening health increasingly—and fundamentally—affected Chopin's personality and temperament in the years to come, all indications are that as a boy he was secure, happy, and often mischievous with a fine sense of humor, easily attracting devoted friends.

It does not necessarily follow, of course, that a child reared in a secure home environment will become a secure adult—or vice versa. And, as it soon became evident, Chopin was quintessentially an emotionally insecure man from what appears to have been a most secure background. It may have been part of the price of genius—and progressive adult personality deformation—linked or not to his illness, or all of the above. Modern psychiatric analysis of Chopin's mental health, based on correspondence, memoirs, and early biographies, does suggest strongly that he was a schizoid or manic-depressive type. The relationship between genius and mental illness remains to this day a theme of controversy among scholars. A recent study of the lives of sixty composers in Warsaw's *Ruch Muzyczny* led to the conclusion that approximately one half of them had a "melancholic temperament"—"melancholy" was a word for depression—and that mood disorders associated with depressions were "easily the commonest and most important of psychiatric illnesses." But the full truth about Chopin's psychological evolution from childhood to adulthood will never emerge: There are just too many gaps in his personal history.

By all accounts, Fryderyk's Warsaw home was a happy environment. Mikołaj Chopin was an even-tempered, warmhearted, well-liked if rather boring paterfamilias. He was a practical man rather than a deep thinker. But he was a fairly authoritarian decision maker—as were most other heads of families at that time. Fryderyk never questioned his views and generous doses of advice, but, unlike the hostile relationship between Mozart and *his* father, he did not resent them: In fact, he often requested them. Chopin clearly loved Mikołaj, plunging into deep depression at his death.

Fryderyk's mother appeared to be much less obtrusive, though, and unquestionably she was equally loving. Lacking Mikołaj's education and background, she tended to devote herself to the care of the family, abstaining from volunteering too much advice.

In a portrait painted in 1829, Mikołaj's clean-shaven, rather elongated face conveys intelligence, seriousness, and openness. Fryderyk resembled him somewhat in physiognomy. Justyna's portrait shows a rather defensive woman; Frycek may have taken his wide-set, soft, vulnerable eyes from her.

His sisters, Ludwika and Izabela, adored Fryderyk. The older and highly intelligent Ludwika was perhaps his best and closest adviser; he would demand her presence at his deathbed. They both wrote him enormously long letters, keeping him abreast of Warsaw gossip and the (very good) local sales of his sheet music. Chopin often sent Ludwika (with whom he had played piano four-hands when they were young) his latest compositions, especially mazurkas. In short, he came from a stable home environment. There was no history of mental illness in the family that would explain his mental crises.

As a child, Frycek was friendly, outgoing, and fun-loving, despite fragile health. Of slight build and limited strength, he shunned physical activity, but diverted his friends and fellow students with mimicry, a gift for caricatures, and occasional piano playing. Four boarders at his parents' apartments became his intimates: Tytus Woyciechowski, Jan

Białobłocki, and Jan Matuszyński, and Julian Fontana; he would share aspects of his Parisian life with the latter two.

Tytus Woyciechowski was the most important and, in his own way, the most mysterious of these friends—at least to outsiders. Two years older than Chopin, he too had studied the piano with Żywny, and, after they met in 1823, the boys often played piano four-hands. Tytus's home was the Poturzyn estate near Lublin, east of Warsaw, and he returned there after lyceum graduation in order to farm. Fryderyk made him his most trusted confidant—the only one in his life—after Białobłocki, his earliest friend, died of bone tuberculosis in 1827.

Actually, they spent very little time together after the lyceum days, with Tytus back at his estate. Reconstructing their relationship principally from the cascade of letters Chopin began writing him in 1828, it appears that they saw each other at some length only three times following graduation. There is nothing in Fryderyk's letters to indicate that Tytus had visited Warsaw subsequently. In 1828 Fryderyk and Tytus met briefly at a mutual friend's country home. Chopin spent about ten days with him at Poturzyn in August 1830—the only time he ever went there—and then, two-and-a-half months later, they traveled together to Vienna. Woyciechowski rushed back to fight in the Warsaw uprising within a month while Chopin remained in Vienna and then moved on to Paris. Woyciechowski married in 1838, and remained content at Poturzyn. They never saw each other again, though they exchanged letters until a month before Chopin's death.

It was a romance by correspondence, with Chopin the aggressive "lover"—yet only in the rhetorical sense. Though Fryderyk addressed Tytus as "my love" and "my life," sent him wet kisses on the mouth, and breathlessly awaited Woyciechowski's much rarer letters, no evidence exists that it was in any way a homosexual relationship. In one missive, Chopin wrote: "I am going to wash up; don't kiss me now because I haven't washed up yet. You? Even if I smeared myself with Byzantine oils, you wouldn't have kissed me unless I forced you to do it magically. . . . Today, you will dream that you are kissing me."

In a letter from Paris, Chopin told him "at this moment, as I start describing a ball, where a deity with a rose in her black hair had enchanted me, I receive your letter. All these romances leave my mind."

While most of Chopin's missives to Tytus have been preserved, there are no extant letters from him. Thus Woyciechowski looms as an invisible and mute partner, always ready to receive Chopin's confidences, but no more (in another letter, Fryderyk wrote, "I know you don't like to be kissed, but allow me to do it today").

It was not that unusual for young men of the Romantic generation, particularly in extrovert Poland, to write in erotic language to men friends. It was the culture of the time and place. "Love me as I love you" was not an uncommon salutation between men in nineteenth-century Polish epistolary style.

It was a relationship that suited Chopin, the youth and the man who eschewed emotional commitments. Because they were apart most of their lives, Fryderyk had the advantage and luxury of sublimating his emotions into frequent and fulsome letter writing, without other commitment. He sent Tytus his musical compositions, dedicating to him the famous "Là ci darem la mano" variations (based on the duet in Mozart's *Don Giovanni*) and an earlier piece—and describing for him the work on the Piano Concerto in F minor, op. 21, and subsequent creations.

The contrast between Chopin's attitudes toward Tytus and those toward Konstancja Gładkowska, a beautiful and talented singer who was Fryderyk's age, emphasizes how he feared commitment. Having met her at a Warsaw concert in April 1829, Fryderyk convinced himself that he had fallen in love, referring to Konstancja in fiery letters to Woyciechowski as "my ideal" and wondering, "Does she love me, does she not?" But while he professed his "love" for Tytus in letters (an emotionally safe gesture), he made virtually no effort to court Konstancja or even get to know her better. It was a satisfying intellectual-romantic state of affairs.

It is quite likely that Konstancja did not know that Fryderyk was in love with her—or possibly she thought he was. They were sufficiently well acquainted that when Chopin was leaving Warsaw for Vienna at the end of 1830, she inscribed a short farewell poem in his album assuring him that "strangers" could never "love you more than we do." Chopin later added: "They can." Writing poems and messages in one another's albums was a custom of the time among friends and good acquaintances—Chopin even put down musical compositions in albums—and Konstancja's contribution had no deeper meaning. Afterwards, Chopin wrote her several politely friendly letters.

Chopin always discouraged relating his musical works to particular events in his life and refused to give actual titles to his compositions (he was furious when his English publisher attempted to do so). He believed that all experiences found their way to music as he progressed through life. An idea, an inspiration, a concept triggered by a specific event may have taken years for Chopin to develop and write. And because he never really explained his music, the date of the completion of a work could be wholly meaningless in terms of its promptings. For this reason, Chopin's remark in a letter to Woyciechowski, as he worked on his Second Piano Concerto, "I'm telling the piano what I might have some time told you," has been taken too literally by commentators.

And the widely held belief that Konstancja was one of the great loves of Chopin's life also is a great romantic myth. When, fifteen months after Fryderyk's departure from Warsaw, she married Józef Grabowski, a very rich diplomat, he wrote Tytus that he had only had a "platonic affection" for Konstancja, which presumably was true. He had no need to lie to Tytus. But Chopin has always been surrounded by myths (which, in turn, have produced romantic motion-picture mythologies).

Long before he reached Paris, Chopin had acquired impressive musical culture through exposure to the best, and most varied, of the world's music.

Spending summer vacations in the Polish countryside, he heard plenty of folk dance music and songs—polonaises, mazurkas, krakowiaks, kujawiaks, obereks, and the very special Jewish music of the village—and these influences were present in some of his greatest work. But Chopin was a man of universal taste and, contrary to much conventional thinking, he was vastly more than a "Slavonic composer." As Jim Samson, a scholar, put it, "His music would indeed prove a useful case study in a history of taste, and maybe too a history of taste-creating institutions."

As previously mentioned, Chopin had the opportunity in Warsaw of listening to the extraordinary violin playing of Paganini, the great singing of Angelica Catalani and Henrietta Sonntag (he attended all eleven of Sonntag's concerts), and the pianism of Johann Nepomuk Hummel. During a brief trip to Berlin, he heard Georg Frideric Handel's *Messiah* oratorio and Domenico Cimarosa's opera *Il matrimonio segreto*. In the course of a two-week stay in Vienna in 1829, Chopin saw Rossini and Meyerbeer operas (he also played at two recitals there). He always thought that the human voice (followed by the violin) was the purest and most basic sound in music; hence his love for opera and recital singers, both men and women. In Dresden, Chopin was exposed to drama in the form of a five-hour performance of Goethe's *Faust,* which deeply impressed him. Goethe, of course, was the father of the great German Romantic literary movement, already infecting music as well.

In May 1829, Czar Nicholas I was sworn in as the new king of Poland after the death of his father, Czar Alexander (the Warsaw ceremony occurred four years later). The festivities included concerts by Paganini and much pomp and circumstance. But the advent of the new emperor-king was ominous for Poland: Unlike the moderate-minded Alexander, his son had from the outset imposed a reign of terror in Russia and unprecedented repression and mass arrests in Poland.

In Warsaw young people—among them Chopin's friends and colleagues—began conspiring against the Russian rule, planting the seeds for the uprising that would burst forth the following year. At that time, Fryderyk was busy and very excited with his new piano concerto, pleased with the just-completed Polonaise in G-flat major, which marked his commitment to the poetry of Romanticism, his first waltzes (though they would only be published posthumously), and his first four mazurkas.

Chopin managed, however, to spend long hours at the Dziurka ("The Little Hole" in Polish) coffeehouse where young artists, journalists, and aspiring politicians talked about the future of Poland—and the future of art. Rebellion against the status quo in politics and the arts was becoming fused with the advent of Romanticism in Poland as in Western Europe, and Chopin was determined to be part of it. The talk was about Byron and Schiller—and national freedom.

It was at Dziurka that Chopin met the young Polish poets with whom he would compose patriotic songs in Paris just a few years later: Stefan Witwicki, Bohdan Zaleski, and Dominik Magnuszewski. He read Adam Mickiewicz's incandescent poetry. And he renewed his friendship with Maurycy Mochnacki, a former Warsaw Conservatory piano student, music critic (he reviewed Fryderyk's concerts, but angered him with a negative one about Konstancja), lawyer, newspaper editor—and secret conspirer against Czar Nicholas. Mochnacki would become a political patriotic leader in the Warsaw uprising and become an exile in Paris where he and Chopin would help to keep the national flame aglow.

The news of the Paris liberal revolution in July 1830 reached Warsaw instantly, adding to the Polish fervor. Chopin wrote Tytus Woyciechowski late in September that with the rising ferment in France and Italy, the Russian authorities might not certify his passport for travel there. But Fryderyk was now determined to go abroad—his career required it urgently—and he told Tytus: "In the next few weeks, I expect to leave for Kraków and Vienna. . . . This is the whole romance!"

Chopin, traveling with Woyciechowski, reached Vienna on November 23, after stops in Dresden and Prague. Six days later, the uprising erupted in Warsaw. Dr. Sielużycki and other Chopin scholars believe that Fryderyk's fragile health was responsible, at least to an extent, for his mounting inner turmoil, and it is quite plausible that this predisposition, aggravated by the shock of the news from Warsaw, resulted in a pattern of personality disorders that would intensify with time.

The first *documented* sign of Fryderyk's emotional condition appears in his letter to Jan Matuszyński at Christmas 1830. Recounting his visit to St. Stephen's Cathedral from Vienna, where he arrived well ahead of time for midnight Mass, he wrote: "I came . . . not for the Mass, but to look at that hour inside this immense building. . . . I stood in the darkest corner at the foot of a Gothic pillar. It is impossible to describe the majesty, the dimension of these huge arches. . . . It was quiet: sometimes only the steps of the sacristan lighting candles in the depths of the temple drew me from my lethargy. Behind me a tomb, beneath me a tomb . . . I only lacked a tomb above me . . . I felt more than ever [my condition of] orphan. I enjoyed drinking in this great spectacle until people and lights began to arrive. . . . Then, shielded by my coat collar, I went for music in the Imperial chapel."

Another example of Chopin's fascination with death—and another rare documented case of his uncontrollable emotional outbursts—is the lengthy entry in his album, or the diary he kept between 1829 and 1831, upon learning in Stuttgart of the fall of Warsaw to the Russians. Based on inflamed imagination, in the absence of specific information, and in parts plainly incoherent, the diary is a cry of despair:

> Strange thing! This bed, in which I shall lie, may have served not just one dying [person], but today it does not disgust me! Perhaps not just one cadaver lies on it for long? . . . But is a cadaver worse than I? The cadaver also does not know anything about father, about mother, about [my] sisters, about Tytus! And the cadaver does not have a [woman] lover! It cannot converse in his own language with those surrounding him! The cadaver is as pale as I. The cadaver is as cold as I feel about everything.

The cadaver has ceased to live—and I have already lived to satiation. To satiation? And is the cadaver satiated with life? If he were satiated, he would look well, but he is so miserable—does it have so much to do with [facial] traits, the expression of the face, the human exterior? Why do we live such a miserable life, which devours us and serves to make cadavers! The clocks on Stuttgart towers ring the nocturnal hour. Ah, how many cadavers were created in the world at that moment! Mothers of children—mothers [who] have lost children—how many plans erased . . . How much sadness from the cadavers at this moment and how much consolation . . . How many creatures suffocated by cadavers. Good and bad cadaver! Virtue and crime! So it is clear that death is the best act of man—but what will be the worst? Birth, as contrary to the best act. Thus I am right to be angry that I was brought into the world. . . . What does anybody have from my existence? I am not useful to people because I have no [leg] calves and no snouts. . . . And even if I had them, I would not have anything else. . . . Does the cadaver have calves?

And it goes on about the fall of Warsaw:

I was writing . . . knowing that the enemy is in [our] home! The suburbs are destroyed, burned down. . . . Jaś [and] Wilus probably died on the ramparts. I see Marcely in captivity . . . [General] Sowiński, this good man, in the hands of those brutes. . . . Oh, God, it is Thee and do not revenge Thyself! Don't You have enough Moscovian crimes, or are You a Moscovian Yourself! My poor father . . . maybe he is hungry and he cannot buy bread for my mother. Maybe my sisters have succumbed to the fury of the unleashed Moscovian trash! The Moscovian dominates over the world? . . . Oh, father, what joy for your old age! Oh, mother, suffering, tender mother, you have survived your daughters so that the Moscovian would break in to mortify you over their bones. . . . Did they respect their graves? A thousand other cadavers covered their grave. They burned down the city! . . . Ah, . . . Ah, why couldn't I have killed at least one Moscovian! Oh, Tytus . . . What is happening to [Konstancja]? Where is she? . . . Maybe in Moscovian hands . . . The Moscovian is strangling, murdering her. . . . Ah, my life, I am alone here—come to me, I shall dry your tears, I shall heal the wounds. . . . And maybe I no longer have a mother . . .[My] unconscious sisters are not surrendering. . . . Father, in despair, does not know how to help. . . . And I am here inactive, with bare hands, sometimes sighing. . . . I suffer at the piano, I am desperate. . . . God, God. Move the earth to bury people of this age. Let the most savage sufferings punish the French who did not come to our aid.

Chopin had experienced dark fantasies and hallucinations since early adolescence—he mentioned such episodes in a forced self-mocking way in letters to friends—but never on the scale of the Vienna and Stuttgart occurrences. And after Stuttgart, he never felt really safe—anywhere—fully confiding only in his music.

His complex personality also included a visceral aversion to decision making about important steps in his life, begging his parents and friends to tell him what to do—whether to leave Warsaw in the first place, stay in Vienna, or go to Italy, France, or England. "You know that I am the most undecided person in the world," Fryderyk wrote Jan Matuszyński, his physician friend, from Vienna a month after the start of the Warsaw uprising; he asked his advice whether he should go to Italy at that juncture.

But Chopin's self-proclaimed hesitations may have been his defense mechanism rather than a true Hamlet trait: He would not be rushed and, after excruciating delays, he followed his own instinct in his own good time.

It was this instinct that finally led Chopin to leave Vienna on July 20, 1831, on a leisurely journey en route to Paris by way of Linz, Salzburg, Munich, and Stuttgart. In Munich he found time to appear at a concert matinee with the local philharmonic orchestra, playing his Concerto in F minor, op. 21, and *Fantasy on Polish Airs,* op. 13.

Actually, Fryderyk turned out to be much more decisive and inventive than he admitted to be. Because the Russian embassy in Vienna had refused to stamp his passport valid for travel to France—relations between the supremely authoritarian czar in St. Petersburg and the new constitutional monarchy in Paris were rather tense—he was authorized to go only as far as Munich. Warsaw, his home, being part of Russia, Chopin had to travel on a Russian passport.

But he would not be stymied by the Russians, later writing his parents, "Never mind, I thought, so long as Monsieur Maison, the French ambassador, signs [my passport]." Monsieur Maison was happy to do so, and Chopin went back to the Russians, this time to request clearance to go to London via Paris. Now the embassy agreed, putting a notation in the passport that he would merely be "in passage" through Paris. Chopin subsequently joked that he spent the rest of his life "in passage" in France.

To be sure, Fryderyk was developing into an exquisite master manipulator and salon diplomat in his quiet, charming manner, and it was never entirely clear how he managed his problems. His relations with the Russian embassy in Vienna, for instance, could not have been hostile on the part of the Russians even during the Warsaw uprising when he sought to have his passport validated, and they certainly were not on his part. Thus, at the time he wrote to friends that he had arrived in Vienna with a letter of introduction to the ambassador from Grand Duke Konstanty, the bloodthirsty ruler of Poland. Though the introduction letter was given him before the uprising, as he was departing Warsaw, Chopin referred freely to several social meetings with the ambassador after the eruption of the rebellion and to being introduced by him to other Vienna luminaries. The painful question is, of course, whether Fryderyk, as an outspoken Polish patriot, was morally justified in socializing with the Russians who were killing his compatriots.

Now with Vienna, the Russian embassy, Stuttgart, and the hallucinations behind him, Chopin set course for Paris and the "romance" of which he had dreamt for so long.

Chapter 3

THE ROMANCE FRYDERYK CHOPIN FOUND in Paris was also history in the making and soon he, too, became part of it. This was a time in Europe when art and politics—and culture and history—influenced and redefined each other in an unprecedented fashion. The process had been further enhanced by the 1830 "July Monarchy" revolution in France. Taken all together, it was the crucible of the Romantic Age.

The Lord Byron of *Childe Harold* and *Don Juan* had died at thirty-six, nearly six years earlier (in 1824) at Missolonghi in Greece, a leader in the Greek independence war against Turkey, after having been involved in the abortive Italian revolution of 1821. He was a poetic genius who hated tyranny. His beloved friend Percy Bysshe Shelley, whose *Hellas* celebrated the Greek rebellion, had died two years before Byron. When Shelley's body was cremated, his heart somehow escaped the fire. Byron had ordered that his own heart be removed before *his* body was burned. Chopin was fourteen at the time, but Shelley and Byron would later serve as inspiration in deciding the disposition of his body and heart.

In Germany, Schiller and Goethe, the great masters of Romantic lyric poetry and tragedy (and close friends), had shared deep concerns over the fate of humanity. Schiller, who died in 1805, wrote about the deplorable condition of the poor. Goethe began publishing his *Faust*—the first great triumph of Romantic art in literature—in 1808, but he is remembered, too, as the "champion of revolt." He was still alive when Chopin landed in Paris.

At the opening of the nineteenth century, artistic genius and a sense of history thus made common cause. Together, they spawned Romanticism, with artists often turning into militant politicians and champions of progress, and politicians seeking out allies among the artists. Some of the century's most powerful and lasting philosophical and political movements—including communism—came into being during that period.

Curiously, the electrifying Romantic impulse was born in England and Germany *before* France, Italy, and Spain—and even William Shakespeare is regarded as a forefather of Romanticism. In fact, Felix Mendelssohn-Bartholdy (a year older than Chopin and soon to be a close friend) had composed the movingly beautiful overture to *A Midsummer Night's Dream* at the age of seventeen. Many scholars believe that Mendelssohn along with Chopin and Robert Schumann, Hector Berlioz and Liszt—all of them born at roughly the same time—represented what already was to be the second Romantic generation, following the groundbreaking Franz Schubert and Carl Maria von Weber.

Mendelssohn, Schumann, and Weber were Germans. Schubert was Austrian. Liszt was an Austro-Hungarian. Berlioz was French. Chopin was Polish. Influences and inspirations in music thus came from all over Europe. But, as in other arts, Paris in the 1830s was Romanticism's great battleground.

In literature, Byron was the model for Alphonse de Lamartine, the poet who would become France's first republican president, and for Victor Hugo, who was as much a novelist and dramatist as a politician (interestingly, Lamartine and Alfred de Vigny, another great Romantic poet, both married Englishwomen). All of Byron's poetry had been translated into French by 1820. In Russia, Byron influenced both Pushkin (in the creation of *Eugene Onegin*) and Lermontov, and in Poland, Adam Mickiewicz and Juliusz Słowacki. Each in his own way was a revolutionary. Wagner and Nietzsche, the philosopher, emerged from the Romantic tradition as well. (In America, of course, the contemporary voice of Romanticism was Edgar Allan Poe, who was a year older than Chopin and died ten days before the Pole in 1849; they never met.)

The Romantic spirit in literature breathed Romanticism into music. Schiller, in fact, insisted that poetic compositions act upon readers like music.

Schubert's 1827 song cycle *Die Winterreise* was set to the poems of Wilhelm Müller (Schubert died in 1828 at the incredible young age of

thirty-one, depriving Chopin of what would almost have been the certainty of meeting him, as he knew so many other composers of his generation in Western Europe). Schumann, like Schubert before him, was
inspired by the poet Heinrich Heine; Heine, too, was a German, and
they were Paris friends, often discussing poetry and music.

Chopin, who probably had never heard about Romanticism as such
at the time, happened to purchase a copy of Mickiewicz's *Ballads and
Romances* at a Warsaw bookstore when he was sixteen. Mickiewicz, who
launched the Romantic movement in Polish literature with this book of
poems published in 1822, was still virtually unknown, but Fryderyk
became fascinated with him. He was particularly attracted to Mickiewicz's argument in the introduction that classical poetry rules cannot
apply to the "new style," which should be based on "country songs."

Almost immediately, Chopin composed the music for at least one of
Mickiewicz's ballads, his first foray into song writing. It was published
in 1826, although the original manuscript is lost. In 1831 (in Vienna or in
Paris), Chopin wrote his own Ballade no. 1 in G minor, op. 23, a work
for piano, and the first of four in this genre, which he conceived. The
ballades are among his greatest musical achievements and, as pianist
Charles Rosen has observed, "the form is the Romantic ballade, modern
in conception although influenced by the medieval originals . . . an
antique verse narrative in stanzas with a refrain." In 1830 Chopin also
composed music for another Mickiewicz poem (along with music for
seven songs by his poet friend Stefan Witwicki).

Answering a question from Schumann, when they first met in
Leipzig, about the meaning of the ballades, Chopin said that Mickiewicz's poems, similarly titled, had led him to "this idea."

Chopin and Mickiewicz met only in 1832, in Paris, becoming warm
lifetime friends. But it is not certain whether all of the former's ballades
were based on, or inspired by, the latter's poetic ballads. While Ballade
no. 1 was composed long before they met, the other three ballades followed their first time together. In any case, the exact inspirational relation is moot. Do words trigger sounds in a musical mind or the other
way around? What matters in the end is that Mickiewicz in poetry and
Chopin in music instinctively thought alike.

With its sense of feeling and living, Romanticism created at the same
time a bridge between landscape and music. Again, the famous examples start with Schubert and *Die Winterreise*. It has barely been noted

that at the age of sixteen, Chopin composed variations on the theme of the German song "Der Schweizerbub" ("The Swiss Boy"), that is, a few years before Schubert started work on the *Winterreise* cycle.

"Der Schweizerbub" is a tale of mountains—Fryderyk must have heard it at home in his musically literate family—and he produced this beautiful though today little-known piece in a matter of days. Given that song cycles are regarded by many as the "embodiment of the Romantic ideal," Chopin was among the forerunners in this field. This is what has made Romanticism so marvelously all-encompassing.

Romanticism, accentuating reality and individualism as well as emotion and sensuality, surged along with the latest French revolution, the "Three Glorious Days" of July 1830—a key turning point in European social history.

If the revolution of 1789 destroyed absolute monarchy and the ancient aristocracy, and the war-minded Bonaparte empire failed to fill the ensuing societal vacuum, the revolution of 1830 did succeed in creating a new order by bringing the bourgeoisie to power. It was a most significant change in French and European history, with the resulting status quo enduring to this day.

Forty-one years after the fall of the Bastille, the 1830 revolution marked the end of the transition period represented by the restoration of the Bourbons in the aftermath of Napoleon's final exile to St. Helena in 1815. Replacing Napoleon in power was King Louis XVIII, brother of the guillotined Louis XVI, who had lived exiled in England for over twenty years. Actually, Louis XVIII became king in 1814, when France's enemies were occupying Paris (the Russian cavalry were bivouacked in Versailles), but he was cast aside by Napoleon's "Hundred Days" return from his first exile on the island of Elba. Louis's resumption of royal functions was known as the "Second Restoration."

His nine-year reign—he died in 1824—presented, as much as anything, a running battle between the past and the future, between the ultras, who wished a return to pre-revolutionary aristocratic rule, and the "liberals," who had a vision of a more modern and tolerant France.

The bourgeoisie and the increasingly powerful bankers (the House of Rothschild was already solidly installed in Paris) favored the more liberal course, principally because it promised reconstruction of the national economy ravaged by the long years of the Bastille revolution and the Napoleonic wars. Intellectuals, artists, and journalists tended to side with the liberals even though men like Victor Hugo and Alphonse de Lamartine at first supported restoration after the years of imperial repression under Napoleon. And the stirrings of Romanticism among the creators were gaining in strength with their nascent movement of protest and innovation.

The movement's center was Victor Hugo's red-walled living room at his home on rue Notre-Dame-des-Champs, where, starting in 1827, young novelists, poets, critics, and painters gathered to discuss feverishly their artistic aspirations and often to read from their own works. Doctrinary literature of Romanticism was born there. In what probably was the first Romantic manifesto, novelist Henri Beyle (Stendhal) wrote that "the nation is thirsty for its national tragedy" and "Romanticism is the art of presenting to the people literary works that, in the present state of their habits and their beliefs, are susceptible of giving them the greatest possible pleasure."

On February 25, 1830, Victor Hugo's drama *Hernani* premiered at a Paris theater, waging Romanticism's first heroic public battle against classicism (organized by Hugo himself). Hugo's young supporters, in wide-brimmed black Andalusian hats and Spanish capes, and the traditional elite clashed during the performance with shouts, whistles, curses, and fistfights. Hugo wrote: "I made a revolutionary wind blow / I placed a red bonnet on the old dictionary / I created a tempest at the bottom of the ink-well."

In *Hernani,* the "tempest" unleashed by the twenty-eight-year-old Hugo took the form of a violent drama in extraordinary lyric poetry bringing together episodes of *hispanique* passion in unprecedented fashion: ghosts of the Napoleonic empire, political prophecies, German brigands straight out of Schiller, an "enchanted" choir, memoirs of a drunken wedding night, and passages from *Le Cid,* Corneille's seventeenth-century epic about the Spanish knight. There was no real "story line" in *Hernani* as far as the audience was concerned, accustomed as it was to straightforward classical plays. As Albert Thibaudet, the French literary historian, has pointed out, "It was poetry of the theater; it was not the reality of theater." Thibaudet also remarked that "the evening of *Hernani* was like *La Marseillaise* . . . the Austerlitz of Romanticism." A late nineteenth-century English critic summed it up: "That Hugo was the greatest tragic and dramatic poet born since the age of Shakespeare, the appearance of *Hernani* in 1830 made evident forever to all but the meanest and most perverse of dunces and malignants." In any event, the "battle of *Hernani*" made Hugo the uncontested chief of the Romantic movement at that point in its history.

In painting, Eugène Delacroix achieved the Romantic breakthrough as early as 1824, when his *Massacre at Scio,* his homage to the Greek independence fighters and Byron, was presented at the official annual *salon* in Paris, ending the dictates of classical rule. Delacroix's monumental contribution in art was his use of vivid color, earlier ignored, and his fascination with great universal themes brought to the canvas in a way none of his predecessors had attempted. This was the essence of the Romanticism of Delacroix described by a friend: "He had a sun in his head and storms in his heart [and] for forty years played upon the keyboard of human passions [and] his brush—grandiose, terrible, or suave—passed from saints to warriors, from warriors to lovers, from lovers to tigers, and from tigers to flowers."

And in music, Hector Berlioz made Romanticism's breakthrough in 1825, when he conducted 150 musicians at a performance of his requiem at Saint-Roch Church. No performance of such magnitude and venturesome boldness had ever been presented before.

Louis XVIII's death precipitated historical change in France and quickened the rise of Romanticism. The new sovereign, Charles X (Louis XVIII's brother, known as the Count d'Artois), made a bad political situation worse with his ultra-hardline inclinations, granting great power to the Roman Catholic Church, one of the main victims of the 1789 revolution. With the tragic history of religious wars in France dating back to thirteenth-century antiheresy crusades, the Reformation, and bourgeois anticlericalism, Charles X had deepened internal political divisions. An economic and financial crisis in the late 1820s added to the tensions, making them unbearable.

Fundamentally, the July revolution ousted Charles X because the bourgeoisie believed that its standing in the changing society and its economic interests were threatened by the policies of his monarchy and its old-line aristocratic allies. Dissolving the National Guard in 1827 as the principal law enforcement institution, the king antagonized still further the middle class, which had long considered the guard as its instrument of prestige and security. It turned the aging Marquis de La Fayette, a most influential politician at home, founder of the guard, and hero of the War of Independence in America, squarely against the royal government of Charles X. By then, La Fayette and his friends were already conspiring to place Louis-Philippe, the Duke of Orléans, in power.

Naturally, revolutions—as distinct from coups d'état—do not happen in a vacuum; they require some sort of social and political context. This was the situation in France at that point in history as both the middle class and the working class—the new proletariat—were growing vigorously and as the national economy expanded, becoming increasingly modernized. Railways were being built, and factories and smaller ateliers established across the country as the industrial revolution dawned.

Consequently, both the middle class and the gruesomely disadvantaged working class began to emerge as potent new political forces, with the better-educated bourgeoisie guiding the workers. Politicians and intellectuals, including La Fayette and a group of young writers, started to pay attention to the "New Christianity" preachings of Count Claude-Henri Saint-Simon, who believed that the time had come to end the exploitation of man by man. This was the birth of serious socialist doctrines in Europe. By the time Saint-Simon died in 1825, they had already taken root.

Meanwhile, Charles X, who serenely played whist with friends at the Tuileries Palace as his regime foundered, at last provided the final push for the 1830 revolution. He restricted press freedoms through new censorship laws and promulgated new electoral legislation that, in effect, deprived the bourgeoisie of political power through the exclusion of voters whose annual property taxes were below a very high minimum line. This allowed only the rich upper-middle-class French citizens to vote along with the wealthy traditional aristocracy. Workers and peasants were automatically deprived of the vote.

The revolution broke out on July 29, when printshops in Paris closed down in protest against censorship, letting their workers go. Other industrial ateliers shut down in solidarity or in fear, and soon there were tens of thousands unemployed workers in the streets, turning into rioters and foot soldiers of the rebellion.

La Fayette reactivated the National Guard in support of the street rebels. After three days of combat in Paris, Charles X fled and the seventy-three-year-old general handed power over to the fifty-seven-year-old Duke of Orléans on July 31. The duke now became King Louis-

Philippe, inaugurating the era of bourgeois ascendancy and affluence, with a banker as his first prime minister and a furled green umbrella under his arm as public trademark.

And under the "July Monarchy," as it became known, Romanticism in the arts and letters experienced a glorious surge. Chopin appeared on the scene at the perfect time to catch the cresting wave.

Chapter 4

CHOPIN'S CONQUEST OF PARIS as the Romantic revolution in arts and politics erupted across Europe was achieved with remarkable alacrity—considering that the city was wholly terra incognita to him. His situation was quite reminiscent of the fortunes of Rastignac, the hero of Honoré de Balzac's great and somewhat autobiographical novel *Le Père Goriot;* Balzac was Fryderyk's romantic contemporary and friend.

Chopin's accomplishment stood tribute to his artistic genius, extremely fortunate musical timing, enormous personal charm and appearance, exquisite manners, supreme self-confidence as a musician (unfailingly overcoming his innate insecurities and self-doubt), iron will, hard work, discipline, and a businessman's talent for organizing and managing his life in an alien environment. He was adored by women of all ages, and cherished and respected by men.

At the same time, Chopin was—and would always remain—a mysterious, secretive, and inviolably private human being. He had erected tall ramparts around his person to protect his ever-deteriorating physical health and the tortured heart and soul that he never really bared to anyone. He craved company, but trusted no one and sought isolation. In a letter to Woyciechowski, he complained: "You would not believe how sad I feel that I have nobody to whom I can cry out loud. You know how easily I form acquaintanceships, you know how I like human company . . . but I am up to my ears with such acquaintances. . . . There is nobody, nobody with whom I can sigh. That's why I suffer, and you won't believe how I search for a *relief,* that is, solitude . . . so that nobody would drop in on me all day, that nobody would strike up a chat. . . . Even as I write to you, I can't stand the ringing of the doorbell."

Indeed, Chopin had two distinct personalities: a private Polish personality, warm and loving, reserved for those to whom he felt the closest (mostly, but not exclusively, other Poles), and a public one, impeccably polite, but cold and distant. He suffered from typically manic-depressive mood swings that were as violent as his shifts from major to minor and back again in the same composition, not to mention key shifts.

During attacks of rage, he smashed chairs, broke pencils, and heaped invective upon hapless piano students or visitors. A former pupil reported that at least once he had seen Chopin's hair stand on end like a dog's hackles. When deeply depressed, he shut himself in his room for days, weeping softly.

Haunted by constant premonitions and fears of impending death and tragedy, Chopin was nonetheless endowed with a puckish sense of humor about himself as well as others, which may have been psychologically his saving grace in the blackest moments. He often spoke deprecatingly about his large nose. He was a natural comedian, caricaturist, and (like Mozart) a mimic, and he loved to imitate other pianists at the keyboard, especially Liszt, with his dramatic, flamboyant style. Chopin had the keen eye of a satirical journalist or novelist, spouting colorful, often malicious descriptions, usually in his letters home, about strangers in the street, concert audiences, other composers and pianists (most of whom he held in deep contempt), and his music publishers, whom he often called "those tricky dog-catcher Jews."

Chopin chastised his Jewish music publishers (most of them *were* Jewish) when they were late in paying him for commissioned works, or he thought they were, or they refused to lend him money (or demanded it back too quickly). In 1839 letters from Marseilles to Polish friends in Paris handling his affairs with publishers, he observed that "Jews are always Jews and Germans [are] always Germans—it is true, but what to do?—I have to deal with them . . . if you have anything to do with Jews, do it at least with the Orthodox." Instructing his friends on how to approach a publisher, Chopin remarked, "but do it politely because he is a Jew and he wants to be regarded as somebody."

Despite derogatory comments about his Jewish publishers, Chopin is not known to have made them about other Jews or Jews in general. In fact, his principal publisher in Paris, Maurice Schlesinger, and his banker,

Auguste Léo, were personal friends. And Chopin was not as viscerally anti-Semitic as was, for example, Robert Schumann, who had told his wife, Clara, that while he revered Mendelssohn, a Jew, as an "Artist," he saw in him Jewish "avarice, greed, and self-aggrandizement."

Chopin's attitude toward Jews was in tune with the Polish language culture of the nineteenth century (still persisting today), which allowed mocking and patronizing—but seldom vicious—remarks about Jews. When he was fourteen, spending a summer at a nobleman's estate, Fryderyk handwrote a "newspaper" reporting on the daily events there. In one of the "dispatches," he provided an amused description of a Jewish family's distress when their horse cart turned over and spilled them on the road, mixing Polish and Yiddish words. In another news item, he wrote about a Jewish musician "sticking his hooked nose into the salon" of his friends' mansion in order to listen to Fryderyk's piano performance of a piece based on Jewish airs. The Jews, he added, had told him that if he wished to play at a Jewish wedding, he "would earn at least ten talers." This comment "encouraged" Chopin to practice playing more Jewish folk music, very much a part of traditional Polish countryside music, to gauge the "possibilities of this kind of music, which, who knows, might in time serve to lead to promising harmonies." And, indeed, it did: There are distinctively Jewish airs in some of his mazurkas. In Mickiewicz's epic poetry, the Jewish fiddler Jankiel is an important individual. Polish-Jewish culture, surviving to this day through synthesis and assimilation, owes much to Chopin and his friend Mickiewicz.

In his day-to-day life, Chopin could be alternately selfish and immensely generous, extremely considerate and extremely inconsiderate of people, arrogant and humble, deeply suspicious and trusting, and explosively irritable. He was a perfectionist, even pedantic at times. A man of supreme good taste, he was naturally "fashionable" in dress ("fashionable" being the word of the day for quiet, distinguished elegance).

He was eminently practical when it came to the money he needed to earn to pay for his high living style, including, not too long after his arrival in Paris, a hired horse, carriage, and coachman, and a full-time butler. An incomparable piano teacher in ever-growing demand, Chopin soon commanded high fees for the lessons. His compositions, published in Paris, London, Vienna, Leipzig, and Warsaw, brought him rising revenues as his fame grew. But he spent every louis and sou he made (ignoring his father's admonitions in letters from Warsaw to save for a "black hour"), and worried about money until the end of his life.

Chopin never married despite many fine opportunities. His longest continuing relationship spanned the nine turbulent years spent with George Sand, the French novelist. In all likelihood, he was asexual, notwithstanding his high sensuality.

What, apart from death, Chopin seemed to fear the most was emotional commitment. He never gave it fully to any person outside his immediate family. The inability to make such attachments may have been his deepest personal tragedy. Perhaps such relationships were sublimated to his musical creation.

Fryderyk's commitment to family—parents, sisters, and brothers-in-law—and theirs to him were the only solid and permanent emotional anchor in his life. With the exception of one personal encounter after he left Warsaw, halfway between his old and his new home, contact was maintained by what must have been quite voluminous correspondence, despite Fryderyk's reputation as a highly reluctant letter writer.

Because most of his letters to Warsaw were lost when the family home was destroyed by the Russians during a new uprising—in 1863—it is the correspondence from the Chopins to him (preserved almost in its entirety) that provides, like a mirror image, the essence of what Fryderyk had chosen to share with his loved ones. The exceedingly meticulous and attentive Mikołaj Chopin made a point of responding to the news and impressions imparted by his son and commenting amply on them in his lengthy letters, first to Vienna, then to Paris. They also exchanged doggerel about Fryderyk's health and his irregular letter-writing habits (*this,* Mikołaj wrote in Polish).

That Fryderyk reported a lot about his life in Paris, certainly more than he told all his friends (except Tytus Woyciechowski), is evident in a typical missive from Mikołaj in the mid-1830s: "I know . . . that you are very busy with lessons as well as with composing, but I notice with sadness that you rest very little. . . . The long evenings which, as you say, are essential, could do you harm, especially during the time of year [winter] when it is so easy to catch a cold. I know that these great receptions allow you to make many valuable acquaintances, but your health?"

Given the frequency and the detail of the letters to Fryderyk from his father and sisters, Justyna Chopin wrote only on the rarest occasions. The girls supplied him with a rich blend of affection, Warsaw gossip, and musical discussions. Elsner, his conservatory teacher, kept up a stream of advice on Frycek's career. This steady flow of family warmth from Warsaw must have given Chopin a modicum of personal stability, allowing him to turn his energies fully to writing piano works; it also allowed him to tell his old teacher Elsner in a long letter why he had no interest in composing operas.

From the very outset, Fryderyk had come under pressure from Polish friends, notably poet friends, to become an opera composer. Some of them firmly believed that he had a patriotic duty to be a "national composer" and that the grandeur of a "Slav opera" was the best vehicle for the propagation of Polish ideas. Others, thinking principally of Mozart, felt that only through opera could a composer achieve greatness; it was the conventional wisdom of the day.

Chopin, however, was always convinced that for *him* the piano was the perfect instrument and that he could and would achieve more with the keyboard than with a hundred voices on an opera stage. He felt the same way about orchestral works. His devotion to the human voice as pure sound led him to use it as the basis for tonality in his compositions. He admired opera and operatic composers, and some of his music was influenced by opera, but Chopin never wished to be an imitator. In fairness to his well-meaning friends, however, it must be noted that the piano's ability to create extraordinary sound had not been fully appreciated until the coming of Chopin.

Elsner was among those urging Chopin to compose operas (he had himself composed an obscure Polish patriotic opera), and Fryderyk undertook in an exquisitely polite letter from Paris on December 14, 1831, to explain that he could not possibly match his musical example and that he had to "postpone for some time the higher artistic vistas that you so wisely set forth in your letter to me." He added: "I shall create a new world for myself."

In sublimating his emotions, in this fashion, Chopin resembled his idol Wolfgang Amadeus Mozart, about whom one of his biographers, Maynard Solomon, wrote: "The artist's personal motivations, experiences, and drives may be . . . thoroughly absorbed—or objectified—in a successful creation. . . . In his work, the artist finds ways symbolically to repair psychic injuries and object losses, to neutralize anxieties." That Mozart, unlike Chopin, did marry and created his own family home made little difference in his emotional makeup. Chopin, however, never could "repair" his psychic injuries or allay anxieties.

*   *   *

Nevertheless, Fryderyk Chopin had reason to feel self-assured as a *musician* when he first set foot in Paris. He had traveled there because he felt competitive as a composer and pianist—and ready to take on the challenge. Much as he talked about his supposedly hesitant nature, he always looked for challenges, both in unheard of innovations in musical composition, the core of his genius, and in arenas of competition.

In the words of Charles Rosen, "[Chopin's] later interests [were] already fully developed" when he turned twenty, a year before he embarked on the conquest of Paris. Though the sheer volume and variety of his musical creation did not even remotely approach Mozart's output at a similar age (Mozart had produced more than 150 compositions over a three-year period in the 1780s, which exceeded Chopin's known lifetime total), the portfolio of published and unpublished manuscripts he had brought along was quite impressive. Moreover, both Chopin and Mendelssohn were more mature composers before the age of twenty than Mozart.

Chopin was helped, of course, by the fact that from late in the eighteenth century there was an intense and growing interest in music throughout Europe and that new compositions were published as sheet music and circulated with astonishing speed, considering the day's technology and communications limitations. New wealth was expanding the middle classes, and every self-respecting affluent French bourgeois home had to have a "modern" Pleyel or Erard piano. Moreover, there were more musical journals and reviews in European capitals in the early 1800s than today.

And high quality music criticism was at its apex with many leading composers such as Schumann and Liszt writing as critics in that innocent age when the notion of conflict of interest in reviewing had not yet been conceived. At the same time, writers like Ernst Theodor Amadeus Hoffmann (better known as E. T. A. Hoffmann) composed fine operas—his *Undine,* for example—and piano sonatas and chamber music. Delacroix, the painter who was deeply interested in all forms of artistic expression, also wrote about music, pronouncing it, in a diary entry, to be superior to literature: "Music is the luxury of the imagination."

But even in such a sophisticated environment, Chopin was no nonentity when he alighted in Paris.

He was best known at that point, at least among musicians, for his

Variations for Piano and Orchestra in B-flat major on "Là ci darem la mano," the duet from Mozart's *Don Giovanni*. He'd written it at seventeen, in 1827. It shows both his devotion to Mozart and his love of opera, and was published in Vienna three years later, on the eve of his appearance in Paris, as his first work published outside Poland. Schumann, three months younger than Chopin (whom he had not yet met), read the variations in the autumn of 1831, proclaiming in a lengthy, if slightly bizarre, review for *Allgemeine Musikalische Zeitung* in Leipzig: "Hats off, gentlemen—a genius!" The review was published on December 7, and immediately read in Paris, where Chopin was preparing for his first public concert. (The review was bizarre because it took the form of a conversation among "Florestan," "Eusebius," and "Master Raro," imaginary companions Schumann had invented for himself as a young man and kept alive in his mind until his ultimate madness.)

It was the greatest public accolade Chopin had received up to that time—though there had been favorable reviews earlier in Viennese, German, and of course Polish publications—but, displaying the discourtesy with which he often treated other contemporary composers, he made no known effort to thank Schumann. The German, too, was a rising star in the newly discovered firmament of Romanticism, publishing his *Papillons* about the time he wrote the review of Chopin's Mozart variations. It is conceivable that Chopin, who had heard *Papillons,* may have resented the rivalry. He admired very few contemporary composers. Schumann had been more generous.

Chopin, in fact, could be downright ungracious. Shortly after the publication of Schumann's review in Leipzig, his teacher Friedrich Wieck (whose pianist daughter Clara would later marry Schumann) wrote an equally admiring article about Chopin's variations for the German periodical *Caecilia.* Wieck then tried to have it reprinted in *Revue musicale* in Paris, but Chopin, having read the German version, succeeded in preventing the proposed publication in French. He thought it embarrassingly cloying—the review described the variations as a "fantastic tableau"—and he remarked in a letter to his friend Woyciechowski that Wieck (whom he did not know, either) "instead of being clever, is very stupid." Chopin added that he did not want to "die"—musically—because of "the imagination of that . . . stubborn German."

In another letter to Woyciechowski, soon after his arrival in France, Chopin commented lightly: "I don't know where there are more pianists

than in Paris—I don't know where there are more jackasses and more virtuosos than here." Plainly, he was not awed by the musical competition.
(In a letter to his friend Julian Fontana in 1839, Chopin suggested that
Ignaz Moscheles, a well-known pianist and composer, should be given "an
enema made up with oratorios by Neukomm, seasoned with Cellini and
the concert by Doehler." Sigismund von Neukomm was an Austrian composer and Haydn's favorite pupil; Cellini was an obscure Italian composer;
Theodor von Doehler was a popular Italian pianist and composer.)

In addition to the variations, Chopin carried with him to Paris numerous unpublished works although some of them were known, as it were,
through word of mouth. Pianists, violinists, singers, and composers
traveled extensively throughout Europe in those days to give concerts and
recitals, and they were generally familiar with new compositions from
hearing them in the cities they visited.

Many knew, for example, Chopin's Concerto in F minor for piano
and orchestra he had composed at eighteen in 1828, and had played at
concerts in Warsaw and Vienna (he first went there for a brief stay in the
summer of 1829), receiving favorable newspaper reviews. This was the
first of only two concertos he would compose for piano and orchestra,
writing the second, in E minor, in 1830 (curiously, the E minor Concerto is known as no. 1 and the F minor as no. 2). Having resolved in
adolescence to concentrate on piano music—and stay away from symphonies, operas, and other genres calling for large instrumental forces—
Chopin did try once again to compose a full concerto, but gave up for
good after writing an *Allegro de concert,* op. 46, a brisk movement of an
unfinished piece, between 1834 and 1841. This was one of the works it
took him years to "chisel," but failing in the end, as he concentrated
simultaneously on a variety of other ideas.

Both concertos were highly regarded from the outset for their inven-
tiveness in both the principal voices and accompaniments and their
power of drama. Each is deeply original in its form. Each represents an
early attempt to throw off the yoke of the classical harmonic system of
composition. Sir Donald Francis Tovey, the eminent historian, pianist,
and musicologist, has remarked that the Concerto no. 2 "is a masterpiece in a form and a mood which neither Chopin nor any other composer reproduced later. The finale is a delightful example of the long
ramble through picturesque musical scenery."

Unquestionably the most fabulous of the works Chopin had brought to Paris were several of the twelve études which would constitute the Opus 10 cycle. Probably eight of them—nobody can be certain because Chopin left no real clues—were written in Vienna late in 1830, after he left Warsaw, and during the summer of 1831, when he began his trek to Paris. Études nos. 1 and 2 may have been completed in Warsaw. Étude no. 12, the "Revolutionary," and no. 7, a fast, toccata-like piece, were most likely completed in Paris. Their numbers do not necessarily reflect the actual sequence of composition because Chopin's concept was that they should form a musically logical progression—and the order may have been established when the whole cycle was completed. Except for friends, who might have heard them privately, the études remained unknown until they were published in 1831.

"Étude" means "study" (in French) and, technically speaking, this is what Chopin's études are. He composed twelve more, published as Opus 25, in 1837, and three "Nouvelles Études" in 1840. But, as Tovey has commented, Chopin's études "are the only extant great works of art that really owe their character to their being Études." Another distinguished musicologist (Rosen) believes that "in the Études, Chopin invents pure piano sound—abstract piano sound, in fact." Chopin was the tireless experimenter with limitless imagination. But, above all, the penning of the first twelve études marked a historic turning point in Chopin's creativity.

Finally, Chopin's musical baggage, as he made his way that first evening in Paris to the rue de la Cité Bergère inn, also included a number of mazurkas and nocturnes—it is uncertain exactly how many—that would be published the following year and afterwards, adding to his rising fame.

Unlike Hugo in drama and literature, Delacroix in painting, and Schumann and Berlioz in music, however, Chopin was not a theoretician or an outspoken champion of the Romantic movement. He was not an artistic *thinker* or intellectual, he was not striving to launch a new school in music, he is not known to have spoken of Romanticism in so many words (it does not appear in his surviving letters), and, at least at the outset, he may not even have been aware that it existed as a novel concept.

Actually, some scholars insist that Chopin was not a "typically Romantic composer" because he adhered to classical rules of construction in his concertos, sonatas, and ballades while contributing fundamentally to purely Romantic forms with his études and préludes. Moreover, as noted most helpfully by the critic Joseph Kerman, there is "confusion between music theory and music, academic musical discourse and musical experience at large."

Chopin himself put it best when he once wrote that "music is the expression of our thoughts with the help of sound." What he had in him was inspiration, instinct, and, naturally, genius. In the mysterious ways of human creativity, he surged onto the stage of universal art attuned to other creators whose inspiration at the same time matched his own divine gift. He must have been guided by destiny.

Chapter 5

WHEN CHOPIN SET FOOT IN PARIS in September 1831, he instantly realized that, indeed, he had come to the cultural and musical capital of the world.

The city was rich in music with the best of opera and singers, orchestras and concerts, pianists and recitals. In comparison, even Vienna was a backwater. Notwithstanding on-and-off rioting in the aftermath of the July revolution (for example, the archbishop's palace was burned down in February) and the continuing poverty of the working class combined with massive unemployment, the Paris elites—and its Romantic creative figures—were enjoying the best of times. *Paris s'amuse,* wrote a contemporary chronicler.

Chopin's immediate problem was his lack of access to the Parisian musical establishment—having only two introductions. But the two letters, plus his charm and amazing talent, were all Fryderyk needed to start the conquest.

The first letter of recommendation came from Dr. Johann Malfatti, the personal physician of the emperor of Austria and once a close friend of Beethoven, to Ferdinando Paër, an Italian opera composer who had settled in Paris and become royal court music conductor in Napoleonic times. Chopin had met Malfatti when he arrived in Vienna from Warsaw with a letter of introduction to the physician's wife, Helena, the daughter of a senator of the Kingdom of Poland, and the Malfattis immediately took to him like a son, feeding and feting him. Fryderyk played for Malfatti at a surprise saint's-day party for him. He wrote to his family: "All goes well for me. I have faith in God and in Malfatti that it will be even better. . . . Malfatti really loves me, and I am not a little proud of it."

The second introduction letter was from Chopin's Warsaw teacher Józef Elsner to the French composer Jean-François Lesueur. He also carried a few letters from Vienna music publishers to Paris publishers, but did not identify them.

Malfatti's letter to Paër turned out to be Chopin's gold key to a new life. The sixty-year-old Italian had superb connections in Paris and became Fryderyk's protector in every sense. Because Chopin's Russian passport restriction allowed him to remain in Paris only "in passage" to London, Paër wrote the French authorities requesting a more permanent status for "this young man . . . [who] is a Pole deported from Warsaw as a result of the revolution [and] who was in Vienna where the press and the society elite received him with great consideration. Chopin is an educated young man."

Chopin, of course, had not been deported and was not a political refugee, but the French granted him permission to stay in Paris indefinitely "to be able to perfect his art." Four years later, Fryderyk became a French citizen and a French passport was issued to him on August 1, 1835. He is not known to have discussed his decision to change citizenship with anyone, including his father. It is unclear whether he did it to avoid renewing his Russian passport at the Russian embassy for patriotic reasons or simply as a matter of general convenience.

And through Paër, Fryderyk very quickly got to know musical *tout Paris:* the brilliant new generation and the older musicians who controlled the establishment. Among the first, in November 1831, was pianist and composer Ferenc Liszt, one of Paër's pupils. Liszt was more than a year younger than Chopin, and their instant friendship—and complex rivalry—developed into one of Fryderyk's closest life relationships.

Liszt and Chopin were a study in absolute contrasts in every imaginable way. While Liszt was tall with dramatically long black hair spilling down his shoulders—he always cultivated the dramatic image—Chopin was of slight stature and never strove to impress with his physical presence. Liszt was an extrovert and Chopin an introvert. With a background even more complicated than Chopin's, Liszt had troubles with his identity at every step of life. He was born on the Esterházy family's Raiding estate sixty miles from Vienna, and both his parents were

Austrian. His public identification as a "Hungarian" musician stemmed from the fact that Raiding, where his father worked as a steward, was part of the huge domains of the noble Esterházy clan, perhaps the greatest Hungarian family. (Austria and Hungary were joined at the time as the Vienna-ruled Austro-Hungarian "dual monarchy.") As a child, Liszt was exposed to Hungarian and nomad Gypsy folk music on the Esterházy estate, and, as a nine-year-old prodigy, he gave his first public concert before an audience composed mostly of Hungarian aristocracy. Folk music deeply influenced him, but he never learned Hungarian and left Raiding when he was eleven for Vienna and Paris, not to return there for eighteen years. With German as his first language, French became his *best* language after he settled in Paris.

What Liszt and Chopin certainly had in common was genius as pianists and composers—and their deep psychological and emotional problems. Like Chopin, Liszt appeared to suffer from manic-depressive illness; at the age of eighteen, he had a major nervous breakdown after the collapse of an ardent adolescent love affair. The greatest difference between them was their approach to life.

In his late teens (as Chopin single-mindedly pursued his musical career), Liszt made plans to become a priest notwithstanding his Europe-wide success as a prodigy recital pianist (he had even played for King George IV at Windsor Castle). Soon, however, he went back to music playing and composing—and to women (his dying father's last words to him were, "I fear for you with women"). About the time Liszt met Chopin, he came upon Countess Marie-Sophie d'Agoult, a wealthy divorced woman, six years his senior, who became his mistress for the next eleven or twelve years (their daughter Cosima would marry Richard Wagner, for whom, along with Chopin, he was the most important musical influence). Countess d'Agoult, who wrote novels under the pen name of Daniel Stern, also happened to be a friend of George Sand—a fact that would before too long become instrumental in changing the course of Chopin's life. Meanwhile, Liszt, together with Mendelssohn, attended Chopin's first public concert in Paris in February 1832.

Years later, following other love affairs and the production of musical masterpieces, Liszt would embrace the Roman Catholic Church at the age of fifty-three, receiving minor religious orders, and becoming a full-fledged priest at the age of sixty-nine. Justly or not, he would be described by contemporaries as "a mixture of priest and circus rider."

Chopin's other new friend, also more than a year younger, was the German composer and pianist Ferdinand Hiller, whom he admired as an artist with "a huge talent . . . something like Beethoven, he is a man full of poetry, fire, and soul." Hiller would write decades later that "Chopin loved me, but I must add that I was in love with him. I do not know how else to describe the sentiment he inspired in me. His presence made me happy, I could never hear him [play] enough; if I did not see him for a longer time, I missed him; in the morning, I left home early to see him before he started his lessons." Hiller came the nearest to replacing Tytus Woyciechowski in Chopin's life in terms of their mutual warmth though Fryderyk never opened his heart as fully to him. Again, there is not even a hint of homosexuality in their friendship.

Hiller, in turn, introduced Chopin to Mendelssohn, still another German musical genius of his generation to make Paris his home. Mendelssohn was a year older than Fryderyk, had heard him at a concert in Berlin three years earlier, but lacked the courage to introduce himself. Now it was Mendelssohn's turn to admire Chopin, and they became fast friends. He called him "Chopinet" or "Chopinetto." Then there was George Alexander Osborne, an Irish pianist, and Camille-Marie Stamaty, a French pianist. Finally, Chopin found a very special friend—for life—in Auguste Franchomme, the marvelously talented, boyish-looking court cellist, two years older than he. Franchomme and the painter Delacroix (whom Chopin would meet only years later) would be Fryderyk's best French friends. Vincenzo Bellini, who was thirty years old when Chopin met him in 1831 (he died four years later) and another transplant to Paris, was venerated by Fryderyk: His opera *La Sonnambula* left a deep impression on him. Hector Berlioz, who had gone to Italy after stunning Paris with his hour-long *Symphonie fantastique* in December 1830, was back home at the end of 1832, meeting Chopin almost immediately.

All these young musicians were men of extraordinary talent and it was unprecedented for so many of them of the same generation—all born between 1803 and 1813—to be so magically assembled at the same time in the same place, and to be friends. They developed the custom of gathering for long dinners at the Café de Paris, one of their favorite restaurants along with the Maison Dorée, or some other fashionable Parisian eatery. The system held that each of the group took his turn paying for

the whole dinner though, naturally, the composition of those participating varied. All were fun-loving, occasionally hard-drinking, and
Chopin startled his companions with unmatched mimicry gifts.

Never before had so young and large a group come together to influence so profoundly the future of music. Nobody had planned it and
none thought of themselves as anything as structured, ponderous, and
pompous as the "Romantic generation." The designation would come
much later. In fact, their individual composing and playing styles dif-
fered greatly under the general heading of "new music," replacing classicism. They often criticized one another, especially as they began to age.
Chopin, for example, thought Berlioz's music was brash and vulgar.
Liszt and Chopin were piano performance rivals, with the latter bad-
mouthing the former.

In fact, Paris, overflowing with first-rate pianists, was a merciless field
of battle for them. Among reasons for Chopin's disdain of Berlioz (who
thought the world of him) was that the Frenchman could not play the
piano. In his up-and-down relationship with Liszt, Chopin joined him in
appearing at major public concerts and confessed his admiration for the
man's keyboard wizardry, but was able to say horrors behind his back. He
disliked Liszt's friendships with the Paris aristocracy (though he cultivated
the very same aristocrats), remarking in a letter to a Polish friend that
Liszt "one of these days will be a member of Parliament or perhaps even
the King of Abyssinia or the Congo." Teaching the piano to the great
singer Pauline Viardot, who was also an outstanding composer of songs
and operas, Chopin criticized her on one occasion, exclaiming, "That's
for the playing of Liszt . . . it's not needed to accompany the voice." Liszt,
on the other hand, venerated Chopin as his book, written a few years
after Fryderyk's death, amply demonstrates. Alan Walker, an English
music scholar, has noted that as a composer Liszt was so intimidated and
influenced by Chopin that he composed "virtually nothing which owes
anything to Chopin while Chopin lived . . . as if there was a deep-
rooted unconscious hostility towards Chopin, which forced him to resist
Chopin while Chopin lived, and embrace him after he died." However,
Liszt and Chopin shared one opinion: that the immensely touted and
popular Swiss pianist Sigismond Thalberg (their contemporary) was
vastly overrated. And as pianists, both were pioneers in the use of the
pedal in a manner that significantly enhanced sound and tonality.

All of them represented many cultures and backgrounds: German,

French, Italian, English, Hungarian, and Polish (French was their conversational lingua franca). Rather than developing into "national" composers—and Chopin, for example, must never be regarded as exclusively a "Slavonic" or "Polish" composer—they created together a quintessentially *European* (or universal) music. They inspired and affected music for the balance of the nineteenth century—and beyond.

Richard Wagner, a contemporary of the Paris group, but growing apart from it in Germany, was undoubtedly influenced by these trailblazers of Romanticism. Chopin was one of many geniuses of the Romantic Age in whose harmonic language, as well as other innovative musical procedures, there are precedents for Wagner's style. Liszt, of course, was another influence on Wagner. And the echo of Chopin and the Romantic generation is heard loud and clear, too, in Brahms, Debussy, Fauré, and Saint-Saëns late in the nineteenth century. Chopin was probably the most innovative with his ballades, scherzos, and nocturnes, but the overall revolutionary impact came from the entire Paris group.

But Paris in the early 1830s was a magnet for writers as well as musicians of Romanticism. Heinrich Heine, the young German poet (and Marx's friend), had exiled himself to Paris because he believed that his Jewishness harmed him in his own country. He, too, was Chopin's friend. Polish poets Mickiewicz and Słowacki chose Paris for *their* exile after the collapse of the "November Uprising" in Warsaw. They and others rapidly built contacts with many of the musicians and with French writers like Hugo, Balzac, and Lamartine. It was the cultural "Internationale."

Inevitably, the influence of the Paris group—in music, literature, and painting—radiated back to their individual countries. Indeed, the degree and speed of cultural communication in the first half of the nineteenth century was astonishing. Book and music publishers and stores proliferated to serve the ever-hungry clientele as did newspapers and magazines. And Paris was on the receiving end of creativity born elsewhere in Europe. Charles Dickens's novel *Oliver Twist,* for example, was published in London in 1837, and read in French translation in Paris the following year.

It was also the time of resurgence in great philosophical thought. German philosopher Arthur Schopenhauer, then in his mid-forties, had been a friend of Goethe in Weimar (and among other works he produced reflections on death and the metaphysics of sexual experience). Wagner was devoted to Schopenhauer's writings because he believed that the philosopher's ideas as he understood them were in accord with his own. Schopenhauer had written that music "exclusively" is a direct "emanation" of "basic forces of nature," and Wagner went on to explore the mystical role of music with his "music drama" creations. In 1854, Wagner inscribed one of the last copies of his *Ring of the Nibelung* text to Schopenhauer with "Reverence and Gratitude." Søren Aabye Kierkegaard, the Danish philosopher, three years younger than Chopin, conceptualized ethical and aesthetic ideas of life in ways intellectually attuned to the Romantic Age. Another German philosopher of profound influence was Georg Wilhelm Friedrich Hegel, who knew Paris well and proclaimed that music was "the archetypal Romantic art" (he died of cholera in Berlin in 1831).

Grand Parisian post-Empire literary salons were built mostly around men—Victor Hugo serves as a good example—in a departure from eighteenth-century traditions. But there were memorable exceptions.

Thus, there was the salon of Germaine de Staël on rue du Bac on the aristocratic Left Bank, which she had established in the early days of the Empire. A renowned novelist and literary critic in her own right, Madame de Staël and her lover, Benjamin Constant, a famous intellectual and politician, but an unimpressive writer, were a magnet for the literati of the day. She died in 1817, but her impact as a Romantic pioneer lived long after her. A French literary historian has written that Madame de Staël "existed less as a producer of works than as the choirmaster and mistress of a house of immense dialogue."

The next great literary hostess was Juliette Récamier, an intimate friend of Madame de Staël and Constant, whose salon on rue de la Chaise was illuminated by the presence of her lover, François-René Chateaubriand, one of the first and greatest Romantic era authors, and Charles-Augustin Sainte-Beuve, the leading literary critic of the period (who would be among George Sand's first admirers). Sainte-Beuve believed that Chateaubriand in literature and Chopin in music were the "bridge" between the classics and Romanticism. Lamartine, the political poet, was a frequent guest *chez* Madame Récamier, who ran her salon for thirty years, until 1849 (the year Chopin died).

Usually, salons were held before or after dinner, and guests were offered orangeade, syrups, and cookies. Often authors were asked to read their latest works (or, at least, some passages) and composers and pianists sat at the keyboard. Chopin, a frequent and highly favored guest at many salons, sometimes sat at the piano almost until dawn, enchanting his audience with variations (responding to requests) on known pieces of music or, better still, brilliant improvisations—and the tomfoolery of imitating other pianists and composers: He imitated the way they hit the keys, their facial expressions, and even their voices.

Delphine de Girardin, the wife of a rich and powerful newspaper publisher, gained a footnote in musical history by organizing one evening—she entertained almost nightly—a piano "duel" between Liszt and Thalberg to determine who was the better (Thalberg was the pianist despised by both Liszt and Chopin). Because the salons were for polite society, the verdict in Madame de Girardin's town house was that while Thalberg was the first pianist in the world, Liszt was "the only one." To be sure, the "truth" will never be known: apart from differences in taste, recordings had not yet been invented and it is a matter of contemporary opinion who played how. The same, of course, goes for Chopin's improvisations that nobody seems to have thought of transcribing as he drew his miracles from the keyboard.

Under the Romantic revolution of the 1830s, women of the new (and old) elites naturally stressed elegance as well, but they were not competing with the brilliant male plumage. In the evening, ball gowns were de rigueur, usually in discreet colors though bare shoulders and decent décolletage were perfectly acceptable. Long gloves were always worn. When the Polish cause dominated Paris in the early 1830s, it was not uncommon for ladies to appear in gowns in the Polish national colors: red and white.

To succeed professionally on the savagely competitive Parisian music scene, the newcomer needed contacts in the establishment. In this endeavor, too, Chopin was greatly helped by Paër, who introduced him to Friedrich Wilhelm Kalkbrenner, the German considered to be the premier living pianist in Europe, and such key personalities as Luigi Cherubini, the director of the Conservatory of Music (where Chopin, understanding its importance, desperately hoped to be invited to play); Gioacchino Rossini, who composed famous operas and directed the Italian Opera in Paris at the Théâtre des Italiens; Giacomo Meyerbeer, who composed the grandiose and immensely successful five-act opera *Robert le diable,* which dealt with religious mythology; and the violin virtuoso Pierre-Marie Baillot.

One of Chopin's first calls was on the chin-bearded, forty-six-year-old Kalkbrenner—"The King of the Pianoforte"—and he chose to play for him solo passages from his Concerto in F minor as a musical self-introduction. It was a distinct honor to play for Kalkbrenner, who was among the few pianists Chopin genuinely admired, at least at the outset. Eschewing modesty, Fryderyk reported in a letter to a friend that "I astonished Mister Kalkbrenner, who instantly inquired whether I was a pupil of [John] Field, told me that I play like [Johann Baptist] Cramer though I have a Field touch. . . . It made my soul rejoice." This was an extravagant compliment because Field, the Irish composer, and Cramer, a German, were legendary figures in pianism, but Chopin could not resist adding that after listening to him, "Kalkbrenner, wishing to impress me, sat at the piano, but he made mistakes and had to stop!"

But they quickly became friends, saw each other frequently, and the older man volunteered to take Chopin on as a pupil for a three-year period. Though this, too, was an extraordinary compliment, Chopin's instinct—and advice from his family and from his Warsaw composition teacher, Elsner—dissuaded him from accepting the offer. Kalkbrenner was the master of the Vienna-developed "Brilliant" piano style, overwhelmingly popular late in the eighteenth century and early in the nineteenth before the advent of Romanticism, and he argued that after his death there would be nobody to perpetuate the tradition of that great piano school unless Chopin became his successor. The "Brilliant" style could best be described as overpowering, a quality the subtle Chopin found offensive.

Moreover, to Chopin, this also meant that he would have to sacrifice composing in order to be a full-time piano virtuoso. His own idea was to do *both*—on his own terms. Chopin, who was for the most part self-taught at the keyboard and an amazing sight reader, had already convinced himself that he could play better than Kalkbrenner and vastly exceed him as a composer. In a letter home two months after arriving in Paris, he wrote: "You should know that I already have a great name among musicians here."

As usual, Chopin wasted no time in making up his mind about whom he liked and disliked in the Paris music power structure. Cherubini, then in his early seventies, was listed (in a letter to Elsner in Warsaw) among the "dried-up mummies" he had encountered in Paris,

Chopin adding that "he mumbles only about cholera and revolution" (actually, he used the Polish word *pupki,* derivative from the word for "derrière," to describe the "dried-up" people). Johann Peter Pixis, a German composer in his early forties, and Anton Reicha, the Czech-born professor of counterpoint at the Paris Conservatory, were also dismissed as "dried-up *pupki.*"

Meyerbeer, who was twice Chopin's age, won his approval because Fryderyk was most impressed with *Robert le diable,* and because the composer had listened to *his* music and was, in Chopin's never modest words (in a letter to his father), "astonished" by it. Meyerbeer himself addressed Chopin in a letter as "Dear and Illustrious Master." Fryderyk had kind words for Kalkbrenner and for Pierre-Joseph Zimmerman, a respected professor at the conservatory, whose musical evenings were famous in Paris—and soon he was a favored guest at his home.

Fryderyk, however, could not stand to be crossed or contradicted even by those he loved and admired. Wilhelm von Lenz, a distinguished pianist who was among Chopin's pupils, recalled a scene at his teacher's apartment when Meyerbeer arrived unannounced while the pupil was playing a mazurka and how an argument erupted over the meter in which it had been notated:

> Meyerbeer took a seat and I continued. "That's in 2/4," said Meyerbeer. I had to repeat it while Chopin, pencil in hand, beat time on the piano; his eyes were blazing. "2/4," Meyerbeer calmly repeated. Only once have I ever seen Chopin lose his temper, and it was at that moment—and what a wonderful sight it was! A faint red suffused his pale cheeks. "It's in 3/4," he said in a loud voice. "Give me that piece as a ballet in my opera," retorted Meyerbeer, "I'll prove it to you." "It's in 3/4," Chopin almost yelled, he who never normally raised his voice above a murmur. He pushed me aside and sat at the piano himself. *Three times* he played the piece, counting aloud and stamping out the beat with his foot; he was beside himself! Meyerbeer still held his own and they parted on bad terms. . . . Without taking leave of me, Chopin had disappeared into his study. He was right, all the same: For though the third beat loses some of its value, submerged as it is in the flow of the melody, still it does not cease to exist.

In public, of course, Chopin was always smiling and polite—in the company of his contemporaries as well as the "dried-up mummies."

Within six months of his arrival, he had met almost everybody who counted (for him) in Paris.

Ironically, however, Chopin would not meet for years at least two persons fated to play extremely significant roles in his life.

Eugène Delacroix, already very famous, had left for North Africa to travel and paint for an indefinite period just before Chopin materialized in Paris.

When he arrived in September 1831, a budding novelist named Aurore Dudevant was still married to Baron Casimir Dudevant, with whom she had two children. She divided her life between a Paris apartment and the family mansion in Nohant in the Berry region, two hundred miles south of the capital. There was no reason or occasion for them to meet at the time, never having heard of each other, but their respective fames began to soar simultaneously.

Within a year, Chopin would be one of the most admired musicians in Paris. Aurore, having shed Casimir, would become a literary sensation with the publication of her novel *Indiana* and metamorphose into the public identity and personality of George Sand. Most likely, they began hearing and reading about each other at some moment—without any particular personal interest.

Chapter 6

"I AM SLOWLY LAUNCHING MYSELF in the world although I have only one ducat in my pocket," Fryderyk Chopin wrote with absolute self-assurance to a friend in Berlin on November 18, 1831, two months after arriving in Paris.

And, indeed, the twenty-one-year-old genius had launched himself in Parisian society to the point where soon he could afford to be insouciant regarding whether he had one or more gold coins in the pocket of his fashionable black frock coat cut for him by Dautremont on rue Vivienne, the best tailor on the great boulevards.

Chopin had moved that same day from the inn where he had lived since September to his first Paris apartment in a narrow building at 27, boulevard Poissonnière in the center of the newly politically powerful French bourgeoisie, just below Montmartre. It was a chic address—many artists lived there, too—but, as Chopin was learning, the ancestral homes of old-line aristocracy were in the Left Bank Faubourg St. Germain, immediately east of the Chamber of Deputies in the Palais Bourbon, and on the Right Bank's Faubourg St. Honoré behind the Louvre. Chopin would before long become an esteemed guest in both faubourgs, but even now he was cheerful and happy.

"You won't believe how nicely I live," he wrote the evening of his move to Norbert Alfons Kumelski, a plant biologist friend who had traveled with him from Vienna to Munich, staying behind in Germany. "I have a room beautifully furnished in mahogany on the fifth floor . . . with a balcony over the boulevards, from where I can see from Montmartre to the Panthéon and the whole lovely world along with it (many envy me my view, but not the stairs)."

Boulevard Poissonnière was a busy, fairly broad street, tree-lined on both sides, and Chopin, ever curious, instantly plunged into the thick of Parisian life in his neighborhood and beyond. Paris at the time was a metropolis of about one million inhabitants—ten times the population of Warsaw—and, always the sharp-eyed observer, he marveled at what he saw. In letters to family and friends, he reported the "impression this great city has made on me after Stuttgart and Strasbourg."

"There is here the greatest luxury, the greatest pigsty, the greatest virtue, the greatest displays, posters about venereal disease at every step," he wrote Kumelski. "[There is] more shouting, noise, and mud than one can imagine. One becomes lost in this beehive, and this is convenient from the viewpoint that nobody asks how you live. . . . One day you eat the richest dinner for 32 sous in a mirrored restaurant lit with gold and gas—the next day you can go to lunch where they serve you as if you were a bird, and you pay three times as much."

Chopin also noted ironically, "so many ladies of mercy . . . they chase after people." But, he wrote, "I regret that the souvenir of Teresa, despite the efforts of Benedict, [who] regards my grief as something very small, I am not allowed to taste the forbidden fruit." Evidently, Fryderyk had caught venereal disease, probably gonorrhea, from (probably) a prostitute named Teresa somewhere between Vienna and Munich, and Benedict was probably his doctor. And, inevitably, Chopin spotted at once the advertisements for the cure of venereal diseases. After mentioning his "grief," he remarked wistfully, "I already know several singers—and the singers here, even more than the Tyrolian ones, would like to [sing] duets." Fryderyk also informed friends in mock seriousness that he had resisted the "temptation" presented by a pretty Paris neighbor to visit her in her husband's absence and warm himself at her fireplace on cold evenings. (Venereal disease was quite commonplace in Chopin's day: Paganini and Schumann, for example, suffered from advanced syphilis.)

From everything known about Chopin, we may assume he was a virgin when he left Warsaw, and his initiation at twenty to sex with "Teresa" (never mentioned again) resulted in a gonorrhea infection, hardly an incentive to further sexual activity for a man who appears to have been asexual in the first place. There are no other references to or hints of a sexual life in his surviving correspondence, and Chopin's asexuality, which did not rule out occasional sexual acts, was a significant aspect of his subsequent romantic relationships with women.

Love, friendship, and the support of women, always there for him, were the backbone of Chopin's existence, from the outset with his mother and adoring sisters, to the very end. And when he embarked upon the conquest of Paris in the autumn of 1831, it was a woman who became one of his most devoted friends, helping to open great Parisian doors to Fryderyk.

She was Countess Delfina Potocka, considered at the time to be one of the most beautiful women in the elegant circles of Europe, and a natural musician. Chopin had met her parents, Count and Countess Komarów, in Dresden the previous year. The Komaróws now lived in Paris, one of the few families there of Chopin's acquaintance, and they were among the first he called upon on his arrival. A few weeks later, Countess Potocka, separated from her husband, Mieczysław, and residing in Paris at that point, invited Chopin to dinner on November 17, the day he moved to his boulevard Poissonnière apartment. Fryderyk recorded that fact, without further elaboration, in his letter to Kumelski, describing Delfina as "the pretty wife of Mieczysław."

A lifetime friendship rapidly developed between them, with Chopin discovering in Delfina a magnificent singer and an understanding companion. Sometimes they made music together. When Fryderyk's Concerto no. 2 in F minor for piano and orchestra was published in Paris in 1836, he dedicated it to her. But their relations were purely platonic even though Delfina had an outstanding European reputation in sexual matters. The poet Mickiewicz called her the "Great Sinner" and her lover of many years, the Polish Romantic poet Zygmunt Krasiński, referred to Delfina good-humoredly as "Don Juan in skirts." (After the Second World War, a colossal hoax was perpetrated with the "publication" of alleged letters from Chopin to Delfina—an epistolary masterpiece by unknown authors—and it took an extensive graphological investigation by the Polish communist secret service and Interpol to demonstrate that they were fake.)

Another important family to welcome Chopin were Count Ludwik Plater and his wife, who "received"—entertained—every Thursday in their house on rue de Londres on the Right Bank. At their "open house" Chopin met Polish and French aristocrats, artists, writers, and musicians, and the new bourgeois elite of Paris. Paulina Plater, their daughter, became Chopin's first piano student, and word soon spread of his extraordinary teaching talents, supplying him with more and more student prospects. From the beginning, however, he had made it an iron rule to accept only students showing exceptional musical background and talent.

The Platers treated Fryderyk like a family member, but it was Countess Plater who most subtly defined his exact role in man-woman relationships. "If I were young and beautiful, my little Chopin," she once told him, "I would take you for husband, Hiller for friend, and Liszt for lover." Chopin, Hiller, and Liszt were roughly the same age, and the Countess knew the three of them well; they played frequently at the Platers' musical Thursdays. The countess chose not to elaborate, but it is a fair guess that she saw in Fryderyk an adorable, docile husband—a lovely convenience, but no more. This was in keeping with the lifestyle of the rich and famous of the day.

Liszt wrote in his book on Chopin that Countess Plater "knew how to welcome and to encourage all the talents that then promised to take their upward flight," and that she was "in turn fairy, nurse, godmother, guardian angel, delicate benefactress, knowing all that threatens, divining all that saves. . . . She was to each of us an amiable protectress, equally beloved and respected, who enlightened, warmed and elevated Chopin's inspiration, and left a blank in his life when she was no more."

As his circle of Polish friends of influence widened, Fryderyk was next adopted by Prince Czartoryski and his family. In the Polish emigré hierarchy in Paris, the prince (who once was the lover of Russia's empress, the mother of Czar Alexander) was the undisputed social and patriotic leader in the first years after the Warsaw uprising. He was also the head of a Polish royal family and he had served briefly as chairman of the rebel provisional government in Warsaw. The prince was a founder of the Polish Literary Society in Paris that Chopin joined in 1833, pledging his services to the organization "with all my strength."

The Czartoryskis lived at first in Paris on the Faubourg du Roule, near Faubourg St. Honoré, then acquired the Hôtel Lambert at the far end of the Île St. Louis, the small island in the Seine, just east of Notre Dame. A vast walled five-story seventeenth-century structure with a spacious garden (and mounting blocks on either side of the wooden portal), Hôtel Lambert had once been the home of Voltaire and his mistress, the Marquise du Châtelet. It was the finest private home in the city, in its most beautiful location. With the Czartoryskis in residence, it functioned as the nerve center of the "Capital of Poland in Exile" that Paris had become with tens of thousands of Poles fleeing to France in the aftermath of the failed uprising.

Chopin was a frequent visitor at the great mansion on Île St. Louis, where the weekly salon took place on Mondays, playing for the Czartoryskis and their friends during long quiet evenings or at fund-raising functions and balls for the benefit of Polish refugees. The extravagant balls were usually held in the garden during the warm months, protected from vagaries of weather by removable canvas covers.

In the course of one of his early visits to the Hôtel Lambert, Chopin was introduced to the "young princess," the twenty-five-year-old Marcelina Czartoryska, Prince Adam's niece by marriage. She, too, became a friend forever and one of the extremely important women in Chopin's life. Born a Radziwiłł (an even older Polish royal family), Marcelina went to live in Vienna as a child—studying music under Karl Czerny (Beethoven's student and Liszt's teacher)—before marrying Prince Aleksander Czartoryski when she was twenty-three. The beautiful black-haired princess divided her time between Vienna and Paris, and, in the early 1840s became Chopin's pupil. In the words of her biographer, in an account published a year after her death in 1894, Chopin had discerned "such an unusual talent in her" that he "forcefully molded it through instruction and conversation . . . into perfection and individual poetry."

Princess Marcelina became by most accounts his most outstanding pupil and a great pianist in her own right. Many Polish critics regard her as the "heiress" of Chopin's piano artistry. But there never was any romantic attachment between them, although she remained devoted to Fryderyk until he breathed his last sigh—in her presence.

In terms of his relations with women, there was, naturally, the long and formidable presence of George Sand. But both Countess Potocka and Princess Czartoryska outlasted her as his friends.

Fryderyk Chopin, the charmer and young man of impeccable manners, had a darker private side, easily displaying contempt, irritation, impatience, and mockery when it came to fellow Poles of less than exalted station, the French nation at large, and most contemporary composers and pianists. But because he depended on the goodwill of a great many of those people, Chopin tended to confine his criticisms to personal letters and conversations with a select few friends, chiefly former Warsaw schoolmates, whom he trusted with his business and day-to-day private affairs—and whom he increasingly used in every conceivable dimension, from manuscript copying to the purchase of clothing. Case in point, Wojciech Albert Sowiński, a pianist, composer, and music journalist, who had lived in Paris since the 1820s: Sowiński, Antoni Orłowski, a violinist who had just settled in France, and Ludwik Norblin, a cellist, were the only Polish musicians in Paris about whom Chopin had heard when he first arrived. Two years earlier, Sowiński had written Chopin, inviting him to become the Warsaw correspondent of the *Revue musicale* of which he was an associate, but Fryderyk declined the offer. Now, however, he was among the first people in Paris whom Chopin visited, and Sowiński busied himself helping the newcomer to find his way around.

But Chopin soon soured on Sowiński, resenting his excessively "familiar" behavior—and taking a very dim view of his piano playing and composing. Shortly after he had moved into his boulevard Poissonnière apartment, Fryderyk wrote about him in one of his typically colorful letters:

> I can't suffer it when the bell rings—and *something* with a mustache, big, tall, obese—enters and sits at the piano, and *it* doesn't know itself what it is improvising . . . *it* hits, bangs senselessly, throws itself around, crosses hands, thunders for five minutes on one single key with a fat finger that somewhere in the Ukraine was meant for whip and reins. Thus you have a portrait of Sowiński, who has no merit except for his good figure and a good heart for himself. If I could ever display charlatanry and stupidity in art, it would never be as perfect as what I now often must hear walking up and down the room. My ears are turning red; I would like to throw him out of the door, but I must manage it, even be mutually tender. You cannot imagine anything like it, but because they ("they" who only know about cravats) regard him as somebody, one must fraternize.

Ryzsard Przyblzski, a Polish music historian, has offered this comment about Chopin's letter: "Beethoven would have surely thrown Sowiński out of the door. Chopin dances around the stupid man because the stupid man can injure his art." And, indeed, there was a definite touch of hypocrisy about Chopin. In letters to his friends, Fryderyk commonly used the expression to "compose à la Sowiński," meaning "to hit the bottom." But less than a month after his savage portrayal of the hapless musician, Chopin found it socially convenient to invite Sowiński to participate in a group concert that was to include his own public debut in Paris as one of its features. It was at about the same time that Chopin referred to Friedrich Wieck, who had authored the admiring review of his Mozart variations, as being "very stupid."

The French, as a people, were equally a target of Chopin's private disdain. Their dedication to the Polish cause, at least in Paris, loomed in his mind as an excellent target for his derision. In Stuttgart, when he had learned of Warsaw's fall, Chopin had—perhaps understandably—wished "the most savage suffering" upon the French for failure to assist the patriotic uprising. But now, less understandably, he was heaping ridicule on the pro-Polish French demonstrating in favor of Poland.

Thus, on December 22, 1831, three months or so after reaching Paris, Chopin and several Polish companions—including the Romantic poet Słowacki—attended a performance of the drama *Les polonais* that had been playing daily before sellout audiences for two months at Francon Theater (also known as the Cirque Olympique). In a letter to a friend three days later, Chopin wrote: "At the Francon Theater, where only drama and tableaux with horses are presented, they are now presenting the entire history of our times, and people rush like mad to see all these costumes."

Chopin then went on to make fun of the misspelling and mispronunciation in the play of the names of heroes of the Polish uprising performed by French actors as well as the title of the great Polish national mazurka anthem, "Poland Is Not Yet Lost." He concluded by adding that he was not making it all up: "I have witnesses who marvel, along with me, that the French are such fools."

General Girolamo Ramorino, an Italian-born officer who had served in Napoleon's armies and, as a volunteer, commanded rebel Polish regiments during the November uprising, likewise earned the epithet of "fool" from Chopin. Ramorino was a friend of the Marquis de La Fayette, and one of the most powerful French political and military leaders.

La Fayette became the chairman of the French-Polish Committee after the fall of Warsaw. His dedication to Poland dated back to his friendship with General Tadeusz Kościuszko, the Polish freedom fighter against the Russians, who had gone to America to join the colonists in their struggle for independence after his own defeat at home. In this sense, Kościuszko, La Fayette, and Ramorino were the world's first "internationalists" to fight for other nations' liberty; Kościuszko's motto was: "For your freedom and ours!" The French-Polish Committee included a powerful contingent of French Romantics: Victor Hugo, writers Théophile Gautier and Émile Deschamps, playwright Casimir Delavigne, and the "King of Song" Pierre Béranger.

There was another American-Polish figure in Paris: James Fenimore Cooper, the novelist of the American wilderness and a devotee of Poland's causes, brought flags of the defeated Polish rebel regiments from Warsaw and presented them to the exiled leaders. Though Cooper and La Fayette were friends, it remains unclear how the American found himself in Warsaw at that historical moment, although he was an active supporter of European democratic movements. He lived in Paris at the time, and Victor Hugo admired him as "a master of the romance."

Chopin tended to be patronizing and dismissive of Ramorino. In a letter to a friend late in 1831, he described a gathering of over a thousand French students in front of Ramorino's temporary residence to greet him upon his return from Poland. It happened to be in Cité Bergère, a square across the street from Chopin's apartment building, and Fryderyk watched the scene from his balcony.

"Although [Ramorino] was at home," Chopin wrote, "he did not wish to incur the displeasure of the government, and did not show himself despite the shouts and chants of 'Long Live the Poles!', which is to say he is a fool." A few days later, a huge pro-Polish demonstration occurred in front of Ramorino's new residence near the Panthéon on the Left Bank, and Chopin provided a graphic account of how mounted hussars and the National Guard violently suppressed what had turned into a citywide riot, with new mobs forming "under my windows" to join those on the other side of the Seine.

The riots finally wound up at eleven o'clock at night with mass singing of *La Marseillaise,* and Chopin commented: "It was expected that the riot would start again the next day, but the fools are sitting quietly." The following week, Chopin attended, by personal invitation, a dinner for Ramorino and hundreds of guests at Au Rocher de Cancal, the best (and Fryderyk's favorite) restaurant in Paris. He had, of course, stayed away from the demonstrations. His father, the supporter of the status quo, in a letter expressed his hope that Poles in Paris took no part in any antigovernment activities, remarking: "Don't they have enough of this madness? . . . They committed so much of it here."

Chopin himself thought little of the French government and, for that matter, of Frenchmen around him. Discussing the social and economic situation in the country, he called King Louis-Philippe a "fool."

"It is a strange nation," Fryderyk commented in the same letter. "When evening comes, all you hear are the shouted titles of . . . pages of printed stupidities that you can buy for a sou: 'The Art of Making Lovers and Keeping Them Afterwards,' 'Loves of Priests: The Archbishop of Paris with the Duchess du Barry,' and thousands of similar fatheadedness, some quite amusingly written."

Chapter 7

AFTER SEVEN MONTHS in the fifth-floor apartment at boulevard Poissonnière, his fortunes steadily improving, Chopin's lifestyle also improved
as he moved in June 1832 to a much nicer, first-floor apartment at 4, rue
de la Cité Bergère, a quiet, narrow street. It was apartment no. 702 in a
residential hotel, only a block north of his old apartment, but easier on
the legs and his increasingly short breath. Cité Bergère and boulevard
Poissonnière were part of the Chaussée d'Antin neighborhood that after
the July revolution became a *quartier à la mode* (fashionable district),
attracting artists, writers, and musicians along with the new upper
classes. Some called it the "New Athens."

As he did at boulevard Poissonnière, Chopin had a fine piano at his
disposal—to compose, improvise, and teach—courtesy of Camille
Pleyel, the leading French piano manufacturer and a new friend. It was
also Pleyel who had helped to sponsor Chopin's public debut in Paris at
his Salle Pleyel, a fashionable concert hall at 9, rue Cadet (not far from
Fryderyk's apartment) on February 26, 1832. It was quite remarkable for
such a young outsider to be invited to play publicly within only six
months of his appearance on the Paris scene (actually the concert had
been scheduled for Christmas Day), but Chopin had made friends
quickly in the music world.

Elegant in his tailored black evening coat, Fryderyk played three
times that evening. First, he presented his Concerto no. 2 for piano and
orchestra, then joined the great Kalkbrenner and four other pianists
(including Sowiński) in Kalkbrenner's own Grand Polonaise for six

pianos (the German piano "king," a business partner of Pleyel, was a fellow sponsor). Finally, as soloist, Chopin performed several of his nocturnes and mazurkas and the variations on "Là ci darem la mano." It was not unusual at the time for concerts to be put together by a number of artists, and on this occasion the program also included a Beethoven quintet, a duet by two female singers, and a solo for oboe.

The concert was a critical, if not financial, success. Most of the tickets were sold to Chopin's Polish friends and admirers (they cost ten francs, which was five times a Paris worker's daily wage) and the rest were sent free to other friends—French musicians, artists, writers, and journalists. Cherubini, Hiller, Liszt, and Mendelssohn were among the "names" in the audience, which made the concert an important Paris cultural event.

Hiller wrote that "Mendelssohn applauded triumphantly," and Antoni Orłowski, the violinist, said in a letter to Poland that "our dear Fryderyk gave a concert that brought him a great reputation and a little money. . . . He utterly destroyed every local pianist and all Paris was stupefied." Liszt wrote that "the most vigorous applause seemed not to suffice to our enthusiasm in the presence of this talented musician, who revealed a new phase of poetic sentiment combined with such happy innovations in the form of this art."

François-Joseph Fétis, the editor of the influential *Revue musicale,* commented:

[H]ere is a young man who, abandoning himself to his natural impressions and without taking a model, has found, if not a complete renewal of pianoforte music, at least a part of what has been sought in vain for a long time—namely an abundance of original ideas of which the type is to be found nowhere. . . . I find in M. Chopin's inspirations the indication of a renewal of forms which may exercise in time much influence over this department of the art.

Three months later, Chopin made his second public appearance, playing at a benefit for the poor organized by the Prince de la Moskowa at his palace. His performance of the first movement of his Concerto no. 2 failed, however, to elicit the same praise as did the February presentation.

The music critic of *Le Temps* observed that Chopin "is a very young Polish pianist who . . . in time will gain wide fame, especially as a composer. Rich in ideas and original, he does not yet know how to express them through an orchestra. . . . The first part of the concerto made a greater impression at private concerts. This must be attributed to the limited power of sound the artist extracts from [his] instrument." Even Fétis wrote in the *Revue musicale* that the second Chopin appearance did not repeat the "superb success" of the first one, "largely because of [his] limited piano sound. . . . The music of this artist will please audiences more and more when it becomes better known."

Painfully thin-skinned, Chopin abhorred all criticism of his music or his piano virtuosity. Fétis's review mortified him though he chose to remain silent publicly (earlier he had informed friends, rather gratuitously, that Fétis had so many debts that he seldom came to Paris from his country home, thus avoiding prison).

He took it even harder when, soon after the publication of the Fétis article, he read a savage attack on his *Don Giovanni* variations, which he had dedicated to Tytus Woyciechowski. The author was the well-known Berlin music critic Ludwig Rellstab, highly conservative despite his relative youth (he was then thirty-three), who wrote in his periodical *Iris im Gebiete der Tonkunst* the following indictment: "Mister Chopin is supposed to be Polish, or so one can guess since he has dedicated his work to a Pole, if one is not to assume it likewise from the vandalism he has perpetrated on the Mozart melody, [which] is a sign that this work grew out of the crude tree trunk of the Slav people." This was the work that Robert Schumann had so extravagantly admired.

Rellstab kept up his assault on Chopin when he reviewed the five mazurkas forming Opus 7 ("if Mister Chopin had submitted this composition to a master, he would most likely tear it up and throw it under his feet, which we wish to do symbolically"); the three Opus 9 Nocturnes ("we plead with Mister Chopin to return to nature"); and the Opus 10 Études ("he who has sprained fingers will be able to straighten them out with these études, but he who has healthy fingers should be careful not to play these études unless surgeons are nearby").

John Field, the obese wine-imbibing Irishman credited with inventing the nocturne and much admired by Chopin, told musician friends after meeting him during a 1832 Paris visit that Fryderyk's compositions were "a sickroom talent." The comment was repeated to Chopin, who later attended the two concerts given by Field.

Rellstab relented seven years later, in 1839, discovering that Chopin had enormous talent after all. "Did we change," Rellstab asked in a favorable review of a new edition of Chopin's nocturnes, "or did the composer change, or did the times change, or is it a confirmation of the old proverb *Tempora mutantur, nos et mutamur in illis?*" But it was too late for Fryderyk, who tortured himself over what he always feared was his inability to please enough—notwithstanding his public and epistolary displays of self-assurance and his very high opinion of himself.

This was the central tragedy of Chopin's life, explaining so much about him, and it was best put by one of his first biographers, Frederick Niecks:

> No artist can at heart be fully satisfied with the approval of a small minority; Chopin, at any rate, was not such a one. Nature, who had richly endowed him with the qualities that make a virtuoso, had denied him one, perhaps the meanest of all, certainly the least dispensable, the want of which balked him of the fulfillment of the promise with which the others had flattered him, of the most brilliant reward of his striving. In the lists where men much below his worth won laurels and gold in abundance he failed to obtain a fair share of the popular acclamation. This was one of the disappointments which, like malignant cancers, cruelly tortured and slowly consumed his life.

Niecks concluded that "opposition and indifference, which stimulate more vigorous natures, affected Chopin as touch does the *Mimosa pudica,* the sensitive plant—they made him shrink and wither."

In what may still be the most insightful judgment of Chopin's personality, Niecks wrote that "there was then, and there remained to the end of his life, something of a woman and of a boy in this man." And Niecks's opinion deserves to be taken most seriously: He knew and interviewed Chopin's contemporaries and friends, from Liszt, Hiller, and Delacroix to a large number of Poles and others who had known him over the years, and he read all the relevant correspondence he could find, along with diaries and journals.

Chopin's exaggerated sensitivity was undoubtedly the main reason for his reluctance to play in public as distinct from salons with only small groups listening to him. He played the fewest public concerts of any pianist of renown in his time: only thirty in thirty years, from childhood in 1818 to 1848, the year before his death. He once explained his feelings to Liszt: "I am not at all fit for giving concerts, the crowd intimidates me, its breath suffocates me, I feel paralyzed by its curious look, and the unknown faces make me dumb."

And Liszt noted correctly that "if Chopin suffered on account of his not being able to take part in those public and solemn jousts where popular acclamation salutes the victor; if he felt depressed at seeing himself excluded from them, it was because he did not esteem highly enough what he had, to do gaily without what he had not."

Fétis had remarked in his first review that he was not necessarily seeking to compare Chopin with Beethoven, but the reference was very much to the point because Beethoven was being rediscovered, at least in Paris, and the Romantic generation was becoming aware of his importance to them. Because he seemed to shock the audiences during the eras of the Napoleonic empire and the First Restoration under Louis XVIII, he was cast aside and forgotten. Moreover, no public orchestra concerts were held in Paris for twenty years until Charles X decided in 1828 to make a grant to the conservatory to resume performing orchestral music.

Not quite a year after Beethoven died, the Paris Conservatory orchestra's opening performance of his *Eroica* Symphony was greeted with what contemporary chroniclers described as "delirium." From there on, Beethoven was a god reborn, his symphonies (sometimes three or four on one program), his opera *Fidelio,* concertos, and chamber music available to the increasingly affluent Parisian bourgeois public as well as to the newest generation of composers.

By the time Chopin had settled in Paris three years later, all nine Beethoven symphonies had been presented to enchanted crowds and the city seemed to be floating on music everywhere, all the time. The ostensibly liberating political spirit of the July Monarchy revolution and the Romantic surge combined to turn Paris into a grandiose musical festival and literary fair. According to music scholar James H. Johnson, "Beethoven's revival was perhaps the first and most dramatic evidence of a new taste for pure music." And Johnson quotes the journalist Jules Janin that "music is the new art of France. . . . it is our new passion, it is our daily study, it is our national pride."

And, as Régine Pernoud, a historian of the French bourgeoisie, has noted, "to study the piano would be the mark of distinction of the young *bourgeoise,* just as Latin for the young *bourgeois.*"

The flowering of the Romantic movement that coincided with the 1830 revolution—and was encouraged by it—provided a rare example of crucial interaction between culture and politics, which then became transmuted into history. It influenced the balance of the nineteenth century and the twentieth century. Voltaire and the Encyclopedists were naturally a major intellectual influence on the 1789 revolution, but they did not match the quality and energy unleashed under the July Monarchy.

For Chopin, of course, it was fantastic timing to find himself in Paris at such a moment. His consuming loves—bel canto opera and the most exquisite imaginable violin music—were his for the listening, and listen he did, night after night. Chopin had always believed that the human voice and the violin were the most perfect sounds in creation, absorbing them as he lived with the mystery of his own inspiration. He could hear the human voice, the divine perfection, in the sound of the violin played by a master.

Now Fryderyk had *three* opera houses at his disposal, in addition to the Paris Conservatory for concerts—piano, violin, and wind instruments—and at least ten theaters for drama. There was the principal Paris Opera (known formally as the Royal Academy of Music) on rue Le Peletier, directed by Louis Véron, a physician and businessman who breathed new life into it after taking over a few months before Chopin arrived in town. It was within walking distance from his apartment, even for the short-of-breath Fryderyk. Then he had Italian opera at the Théâtre des Italiens on the boulevard des Italiens, directed by Rossini, and the Opéra-Comique on rue Feydeau, offering lighter operatic fare, a little farther away, but easily accessible by carriage, which was always available to Chopin. He disliked traveling in the cheap horse-drawn omnibus, a new Parisian service and forerunner of urban transit.

During his first and second year in Paris, Chopin went to the opera almost every night, most frequently to hear the great voices at the Théâtre des Italiens. After a performance there or the nearby Opéra-Comique, Fryderyk often stopped for an evening of drinks at the Café Feydeau (across the street from the latter). After performances at the Royal Academy of Music, the favorite spot for post-opera conversations was the Café du Divan, across the street at 3, rue Le Peletier, where the writers Honoré de Balzac and Théophile Gautier often held court. The private parties, with Chopin, Liszt, or Hiller playing for their friends (often at Chopin's apartment), usually started around midnight and went on into the small hours.

Chopin was absolutely enchanted with opera—and the voices. In enthusiastic letters home, he wrote that "only here one can learn what singing is. . . . now I have everything in Paris." The singers were truly fabulous, and Fryderyk breathlessly listed them: Luigi Lablache, Giovanni Rubini, Giuditta Pasta, and María Malibrán at the Théâtre des Italiens (where Chopin felt Rossini was producing the "best" opera in Europe) and Adolphe Nourrit and Laura Cinti-Damoreau at the Royal Academy.

Chopin regarded Malibrán, a Spaniard, as "the first in Europe—a marvel!" although he admitted that he preferred Cinti-Damoreau's singing: "Malibrán astonishes, Cinti enchants. . . . It is impossible to have a more perfected voice—it costs her so little [effort] that it seems that she is just breathing lightly at the audience." Of Nourrit, the tenor (who would become a personal friend as would Malibrán), Chopin wrote: "He astonishes with his feeling." He criticized a performance of Rossini's *Otello* because he thought the stout German singer Wilhelmine Schröder-Devrient as Desdemona would "smother" the "little Malibrán" who played the tenor role of Otello as a soprano wearing a black mask.

Fryderyk saw Rossini's *Il barbiere di Siviglia* as well as *Otello* and *L' Italiana in Algeri* several times at the Théâtre des Italiens. At the Royal Academy, Chopin joined the audience in a standing ovation at a performance of Rossini's *Guillaume Tell* (a highly romantic oeuvre with libretto based on a Schiller play). After attending the première of Meyerbeer's *Robert le diable,* Fryderyk described it as "the masterpiece of the new school . . . Meyerbeer immortalized himself."

Chopin's devotion to violin music as being like the human voice was again gratified when the great Paganini came to Paris late in 1831 for a series of ten concerts. He went to all of them, alternating Paganini concerts with opera performances in what was to him a sequence of pure logic. But Chopin, always ready for a new musical experience, also went to the conservatory during his first Parisian years to hear the Society of Concerts Orchestra under violin-wielding François-Antoine Habeneck play Beethoven's symphonies; he listened to the Third, Fifth, and Ninth Symphonies.

Because opera was so popular (and profitable) all over Europe—Mozart and Beethoven as well as Rossini, Bellini, and Verdi composed them—powerful pressure was again placed on Chopin to turn to composing an opera himself. His poet friend Witwicki (whose poems he had set) argued forcefully that he owed it to Poland to be its "national composer" in the field of opera. Józef Elsner and his sister Ludwika joined the chorus of persuaders.

Chopin, however, remained firm. He did not hesitate, as he might have in other situations. Just as he did not believe that it was his destiny to write "large" compositions for piano and orchestra, as Mozart and Beethoven had done, and notwithstanding the success of the two concertos he did produce, he had no intention of entering the world of the opera that he adored as a listener. His true destiny, Fryderyk was convinced, was to continue composing for the piano. It was the calling of his genius.

Addressing him with utmost respect in a lengthy letter, Chopin explained to Elsner that it was simply impractical and unrealistic for him to think about opera. "Several talented young people, students at the Paris Conservatory," he wrote, "are waiting with crossed arms for performances of their operas, symphonies, and cantatas that only Cherubini and Lesueur have seen on paper. . . . Meyerbeer, favorably known for years as a composer of operas, sat, paid, and worked in Paris for three years before he could stage his sensation-creating work, *Robert le diable*." Chopin continued: "Today, I have a unique opportunity of fulfilling my natural promise. Why shouldn't I grab it?"

Now solidly established in Paris as a composer and piano virtuoso, Chopin had a clear vision of his fate—and of the inner torments and lonely daily battles that lay ahead as he sought to fulfill that promise.

"I have entered high society, I sit among ambassadors, princes, ministers," Chopin informed his childhood friend Dominik Dziewanowski in a letter in mid-January 1833—not quite a year and a half since he had made Paris his home forever. "For me today this is the most necessary thing because good taste seems to come from there; you, at once, have a greater talent if they have heard you at the English or the Austrian embassy; you play better right away if Princess Vaudemont protects you."

Fryderyk must have felt a bit self-conscious about this triumphant announcement because a few paragraphs later he undertook to justify it in terms of the professional standing he had attained.

"Among artists I have friendship and respect," he wrote. "I would not be writing this, after barely a year of being here, but the proof of the respect that people with enormous reputations have for me is that they dedicate their compositions to me, before I do it for them. [Friedrich Wilhelm] Pixis dedicated to me his recent variations for a military orchestra, and [others] are composing variations on my themes. Kalk-brenner [wrote] variations on one of my mazurkas. Conservatory stu-dents—pupils of [Ignaz] Moscheles, [Henri] Herz, and Kalkbrenner, in one word complete artists, take lessons from me."

Never self-effacing, Chopin knew at the same time when to be self-deprecating—it was the defense mechanism he had perfected—and he went on telling Dziewanowski: "If I were more stupid, I would think that I was at the top of my career, but I see how much I still have ahead of me, especially because I live intimately with the leading artists and I know what each lacks. But I am ashamed of all the silliness I have writ-ten; I have bragged like a child or like someone whose cap is burning and defends himself beforehand. I would erase, but I have no time to write a new sheet. . . . You know my character."

Undoubtedly, high-level access to Paris society—members of the French royal family, the aristocracy, powerful bourgeoisie, and foreign diplomats—was essential to Chopin's advancement in the ruling estab-lishment (and acquisition of pupils who were both talented and well-heeled). He was practical and cynical enough to understand it, and would keep building these relationships for the rest of his life.

Chopin was, of course, right about his approach to high society. Until not long before, musicians who came to play at soirées had to use service entrances, were treated like tradesmen because they were paid for performing, and were often even refused a meal. Once Chopin protested that he "had so little to eat" when commanded to play to earn his fee after having been given a light collation. It was not even a matter of "singing" for one's supper. In Fryderyk's case, his charm and attrac-tion to older women who ran the salons for their husbands made him in time a social equal.

And clearly Chopin enjoyed his high society life and friends. Often, he stayed at receptions until dawn, enthralling salon audiences with hours on end of heaven-inspired improvisations. It is a tragic loss that none of the improvisations were transcribed by fellow musicians who listened to him, especially since several of them believed that in many cases the improvisations exceeded in sheer beauty and imagination the composi-tions that Chopin had painstakingly written down over the years.

His propensity for staying up late and surviving on insufficient sleep—he started giving lessons daily midmorning—must have con-tributed to the deterioration of his health, but Fryderyk felt it was the price he had to pay, and did it with pleasure. In fact, his life had become something of a vicious circle. He wrote Dziewanowski: "I have to give five lessons today, [and] you may think that I shall make a fortune, [but] the cabriolet costs more as do the white gloves without which you would not have good style. . . . Besides, I do not care about money; I only (care) about friendship for which I beg and ask you."

Fryderyk's father, for his part, cared considerably about Chopin's health and offered admonitions along with loving understanding. In April 1833, he wrote him from Warsaw: "I see from your letters that you are very busy; at your age there is never too much activity—idleness is often damaging—but work should not suffocate you [and] you must remember your health. . . . I do not condemn you for seeking recreation in distinguished society. . . . I only fear prolonged evenings because you need much rest." Fryderyk's older sister, Ludwika, who was married the previous November to Józef Kalasanty Jędrzejewicz, a professor of administrative law, bombarded him with similar advice.

Chopin's pragmatism and the sense of how he envisioned his future were demonstrated again in mid-1833 when Czar Nicholas decreed an amnesty for all the Poles who had been involved in the November uprising. His father consequently urged Fryderyk to renew his passport at the Russian embassy in Paris. This would have made it possible for him to return to Poland without fear of punishment, had he wanted to do it—in any case, he had left before the uprising and was engaged in no active conspiracies abroad—but Chopin had made up his mind that only Paris could assure the continuation of his career and further growth of his fame. Having declared himself a permanent "emigrant," it was logical for him to request a French passport.

But an exiled friend of Chopin's indignantly wrote home that after the Russian embassy had announced that any Pole applying for amnesty who admitted to having fought in the uprising would have to serve fifteen years of hard labor, "two hundred [men] instantly accepted this condition."

To be sure, Chopin was already regarded at home as something of a national hero and his polonaises and mazurkas were perceived as expressions of patriotism at a time when it was vital to keep the national culture alive. Robert Schumann, his foremost admirer, wrote in an article in 1836 that "if the powerful ruling monarch in the north knew what a dangerous foe threatens him in Chopin's works—in the simple melodies of his mazurkas—he would have forbidden this music. . . . Chopin's works are cannon concealed among flowers."

It may have been true, but Fryderyk preferred to fire his cannon from among Parisian flowers.

Chapter 8

LIFE AMONG PARISIAN FLOWERS was not always easy, although Chopin weathered it with aplomb. A cholera epidemic swept Paris during the spring of 1832, killing over a thousand people daily over long weeks, including King Louis-Philippe's prime minister Casimir Périer. Despite his delicate health, Chopin escaped contagion. But tens of thousands of well-to-do Parisians fled the city fearing for their lives, including a number of Chopin's students—and his income dropped accordingly.

When he first arrived in Paris, Fryderyk still had some of the funds his father had sent him while in Vienna and Munich. Some of the money came from the sale, at his request, of the diamond ring the late Czar Alexander had given him in Warsaw; he had left it with his parents.

By the end of 1832, however, Chopin was earning enough from his lessons to make his rather expensive ends meet. He was charging twenty francs per lesson and teaching five hour-long lessons daily (though sometimes, when he was interested in the pupil, he let lessons run much longer); he could earn as much as five hundred francs a week. (A Parisian doctor charged ten francs for a house call and a Paris worker earned at the time between ten and fifteen francs weekly.) Before long, Chopin began earning respectable sums from music publishers in Paris and elsewhere in Europe, as well. But he had to work very hard teaching and composing to ensure that enough money flowed in.

His father's warnings notwithstanding, Fryderyk was a spendthrift, buying luxurious furniture for his apartments, paying for expensive dinners out—the famous Au Rocher de Cancal restaurant on rue de Montorgueil, specializing in fish, and Tortoni Café for after-dinner coffee were among his favorites—and ordering the most elegant clothes money could procure. A suit would cost him around 150 francs. He also bought presents for friends and lent money to needy Poles.

Józef Brzowski, a Polish musician who spent several years in Paris, has described in his diary a dinner Chopin had hosted for him and Jaś Matuszyński (Chopin called Jan Matuszyński by the diminutive "Jaś") one evening at Au Rocher de Cancal. Chopin had reserved a private dining room upstairs in the restaurant and, after consulting the menu in the shape of a book, he ordered the meal for all of them. They started with oysters, then had soup, venison, matelote (fish cooked in wine sauce), and fresh asparagus. The best champagne was served to wash down the dinner, and fine cigars were passed around. Cognac was at Tortoni Café of which Fryderyk was particularly fond because he could have his favorite ice cream brought from the café to his carriage whenever he stopped there.

As a well-sheltered member of the Paris elite and a foreigner, Chopin stayed away from social and economic tensions sweeping France under her "Bourgeois King" as hopes of justice and democracy promised by the July revolution were quickly forgotten. Chopin's attitude would change somewhat when he established his relationship with the socially conscious George Sand. Meanwhile, he was certainly aware of the realities around him. He knew that in November 1831, two months after his arrival, the king had dispatched the army to Lyons to put down what was the first workers' uprising in French history. In June of the following year, Chopin heard cannon firing on rioters in the streets of Paris when it took twenty-five thousand troops of the National Guard to quell a rebellion by unemployed workers.

A keen observer, Chopin wrote shortly after reaching Paris that "there is much misery here, there is little money in circulation, you encounter many in tatters. . . . The lower classes are completely furious and . . . urge a change in their condition of poverty, but the government . . . disperses street assemblages with mounted gendarmerie."

After the 1832 riots, he wrote: "I cannot stand the Philippistes. . . . I am a revolutionary" ("Philippistes" were followers of King Louis-Philippe). Inasmuch as Chopin's letters often jumped from subject to subject to the point of occasional incoherence, it is difficult to judge what, if anything, he meant by this remark. There is no comment in his surviving letters on the events of April 1844, when the regime deployed forty thousand troops in Paris to control a wave of street riots; all the inhabitants of rue Transmontain in the Marais (workers' district) were massacred by the soldiers in the terrible episode immortalized in the lithographs of Honoré Daumier.

Whatever Chopin did think of Louis-Philippe, he remained a faithful pragmatist. In February 1838, for example, he would play for the king and the royal family at the Tuileries Palace. The invitation had been arranged by Count A. de Perthuis, the king's aide-de-camp, whose wife, Émilie, was Chopin's pupil. After each royal concert, Chopin received a precious gift from the sovereign—a tea service, a Sèvres dinner service, and Sèvres vases—inscribed *Louis-Philippe, Roi des Français, à Frédéric Chopin.*

Chopin's personal life became infinitely more pleasant with his next Paris move, this time to share an apartment with a Warsaw friend. The new apartment was at 5, rue de la Chaussée d'Antin, just a few blocks from Cité Bergère, by now the center of the expanding neighborhood of the upper-middle class and successful artists. The prestigious Perregaux Bank was down the street. The Chaussée had become by then an enclave of elegant Parisian life, encroaching on Montmartre, and "it was in very bad style to be seen beyond it," as a city historian, André Castelot, has put it.

Fryderyk had visited the apartment many times in the past as a guest of Dr. Hermann Franck, a scientist, journalist, and music lover, who frequently entertained writers and musicians at his lodgings (often playing chess with Mendelssohn). When Franck left Paris, Chopin rented the apartment for himself and his friend Dr. Aleksander Hoffmann, a pipe-smoking physician and pianist.

Chopin's and Hoffmann's fathers were close friends back home, and when Aleksander, five years older than Fryderyk, came to Paris to practice medicine after fighting in the November uprising, they decided to share the Chaussée d'Antin apartment. They moved in mid-June 1833. (It was at about the same time that the young poet Alfred de Musset, whom Chopin knew slightly from artistic soirées, started a troubled romance with the increasingly famous woman novelist George Sand, whom Fryderyk somehow had not yet met.)

Hoffmann was one of the best things to happen to Chopin. He was calm, quiet, and thoughtful, where Fryderyk was hypernervous and high-strung, and he exercised the most beneficial influence on him. As a physician, he was in a position to make him look after his diet and go to bed early. To Chopin, who hated loneliness and always tried to surround himself with people, Hoffmann was a godsend. Hiller, who saw Chopin frequently, has observed that "even if Chopin did not go out and played at home in the evening, he always had to have at least one of his friends with him."

The doctor also convinced Chopin to rest at the home of his cellist friend Franchomme near the village of Côteau in Touraine with its fresh country air. Fryderyk loved his visit to the Loire Valley, telling Franchomme in a thank-you letter: "I shall never forget my stay in Touraine . . . so much kindness has made me forever grateful. People think that I am stouter and look very well, and I feel wonderfully well, thanks to the ladies who sat beside me at dinner, who bestowed truly maternal attentions upon me."

Hoffmann went back to Poland after nearly two years of conviviality with Chopin. (Fryderyk must have greatly appreciated Hoffmann's presence because he is not known to have complained to him about his pipe smoke, although it inevitably irritated his weak lungs. He did complain, however, in a letter to his father. But why did Hoffmann, a physician, smoke in Chopin's apartment, aware of his condition?)

Emilia Hoffmann, the doctor's widow, recalled in her memoirs: "My husband was extraordinarily musical and had much artistic feeling. Chopin, living with him, very frequently heeded his comments about matters of composition." She wrote that when Chopin was working on his very familiar Étude op. 25, no. 11 (known as the "Winter Wind")—in the second cycle of études—Hoffmann told him that opening "with savage right-hand passages" (as it did in the first draft), the piece "started too brusquely, splendid as it was," and "would produce a much stronger effect if it began with a few bars of an introduction."

Mrs. Hoffmann, who had heard the story after her marriage to the doctor, added that "Chopin, who having already written something, never liked to alter it, had decided, despite my husband's comments, to leave the étude as it was, at least because no better beginning came to his mind. But his friend's remark, considered by Chopin as justified, did not leave him in peace until one night he conceived the idea for a beautiful, melancholy four-bar introduction preceding the emotional fortissimo of the original beginning of the étude. . . . Getting up from his bed, he wrote it down. The next day, he played it for my husband who, enchanted by it, approved without reservations."

Chopin was not alone long after Hoffmann departed. Jaś Matuszyński, a childhood friend (probably the closest after Tytus Woyciechowski), arrived in Paris in mid-1834 from Tübingen in Germany, where he had graduated from medical school, and Fryderyk invited him to share the Chaussée d'Antin apartment. They had not seen each other in five years. This way Chopin not only had another physician friend to look after him, but, again, someone with whom he could speak Polish whenever he wished it; to be able to do so was one of his permanent concerns. Moreover, Matuszyński knew music and played the flute.

Not long before he died, Chopin explained in a letter to Marie de Rozières, a French pupil and friend who helped him manage in his final, lonely years: "It may seem like a small detail, but the greatest consolation in a foreign country is to have someone who takes us back to [our] country whenever we look at him, speak to him, or listen to him."

Matuszyński, who was a year older, was delighted as well. He wrote his brother-in-law: "The first thing I did in Paris was to call on Chopin. . . . He has grown strong and tall; I hardly recognized him. Chopin is now the first pianist here; he gives a great many lessons, but none under twenty francs. He has composed much, and his works are in great demand. . . . I have weighty reasons for staying with him—he is my all! We spend the evenings at the theater or pay visits; if we do not do one or the other, we enjoy ourselves quietly at home." And Chopin had come to regard his home at that stage as a "lion's lair" or a "gentleman's grotto," where he could hide from the outside world when melancholy seized him. Then he often hid in his study behind the parlor.

The year 1834 was a good one for Chopin whose life, like the chord spread of an arpeggio, went alternatively from the bottom upwards or from the top downwards. In parallel with Matuszyński's upbeat report, the violinist Orłowski informed a friend that "Chopin is well and strong; he turns the heads of all the Frenchwomen, and makes men jealous of him. He is now the fashion, and the elegant world will soon wear gloves *à la* Chopin."

Fryderyk, who had a natural penchant for elegance, materialized on the Paris scene just as fashion in the Romantic era flowered as a reaction to the aesthetic egalitarianism of the 1789 revolution when, to cite a historian, "full-length trousers, boots, and shirts, the same on everybody, filled the world with somber uniformity. . . . Dress began to erase differences between social classes."

Under the July Monarchy, a "cult of diversity" was born and Paris became peopled with "dandies" and "*incroyables*," the latter being true eccentrics in dress. Chopin, however, tended toward quiet, moderate elegance—usually dressing in a fitted black frock coat, buttoned at the neck or open with a cravat—and was regarded in the parlance of the day as "a fashionable man." The "*incroyable*," "*merveilleux*," and "*miriflore*" were in the category of peacock-style dress, harking back to the eighteenth century.

The peacock-style attire was also reflected in public arrogance, the hauteur and affectation displayed by English dandies and imitated in Paris. Such behavior, naturally, was beneath Chopin.

The whole question of fashion was so important during the Romantic Age that Balzac not only wrote about it in articles for the periodical *La Mode,* but devoted a whole book—*Traité de la vie élégante* ("Treatise on Elegant Life")—to it. And, of course, that was the time of Beau Brummell—George Bryan Brummell—the Englishman who became famous as arbiter elegantiarum, the dictator of male fashion, whose influence reached every corner of Europe. Byron had written that the most remarkable thing about Brummell's dress was "a certain exquisite propriety."

This applied perfectly to Chopin. His redingotes were tailored in black, pale gray, mauve, or royal blue. His shirts were of white batiste. While the dandies strove to outsmart one another with vests in many hues and bizarre color patterns, and with off-white or off-yellow gloves, Fryderyk opted for "a black, modest vest . . . with a tiny, nonscreaming design, something very modestly elegant." And he chose immaculate white gloves over any color. When he composed at home, Chopin liked to wear an unbleached muslin blouse with mother-of-pearl buttons. He was conscious of footwear, patronizing a Mr. Brown's and Chez Rapp, shoemaking establishments that custom-made shoes for his small feet (Rapp specialized in varnished boots). And he had a hatmaker, Dupont on rue Mont-Blanc, who remembered that Fryderyk liked hats light in weight.

Unlike the dandies, Chopin preferred muted cravats. A former pupil recalled that in daytime Fryderyk wore "a long and wide cravat, covering his shirt" and a broad white silk cravat when he performed in formal surroundings. To tie a cravat was an art, and, according to *L'Art de la toilette,* a book then in wide circulation, there were seventy-two ways of doing it. It is lost in the mists of history how Chopin tied his cravat, but he may have been familiar with his friend Balzac's essay on *The Cravat Considered in Itself and Its Relation to Society and Individuals.* Finally, Chopin was most meticulous about "good soap" and "scented water."

The overall effect was stunning. Liszt wrote: "There was so much distinction in his posture and his manners had the mark of such good upbringing that he was treated like a prince."

But Chopin was also having a fine time in every possible way at that point in his life. The poet Juliusz Słowacki, describing a dinner at the home of a Polish historian in Paris, wrote his mother that "we were bored to death from ten o'clock until two o'clock [in the morning]—in the end, Chopin got drunk and he improvised beautiful things on the piano." On another occasion, according to a contemporary, Chopin came to the "salon" of his friends, the Platers, "acting the part of Pierrot, and, after jumping and dancing for about an hour, left without having spoken a single word."

Chopin and Matuszyński entertained regularly at the Chaussée d'Antin apartment that Fryderyk had furnished in the most expensive fashion (his nephew Antoni Jędrzejewicz would say later that the composer had "assembled a veritable museum of the most elegant furniture") and filled it with flowers that had to be changed daily. Liszt was a frequent visitor and, almost inevitably, the two men fought piano duels over how different pieces of music should be performed. Liszt, for example, had his own idea how Chopin's exceedingly difficult études should be played. Fryderyk described it on one occasion in a letter to Hiller, another great pianist:

> I write not knowing what my pen is scribbling because at this very moment Liszt is playing my études, and transports me beyond the limit of rational thought. . . . I would like to steal from him his way of performing my own creations.

The "quiet" evenings Matuszyński had mentioned included once in a while games of whist with their Polish pianist friend Julian Fontana and the French banker Auguste Léo, who knew most of the top musicians and writers in Paris and provided Chopin with interest-free loans as required. But when Léo, known as Léon to his friends, once asked for repayment before the composer could collect for his préludes from his music publisher, Chopin called him "a tricky Jew" in a letter to Fontana, threatening to send him "my thanks that would go up . . . where you want it to go up." He used the same epithet for Maurice Schlesinger, his Paris publisher since 1832, and a good friend. But soon Chopin dedicated to Léo his Polonaise in A-flat major, one of the more ambitious ones, which has become famous. Increasingly, he was becoming a man of quick and vicious anger—but then astonishing generosity.

Chopin was generous in the same way to Paul Émile Johns, a Polish-American pianist, composer, music store owner, and New Orleans cotton merchant whom he'd met in 1832 through Pleyel, the Paris piano manufacturer, and befriended to the point of dedicating the Five Mazurkas Opus 7 to him. Fryderyk had developed the custom of dedicating his works to special friends (such as Tytus Woyciechowski, Delfina Potocka, and Liszt [three times]) or to influential persons whom he owed favors—or from whom he hoped to obtain them.

Johns, about whose relations with Chopin very little is known, evidently came under the heading as Fryderyk's only American friend. They appear to have met only during the short period the black-mustachioed Johns spent in Paris in 1832, presumably arranging with Pleyel for imports of pianos for his store in the United States. Johns was actually born in Kraków in 1800, to a Polish father and Czech mother, but grew up in America. He performed at least six piano concerts in New Orleans.

Chopin's acquintanceship with Johns may have been the origin of reports, circulating at the time in Paris and subsequently repeated by several biographers, that the composer was seriously contemplating moving permanently to the United States because supposedly things were not going well for him in France. According to this version, Chopin was dissuaded from the American idea after meeting in the street one morning his friend Prince Walenty Radziwiłł, who, in turn, took Fryderyk to a dinner at the Rothschild mansion, where he met the rich and famous of Paris, arranged for additional well-paying piano lessons, and decided to stay put. The story is at best apocryphal.

Where Chopin did go, though briefly, was to the Lower Rhine Music Festival in Aachen, the medieval German city (better known at the time as Aix-la-Chapelle), where Charlemagne was born in the eighth century. This trip, in May 1834, was the first Chopin had taken abroad since his 1831 arrival in Paris, and he made the most of it. He and Hiller traveled together, and they were enthusiastically greeted by Mendelssohn, their host, who had become music director at Düsseldorf. In March of the previous year, Chopin had come out of his shell to join Liszt in playing a benefit for Berlioz's ailing fiancée, Harriet Smithson—it was his second appearance in a concert hall—and the next day he played publicly with three other pianists. In December, Chopin, Hiller, and Liszt performed together in a concert at the Paris Conservatory, where they played works by Bach, their idol, and Hiller played his own Second Symphony.

Between appearances at the Aachen festival, Chopin, Hiller, and Mendelssohn spent all of their time together, except when Fryderyk rode a donkey to take some fresh air; then they continued chatting and playing the piano together at Mendelssohn's house in Düsseldorf. Afterwards Mendelssohn wrote his mother that Chopin "astonishes with his innovations, as Paganini has done on the violin, and he introduces marvels that would seem to be almost impossible."

Chopin and Hiller next sailed up the Rhine to Cologne on their way back to Paris. Aboard the river steamer, Chopin wrote Hiller's mother: "I am today like the steam from our steamer. . . . I dissolve in the air, and I feel as if part of me is traveling to my motherland, to my [people], and the second part to Paris to you." He had seldom expressed his ambiguities so explicitly, and Ryszard Przybylski, the Polish Chopin scholar, has suggested that this letter was an indication of the composer's schizophrenia—as were his Vienna and Stuttgart "living corpse" hallucinations.

Chopin's visit to the Rhineland and the time he spent together with Hiller and Mendelssohn were an important example of how these young but great composers maintained a human and musical rapport while they created their works. For Chopin, similar relations existed with Liszt and Berlioz as well as with Hiller in Paris. Fryderyk may have resented Liszt as a person, which he increasingly did, and he and Berlioz heartily disliked each other's music, but in this unprecedented situation—probably never repeated again on such a high artistic level—they had the opportunity to share and compare thoughts and sounds, ideas, and execution. It would be reasonable to assume that in many ways each of them was enriched by the experience.

Back in Paris from his German foray, Chopin resumed his usual routine of teaching and composing—and occasionally playing in public. He and Berlioz may not have been mutual admirers, but Fryderyk readily agreed to participate in a concert the Frenchman had organized at the conservatory in December 1834. It was a matter of noblesse oblige. The program included Berlioz's symphony concertante *Harold in Italy,* based on Byron's poetry, and the Larghetto (middle movement) of Chopin's Concerto no. 1 in E minor that had not yet been publicly heard in Paris. Ten days later, Chopin and Liszt appeared together at a concert at Pleyel's chandelier-lit elegant new hall on rue Rochechouart. The *Gazette musicale* announced that Chopin and Liszt were "the greatest two pianists of our epoch."

Chopin performed in public four times during the first half of 1835, before facing a series of events that formed major turning points in his life. In February, he played together with Hiller at the Erard Hall (Erard was another leading piano manufacturer), but their two-piano performance brought the comment from *Le Pianiste,* a Paris periodical, that "Chopin's talent . . . is so delicate and so full of incredible nuances, which can be captured only by a subtle and trained ear, that it is not useful to listen to him [playing] with others." In mid-March, however, Chopin was back at the Salle Pleyel at a concert with three other pianists.

When it came to organizing a benefit for needy Polish emigrants, Chopin's musical friendships in Paris paid off handsomely. It was another case of professional noblesse oblige. Chopin and Princess Anna Czartoryska were co-chairs of the concert, which became the highlight of the year's musical season. François-Antoine Habeneck, the director of the Paris Conservatory, conducted the orchestra. Liszt and Hiller joined Chopin during the piano part of the program. Tenor Adolphe Nourrit and soprano Marie-Cornélie Falcon sang. Heinrich Wilhelm Ernst played the violin.

The Théâtre des Italiens was full that evening and the benefit was most successful financially. Chopin, however, suffered a painful personal disappointment when the audience reacted coldly to his Concerto no. 1 in E minor; the *Gazette musicale,* which belonged to Schlesinger, his music publisher, commented that "it is very difficult not to be monotonous in a piano concerto." Fryderyk could not stand criticism, no matter how small.

The experience of the Polish benefit reinforced Chopin's reluctance to play in public. But when Habeneck invited him to appear at *his* concert three weeks later, he could not refuse. And he was pleasantly surprised with the applause for his *Grande polonaise brillante* in E-flat major, the last composition for piano and orchestra he would write.

Fryderyk was feeling fairly well despite the stress of composing, teaching, and appearing at concerts (plus his social life), but his physician friend Jaś Matuszyński persuaded him to take another vacation. They spent the second half of July at Enghien health resort near Paris, with Chopin taking walks in the beautiful park on the lake shore, bathing in the lake, and chatting away with Polish acquaintances who had settled in the nearby village of Montmorency.

The vacation was cut short, however, when Fryderyk received word that, on doctor's orders, his parents were planning on taking a cure at the Bohemian spa of Karlsbad (today, Karlový Varý). He had not seen them in nearly five years and decided, in a rare display of action without hesitating, to surprise them by turning up there, too. His younger sister, Izabela, had married Antoni Barciński, a mathematics teacher, seven months earlier, and Chopin was anxious to hear everything about the family directly.

Fryderyk's departure for Karlsbad by stagecoach the first week of August 1835 marked the end of an extraordinary phase in his musical career. It brought an impressive surge of creativity and innovation. Yet, the personal life of Chopin, the Romantic genius, was wholly bereft of romance, emotional commitment, or even sexual content.

Chapter 9

THE QUESTION OF WHAT CONSTITUTES INSPIRATION—for Chopin or any other composer—will presumably remain unanswered forever.

There are no definitions, formulas, or formats to apply to creativity. By the same token, as the examination of Chopin's life suggests, it is impossible to try to relate the time of composition or appearance of specific works to specific events in his (or even Polish) history. As Karol Szymanowski, a leading Polish composer of the early twentieth century, remarked, "Chopin's music is not a diary of personal suffering."

Any attempt at reconstructing the chronology of Chopin's creation, quite apart from the actual relationship to events, is rendered even harder by his immensely complicated and confusing work and publication habits. Often, years would elapse between the start and the completion of a single composition, no matter how short (the length never being a defining element), because Chopin's mood or concentration would shift or he would become more interested in something else before returning to the original project. (This was not atypical: It took Liszt twenty-one years to complete one of his concertos.)

Moreover, it was excruciatingly difficult for him to put down on paper the melodies that filled his mind. George Sand has recounted that during their walks near her country home in Nohant, for example, Chopin would hum a new melody, then later struggle at home to write it in coherent form. Delacroix, who knew Chopin well, believed that his creativity was "to a greater degree the result of work rather than of inspiration."

On a less vital but symptomatic scale, Fryderyk, by his own admission, hated writing letters (though he actually wrote a large number of them), and it was not uncommon for him to start a letter, say, on Saturday and complete it the following Friday; in numerous instances, weeks and even months would elapse before the beginning and the end of a missive prior to posting.

For reasons dictated by his own desires or those of his music publishers, the publication of a finished score could be delayed sometimes for many years. Chopin, the perfectionist, almost never explained precisely why he held a piece back, simply announcing that, in terms of quality, it was not ready for the public. This was so even though he was always keen to sell and deliver a work (they were often precontracted) and collect payment. Fryderyk was able to advise his publisher that, for instance, he was embarking on composing the Twenty-four Préludes—evidently the construct already existed in his mind—and even promise a delivery date. But often weeks stretched into months and years in the mystery of inspiration. As Schlesinger, the publisher, once remarked, "Chopin still worked on creations finished a long time ago."

Publishers were normally guided by their business sense of whether, in their judgment, a given composition would sell well at an earlier or later time. In immutable fashion, public tastes had to be guessed or predicted. Finally, a surprising number of Chopin's works were published only posthumously (at least ten in the twentieth century, the most recent as late as 1968) because he had forbidden publication in his lifetime or because some were lost for a very long time.

As a rule, Chopin did work hard to deliver on time as specified in a presale agreement (he usually received generous advances). But when he decided he did not like a publisher, as happened several times in the early days, he would contrive to break the contract. He would, for example, deliver entirely unreadable, partly erased, or incomplete manuscripts, without required notations, then promise to provide corrections, but fail to do so, by invoking forgetfulness, indolence, and "no head for business."

This occurred with Jacques-Hippolyte Aristide Farrenc, his first Paris publisher, when Chopin decided to sign up with Schlesinger (Farrenc allegedly was only interested in orchestral and chamber music works while Fryderyk wished to concentrate on the piano). After Chopin's treatment, the infuriated Farrenc chose to cancel their agreement, describing Fryderyk as "a lazy and extremely weird" individual.

A reconstruction of Chopin's creativity during his first Paris phase—

1831 to mid-1835—in terms of presumed dates of *composition* shows that he had really labored exceedingly hard on his music while teaching at the same time. Inspiration seemed never to leave his soul. From the Opus 6 and 7 Mazurkas to the Opus 27 Nocturnes, it is a most impressive body of work, including such gems as the first cycle of études, the Ballade no. 1 in G minor, the Scherzo no. 1 in B minor, the aforementioned mazurkas and nocturnes, and, possibly, the Fantaisie-Impromptu, op. 66. This alone would make any composer proud.

Most likely, Chopin spent his first year in Paris feverishly completing his cycle of the twelve *Grandes Études* Opus 10, including the "Revolution-ary" Étude, that he had begun in Vienna or perhaps even in Warsaw (all but one were written in pre-Parisian days). The full cycle of these "miniatures" was published by Schlesinger in 1833, enchanting and intriguing most of Chopin's fellow pianists and composers (though bringing down on him the wrath of the German critic Rellstab).

But he also produced or completed during that first year or so the Ballade no. 1 in G minor and Scherzo no. 1 in B minor in their earliest versions (later recast), the two sets of mazurkas, two sets of nocturnes, his first waltz, and his only boléro. The Boléro in C major, op. 19, was meant to be Spanish in flavor, but is rich, instead, in polonaise themes (it was written before his trip to Majorca). Chopin liked to experiment. There is not much doubt about the approximate accuracy of these composition dates because all of the works were published in 1833; the waltz and the boléro, his lesser works, came out in 1834.

Tovey, the musicologist, had concluded at the turn of the century that "Chopin's Études stand alone [as] the only extant great works of art that really owe their character to their being études." Simon Finlow, a Chopin scholar, has written almost a century later that the publication of the first cycle of the études "provided the musical world with its first conclusive evidence of Chopin's creative talent." Most of them were written when he was in his early twenties.

Chopin, to be sure, did not invent the idea of an étude as an instru-mental study. Jon Newsom, the American musicologist, points out that "Bach was among many earlier composers who composed keyboard studies. What Chopin did in his Études was to create a new genre: the keyboard study as a vehicle for brilliant public performance."

Technique is naturally important, remembering that études are *studies.* And Chopin has made them almost impossibly difficult for pianists while maintaining beauty and artistry. Étude no. 3 in E major, op. 10, calls for both melody and accompaniment to be played by the same hand at the outset and toward the end. In the dramatic Étude no. 4 in C-sharp minor, op. 10, the endless chromaticism is written to be played exclusively by the right hand, which provides accompaniment for the left hand's "tree trunk" staccato melody. Chopin was one of the pioneers in commanding the use of the fifth finger and the thumb of the right hand, believing that each finger has different characteristics and should therefore be fully employed. Étude no. 5 in G-flat major, op. 10, is confined to the black keys in the right hand, a limitation that makes it, besides being of technical interest, something of a compositional tour de force. And in most of the Opus 10 Études, from the first to the last (or "Revolutionary"), Chopin makes enormous pianistic demands. Étude no. 2 in A minor, op. 10, is considered so difficult technically that many contemporary pianists choose not to play it.

Late in 1831 or early in 1832, Chopin composed the first version of his Ballade no. 1 in G minor. Mieczysław Tomaszewski, the author of the exhaustive and authoritative Chopin section in the Polish *Musical Encyclopedia,* describes the ballades as "a new kind of piano music, typically romantic," adding that no earlier ballades "are known in instrumental music."

The history of Ballade no. 1 perfectly illustrates Chopin's bizarre composing habits. Though the first version was written possibly as early as 1831, the final version was finished only late in 1835 or early 1836 (it was published in 1836), and Chopin has left no explanation for this delay. He may have laid it aside for four or so years because he disliked the first version, preferring to concentrate on other compositions, or just kept rewriting it (occasionally or until he reached what he regarded as perfection). It also took from 1836 to 1839 for Ballade no. 2 to be completed; nos. 3 and 4 came easier in 1841 and 1842.

His Scherzo no. 1 in B minor had a similar history: Chopin wrote the first version probably in 1831 and the final version between 1834 and 1835 (it was published in 1835).

Along with the études, the ballades and scherzos were Chopin's most imaginative musical forms, although in the latter he followed an existing tradition, looking especially to Beethoven's late scherzos. The ballade is storytelling, and, in Charles Rosen's words, "The fusion of narrative and lyric . . . is perhaps Chopin's greatest achievement: he realized in music one of the major ambitions of the Romantic poets and novelists." The scherzo, which once meant a "joke" in music, became in Chopin's hands a work of high vigor and high emotional intensity. To Eugene Istomin, the American pianist, Scherzo no. 1 begins with "two explosive screams of protest" and ends with "two explosions of final protest." To Tomaszewski, the scherzos—there would be four in all—"mark the culminating point in the history of the genre." Rosen believes that Chopin produced an "astonishing effect" in Scherzo no. 1 by having the left hand, on its own, "resolve the cadence of a measure before the right." Chopin's spectacular device entailed dropping harmonization long enough to create that startling effect.

The ideal experience in pure sound would be if one could imagine the singing of María Malibrán followed by Chopin's rendition of his Ballade no. 4 in F minor. This ballade in Charles Rosen's opinion is "one of the most moving pages in all nineteenth-century music."

John Field (who played in Warsaw when Chopin was thirteen, then criticized his music in Paris) was then considered to be the father of the nocturne. But it was Chopin, composing his first nocturne at the age of eighteen, who made the genre so greatly admired. In its standard definition, a nocturne is a short, slow piece in which a melody in the right hand is accompanied by broken chords in the left; it is supposed to convey the calm beauty of night. Tomaszewski writes in the Polish *Musical Encyclopedia* that Chopin's Nocturnes brought together "the erotic and the heroic."

While Chopin's first nocturne was published only posthumously (he had not revealed its existence in his lifetime), the eight nocturnes in three opuses he completed in Paris and had published between 1832 and 1836 made his name virtually synonymous with this genre of music. Supremely romantic in their rocking meter (as in rocking to sleep), Chopin's Nocturnes are rich in Italian bel canto opera influences in their mode of expression such as in their ornamental fiorituras. Given his passion for the opera—and his friendship with Bellini—this is not surprising. Liszt, in fact, attributed it to the influence of Bellini's arias. A contemporary critic called Chopin's Nocturnes "bel canto of the pianoforte."

But the closest to Chopin's heart were the mazurkas. He composed or completed seventeen of them in four opuses between the time he settled in Paris and his departure for Karlsbad. Together with his polonaises (of which he wrote only three during his first Parisian phase), the mazurkas were his way of expressing his Polishness, Polish sentimentality, and devotion to Polish independence; they were the only genre Chopin composed uninterruptedly throughout his life—from the first two written when he was fifteen to his last work in 1849—for a total of fifty-seven, many published posthumously. Pianist Wilhelm von Lenz, a pupil of Chopin, wrote in his memoirs that through the mazurkas "Chopin . . . represented Poland." This, he went on, "was the only political pianist . . . he incarnated Poland, he put Poland to music."

Tomaszewski explains that Chopin's Mazurkas had evolved from a "semiutilitarian" character intended for dancing—the original mazurka (or *mazurek,* in Polish) is a folk dance named after the central Mazury region—to "a form of reflective lyricism, a most personal expression . . . a longing for his native land." Having listened avidly to folk music during his childhood and adolescent vacations in the countryside, Fryderyk carried forever the seed of inspiration that created the treasury of mazurkas.

Chopin's genius shielded him, however, from simply transmuting dancing and singing mazurka tunes into *his* piano mazurkas, unlike Liszt and Brahms, who would both adapt Hungarian folk melodies. (Liszt even wrote a 450-page book on Gypsy music.) What he took from the Polish villages were the rhythms, the accents of joy, hope, wistfulness, sadness, and defiance, and he molded them with his artistry into forms of pure or abstract music. In so doing, he filtered them through his own personality, which, indeed, was the sum of all these feelings and their extremes.

Outsiders tend to perceive the Mazurkas as being essentially dramatic, if not downright tragic, in their beauty. Poles respond on various levels of perception. Ludwika Jędrzejewicz, his older sister, conveyed it to Fryderyk in a letter from Warsaw in February 1835:

> Your Mazurka, the one that goes Bam Bum Bum in the third part . . . was performed by the full orchestra at the Variety Theater [and] played all night at the ball at the Zamoyskis, [who] were extremely pleased with it for dancing. What do you say about being profaned like that? . . . The Mazurka is more properly for listening. . . . What will you say about my being at the Lebruns one evening and having had to profane you? They had asked me if I could play your magnificent Mazurka, and . . . I played for dancing with

the approval of the dancers. My dear, tell me whether you wrote it in the spirit of a dance; perhaps we have understood you incorrectly.

Chopin, not normally given to discussions of his feelings, seems to have tried on at least one occasion to make himself understood by foreigners. According to Liszt, Fryderyk was asked by Princess Carolyne Sayn-Wittgenstein (Liszt's cigar-smoking new mistress), as he played for them one afternoon, from where he drew the unusual sentiment in his compositions.

He replied that he could never be free of what was known in Polish as *żal,* a word for which there is no equivalent in other languages. In his book about Chopin (which some scholars suspect was actually dictated by the Polish-born princess), Liszt has written that Fryderyk "repeated this word repeatedly as if his ear could not be sated by the sound of this expression, containing the full scale of feelings set off by deep pain—from contrition to hatred."

The word *żal*—pronounced JAHL (as in *joli* in French)—conveys to the Polish ear and soul sadness, longing, nostalgia, regret, resignation, contrition, resentment, complaint, and even anger. *Żal* therefore fits Chopin perfectly as a person as well as with reference to his music. It is the common thread throughout his works.

Ryszard Przybylski writes (in Polish) that *żal* is a word that contains "remorse as well as a threat of protest, humiliation, and a rise of complaint . . . in *żal* one can weep, but from *żal* one can prepare vengeance. One can accept one's deserved defeat, but anger over undeserved injury may be born from it. A person plunged in *żal* may judge in justice actions against oneself." Przybylski believes that Chopin had acted in this fashion when he wrote to Tytus Woyciechowski shortly before leaving Poland for good that "when I reflect about myself, I feel *żal* that consciousness leaves me [so] often." He was alluding to the loss of a sense of reality that was beginning to haunt him, leading to hallucinations and otherworldliness.

Preparing for the journey to Karlsbad, Chopin had also moved well ahead with work on the second cycle of études. With less than four years behind him in Paris, at the age of twenty-five, he had achieved his goal of conquest.

But before long, Fryderyk would be deeply plunged in *żal*.

Chapter 10

THE SIX WEEKS in the latter part of the summer of 1835 were the most emotion-filled and perhaps happiest in the life of Fryderyk Chopin. His time was divided between two families he loved: his own and one he may have hoped to become his own, too. But, like so much about Chopin's life, it was only a brief interlude—with a touch of the pathetic.

Having received his French passport on August 1, 1835, and being free to travel across European borders, Fryderyk raced by public stagecoach over northeastern France, Germany, and Austria to the Bohemian spa of Karlsbad (Karlový Varý), a truly heroic feat in exhausting heat for one in such weak health. He arrived on the evening of August 15, after ten days on the road, unaware that his parents and their manservant Stanisław Nadolski had reached the resort a few hours earlier and gone to sleep.

The elder Chopins, of course, had no idea that their son was in town. Mikołaj had written Fryderyk in April that they still planned to spend their vacation in Karlsbad, but, clearly, it never occurred to him to suggest a meeting. He assumed that Frycek would be too busy in Paris, and inquired wistfully at the end of a long, chatty letter, "What do you plan to do? . . . To which side will you turn?"

Mikołaj and Justyna were therefore mightily surprised—and delighted—when at seven o'clock in the morning of the next day a fellow Pole named Zawadzki knocked on their door at the Golden Rose Hotel to say that Fryderyk had been looking for them all over Karlsbad. They rushed to wake him up. Mikołaj described the joyous scene in a letter to their daughters and sons-in-law back in Warsaw, reporting that Fryderyk "hasn't changed a bit, he looks to us just as he was at the moment of departure" nearly five years earlier.

In an exalted addition scribbled in his own hand, Chopin announced that "our happiness is indescribable! We embrace one another, and embrace, and what more can one do? . . . How kind is the Lord to us." He let himself go this time: "What I write is without order; it's better not to think about anything today: to enjoy the happiness for which one has lived. That's what I have today. The same parents, always the same, though they have aged a little bit. We stroll . . . talk about you . . . say how many times we had thought about each other. We drink, eat together, caress each other, shout at each other. I am *au comble de mon bonheur* [at the height of my happiness]. The same customs, the same movements with which I grew up . . . the same hand I haven't kissed in so long. . . . It's impossible to collect my thoughts and write about anything else other than we are happy at this moment, that I always had only the hope, but today the fulfillment of this happiness, happiness, and happiness. . . ."

Fryderyk's moment of happiness with his parents lasted four weeks, and it probably was never surpassed for any of the three of them. Apart from Mikołaj and Fryderyk's joint letter to Warsaw that first day, there is no record of how they spent their time. Maurycy Karasowski, one of Chopin's early biographers, has written that Fryderyk "anticipated [his parents'] wishes, told them about life in Paris, about people who were his friends . . . and, above all, played the piano for them." Once, he joined cellist Joseph Dessauer at a musical soirée. According to another biographer, the Chopins could tell Fryderyk in detail about life in Russian-occupied Warsaw, unconstrained, as they were in their letters, by Russian mail censorship.

After three weeks, on September 6, the three Chopins left Karlsbad for the castle of Count Bedřich Thun-Hohenstein in Cieszyn in Silesia for an eight-day visit. The count's two sons had been Chopin's pupils in Paris, and during his stay at the castle Fryderyk gave lessons to his twenty-year-old daughter, Josefina. He also presented her with a manuscript of his *Grande valse brillante*, op. 34, no. 1, one of his loveliest waltzes, probably composed in Karlsbad.

On September 14, the Chopins bade farewell to their son to start the journey back to Warsaw. It was to be the last time they would see him. Countess Thun-Hohenstein wrote her mother that she was "especially sorry" for Madame Chopin "who barely kept her tears at dinner. Fryderyk was so moved," she added, that "he spent the rest of the day in his room, unable to come out to join us." But there is nothing to corroborate the version contained in one of the early biographies that Chopin had contemplated returning to Poland with his parents.

Fryderyk stayed five more days at the castle before departing for what would turn out to be an unexpected episode in his quest for happiness. He was to spend the night in Dresden en route to Leipzig where Felix Mendelssohn awaited him.

The instant he arrived at the Stadt Gotha Hotel in Dresden on the evening of September 19, Chopin ran into Feliks Wodziński, one of his oldest childhood friends. Dresden was one of Fryderyk's favorite cities (here he had first seen Goethe's *Faust*) and now it welcomed him with a most pleasant surprise.

Feliks and his brothers, Antoni and Kazimierz, and sisters, Maria and Józefa, were the children of Count Wincenty and Countess Teresa Wodziński, who had known the Chopins for many years. The Wodzińskis owned land on both sides of the border between the Russian-ruled kingdom of Poland and Prussia—they were said to own twenty thousand hectares and several villages—but prior to the 1830 uprising, the family spent most of its time at their Warsaw apartment not far from the Chopins. The boys attended the lyceum together with Fryderyk, and they boarded at the Chopins' for a year while their mother was readying the apartment. The girls took lessons at home.

The relations between the two families were very cordial. They alternated receiving one another for Sunday dinners. Fryderyk was a summer guest at the Wodzińskis' Służewo countryside mansion at least once. Józefa Wodziński Kościelska (the latter her married surname), the younger sister, wrote many years later that although "Frycek was already considered the best pianist in Warsaw," he played children's games with her and Maria,

> mimicked different acquaintances, at which he excelled, drew caricatures, and, in one word, tried to amuse us the best he could. We were never bored. . . . Sometimes he would sit at the piano, but because we were too childish to feel the beautiful music, he fooled at the piano or played waltzes, polkas, and mazurkas for us to dance to. . . . He exceeded all his contemporaries not only in merriment, but in charm. . . . Simply, it was impossible not to like him.

Maria was six or seven years old and Frycek fifteen or sixteen when they first got to know each other.

The links between Fryderyk and the Wodzińskis were severed when he left Warsaw in November 1830. Antoni and Feliks fought the Russians in the uprising that started four weeks later. After the fall of Warsaw, they joined the rest of the family in Dresden where Senator Maciej Wodziński, Wincenty's brother, had taken refuge earlier. In 1832, Count Wodziński moved to his border properties to rebuild the war-shattered villages while the countess and the children went to live in Geneva.

In Geneva, the countess established an elegant salon for aristocrats and great writers and artists of Romanticism, but it was her daughter Maria who shone as the brilliant star of the household. Even at the age of fourteen or fifteen, she was striking in every sense. With her dark hair, black eyes, and olive-toned skin, Maria had a touch of the Mediterranean about her, inherited from her maternal grandmother, an Orsetti from the Milanese nobility, who had come to Poland with Princess Bona Sforza to wed a Polish king. Maria was not a classical beauty, but "very interesting," as people put it in those days, and certainly most charming.

In Geneva, Maria was learning French from a French governess, English from an English governess, and piano from the Irish composer John Field, who was living there at the time. She was a highly talented sketch artist, taking lessons at the Geneva Arts Academy. Słowacki, the Polish Romantic poet, and Prince Louis-Napoleon, who would become Emperor Napoleon III, were in love with Maria. Both were frequent callers at the Wodziński villa. Słowacki dedicated his poem "In Switzerland" to her. Adam Mickiewicz, the other Polish bard, visited the Wodzińskis often before his 1834 marriage to Celina, the daughter of the famed pianist Maria Szymanowska.

Chopin had not heard from the Wodzińskis since leaving Warsaw (nor they from him) until, out of the blue, he received a letter from Feliks in June 1834, inviting him in his mother's name to visit them in Geneva. Maria added a few warm sentences of her own, enclosing a piano piece she had composed. It is quite likely that it was Maria, obviously aware of Fryderyk's growing fame, who had persuaded her celebrity-adoring mother to invite him. It was perfectly proper for Feliks, as an old schoolmate, to write the letter. But what precisely had inspired Maria to engineer the invitation remains obscure: romantic childhood memories, admiration for Fryderyk's creations with which she was surely familiar as an aspiring musician, or both?

In any event, Chopin could not, or did not wish to, accept the invitation at that moment. On July 18, he sent his regrets to Feliks in a gracious, rambling, amusing, evocative letter. He wrote that "were it not that I have only recently come back from the banks of the Rhine and have an engagement from which I cannot free myself just now, I would immediately set out for Geneva. . . . But cruel fate—in one word—it cannot be done." Chopin failed to explain what sort of "engagement" would prevent him from visiting the Wodzińskis, and he did not actually stir from Paris for the balance of 1834. He may have meant, of course, his piano-teaching engagements (though the summer was a slow time for lessons) or his work on a number of compositions then underway, including the second cycle of études (op. 25). But it is equally possible that Chopin simply had no desire—or interest—in what he may have feared would be wasting time in Geneva.

Still, Fryderyk went out of his way to show his appreciation for the piano composition Maria had sent him. He wrote Feliks that it had given him "the greatest pleasure," adding, "as I happened to be improvising the very evening of its arrival in one of our salons, I took for my subject the pretty theme by a certain Maria with whom in times bygone I played at hide-and-seek." This improvisation, according to Antoni Marceli Szulc, a Chopin scholar, may have been "the very simple and naïve Nocturne in C-sharp" found among Fryderyk's manuscripts after his death.

And Chopin attached to his letter a copy of "a little *valse* I have just published" for "my esteemed colleague Mademoiselle Maria," hoping that "it may afford her a hundredth part of the pleasure which I felt on receiving her variations." It was the Waltz Brilliant in E-flat major, op. 18. He concluded by asking Feliks to make "a graceful and respectful bow" to Maria: "Be surprised and say in a whisper, 'Dear me, how tall has she grown!'"

Fryderyk did not follow up on this exchange, but Countess Wodzińska was evidently determined to snag him socially, one way or another, possibly again at Maria's behest. On February 28, 1835, she wrote him inquiring about the Chopin family in Warsaw and asking, "Aren't we going to have the pleasure of seeing Mr. Fryderyk?" The countess advised him that she did not know how much longer she would remain in Geneva, "but before I leave these parts, I shall first visit

Paris and the persons there who interest me." Then she asked for "a collection of autographs of famous people whom, naturally, you know: a Pole, a Frenchman, a German, etc., it doesn't matter, [and] even a Jew with a beard, like at home, but only if he is worthy."

It is unknown whether Chopin obliged, but he seems not to have had further contact with the Wodzińskis until the surprise meeting with Feliks in Dresden on September 19, 1835, after the visit with his parents in Karlsbad. The Wodziński family had moved from Geneva to Dresden the previous month, presumably to be close to the count's brother Maciej and many of their friends residing there, but Chopin had no way of knowing about it. Several of his biographers suggest that Antoni Wodziński, the eldest of the brothers, may have informed Fryderyk of the move. However, Józefa Kościelska, the younger sister, reports in her diaries that "we knew nothing about Chopin's arrival" until "suddenly, one day, Feliks comes home to say that he had just met Chopin in the street, and both were immensely surprised because neither of them had expected such a meeting."

Fryderyk was immediately invited to the Wodziński home for an evening of reminiscences and music. He remembered Maria as a girl of eleven, and now he encountered an unusually mature, interesting, and attractive young woman of sixteen. She had eyes only for him, and that first Dresden evening marked the birth of what has become known as Chopin's "second great romance," the first having been his rather inconclusive pining for Konstancja Gładkowska in Warsaw. Or, put another way, it was the birth of another enduring Chopin myth, one which he actually might have shared for a time.

For now, he delayed his trip to Leipzig, spending two weeks in Dresden and seeing the Wodzińskis—chiefly Maria—from morning until night at their Rampischestrasse apartment. Józefa Kościelska recounts that Fryderyk spent much time at the piano—"and how he did play!" She noted that "although he looked unwell, his playing was distinguished by incredible magnificence, and, when needed, by titanic strength." But Fryderyk and Maria also went for walks, talked for hours about music— especially his music—and, unquestionably, they were mutually attracted though Chopin tended to remain passive in his attitudes.

It was apparently at Maria's request that he composed a waltz for her, the very moving, sentimental Waltz in A-flat major (published posthumously as op. 69, no. 1). He inscribed the manuscript on the right *pour Mlle. Marie,* and signed it *F. Chopin, Drezno (Dresden), septembre 1835.* As Józefa tells it, Fryderyk presented the manuscript to Maria just before leaving for Leipzig at noon on October 3. He played it for the family as a farewell gesture, then climbed aboard the stagecoach. Józefa wrote that "in this waltz, passionate and lyrical at the same time, the trio was composed in such a way that the note repeated twelve times in the left hand is reminiscent of the sound of the clock at Frauenkirche [church] striking twelve o'clock; the middle part is a passage with a rhythmic crescendo, turning into appassionato to imitate the sinister creaking of the wheels of the carriage approaching the house."

Fryderyk and Maria vowed to meet again the following year—her parents treated him like a family member and the countess clearly favored the relationship with the famous composer—but Maria wasted no time. Within days of Chopin's departure, she wrote him a long, gushing letter in French, describing how much he was already missed.

"On Saturday, when you left us," Maria told him,

> we all went sadly, our eyes full of tears, around the parlor where a few minutes earlier you still belonged to our circle. . . . My mother, in tears, reminded us time after time in some detail about the stay of her 'fourth son, Fryderyk.' . . . My father joked about us and laughed himself only not to cry. The singing teacher came at eleven o'clock: The lesson went rather poorly, we couldn't sing. You were the subject of all the conversations. Feliks kept asking me for the Waltz (the last thing we received and heard played by you). We found pleasure: they in listening, and I in playing because it reminded us of the brother who left us a while ago. . . . Nobody ate dinner: We kept staring at your usual place at the table and then at Frycek's corner. The chair remains in its place and it will surely so remain as long as we stay in this apartment. . . . Mother talks to me only about you and about Antoni. When my brother comes to Paris, I beg you to think at least a bit about him. If you knew what a devoted friend you have in him. . . . Antoni has a good heart, too much so, and he is always exploited by others; because he is very careless, he doesn't think about anything. . . . We have appealed many times to his reason, but I think it will have a greater effect if he hears it from you. . . . But I'm writing too much. Your time is so precious that it is a crime to take it to read my scribblings. Besides, you surely will not read them in their entirety. Little Marina's letter will wind up in a corner after the reading of a few words. . . . God be with you.

In a postscript, Maria informed Chopin that he had left behind his pencil on the piano and that "we keep it here with respect, like a relic."

It is safe to assume that Maria had fallen in love with Fryderyk, or thought so. In Geneva, she had rejected the courtship of the poet Słowacki, who was too much of a "dandy" for her taste (he also happened to dislike Chopin). As for Fryderyk, as usual, it is very hard to gauge his emotions. There is no trace of any reply to Maria's missive, but Chopin evidently conveyed some of his feelings to his family in Warsaw because his father noted in a letter to him later that year: "As I see from your letters, the stay in Dresden was pleasant for you since you plan to go there next year" (these letters from Fryderyk are among those that have vanished). In another letter, Mikołaj Chopin observed that "I see that Dresden has become a very interesting place for you and it seems to attract you." He also informed Fryderyk that Count Wodziński had visited the family in Warsaw, inquiring about news from Paris.

The two families now appeared to be encouraging the rapport between Maria and Fryderyk. Meanwhile, Antoni Wodziński reached Paris, as planned, and wrote his mother that he was seeing Fryderyk every day, including the very moment he was penning his letter: "Fryderyk gets up from the piano and says, 'tell them that I love them all terribly, but terribly.'"

Fryderyk, of course, used the word "love" with extravagant abandon and generosity, to men and women. Was he really in love with Maria in the normally accepted sense of the word, or was it another romantic abstraction, like Konstancja? Nearly another year would elapse, in apparent silence, before the next episode in Chopin's "second great romance."

Chopin spent two days in Leipzig, the German music capital, early in October, visiting Mendelssohn and finally meeting for the first time his great admirer Robert Schumann as well as Schumann's fiancée, Clara Wieck, herself an outstanding pianist. Mendelssohn, recently named director of Leipzig's Gewandhaus, and Chopin spent all day Sunday, October 4, playing for each other. Chopin performed the piano passages of his Concerto no. 1, his new Opus 25 Études, and his new Nocturne in D-flat major, op. 27, no. 2; Mendelssohn liked the nocturne so much he memorized it in the shortest imaginable time. Mendelssohn played his new St. Paul oratorio. The next day, he introduced Fryderyk to Schumann, Clara, and her father, Friedrich Wieck, another admirer, at their home (it was Wieck whom Chopin had called "stupid" in a letter to a friend after reading his review of the Mozart variations three years earlier).

While Chopin's new works evinced fresh admiration from Mendelssohn—and would command it the next day from Schumann—Fryderyk is not known to have reciprocated in this case or in any other case with contemporary composers. While so many of his fellow musicians—Schumann, Liszt, Berlioz, Mendelssohn, Hiller, and others—have published insightful and generally favorable articles about and reviews of Chopin's work, Fryderyk maintained a studied silence about his living colleagues and their compositions though he was a bit more forthcoming about pianists. For example, Chopin commented favorably only on the design of the title page of *Kreisleriana* that Schumann had dedicated to him. By contrast, there is ample documentation of Fryderyk's enthusiasm for a number of new operas, notably Meyerbeer's *Robert le diable* and *Les Huguenots*. Chopin seems to have resented potential competition as much as criticism, which, for example, was among the reasons for his increasingly difficult and complex relationship with Liszt. But he was moved to tears when Clara Wieck played two of his études, a Schumann sonata, and two of her own pieces.

Perhaps the most intriguing of these new études—and one of the deepest works of the genre—is no. 7 in C-sharp minor, op. 25, sometimes called the "Cello Étude." And it is fascinating how music scholars from distinct cultures and backgrounds hear it (or read or interpret it). To Zieliński, the Polish scholar, writing in the early 1990s, this étude moves from a Baroque oratorial style to reminiscences of the baritone *"O Freunde, nicht diese Töne"* recitative from Beethoven's Ninth Symphony, to chords of great solemnity and elegiac sadness. He hears in the right hand a gentle soprano voice that in the first phrase follows the melody of the Polish lullaby "Little Jesus." Charles Rosen, also writing in the 1990s, observes that this étude is "derived" from a scene in the third act of Bellini's opera *Norma*. Clearly, there are multifarious ways of understanding and defining Romanticism in music.

The enchantment of making music with piano companions did not deter Chopin from visiting his Leipzig publishers—Pröbst-Kistner and Breitkopf & Härtel (the latter probably the oldest publisher in Europe, dating back to 1542)—from whom he derived growing revenues for sales of his sheet music in the German-speaking world and much of Eastern

Europe. Fryderyk could be an ethereal musician one moment and a keen-minded businessman the next.

On October 6, Chopin traveled to Heidelberg to visit the family of his favorite student, sixteen-year-old Adolf Gutmann, and the two Pereire-Diller sisters, who were family friends of the Chopins. But his frenetic activities since he left Paris for Karlsbad in August, the fatigue of hot diligence travel, and severe autumn weather at the end combined to weaken him to the point where he had to interrupt his trip home and rest for nearly a week. Józefa had already observed in Dresden that he did not look well.

Finally, Chopin improved sufficiently to undertake the three-day stagecoach journey to Strasbourg and Paris, arriving in the capital on October 16. He was enough of a celebrity by then for the *Gazette musicale* to report his return, calling him "one of the most eminent pianists of our epoch" and noting that during his "tour in Germany" his "admirable talent obtained the most flattering reception and excited enthusiasm." The *Gazette* added that the tour had been "a real ovation." Chopin, to be sure, had made no public appearances abroad, but such was the journalism of the day.

Back at the Chaussée d'Antin apartment, Fryderyk collapsed into bed with what may have been pneumonia. He had high fever, coughed long and hard, and, for the first time, spat blood (he was given ice to swallow to halt the bleeding). His physician friend Matuszyński was there to look after him and ultimately brought him back to recovery—"Jaś gives me medicine instead of dinner," Fryderyk wrote a friend—but this was the most serious illness of his life. Chopin was so scared that he prepared his will; he was only twenty-five years old. At the same time, rumors spread in Germany that he had died, and they soon reached the Chopins in Warsaw. The subsequent arrival of friends from Paris reassured them, and *Kurier Warszawski,* the main newspaper, informed Chopin's "many friends and admirers of his great talent" that the reports of his death "are without foundation."

By December, Chopin was back to normal, relatively speaking, but the autumn illness marked the start of the process of the gradual, if slow, deterioration of his health, leading to the final denouement with the inexorability of a Greek tragedy.

It has long been established that Fryderyk suffered from tuberculosis—then known as consumption—for much of his short life and presumably died of it in 1849 (although cardiac arrest may have been the specific cause of death); by the mid-1830s Fryderyk certainly qualified as a full-fledged consumptive.

Though it was hardly a consolation from a medical (or survival) point of view, it was most fashionable in the first half of the nineteenth century to suffer from consumption. Dr. Jean-Claude Davila, the French pulmonary specialist, has commented recently that "tuberculosis in the nineteenth century was part of the cultural tableau, holding a preponderant place in the expression of Romantic thought," adding that "phthisis was the fever of the Romantics." Dr. Davila also concluded that "thinness and a pale face were an extreme distinction: women loved thin and fragile men, considering it symbols of virility." Again, Chopin fully qualified in this dimension.

Whether or not his opinion is solidly scientific, Dr. Davila believes that "through a curious law of compensation, [this] illness gave consumptives a more exalted inner life." And he is borne out to a degree by the impressive gallery of famous consumptives who, in addition to Chopin, included Schubert, Goethe, Balzac, Chateaubriand, and Paganini. And, of course, Violetta in Verdi's *La Traviata,* inspired by Dumas *fils*'s *La Dame aux camélias,* and Mimi in Puccini's *La Bohème* (based on Murger's *Scènes de la vie de bohème)* were tragically and romantically consumptive. Dumas, a friend and admirer, loved Chopin's Berceuse, written in 1844, describing it as "pure tone color" music and calling it a source of inspiration. "Human soul," he said, "flees in the Berceuse to 'the land of dreams.'" Curiously, then, Chopin's and Puccini's music and Dumas's work converged in the cult of consumption.

No effective treatment for tuberculosis existed in those days (opium-based laudanum drops given Chopin served only to alleviate the suffering in the more advanced stages of the illness) and, as Dr. Davila writes, "the evolution of this pathology was inexorable." Fryderyk had at least thirty-three doctors in his lifetime, but they could do little for him.

And untreated tuberculosis, many specialists believed, produced growing psychological distortions and changes over the years, including schizophrenia, schizoid personality, and obsessional neuroses. Chopin may have been severely victimized in this realm, and Dr. Davila, having studied his life from a clinical perspective, lists "self-isolation, abstention from sex (even as a young man), the apparent cold and haughty public demeanor, over-orderliness, and meticulous dress" as symptoms of such disturbances along with rising irritability, inability to display affection, and bouts of "melancholy."

These symptoms, described as schizophrenia by earlier medical authorities, tend more recently—since the early 1970s—to be associated with manic-depressive illness. Dr. Kay Redfield Jamison of the Johns Hopkins University School of Medicine wrote in her seminal study *Touched with Fire: Manic-Depressive Illness and the Artistic Temperament* that "an inevitable confusion between schizophrenia and manic-depressive illness" has persisted until not too long ago. She observed that "psychotic features such as flagrant paranoia, severe cognitive disorganization, delusions and hallucinations . . . are in fact relatively common in manic-depressive illness," adding that "a lifetime course of manic and depressive episodes interspersed with long periods of normal thinking and behavior, and generally healthier personality and social functioning prior to the onset of the illness" can be distinguished from schizophrenia.

Symptoms exhibited (or suffered) by Chopin from early adolescence and over the ensuing years match many of the diagnostic criteria for major depressive and manic episodes listed by Dr. Jamison: among them, diminished ability to think or concentrate, or indecisiveness; recurrent thoughts of death; a distinct period of abnormally and persistently elevated, expansive, or irritable mood; inflated self-esteem; distractibility (i.e., attention too easily drawn to unimportant or irrelevant external stimuli); uninhibited people-seeking alternating with introverted self-absorption; irritable-angry-explosive outbursts that alienate loved ones; increased productivity, often with unusual and self-imposed working hours; sharpened and unusually creative thinking; and inappropriate laughing, joking, and punning. "Melancholy," of course, is equated today with depression.

While Dr. Jamison cautions about "the difficulties in doing diagnostic studies based on biographical material," her research and other parallel research inevitably raise two fundamental questions about Chopin as well as other highly creative individuals. One is whether, indeed, Chopin's apparent manic-depressive illness really resulted from untreated tuberculosis, as suggested by Dr. Davila, or whether the two were wholly unrelated and coincidental. The other question is the extent to which mental illness and genius may be related. This is an ongoing controversy among scholars, but is a most relevant theme in studying Chopin in the light of Dr. Jamison's remark that "nineteenth-century Romantics . . . emphasized not only the melancholy side, but also the more spontaneous, inspired and swept-by-the-muses qualities of genius."

Her list of writers, artists, and composers with "probable cyclothymia, depression or manic-depressive illness" includes, in the Romantic generation, such figures as Byron, Baudelaire, Hugo, de Musset, Shelley, Balzac, Berlioz, Rossini, and Schumann—but, surprisingly, not Chopin.

Be it as it may, manic-depressive illness or schizophrenia usually lead to a loss of contact with reality, and Chopin himself had reported episodes of hallucination (the Vienna cathedral, entries in his diary in Stuttgart, and subsequent incidents), the sense of being "drunk" and not knowing his own whereabouts. His penchant for self-isolation was illustrated by the shield he had erected against intrusions and violations of his privacy. Though he hated being completely alone, he abhorred being with people whom he did not know or like. The pianist Antoine-François Marmontel, who knew him well, recalled that "Chopin was surrounded, adulated and protected by a small entourage of enthusiastic friends who defended him from unwelcome visitors or second-rate admirers. Access to him was difficult; as he himself told his pianist and composer friend Stephen Heller, one had to make several attempts before one could succeed in meeting him."

According to Niecks, Fryderyk's nerves "reached the point of an almost complete breakdown . . . as a result of the illness [that was] growing with unforgiving speed," leading to outbursts of irritability and uncontrolled anger. When a pupil committed an error, "pages from music books flew through the air, and the pupil's ears were filled with bitter remarks and unpleasant words" and "this weak and slim hand, armed with the ever-present pencil, smashed it, and even broke chairs." The biographer relates that when on one occasion a pupil hit the keyboard too roughly, Chopin jumped out of his chair shouting, "What is this? Was that a dog barking?" Such occasions were known to pupils as "stormy lessons," with men more often the targets than women. But the "explosion of anger was only momentary" and his "kind heart searched for ways of compensating for the harm he had caused," in the words of the biographer recounting the displays of Fryderyk's mood swings.

Did depressions account for morbidity in his music? Chopin did compose his first funeral march when he was sixteen, and his famous *Marche funèbre* (the third movement of his Sonata in B-flat minor, op. 35) was written when he was twenty-eight, the rest of the work being completed two years later. Though both periods were reasonably happy in Fryderyk's life, Schumann found that the *Marche funèbre* was "repulsive," breathing "a strange, horrible spirit which annihilates with its heavy fist anything that resists it." But this was not a universally shared opinion. Moreover, funeral marches were also composed by Handel (in *Saul*), Beethoven (in the *Eroica* Symphony and the Piano Sonata in A-flat major), Mendelssohn (in *Songs Without Words*), Wagner, Grieg, and Berlioz. As usual, then, care must be exercised in relating Chopin's compositions to his state of mind and health at any given time.

Schumann, who died at the age of forty-six of self-starvation in an insane asylum, is regarded in medical literature as a classic case of manic-depressive illness from at least late childhood. During his last five years, general paresis, resulting from the late stages of syphilis, led to a severe, general physical and mental decline, according to Dr. Robert W. Weisberg of Temple University (Schumann's older sister Emilie became mentally ill at the age of seventeen and drowned herself at twenty-nine, and his son, Ludwig, spent thirty years in an asylum).

Dr. Richard L. Karmel of the Montreal General Hospital believes that "as a young adult, Schumann lived simultaneously in two worlds of self-representation." He invented the key personalities of Eusebius and Florestan (the latter borrowed from Beethoven's opera, *Fidelio,* in which he is the imprisoned hero), both appearing in Schumann's 1835 piano work *Carnaval.* Eusebius was his "Self-Portrait as Introspective Artist" and Florestan, the second part of this self-portrait, was a violent extrovert. Charles Rosen observes that the two self-portraits were "expressly and eccentrically designed as representations of the divided personality of the composer." *Carnaval* includes a short piece titled "Chopin."

Schumann's famous review of Chopin's Mozart variations is an account of how Eusebius and Florestan had reacted to it; it was Eusebius who exclaimed, "Hats off, gentlemen—a genius!" Finally, Schumann sums up the review with a discussion with Florestan. Several years later, Schumann came back to the review, asking: "Can you hold it against Florestan if he brags about being the first to present to the world a young man hailing from an unknown world? Look how Chopin vindicated his predictions, how victoriously did he emerge from the battle with the Philistines and ignoramuses."

In any event, Schumann himself was a towering musical genius. But his manic-depressive illness has served to encourage endless hypotheses about possible links between it and creativity and genius, dividing scholars. Some of them have been invoked in the case of Chopin though less convincingly; he was more elusive in terms of specific mood (or mania) and specific works.

Fryderyk Chopin's health was a considerable problem long before his milestone sickness in 1835—indeed since boyhood. But Dr. Czesław Sielużycki points out that all reconstructions are incomplete and possibly inaccurate because Chopin, "unlike other great Romantics, not only concealed his ailments over long years (especially from his family), but dissimulated them, under-estimating the resulting dangers—although he sought to heal himself."

Nevertheless when Stephen Heller, in Warsaw for a piano recital, met the nineteen-year-old Chopin, he described him as being "slim, with sunken cheeks . . . it was generally said that, like many geniuses, he will die young." Another visitor spoke of Fryderyk's "sunken chest" and of concern that he was "condemned to consumption." Konstancja Gładkowska, whom Chopin once thought he loved, remarked many years later that "he would not make a good husband because he was nervous, full of all sorts of fantasies, and weak."

After settling in Vienna in November 1830, twenty-year-old Chopin kept up a drumfire of complaints about his health and mental and nervous condition. He wrote to his friends about "weakening," "losing balance," and "mistaking night for day and day for night." In one letter, Fryderyk said that "instead of gaining strength, I get tired and I weaken," underlining the last word. In the spring of 1831, before finally departing for Paris, he advised another friend: "I think that instead of going abroad this year, I'll catch a fever and it will be all over." In September, already en route, Fryderyk announced: "Even my forehead hurts. . . . I think I'm on my way to die. . . . If my health would just serve me. . . . Somehow, consciousness often leaves me."

In Paris, Chopin's physical condition improved markedly, apart from tension headaches and pain from rotting teeth. The four-year period until his serious illness in the autumn of 1835 represented "a happy era" for him, in Dr. Sielużycki's words. And now his tuberculosis was again in "apparent remission," and Fryderyk could concentrate on his continuing conquest of Paris. His health "served" him well notwithstanding his frantic activity; his father was able to comment with pleasure that he enjoyed "good though delicate health."

Chapter 11

INDEED, CHOPIN'S PHYSICAL AND, PRESUMABLY, mental health was so improved in the new year—1836—that he seems to have allowed himself to think seriously for the first time about such things as love and marriage. His thoughts and perhaps hopes centered naturally on Maria Wodzińska, whose company he had so greatly enjoyed during his stay in Dresden the previous September. Before leaving, he had penned the words *"Soyez heureuse"* ("Be happy") under three bars of his Nocturne in E-flat major he had sketched on a page of her album. Written in 1831 or 1832, this was a pioneering piece of music, introducing a new use of the pedal to bring out the best imaginable resonance from the piano. Fryderyk had also dedicated to her his youthful Waltz in A-flat major.

With Chopin, however, it was impossible to judge what was love—or his idealized notion of it. There was the adolescent flirtation with Alexandrine de Moriolles, the daughter of the tutor of Prince Paweł, the son of Grand Duke Konstanty; he called her "Moriolka" and played with her and Paweł when they were children, at Belweder Palace. Later, the friendship became more serious, and Fryderyk wrote Tytus Woyciechowski about her: "You know, those are my amours, which I very willingly admit." But they never saw each other again after he left Warsaw. Then, there was the platonic veneration of Konstancja Gładkowska—"my ideal"—whom Fryderyk forgot quite easily once he was abroad. In the course of his first visit to Vienna, in 1829, he flirted enthusiastically with eighteen-year-old Leopoldina Blahetka, a beautiful pupil of Czerny and already a leading Viennese pianist. But it was a short visit and Chopin never saw Leopoldina again, though he mentioned her admiringly in letters to Woyciechowski. Chopin, as a matter of fact, had a pronounced propensity for falling in love, or thinking he was in love, with countless women, but always ever so briefly.

Chopin's biographer Niecks observes that "tender passion was a necessary of his existence . . . he would passionately love three women in the course of one evening party and forget them as soon as he had turned his back, while each of them imagined that she had exclusively charmed him." He adds that "Chopin was of a very impressionable nature: beauty and grace, nay, even a mere smile, kindled his enthusiasm at first sight, and an awkward word or equivocal glance was enough to disenchant him."

But Maria Wodzińska was the first real test of Fryderyk's desire and willingness to make a lifetime commitment, something he had always evaded, as he approached his twenty-sixth birthday. Hesitations were his hallmark and, once more, he acted as if he wished that a decision be made for him. Nevertheless there were signs that Chopin was finally considering in earnest a family life for himself even if he had no idea under what circumstances it might occur and what it might entail in terms of his work, habits, surroundings, and quality of life.

For one thing, more and more of his friends and colleagues were getting married or preparing to do so. Mickiewicz and Berlioz were among the newly married. Jaś Matuszyński, the doctor who shared his apartment, was about to wed. Mendelssohn and Schumann were engaged. Liszt's liaison with his mistress—he had children with her—was a de facto marriage. Conceivably this matrimonial spectacle had an impact on the impressionable Chopin.

More to the point were the sentiments and information about Maria and their Dresden encounter that Fryderyk was conveying to his family in Warsaw. Inasmuch as none of it appears in his surviving correspondence, Mikołaj's letters to his son, in response to letters from Fryderyk, allow a reconstruction of the story—again, in mirror-image effect.

Thus, Mikołaj Chopin had written him on December 15, 1835, that he judged from Fryderyk's letters that he planned to return to Dresden the following year. Obviously, Fryderyk's autumn illness did not prevent him from reporting on what seemed to be very much on his mind and in his heart, including the fact that Maria's mother was remaining permanently in Dresden and that he was expected to return there when the children rejoined her in the summer. On January 9, 1836, Mikołaj came back to the subject, commenting: "As I can see, Dresden has become a place greatly interesting to you and it seems to be attracting you. At your age, one isn't always the master of one's will, and one may experience impressions that are not easily erased. But who can keep you from making a small trip next spring to come to know what you do not yet know?"

Rather puzzling was Mikołaj's statement that "one must save [money]as much as possible because I could send you a traveling companion to Berlin or Dresden, but at your expense." He may have been responding to a query from Fryderyk about the possibility of a family member accompanying him during the next visit with the Wodzińskis to sanction his relationship with Maria although the two families knew each other well. Mikołaj went on to propose, in effect, that Fryderyk's mother be the companion. "What do you think?" he asked. "I think that if this could be arranged, you could have no better care than having your mother with you. . . . But this requires health and [financial] means, and therefore you must think about one and the other; this is the only way for you to see Dresden again and that which may interest you there, if that impression has not been erased."

He informed Fryderyk that Maria's father had visited the Chopins in Warsaw just before Christmas, adding that "from the anxiety with which he inquired about news from you, we realized that he had heard the rumors about [your] illness." At this stage, both families appeared to be seriously and favorably disposed to the idea of a continuing relationship between Fryderyk and Maria. And this friendship was further enhanced by the long stay in Paris of Antoni Wodziński, Maria's brother, under Fryderyk's care. Now it was up to Chopin to make the next move, but he had to wait until late summer to see Maria again.

Meanwhile, professional and social life kept Chopin extremely busy composing, giving piano lessons, and enjoying late hours of socializing, music, and persiflage with his Polish and French friends and fellow artists. He was so busy that his father complained in a May letter that the family had not heard from him in seven weeks. Chopin also regretfully turned down an invitation from Mendelssohn and Schumann to join them at a spring music festival in Düsseldorf. Instead, he attended the première of Meyerbeer's opera *Les Huguenots,* a major musical event in Paris, and played with Liszt at the Erard Hall on the eve of Lizst's April departure for Switzerland with his mistress, Marie d'Agoult; it was organized as a farewell concert because Liszt had decided to leave Paris for good. On the occasion of the anniversary of the prepartition Polish Constitution on May 3, Chopin improvised the music for seventeen patriotic poems though only one ("Leaves Falling from a Tree") was transcribed. Also in May, two new nocturnes and two polonaises were published in Paris, London, and Leipzig.

Most often, Chopin's works were published within a year or less of their completion (except for those he chose to hold back during his lifetime), but the rate and wealth of his musical production could not be judged by publication dates alone. While working on the nocturnes and polonaises in 1834 and 1835, he was also occupied with composing the famous Twenty-four Préludes, opus 28, four mazurkas, and a scherzo—and so on. During the 1830s and the first half of the 1840s, Chopin, a slow worker, toiled hard on composition, day in and day out, on top of at least six hours of daily lessons—and his social life.

In the social realm, one of the most interesting acquaintances Chopin made in Paris was Astolphe Louis Léonor, Marquis de Custine, the man who, after visiting Russia in 1839, would produce a study of that country that has not been surpassed in a century and a half—and is still being published around the world. Custine did for Russia what Alexis de Tocqueville, another French aristocrat, did for the United States a few years earlier. Prior to his Russian expedition, Custine presided over a very influential artistic salon in Paris and his countryside château, and one of his top priority projects in the mid-1830s was to attract Chopin to his constellation of literary and musical stars.

The handsome, clean-shaven, and soulful-eyed forty-six-year-old Custine had made a remarkable social comeback from a scandal twelve years earlier resulting from his homosexuality. He was beaten almost to death by soldiers of a cavalry regiment and left naked on the pavement after making advances to a young trooper, and the disgrace turned him into a virtual pariah. His first tragedy was the death of his infant son and soon thereafter of his wife—they had a so-called "social marriage"—a year before the scandal surrounding him in 1824.

But his literary talent (he was the author of *Beatrix Cenci*, a highly appreciated tragedy in verse), his charm, and surviving friendships in the Parisian artistic community (his mother had been a mistress of René Chateaubriand, the great romantic novelist) helped him to create a new life and respected identity. He received in style in the grand ornate salon of his town house at 9, rue de La Rochefoucauld, a fashionable Right

Bank address, and at the château in Saint-Gratien, on Lake d'Enghien, near Paris. Until his death he was regarded as France's most distinguished homosexual.

It is not known when Custine and Chopin first met, but the marquis wrote him a letter on March 4, 1835, addressing him as "Dear Chopinet" and inviting him to dinner with Hugo and Lamartine—and hoping that he would hear Fryderyk play. The salutation was: "Expressions of friendship given to friends whom one loves."

There is no reason to believe he was sexually interested in Chopin—he was interested in the celebrity of the musical genius. The marquis had lived since his wife's death with an English friend, Edward St. Barbe, who would remain his constant companion for thirty years. Occasionally, Custine and St. Barbe had a ménage à trois, and the guest in residence when Custine befriended Chopin was a young Polish political exile named Ignacy Gurowski (he stayed for five years). In any event, Chopin did not attend the March dinner, and Custine waited until January of the following year to invite him again. Chopin agreed to come this time—the dinner was on February 3—and it marked the beginning of a long friendship.

The month of May brought Chopin two more lasting friendships: the painter Delacroix, just back from four years in North Africa, and the singer Adolphe Nourrit. He met them at a reception given by Liszt, who had come back from Switzerland for a few weeks.

Long months had elapsed since Fryderyk took leave of Maria in Dresden, but this time the birth of a romance was a reality to him and he seemed determined to nurture it—although he chose not to write to the Wodzińskis—and to see her again before too long. He was encouraged in his plans to return to Dresden in the summer by an extravagantly loving letter early in February from Teresa Wodzińska, Maria's mother, asking: "When can we see you? . . . If you would write at least two words and tell us whether it is true that you will be here this summer." Quite likely, Chopin had been waiting to hear from the Wodzińskis before daring to write to them first (it would not have been proper to write to Maria directly in any case) to avoid any possible rebuff, a prospect he always feared. That his interest, not to say love, remained alive was made clear, of course, in his letters to Warsaw. But still, he preferred when others—or events—made decisions for him.

Madame Wodzińska provided the needed assurance in the letter sent from Dresden on February 5, under the pretext of asking Chopin to deliver to her son Antoni a money draft she was enclosing. She did not explain why the draft did not go directly to her son, but went on at length beseeching Chopin to look after Antoni, who was something of a spendthrift and playboy, and convince him to find work because "idle life is the cause of disasters." God, she assured Fryderyk, "will repay you a hundred times. . . . I know that your time is dear, but I also know your good heart." Next, she turned to what really interested Fryderyk: "Maria . . . sends tender regards and is overcome with joy upon learning that she might receive sheet music from you." Of her youngest daughter, Józefa, she said that "she often associates her brother with you, saying that 'I have much grief over my brother Antoni and Chopin, too.'" Madame Wodzińska ended her letter on this note: "I embrace you, my dear Frycek, along with Antoni, and I bless you both." He was already being treated as a beloved member of the Wodziński family, though perhaps a bit prematurely.

As Chopin firmed up his plans to travel to Dresden, he received word early in July that Madame Wodzińska and her daughters were first going to the Bohemian spa of Marienbad (Mariánské Lázně). He changed his plans quickly, leaving Paris in mid-July and arriving in Marienbad on July 28, tired but happy.

Shortly before he left Paris, Chopin received a letter from the Marquis de Custine informing him: "You are the only person whom I authorize to arrive in Saint-Gratien whenever you wish and without advising me beforehand. This is all I wanted to tell you with thousands of expressions of friendship."

In Marienbad, Chopin took rooms where the Wodzińskis were staying, Zum Weissen Schwann ("At the White Swan"). They all planned to spend a month at the spa; the idea that Fryderyk's mother would travel with him was evidently dropped. As in Dresden the past September, Fryderyk and Maria shared long hours at the piano, Maria displaying for him how she had learned to play his earlier works and Fryderyk teaching her the first two études from the new Opus 25 cycle. A gifted artist, Maria made sketches of Chopin's head as he played the piano and talked, then sat him down in an armchair to paint his portrait in watercolors. It is one of the best portraits of Chopin extant—after that by Delacroix—with the composer looking relaxed, pensive, and at peace.

Chopin's presence in Marienbad was described by Maria's sister, Józefa Kościelska, in her diary (as she had done in Dresden in 1835). It is the most authoritative, firsthand account of the relationship between Fryderyk and Maria at that stage, and Józefa stresses that she had many conversations with him on this subject.

"This time, Chopin arrived in Marienbad especially to see us," she wrote, "so we spent nearly a month together . . . All the Poles visiting Marienbad at that time, and very many of them came this year, formed a self-contained circle. Chopin moved exclusively in that circle, mainly because he was never separated from us. He played a great deal because whoever came to see us immediately asked him to play something freshly published of his works. . . . He played several études from the second cycle, opus 25, especially the first two ones. . . . The first [he played] expressing feelings of strange uncertainty, was, as he said, the musical portrait of my brother Antoni while the second painted with its tones the character of Maria." (Chopin delighted in "painting" amusing musical portraits of his friends, especially women, in impro- vised piano miniatures, usually at late-evening parties when he was in good humor.)

"Good humor kept him company in Marienbad the whole time," Józefa continues. "He had many friends, especially among [Polish] emigrants and in the Parisian musical world. He was so nice that everybody was in love with him, not concealing their veneration for his genius."

Eleonora Ziemięcka, a Polish writer and a friend of the Chopins, who was also spending the summer in Marienbad, said in her diary that "for patriotic reasons Chopin had decided not to return to his motherland from his voluntary exile," presumably because he did not wish to live under Russian occupation. But, she added, "there was one moment when he was inclined to sacrifice these considerations, abandon his adopted country [and] his beloved Paris, the charm and the softness of the salons where he was a favorite, give up everything he had accus- tomed himself to love, and settle forever in Poland . . . to confine his genius to a Polish village, not far from his birthplace, his beloved War- saw and the most precious family." There are no indications that Chopin entertained such thoughts at any point, but Ziemięcka may have been reflecting the hopes held by the Wodzińskis that Fryderyk would come home to marry Maria—and stay.

"That moment was his stay in Marienbad," she noted,

where he came especially to visit with one of the most distinguished Polish families. . . . The older daughter, known to him from childhood through the friendship of [their] parents, conquered his heart. How deep must have been Chopin's attachment [to Maria] as all the temptations, discussed earlier, were vanishing. Their union seemed to be in accordance with the wishes of the parents on both sides. . . . Chopin, full of love for his people and desiring all the good for his nation, talked about rural schools he would establish and educating the people that he would undertake with his promised one.

Madame Ziemięcka was too optimistic and putting words in Chopin's mouth, assuming erroneously that Fryderyk and Maria's engagement was a fait accompli. She and Józefa Kościelska also painted too bright a picture of Chopin's mood in Marienbad. Others remembered him as wholly self-centered and brusque. When Mendelssohn's sister Rebecca, in Marienbad with her husband, asked him to play "at least one Mazurka," Chopin refused in such a brutal way that she wrote a letter of bitter complaint to her brother. He also left unanswered a letter from Schumann proposing a meeting in Marienbad, Leipzig, or anywhere. To many acquaintances, Fryderyk appeared tense and irritable—except when he was with the Wodzińskis.

Madame Wodzińska for her part, as it turned out, was unconvinced about the wisdom of Maria wedding Fryderyk, much as she liked him. She was principally concerned over the state of his health in terms of the future. He was coughing a lot and pale. But Madame Wodzińska was prepared to give it a chance, and she invited Chopin to join the family in moving back to Dresden at the end of August for more time together for all concerned. For openers, the Wodzińskis' physician there examined Fryderyk at her request, concluding that to protect his fragile health, he had to lead an exceptionally careful lifestyle. Chopin was to avoid catching cold, making physical efforts, and attending late-night receptions. He was to go to bed early and take prescribed medicines. He was to dress warmly even at the sacrifice of fashion and elegance.

Chopin apparently agreed to follow this advice to please the Wodzińskis. But it would have been entirely out of character for him to accept the life of an invalid or hermit. Moreover, Madame Wodzińska decided that Fryderyk's compliance must be tested for a year, until his next summer's meeting with Maria. Whether she realized it or not, her ultimatum killed the whole enterprise in the long run, sparing Chopin from having to make a final decision about his future. In this sense, Fryderyk might have been grateful to her—consciously or not—for making a decision, instead of him.

Count Wodziński was even more worried about the health of his prospective son-in-law. Józefa Kościelska recalls:

> Father liked Chopin very much and in principle he was not at all opposed to his marriage with Marynia. If he did oppose it . . . the reason would have been Fryderyk's state of health, which even then caused the most serious fears. Naturally weak and very delicate, he was always exceedingly pale; looking at him, one often had the impression that he is a consumptive whose days are counted. Overall, he was nervous beyond words. At the piano, because of the nervous excitement music created in him, his face would be altered like a person who is about to faint. When he got up from the piano, he was always so exhausted and enervated that he simply did not know what was happening with him. He did not respond to all the compliments and expressions of admiration with which he was being thanked because he could not articulate a single word. He needed a long time to calm down and regain his equilibrium. Only then I had to tell him what different people said about his playing because he always asked me to listen to what people were saying so that I could repeat for him their different opinions. Indifferent, he was not.

It is actually far from clear how far the romance had progressed in Dresden. Antoni Wodziński wrote in his book *The Three Romances of Frédéric Chopin* that Fryderyk had proposed to her under a flowering tree in Marienbad, a claim not borne out by any other account. Other biographers say flatly that he proposed in Dresden on September 9. Fryderyk, Maria, or her mother are not known to have confirmed that he had ever proposed at all, which suggests that he had never summoned the courage (or will) to pop the question. Hesitation? Fear of commitment as deep in Chopin as the Devil's fear of holy water?

Chopin's discussions—almost negotiations—on this whole topic seem to have been conducted face-to-face with Madame Wodzińska in the course of a long twilight meeting on the eve of his departure. She would refer to it as the "gray hour." Antoni Wodziński was correct, however, in writing that his sister had subsequently told him that "she would never go against her parents, that she did not expect to change their [negative] views, but in her heart she would always, always keep a grateful memory" of Chopin. The family had by then ruled out the marriage.

This, inevitably, raises the question of whether Maria was truly in love with Chopin or simply infatuated and flattered by the great composer's attentions. She certainly went along with her mother's wish to postpone decisions for a year, and, for that matter, there are no reasons to believe that Fryderyk opposed it very forcefully. And he accepted her request, repeated in a letter sent to him in Paris a week later, to keep the test idea secret. "It was necessary," she wrote, "to embark on the road that must be followed . . . until then, I shall ask you only for silence; stay healthy because everything depends on it." She urged him to take gum arabic, a remedy favored at the time for lung ailments. Madame Wodzińska also told Fryderyk that she expected to see his parents in Warsaw, but would not mention the "gray hour."

After two weeks in Dresden, they separated. The Wodzińskis traveled on September 10 to their estate in Służewo to rejoin the count and Chopin went to Leipzig, surprising and delighting Schumann, who had assumed that he had simply ignored his invitation. As a farewell gesture, Fryderyk dedicated the song "The Ring" (a Stefan Witwicki setting) to Maria. Symbolically or not, this was the only ring Chopin would give her, for they would never meet again—though Maria knitted warm slippers for him and wrote late in September: "*Adieu, mio carissimo maestro:* don't forget Dresden now and Poland later. *Adieu,* until we meet again! Ah, let it be soon." But Chopin, so susceptible to real or imagined rebuffs, must have read a rebuff in Madame Wodzińska's test ultimatum. Perhaps, subconsciously, he was ready for another adventure of the heart.

In Leipzig, Chopin appeared to be in the best of humor, as if nothing had gone wrong in Dresden. He spent almost an entire day at the piano, playing études, nocturnes, mazurkas, and a freshly composed ballade—whatever Schumann wished to hear. It was, Schumann wrote, one of the best days of his life. Then Chopin played for Schumann's friend Henriette Voigt, a fine pianist, who had had reservations about his innovations in harmony, but wrote after listening to him that "he charmed me . . . with his velvet fingers flying over the keyboard." Next, Chopin listened to Clara Wieck. After Leipzig, he set course for Paris and home, stopping to visit friends in Kassel, Frankfurt, and Heidelberg.

In great form, Chopin resumed his Parisian life by moving early in October to a "nicer apartment" a block away on the same street—from 5, rue de la Chaussée d'Antin to 38, but his friend Matuszyński did not follow him; he was preparing to get married. Fryderyk engaged a Polish butler whose command of French was confined to telling visitors: "Mosieu café" or "Mosieu leçon." His instructions were to keep away people who were not expected. In more ways than one, in the autumn of 1836 Chopin stood on the threshold of a great new chapter of his life.

Rondo
1837—1847

Chapter 12

AND THAT GREAT NEW PERIOD in Chopin's life began, as if on cue, exactly six weeks after he bade farewell to Maria Wodzińska in Dresden. It happened on the evening of October 24, 1836, when Chopin met George Sand at a small artistic reception given by Liszt and his mistress, Marie d'Agoult, at their lodgings at the Hôtel de France, 23, rue Lafitte, just a few minutes away from Fryderyk's Chaussée d'Antin digs. Sand heard Fryderyk play for the first time, never having attended any of his rare public concerts.

George Sand (whose real name was Aurore Dupin Dudevant) had already become one of France's most famous—and controversial—novelists and personages. Her novels, notably the largely autobiographical *Indiana* and *Lélia,* had been praised to the skies in print by such literary luminaries of the Romantic Age as Honoré de Balzac and Charles-Augustin Sainte-Beuve, who were among her myriad friends and acquaintances in the Parisian artistic world (Balzac had also flatteringly modeled Félicité des Touches, one of the main characters in his novel *Béatrix,* after Sand). Because her books were serialized in newspapers and magazines before coming out in bound editions, according to the custom of the day, Sand also enjoyed an immense audience among the highly literate French masses, chiefly in the cities.

Writing during a time of profound social change, Sand dealt sympathetically (yet with brutal frankness) with the fate of women in love—happy or tragic, but always romantic. She attracted huge attention from the feminine reading public (over sixty percent of Parisian women were fully literate in the 1830s). Her tales reflected as well the realities of the deep social inequities persisting in France under the July Monarchy. Above all, George Sand was a prolific writer of astonishing talent.

A defiantly independent woman, she did not mind shocking the more conventional segments of society with her public behavior. She often dressed in masculine clothing, smoked cigars and cigarettes, and, even while still married, had an impressive string of lovers about whom she made no effort to be discreet. All of them were talented and brilliant, though quite a few were psychologically unstable. A friend called Sand "the insatiable coquette."

And, most remarkably for Fryderyk Chopin, George Sand descended directly from King Fryderyk-August II of Poland (even if her ancestor, the king's son, was a royal bastard)—and she was exposed to music from birth. The Polish-French tie dominated Chopin's life.

The musical soirée given by Liszt and d'Agoult celebrated their return from Switzerland to Paris; they had finally tired of their self-exile in Geneva and they had taken rooms together with Sand, their close friend, who had visited them in Switzerland, at the rue Lafitte hostelry earlier in the month. Sand's bedroom was on the mezzanine and Ferenc and Marie's on the first floor. They shared the large parlor that Marie used principally to establish herself as a Parisian salon hostess, and Sand partook of the social activity. The cultural *Tout Paris* came there, and George wrote that "admirable music was performed . . . and in the intervals one could instruct oneself by listening to the conversation."

On that particular occasion, Chopin had been invited along with the pianist Hiller and a few other friends. Liszt, Hiller, and Chopin took turns at the piano, as they often did at parties, while George Sand listened pensively, smoking her thin cigar. She was in man's attire. Niecks, Chopin's biographer, writes that Liszt told him that he had invited Chopin that evening because Sand, who had heard about Fryderyk's music, had repeatedly asked him to arrange a meeting. Chopin resisted, arguing he had no interest in "literary women," but finally gave in.

As it was, Chopin and Sand had very different first impressions of each other. Hiller wrote Liszt that on their way home, Chopin had remarked, "What a repulsive woman Sand is! But is she really a woman? I am inclined to doubt it." Sand, on the other hand, wrote shortly after they met that in Chopin's person there was "something so noble, so indefinably aristocratic." Niecks himself has observed that "in the case of Chopin I am reminded of a saying [by a friend about another couple]: I do like them both so much, for he is so lady-like, and she is such a perfect gentleman."

To her admirers, however, George was a very special and unusual vision of beauty. The poet Heine found, for example, that

> like the genius which manifests itself in her works, her face is rather to be called beautiful than interesting. The interesting is always a graceful or ingenious deviation from the type of the beautiful, and the features of George Sand bear rather the impress of a Greek regularity. Their form . . . is not hard, but softened by the sentimentality which is suffused over them like a veil of sorrow. The forehead is not high . . . and the delicious chestnut-brown curly hair falls parted down to the shoulders. Her eyes are somewhat dim . . . and their fire may have been extinguished by many tears. . . . [She] has quiet, soft eyes, which remind one neither of Sodom nor of Gomorrah. She has neither an emancipated aquiline nose nor a witty little snub nose. It is just an ordinary straight nose. A good-natured smile plays usually around her mouth, but it is not very attractive; the somewhat hanging underlip betrays fatigued sensuality. The chin is full and plump, but nevertheless beautifully proportioned. Also her shoulders are beautiful, nay, magnificent. Likewise her arms and hands, which, like her feet, are small. Let other contemporaries describe the charm of her bosom, I confess my incompetence. . . . She is as beautiful as the Venus of Milo; she even surpasses the latter in many respects: she is, for instance, very much younger.

Alfred de Musset, another great Romantic poet and formerly Sand's lover, saw in her

> the kind of woman I like—brown, pale, dull-complexioned with reflections as of bronze, and strikingly large-eyed like an Indian. . . . I have never been able to contemplate such a countenance without inward emotion. Her physiognomy is rather torpid, but when it becomes animated it assumes a remarkably independent and proud expression.

And Chopin's first negative impression of Sand did not last very long. On November 5, two weeks after the Hôtel de France reception, he invited her to an intimate dinner with Liszt and Marie d'Agoult at his new Chaussée d'Antin apartment. On December 13, George was the guest of honor at a party for a group he especially liked: Liszt, Marie, the Marquis de Custine, the tenor Adolphe Nourrit, and five of Fryderyk's closest Polish Paris men friends. The pianists played and Nourrit sang. Ice cream and tea were served after Chopin and Liszt performed Moscheles's Sonata for four hands. This time, George wore a white dress with a red sash—the Polish national colors.

Chopin was now smitten by Sand. He wrote in his album (the same diary he kept intermittently during the 1830s and in which he had recorded his Stuttgart hallucinations):

> I now have seen her three times. She looked deeply into my eyes while I played. It was rather sad music, the legends of the Danube; my heart danced with her. . . . And her eyes in my eyes, somber eyes, singular eyes, what were they saying? She was leaning on the piano and her embracing gaze flooded me. . . . Flowers around us. My heart was captured! . . . I've seen her twice afterwards. . . . Aurora [sic], what a charming name!

Given Chopin's proclivities for thinking he was in love and his sentimentality, such musings could easily be discounted. Yet this time he must have been in love. A strange relationship, often loving, often stormy, but infinitely necessary to each for wholly different reasons was born that cold autumn of 1836, although nearly two years would elapse before Fryderyk and George began living together. Both still had other unresolved affairs of the heart overlapping their new rapport. But, as much as anything else, Chopin's paralyzing hesitations and fears of commitment (he declined until late in 1838 all invitations to spend time at her countryside home in Nohant) contributed to the long delay and placed George in heartbreaking uncertainty.

In George Sand, Chopin had found an extraordinary human being with an extraordinary history. Together, of course, they formed a unique coming together of rare talent, if not genius. That George was six years older than the twenty-six-year-old Fryderyk was a fundamental aspect of the relationship they both, consciously or subconsciously, nurtured from the outset. In any case, Sand was an absolutely essential factor in Chopin's life: Their stories cannot be contemplated separately.

But they could not have been more different and were always a study in contrasts. Whereas his childhood had been emotionally happy and secure despite his catastrophic health, hers was one of overwhelming sadness, loneliness, and unhappiness—though her health was perfect and energy volcanic.

She was born Aurore Dupin, a child with a legendary family history—she adopted the literary name of George Sand as a young adult—
and the formation and molding of her character and personality is
superbly described by her biographer André Maurois:

> Having lost her father in childhood, she wished to replace him for her
> adored mother and thereby acquired a virile comportment, being con-
> firmed in this attitude by a boy-like education given her by a slightly
> crazy tutor and by the men's garments he made her wear. . . . At the age
> of seventeen, she found herself independent, the mistress of a domain
> and a house in Nohant, and, subconsciously, she always sought to re-
> create this free paradise of her adolescence. . . . She could never tolerate a
> master, and demanded from love that which she had found in maternity:
> for protecting weaker beings. . . . Impatient of all masculine authority,
> she fought to emancipate women from it and to assure the control over
> their bodies and sentiments.

Though Maurois himself cautions against the temptation of explaining a person's character through heredity, he admits that this is permissi-
ble in the case of George Sand, among whose ancestors "all the
personages are extraordinary: kings involved with mothers superior,
great soldiers with girls of the theater. . . . All the women are named
Aurore, all have sons and lovers, preferring the sons to lovers. . . . Natural children are recognized, exalted, royally brought up. . . . All are
seductive, anarchist, tender and cruel."

Thus Aurore Dupin's family history may be traced back to the six-
teenth-century German-Swedish clan of the Koenigsmark, founded by
Field Marshal Johann Christophe de Koenigsmark, who fought in the
Thirty Years' War. The beautiful Aurore de Koenigsmark, the first
Aurore, was the sister of Phillip de Koenigsmark, assassinated in 1694 on
the orders of the grand elector of Hanover, the future King George I of
England, for reasons of jealousy. Inquiring about her brother's death,
Aurore met Friedrich-August, the grand elector of Saxony, who soon
thereafter became the king of Poland as Fryderyk-August II, "the
Strong," and became his mistress.

Their bastard son, born in 1696, was baptized Maurice and given the
title of count of Saxony—he became known as Maurice de Saxony.
Aurore, however, broke up with her royal lover, taking refuge at a
Protestant abbey in Quedlimbourg, which she promptly turned into

what was described at the time as a "love court." Aurore threw a fabulous reception for the visiting Peter the Great of Russia, dressed as a muse, and recited French poetry of her own composition; the aging abbess took her for a saint.

Aurore's son, Maurice, handsome and sentimental, was destined for a military career. His father prepared him for it the hard way. He was allowed to eat only soup and bread as he crossed all of Europe on foot, carrying his full battle equipment. At the age of thirteen, he was commissioned ensign on the battlefield, then ran away with a girl, also thirteen, whom he impregnated.

As a young officer in Paris, Maurice, having inherited his father's libertinism, conducted widely known affairs with the Princess de Conti, the Duchess de Bouillon, and innumerable other well-born ladies. Hoping to be elected duke of the Courland provinces of Russia on the Baltic, he proposed marriage to Duchess Anna Ivanovna, the widow of the last duke. Maurice committed, however, the imprudent act of smuggling a young mistress into the palace: He was caught red-handed and chased away. Anna Ivanovna later became the empress of All Russias.

Back in Paris, Maurice offered his services to the French army, rapidly attaining the rank of marshal of France. His niece, Marie-Josephe de Saxe, married into the royal family: As the spouse of Louis, the son of Louis XV and dauphin of France, she would be mother of Louis XVI, Louis XVIII, and Charles X. Aurore Dupin (or George Sand) consequently was a blood relative of three kings. Maurice also turned into a champion of societal reforms, proposing, among other ideas, that marriages be limited to a period of five years and could be renewed only if there had been no issue. This curious notion by Sand's great-grandfather may have inspired her in her marital conduct.

The marshal himself never married, but, at age fifty-two, acquired a new mistress in the person of the beautiful seventeen-year-old Marie Rinteau. Their illegitimate daughter, Marie-Aurore, as beautiful as Marie and the first Aurore, was born in 1748. Maurice left her nothing, but Marie-Aurore threw herself at the feet of her cousin, the royal mother, and Louis XV awarded her eight hundred livres as pension, a respectable amount. Next, this feisty lady persuaded parliament to recognize her formally as "the natural daughter of Maurice, Count of Saxony, the General Marshal of the Camps and Armies of France, and of Marie Rinteau." Her half-brother was the Chevalier of Beaumont, whose father, the Duke of

Bouillon, had been her mother's lover after Maurice (who, of course, had been the lover of the Duchess of Bouillon some time earlier).

Marie-Aurore, the grandmother of George Sand, subsequently married an infantry captain named Antoine de Horne, but he died within six months. When the war ministry, not surprisingly, refused her request to inherit her husband's military command—it was a *job*—she went to live with her mother and her aunt at their elegant town house at the Chaussée d'Antin (the street where Chopin would make his home a half century later). Marie Rinteau, her mother, had prospered with a long line of lovers after Maurice's death, including the kingdom's Farmer-General (in charge of France's agriculture) and the composer Antoine-François Marmontel. Another lover was Claude Dupin de Franceuil, a financier and an outstanding musician.

After Marie Rinteau died in 1775, Monsieur Dupin developed an ardent interest in Marie-Aurore (who called him "papa"), a highly accomplished grande dame, a talented actress, and an excellent musician. André Maurois has described her as "one of the most remarkable women at a time when many of them shone with their culture." Dupin had evidently formed the same opinion and, three years later, married Marie-Aurore. He was thirty-two years older than his wife, but it was a very happy marriage until he died on their tenth wedding anniversary.

The Dupins lived most of the time at his old castle in Châteauroux in the Berry region of central France, entertaining the great musicians, writers, and philosophers of the time—even the great Jean-Jacques Rousseau. Marie-Aurore Dupin would be a great intellectual influence and inspiration in the life of her granddaughter George Sand, and Berry would be forever her favorite corner of the world.

Following Dupin's death, Marie-Aurore and their son, Maurice (naturally named after her father and as handsome as the marshal), moved to Paris. Maurice Dupin was eleven years old when the revolution erupted in 1789 with the storming of the Bastille, and Marie-Aurore decided that life would be safer in Berry. She purchased land at Nohant, a village between Châteauroux and La Châtre, and built a spacious mansion to replace a fourteenth-century castle in ruins.

Maurice Dupin, a gifted musician and actor, chose to join Napoleon Bonaparte's armies because, in his judgment, a grandson of the marshal of France had to be a soldier. As Napoleon prepared to conquer Europe, Maurice engaged in amorous conquests around Nohant before joining his regiment. Among his conquests was one of his mother's maids, a Mademoiselle Châtiron, and presently a son was born to her. The baby was named Hippolyte Châtiron (Maurice would not give him legal recognition), but Marie-Aurore decided to look after her illegitimate grandson and kept him at the Nohant mansion. In fact, the old lady became very fond of little Hippolyte.

As for Maurice, he had met at the army headquarters in Milan a young woman, Antoinette-Sophie-Victoire Delaborde, who was the mistress of his commanding general and had a daughter from an earlier liaison. Almost instantly, she abandoned the general for Maurice who, taking advantage of a furlough, brought his new mistress to Berry and installed her at the Tête Noire Inn in La Châtre—to his mother's overwhelming distress. Sophie, as she called herself, was the daughter of a Parisian carpenter and street hawker, and, in Maurois's words, "She had a stormy youth of a poor girl in times of troubles." Marie-Aurore trembled with fear at the thought of a marriage.

In 1804, a pregnant Sophie joined Maurice at the army headquarters in Boulogne, insisting on marriage and a return to Paris before the baby was born. He agreed and they were married—in secret—on June 5. Maurice dared not tell his mother (who would later call it an "army barracks wedding").

On July 1, spending an evening at their Paris lodgings, Maurice improvised songs on his violin as Sophie, wearing a pretty pink dress, went through contredanse steps around the room. Suddenly, she felt ill and retired to the bedroom. A few minutes later, her sister Lucie called out to him: "Come, come Maurice! You have a daughter!" Maurice told her, "She will be named Aurore, like my poor mother, who is not here to bless her, but will bless her one day." Lucie replied: "She was born to music and in pink: She will have happiness."

Nearly a half century later, George Sand would write in her *Story of My Life* that "my mother was from an ugly and vagabond race of bohemians of this world. She was a dancer, less than a dancer: an actress at the lowest of the theaters of the boulevards of Paris, when the love of a rich [man] dragged her out of this abjectness to make her suffer even greater ones. My father met her when she already was thirty years old and in the midst of such confusion! But he had a big heart. He understood that this beautiful creature could still love."

George Sand also had a big heart, loving until the end this crass, difficult, often ill-tempered, but well-meaning woman after whom she looked over the long years. She was still grief-stricken over her mother's death in August 1837, when her attraction to Chopin kept growing, and she was more vulnerable emotionally than usual. Her maternity streak—"the opportunity for protecting weaker beings," as André Maurois put it—reasserted itself upon encountering the weak, ill, feverish musician, with "irresistible [character] traits for a maternal nurse."

That her mother had been seven years older than her father clearly had enormous relevance in Sand's life and her choices of men. Chopin was almost six years younger than George; six of her earlier lovers—notably Musset, who was Chopin's junior by eight months—were quite a bit younger, too. (Liszt was six years younger than his mistress, Marie d'Agoult.) But, just as clearly, George's chosen men must have desired to be her children, needing her as she needed them, Fryderyk being the latest and most dramatic case in point.

Aurore Dupin had a truly atrocious childhood. Because her mother was not welcome in Nohant, the baby lived with her at first in utter poverty in an attic room in a rundown Paris apartment building. When Aurore was barely a year old, Sophie spent two years or so in Italy, probably with her husband, leaving the little girl and her cousin Clotilde (her aunt Lucie's daughter) with a farming family in the nearby village of Chaillot. Sand recalled that "we were brought to Paris on Sundays on a donkey, each in her basket, with cabbages and carrots to be sold at the market hall."

Back in Paris for about a year, Sophie was, surprisingly, a model mother, winning Aurore's eternal love. As for Maurice, he was always away with the army and Aurore simply had no father. Charming, gay, with an innate sense of beauty, Sophie did everything she could for her little daughter during their short period together in the rue de la Grange-Batelière attic room. She cooked and sewed. She spent hours showing Aurore picture books with mythological figures and scenes from the Bible, explaining them as best she could. She told Aurore fairy tales and made her say her prayers in the evening. Aurore adored these moments with her mother, memorizing the stories and the fairy tales, and beginning to dream her own fables. George Sand, the novelist, thus came into being in that Parisian attic. She would always remember with tenderness this life of "enchantment and poverty," as Maurois put it.

In the spring of 1808, an eight-months pregnant Sophie dragged the four-year-old Aurore on a murderously hard voyage by coach from Paris to Madrid, much of it through guerrilla-infested Spanish territory, to make sure, in a fit of jealousy, that her husband was not succumbing to the charms of beautiful *madrileña* ladies. Colonel Maurice Dupin of the roving eye was serving as aide-de-camp to Marshal Murat, the commander-in-chief in the Spanish war, and he was a dazzling presence in the capital. Sophie, who presumably became pregnant during her stay in Italy or in the course of one of Maurice's visits home, was taking no chances. In any event, the colonel did not doubt the legitimacy of the boy born in Madrid on June 12, and presently took the whole family to Nohant in a two-wheeled calèche he had purchased. It was a horrible trip, with the two children near death from fever and hunger.

Aurore survived it, but the baby died soon after they reached Nohant, where her grandmother smothered her with love. And a few weeks later, Maurice was killed when his fiery Spanish stallion Leopardo crashed against a pile of stones just outside La Châtre one festive night of celebrations. Aurore now found herself living with two widows: her mother and her grandmother—and no father.

It was not a tenable arrangement. The two women disagreed over everything. The elder Madame Dupin refused to let Sophie bring her first-born daughter, Caroline Delaborde, to Nohant. Aurore was caught between them, defending her mother against her grandmother, albeit Sophie often slapped her in one of her rages. She loved them both, but Sophie came first in her heart, her cruelties notwithstanding. Later Aurore wrote: "Oh, my mother! Why don't you love me [when] I love you so much?"

Inevitably, they were separated. Sophie had decided to return to Paris, leaving Aurore in Nohant where she thought the girl would receive a better education and live in greater comfort. Aurore protested and wept, even when she was promised a visit to her mother every winter. Still, the next nine years were relatively happy ones for Aurore in the Berry countryside that she would regard as home for the rest of her life. She played with her half brother, Hippolyte, and other village children, and learned the ways of the country, feeding chickens, looking after lambs and becoming an accomplished horsewoman—in a boy's attire. But Aurore also learned to read, learned Latin and natural sciences from the administrator of the estate, and was the best-educated child in Berry. She read the *Iliad* before she was ten. Madame Dupin taught her the piano and turned her into a fine musician. She began to write descriptions of life in the fields, her literary awakening.

Still, nothing lasted forever in Aurore's life. She developed personal, religious, and political disagreements with her grandmother, who was a rock-ribbed conservative, and she continued to miss her mother. When she was fourteen, Aurore and the old lady had a terrible scene. Madame Dupin told her that Sophie was "a lost woman" and Aurore herself "a blind child who wants to plunge into an abyss." She then announced that she had resolved to put her in a convent in Paris.

The convent she chose for Aurore was that of English Augustine sisters, established when Cromwell was persecuting Catholics in England, and located in the Faubourg Saint-Germain on the Left Bank. It counted among its pupils the daughters of the most distinguished French noble families. Napoleon's empire had vanished, the Restoration brought new prosperity to Paris, and an optimistic mood pervaded the city. At first, Aurore had been delighted about being sent to Paris, anxious to see her mother more often. But she encountered rejection again: Sophie was cold and indifferent, deep in her new "free" life, and insultingly critical of the idea of Aurore entering a Catholic convent school. As always, the French were divided over the Roman Catholic Church.

Yet, nothing could discourage Aurore in the long run. She took to school life with joy, was extremely popular with her fellow students, learned English well, became known as "Madcap" to the sisters (because she was *that*), and acquired a trusted friend in Sister Mary Alice, her favorite teacher. She also discovered mysticism as her very personal religion. Sand's strong penchant for Christian socialism in her writings and political attitudes may have had its roots at that English convent.

Aurore's life changed again after two years when she completed her schooling at the convent and returned to Nohant to rejoin Madame Dupin in the spring of 1820. She was nearly sixteen, but quite mature—and she was hurt once more when Sophie flatly refused ever to come to see her in Nohant. With her grandmother, on the other hand, Aurore finally developed warm relations, though she would not hear about an arranged marriage in Berry that Madame Dupin favored for her. And Aurore adored life in Nohant. She made music, improved her Italian, read great philosophers and poets, raced on her horse across the Berry fields, hunted hare with a shotgun, and learned all she could about managing the estate.

On Christmas Day 1821, Madame Dupin died. At the age of seven-teen, Aurore Dupin became the mistress of Nohant (and inherited the Dupin town house in Paris), with an annual income of twenty-five thousand livres, a small fortune. She now enjoyed absolute independence as a young woman with firmly held ideas. A descendant of a long line of tough, stubborn, and imaginative women, Aurore was ready for life.

But love would continue to elude Aurore.

Impatient and starved for love, she reached out for it the following year, shortly after she turned eighteen, by marrying Casimir Dudevant, the handsome bastard (but fully recognized) son of Baron François Dude-vant and Augustine Soulès, a servant. The baron was a retired colonel and had been a friend and army comrade of Aurore's father. The Dude-vants owned property in Guillery in Gascony in southwest France and had an annual revenue of seventy or eighty thousand livres. Aurore, who had fallen in love (or thought she had) with Casimir, needed not worry that he was marrying her for *her* money—unlike several Berry suitors—and was full of hope for marital bliss.

Casimir, whom she had met through friends in Paris, had been her first serious romantic experience, apart from a brief Nohant flirtation with Count Stéphane Ajasson de Grandsagne, a medical student, and she rushed headlong into marriage. They were wed in September 1822, barely six months after they first met, and went to live in Nohant. Aurore, as was her nature, made a total commitment to the marriage, writing a friend that "every privation is a new pleasure; one sacrifices oneself at the same time to God and conjugal love, fulfilling one's duty and one's happiness. . . . One must love, and love very much, one's hus-band to achieve it and to know how to make the honeymoon last for-ever. Like you, I had a sad opinion of marriage until the moment I became attached to Casimir."

By October, Aurore knew she was pregnant. Casimir surrounded her with gifts and attention and, as the time approached, they moved to the town house in Paris. Their son, naturally named Maurice, was born on June 30, 1823, and presently they returned to Nohant. Soon, however, Aurore realized that she had trapped herself in a hopeless and increas-ingly unhappy marriage.

Being married to Casimir, she discovered, was not at all what she had imagined as a trusting virgin—sentimentally, sexually, and intellectually. Her belief in the joy of marriage—those first impressions relayed in the letter to her friend shortly after the wedding—were deeply deceived, if not downright betrayed, as Aurore recounted in her memoirs. She had been prepared for sentimental love, and physical love had surprised her without offering rewards. As André Maurois had noted, a woman needs, especially in her first experience, "to feel loved and also to admire her partner." But Casimir was loud and vulgar—and a "sensual egoist" when it came to sex. Inevitably, Aurore drew back; Casimir complained of her "coldness" and of rebuffing his "embraces."

Though Casimir now administered the Nohant estate, he spent much of his time hunting, drinking, and carousing with his friends. Living "always in solitude," Aurore went back to books, reading at one stage Montaigne's essays on morals ("my favorite author"). When she tried to interest Casimir in reading, "boredom and sleepiness" made him drop the books to the floor. When she spoke to him of poetry and morals, he called her a "romantic fool." When she described her emotions to him, Casimir accused her of being victimized by "a bilious temperament, aggravated by a neuralgic disposition." As for music, he fled at the sound of the piano. He seemed interested only, Aurore concluded, in hunting, drinking, and local politics.

Still, Aurore strove to make the best of a situation that had reached the point where both of them dreaded tête-à-tête evenings at home in Nohant, having nothing to say to each other—except when it concerned little Maurice and the estate's deteriorating financial condition under Casimir's stewardship.

Before too long, Aurore developed a "horror" of physical love under her husband's constant demands. When the daughter of her half brother, Hippolyte, prepared for marriage, Aurore warned him that his prospective son-in-law might "brutalize" the bride on the wedding night. "Tell him," she added, "to manage his pleasures a bit and wait for his wife to be, little by little, brought to him to understand them and to respond." She would spend the rest of her life searching for the "exclusive love" the unfaithful Casimir had denied her. She was only nineteen years old.

As Maurois has noted, "When a woman with beautiful eyes looks for a sister soul, she will find him." In Aurore's case it was a twenty-six-year-old Bordeaux lawyer with a poetic soul named Aurélien de Sèze, whom she had met during a vacation in the Pyrenees, where the Dudevants stopped en route to the old baron's estate in 1825. They fell in love, met again in Bordeaux during the next visit to Gascony, stole precious moments together, and exchanged ardent love letters, but Aurore resisted "giving myself to him" out of a residual sense of virtue. On Aurélien's suggestion, however, she wrote Casimir an eighteen-page letter to explain her sentimental dilemma while assuring him of her faithfulness. Indeed, she drafted an eight-point agreement—she called it a "charter"—outlining a more rewarding relationship for both, but allowing her to write Aurélien once a month; she hoped rather implausibly that Casimir would think of him as a "brother."

Curiously, Casimir agreed to Aurore's highly structured proposals for a happy conjugal life, himself catching the romantic fever of the day. But, ironically, he lost her respect—even though he tried to read great philosophical works and learn English while protesting his love in letters from his father's estate, where he visited frequently, and even though he promised to give up hunting and never to go out alone. Aurore thought that, compared with Aurélien's missives, Casimir's letters were pathetic. When Casimir made a vulgar joke at a dinner party, she said to him, quite audibly, "My poor Casimir, how stupid you are! Nevertheless I love you like this."

Aurore had gained the upper hand in the marriage, the roles were reversed, and a pattern was set for the future in her relations with men. She was happy for the first time in a long while and, disgusted with "natural and complete love"—conjugal sex—she now hoped to save herself, in her words, by "great Platonic love." Aurore regularly saw Aurélien in Bordeaux under her charter with Casimir, keeping their rapport Platonic, but she could "make his heart beat faster" with a mere handshake. And Casimir occasionally carried her letters to Aurélien when he came through Bordeaux on the way to his family home. Aurélien ultimately tired of the Platonic relationship and exchanges of poetic letters and his communications with Aurore became increasingly rare.

Aurore now had to face her next dilemma: Is it possible to retain a man without a carnal link, to be loved without giving herself, to be, at the same time, a horseback Amazon in men's clothing and a femme fatale, a perfect wife, and an adored mistress?

Before long she reached the conclusion that, yes, she could be all things to all people and, in the most rational manner, she decided to take a lover. She was twenty-four years old, had been married for five

years, and was ready for a new phase in her life. The love affair she initiated later in 1827 thus marked a major turning point in Aurore's attitude
toward men and toward society in general.

The lover Aurore had selected for this act of feminine emancipation was
her beau from premarriage days, Stéphane Ajasson de Grandsagne, who
became a classics and science scholar at the Paris Museum after having
abandoned his medical studies. His health was precarious—Maurois
describes him as "half consumptive, half crazy"—and he came back to
Berry to convalesce. Soon Stéphane and Aurore rediscovered each other
and, as much as anything else, she saw him as a sick man whom she
liked to look after and tried to help regain his health. Aurore thereby set
another new pattern in relations with men: Stéphane was, physiologi-
cally and psychologically, the perfect emotional prize for her. And she
could not care less what anybody thought or said about her behavior.

With a very passive Casimir, Aurore did not try to conceal the liaison
even in Berry where everybody knew everybody—and everybody's business. She traveled with Stéphane and visited him in Paris under the pretext of consulting physicians in the capital for her health. And when she
returned to Nohant from Paris in August, she was pregnant—quite possibly by Stéphane. Her daughter was born on September 13, 1828, and
was named Solange. Though Aurore occasionally referred to Solange as
Mademoiselle Stéphane, her husband acted as if he were the father
(which he may have believed). In any case, Casimir had his affair with
their Spanish maid Pepita, making love to her in a room adjacent to the
bedroom where Aurore was in the process of giving birth, as well as at
other times with another family maid. And Stéphane himself joked with
his friends in Paris whenever he left for Nohant: "I'm going to see my
daughter!"

Aurore no longer shared the bedroom with Casimir, moving to a
ground-floor boudoir next to her children's room. She slept in a ham-
mock, read a lot, and began sketching what would become her first novels. She engaged a young man named Jules Boucoiran to tutor Maurice
and Solange in Nohant. She may, or not, have had a brief affair with
him though she continued the liaison with Stéphane, often still visiting
him in Paris. It was a deliciously complicated situation with Stéphane
and Boucoiran her on-and-off lovers, a pliant (though mostly drunk)
husband at home, and the residual amorous letter contact with Aurélien

in Bordeaux. Aurore finally could have sex on her own terms, but it does not follow from her comments and observations in her memoirs and letters that she had actually craved or desired sex for its own sensual sake. From the very outset there always was the question of whether it ever satisfied her—or was actually sought as a form of sentimental love she lacked.

On July 31, 1830, the day liberal revolutionaries overthrew King Charles X in Paris, Aurore (in the Berry countryside) again fell in love and acquired a new lover. He was Jules Sandeau, a law student spending his summer vacation in La Châtre, his hometown, and Aurore met him when she rode her mare Colette to a nearby château to visit a friend. As it happened, Jules, then nineteen, was seven years younger than Aurore. He was thin, his health was fragile, he was lazy—preferring to fall asleep with a good book atop a haystack rather than hunt and drink with his friends—and Aurore found him and his pink-and-white cheeks and curly blond hair charming and adorable. He was known to his friends as "Le Petit Jules," but she called him "colibri" (hummingbird). Of course, he was madly in love with her, too, and probably flattered by the attentions of this amazing older woman.

Aurore's taste in men now seemed firmly set. Jules was a worthy successor of Stéphane (whom she had not cast aside altogether) in fulfilling her powerful sentimental, maternal, and nurturing needs. "If you knew how I love this poor child," she wrote a friend, "[with] his expressive glances, his timid gaucherie toward me, which gave me the desire to see him, examine him." This desire was satisfied almost immediately as Aurore brought Jules to a secluded *pavillion* she had built some years earlier at the edge of her Nohant property, with a direct entrance from the highway, to serve as a love nest. They enjoyed complete privacy (Casimir remained busy anyway with Pepita), but Aurore left no written observations on the sexual aspects of the new friendship. Perhaps it was not much on her mind at that time.

What *was* very much on her mind, however, were politics and arts, which the "Glorious" July revolution had joined together, sanctifying the emergence of the Age of Romanticism. Both Aurore and Jules responded with passion to the works and appeals of the new poets, playwrights, novelists, and philosophers, from Victor Hugo to the social justice teachings of Saint-Simon. Aurore was dying to meet Hugo, Balzac, Lamartine, and all the intoxicating geniuses of the new epoch. Her liberal and social instincts were unleashed. She craved to be part of the scene. Besides, "Le Petit Jules" was back in Paris, ostensibly studying law.

Being Aurore, she wasted no time on just craving. With her marriage to Casimir so clearly a fiasco beyond repair, she decided to reorganize her life altogether. She informed her husband that she would spend six months of the year in Paris—where Jules and the action were—and six months in Nohant. The children would remain with him, and a tutor would be hired. She would receive a monthly allowance from Casimir from the Nohant estate revenue. In exchange, Aurore promised Casimir to preserve the fiction of the marriage; husbands preferred to be spared the public humiliation of being abandoned by their wives, and Casimir agreed to her terms.

On January 4, 1831, Aurore left Nohant for Paris. It was the beginning of the great metamorphosis of Aurore Dupin Dudevant.

In Paris, Jules Sandeau awaited her breathlessly at the apartment that Aurore's half brother, Hippolyte, had lent them at 31, rue de Seine, an elegant Left Bank street leading from boulevard Saint-Germain to quai Malaquais on the river. Aurore, familiar with Paris from childhood, felt instantly at home. Apart from Jules, a large group of men friends from Berry, most of them infatuated with her, as well as Stéphane were there. So was Aurore's mother, with whom she kept alive a depressing relationship which, however, she would never let go.

Her monthly allowance of 250 francs was hardly enough to live on in Paris, and Aurore was determined to start earning money as soon as possible, preferably by writing. In the meantime, she loved the July Monarchy and the explosion of Romanticism. "One lives as gaily amidst bayonets, riots, and ruins as if one were in full peacetime," Aurore wrote a friend. "It amuses me!" She joined her friends at the opening of Alexandre Dumas's new play *Antony,* a defense of adultery and illegitimacy, starring the beautiful actress Marie Dorval in the lead role. It was, Aurore recalled, an evening of "agitation, tumult, effervescence," similar to the première of Hugo's *Hernani* a few years earlier. She also attended a Paganini concert. And to move more freely in Paris streets and to save money, she dressed in men's attire: a gray redingote, wool necktie, gray hat, and black boots.

Through Berry friends, Aurore met Henri de Latouche, a publisher, who pronounced *Aimée,* a novel she had written in Nohant (her first), to show no promise. But he hired her as a writer-reporter for *Le Figaro*, a satirical opposition journal he had just purchased and installed at his apartment on quai Malaquais. Next, Latouche hired Jules Sandeau. Before too long, another magazine published an article written together by them, but signed by him alone because Aurore did not wish to have her name in print—to avoid embarrassing Casimir. And much of her daily effort went into mothering Jules: She made sure he ate his meals and forced him to sit down and write; he was still excessively lazy. As Maurois put it, "She liked to exercise this sweet tyranny."

Above all, Aurore was convinced that she and Jules had embarked on real literary careers. Balzac had befriended them, often visiting their new mansarded flat on quai Saint-Michel, offering helpful advice. Dividing their time between Paris and Nohant (Jules actually stayed at his home in La Châtre), they worked on a five-volume novel titled *Rose et Blanche* ("Pink and White") for which a Parisian publisher promised to pay 625 francs when delivered. It was a "realistic" story of a woman comedienne and a nun, and Aurore had done most of the writing.

Aurore was following in the footsteps of great women writers who preceded her by less than a generation. There was Madame de Staël, but perhaps a better model for Aurore was Jane Austen, whose *Pride and Prejudice* was published in 1813; she may have read it after learning English at the Paris convent. And Aurore was a contemporary of Mary Ann Evans, who wrote under the name of George Eliot and who noted that "there is no sex in genius."

Jules, whose name alone appeared on the cover of *Rose et Blanche*, was becoming quite ill, with constant high fever. He seemed, indeed, to be dangerously consumptive, but Aurore chose to believe that she had ruined his health by forcing him into sex. She wrote a friend: "You have no idea of the terrible remorse in seeing . . . that your caresses are poison, your love a fire that consumes and devours, that destroys and leaves only ashes." Still another pattern was emerging in Aurore's dealings with the men she loved—these were consistently men who suffered poor health.

The novel was published in December 1831, and sold remarkably well. Aurore returned to Nohant for the winter, having become ill herself, but she was back in Paris the following spring with a new novel, *Indiana*, which she had written exclusively. Jules read it and proclaimed the book to be admirable. However, he insisted, it should carry her name alone, despite their earlier agreement on joint bylines. When

Aurore refused, Jules came up with a solution that also satisfied her desire to use a man's name. He proposed that the first name in her nom de plume be George because the day this conversation took place happened to be St. George's Day, and the last name Sand, a contraction of Sandeau, to immortalize their tie as lovers. From that time on, Aurore used the new name on all occasions, personal and professional.

Thus George Sand was "born" on April 23, 1832. Only two months earlier, a young Polish composer who had reinvented himself as Frédéric Chopin had played his first concert in Paris, performing his variations on Mozart's "Là ci darem la mano" and his Piano Concerto no. 2 in F minor and had been hailed by reviewers for the "rebirth of piano music." Sand's *Indiana* received an ecstatic review from Balzac: "This book is a reaction of truth against the fantastic, of the present time against the Middle Ages, of intimate drama against the tyranny of the historical genre." It was a fabulous coincidence, two stars rising at the same time on the firmament of Romanticism, both bringing the rebirth of artistic truth!

After *Indiana,* George Sand became a hot literary property in Paris. François Buloz, the publisher of the influential *Revue des deux mondes* magazine and a new friend, signed her up to provide, every week, thirty-two pages of material for 4,000 francs annually. The publishers of *Indiana* gave her an advance of 1,500 francs for her next novel. Suddenly she was rich and famous.

Indiana, like most of her novels, was essentially autobiographical: "It is the woman, the weak being, representing the passions compressed or, if you prefer, suppressed by the laws . . . it is love crashing its forehead blindly against all the obstacles of civilization." In the novel, the lover who disappointed her resembled Aurélien de Sèze, and the heroine's husband sounded like Casimir—brutal, vulgar, but not evil. The public adored George's themes and style.

Latouche, the publisher of *Le Figaro,* turned his quai Malaquais apartment, across the Seine from the Louvre, over to Sand when he decided to live permanently in the countryside. One of her first visitors there was the celebrated actress Marie Dorval, whom George greatly admired and hoped to meet after seeing her in Dumas's *Antony.* It was the beginning of a lifetime friendship—and more. A widow with three daughters at twenty-two, Dorval had married the director of the Porte

Saint-Martin Theater, then took Count Alfred de Vigny, the great Romantic poet, as her lover.

Soon after their meeting, Dorval invited Sand and Sandeau to dine with her husband and Vigny. George Sand and Vigny developed an instant dislike for each other, but intimacy grew between her and Marie Dorval. André Maurois summed it up precisely: "Despite the appearances and despite the frenzy of certain letters, Sand had never found in the love of men an absolute passion, that happy delirium, that release she sought. The weak Sandeau lacked human warmth. Sand had done her best to convince herself that she loved him passionately; she had pursued sensual pleasure with him with rage and never achieved it. Marie Dorval was all that Sand would have wished to be."

George herself wrote: "God had given her [Marie Dorval] the power to express what she feels. . . . I do not know the words to explain what is *cold* and incomplete in my nature; I do not know how to express anything. . . . When this woman appears with her nonchalant walk, her sad, penetrating gaze, it seems [to me] that I see my own soul." And in a letter to the actress she announced: "I feel that I love with a heart made younger, made new again by you. If it is a dream, like all that I had ever desired in my life, do not take it away from me too soon. It does me so much good! *Adieu,* [my] big and beautiful! Anyway, I shall see you tonight."

Not surprisingly, George dropped "Le Petit Jules" as her lover shortly after meeting Marie Dorval and made him move out of the quai Malaquais apartment. Whatever went on between her and Marie, George did not give up her quest for the perfect man. She wrote amorous letters to a number of her men friends, but she did not seem to have settled on anyone in particular. Maurois compared her to a sultan surveying the "odalisques in the secrecy of his harem." Sandeau, who suffered from manic-depressive illness and attempted to commit suicide after being ditched, went to Italy and wrote a novel titled *Marianna,* which, of course, was about George. It was his revenge: "The silence of the fields, her studies and readings, and daydreaming had developed in Marianna more strength than tenderness, more imagination than heart, more curiosity than true sensitivity. . . . She arranged for herself in advance a heroic existence, well filled with beautiful devotion and sublime sacrifice. She had anticipated battles, combat, betrayed loves, and tormented felicities. Before having enjoyed them, she had exhausted it all."

In real life, George, free and alone, could not remain long a woman without a man. Her novel *Lélia,* the best and most famous of all her works of fiction, had been published to overwhelming applause early in 1833—she had no trouble creating a great novel in a matter of a few months, working virtually around the clock—and it was nothing less than a deep, intimate personal confession about her own coldness and rejection of love. Sténio, the poet who loved her passionately, complains that "Lélia is not a complete human being. What, then, is Lélia? A shadow, a dream, an idea, at best . . . where there is no love, there is no woman." Lélia went from man to man because none of them had given her pleasure. In subsequent editions, George excised much of this confessional material as her children and grandchildren would later excise much intimate detail from her voluminous correspondence that, together with her *Journal Intime* and the *Story of My Life,* filled ninety-seven published volumes—in addition to one hundred novels, essays, and travelogues.

An embarrassingly failed short affair with the writer Prosper Mérimée (who had contributed in one of his novels the memorable observation that "the road to hell is paved with good intentions") was George's first liaison of note after dismissing "Le Petit Jules." She had told Marie Dorval: "I had Mérimée last night; it is not a big thing," and the comment was repeated instantly all over Paris.

Then, at a dinner in the spring of 1833, Sand met the poet and playwright Alfred Louis Charles de Musset—blond, "beautiful like God," a "dandy," and six years younger than she. Hugely talented and already famous at twenty-three, Musset had devoted himself (like his hero, Byron) to debauch, alcohol, opium, and "easy" women. Like Byron, he believed that in debauch women resume their ancient role of witches. Like Byron, Musset had a full-fledged manic-depressive personality.

But Musset made Sand laugh and she, in turn, inspired him to address a beautiful poem to her after reading *Indiana.* It was the most subtle of seductions. They became lovers and Musset moved to the quai Malaquais apartment. It would be one of the most complicated, dramatic, and exalted liaisons of the Romantic Age. Sand was now thirty and the freshness of youth was already gone, but she had not lost that magic quality which made men of all ages desire her with fervor.

But, again, Sand discovered that she was perceived more as a mother than mistress and, again, her hope of pure love was unattainable. Her own strength as well as her sense of maternity and her weakness for very young men—Musset was the third to come under this heading, after Aurélien and Jules—made it inevitable. Yet, Sand was in despair when Musset wrote her: "I love you like a child [would]." In her memoirs, she exclaimed, "He loves me like a child! What has he said, my God? And does he know the pain he causes me?" But a few months later, George wrote Sainte-Beuve: "I am in love, and this time very seriously, with Alfred de Musset. It is no longer a caprice, it is a deep feeling. . . . I loved once for six years, another time for three, and now I do not know of what I am capable."

She certainly was capable of being a mother and a governess, forcing him to get up and write when he preferred to sleep late (George herself met all her deadlines, often getting up in the middle of the night to work). Musset laughed it off at first: "I have worked all day and by evening I did ten verses and drank a bottle of firewater; she had drunk a liter of milk and wrote half a volume." But George also learned that she dealt with a psychologically unstable individual when, during a romantic moonlight stroll across a cemetery in the woods of Fontainebleau, Musset suddenly succumbed to hallucinations. He thought he saw a pale specter running past him, clothing torn and hair blown by the wind, and, as he later wrote, "I was scared and I threw myself facedown on the ground because this man . . . was me!" Other episodes of hallucination followed, and George began to call him "my poor child." Musset called her "my big George." Maurois observes that "once more, she was the man of the couple." But Musset celebrated the new relationship with one of his most moving poems, "Rolla."

In December 1833, the lovers traveled to Venice in quest of amorous and literary inspiration, Sand having first visited Musset's mother with assurances that he would receive the best maternal care from her. She informed Casimir that the voyage was intended for her "instruction and pleasure." He evidently interposed no objections.

As for Musset, he soon discovered that the voyage and the Venice sojourn held no pleasure for him. Indeed, it nearly killed him. Instead of a romantic lovers' escapade, he found himself ignored much of the time as George spent eight or more hours a day working on one novel after another and her *Letters of a Traveler*. Musset countered with accusations—doubtless with reason—that she was cold and reserved toward him (presumably in bed). When she came down with a fever in Genoa, where they stopped en route to Venice, he vanished for the duration of the stay, drinking heavily and finding sex in the streets of the port city.

Upon arrival at their Venice hotel, Musset informed Sand: "I've made a mistake . . . I don't love you." Her first instinct was to flee, but she was still ill and apparently did not wish to leave her "child" alone in a foreign city. Musset continued to drink and womanize while George aggravated the situation even more by refusing him sex—out of petulance. Next, Musset suffered a frightening nervous breakdown, complete with burning fever, hallucinations, and suicide attempts. What followed could have been taken straight out of one of George Sand's most romantic and dramatic novels. And with Sand, reality and fiction were often confused in terms of her own life: It was hard to tell whether she drew on reality for fiction or the other way around.

While Musset lay delirious for three weeks, George fell in love with the blond twenty-six-year-old Italian physician, Pietro Pagello, four years her junior, who had been summoned to try to heal the poet. They presently became lovers, largely on her initiative, although George insisted in a letter during that period that Musset "is the person I love the most in the world" and Pagello already had a Venetian mistress. In a feverish note she slipped him one night while they sat at Musset's bedside, Sand seemed to sum up all her emotional anxieties, fears, and hopes (though probably addressed to the wrong person): "Will you be my support or a master? . . . Will you know why I am sad? . . . Shall I be your companion or your slave? Do you desire me or love me? When your passion is satisfied, will you know how to thank me? Do the pleasures of love leave you breathless and stupefied or do they throw you into divine extasis? . . . Hide your soul from me so that I can always believe it to be beautiful."

Musset recovered, but he and George no longer lived together, exchanging notes delivered by gondoliers. On March 29, 1834, three and a half months after they had undertaken the Venice journey, Musset left for Paris and Sand moved in with the young doctor. But during the five months she remained in Venice, George kept writing Musset with peremptory requests to shop for shoes and gloves for her, look after her son, Maurice, and perform endless other errands. Musset, still (or again) in love with her, obliged and defended her from criticism by mutual friends over the liaison with Doctor Pagello, which, naturally, was common knowledge in Paris. She also wrote a novel (*Jacques*) during that time. Musset recounted the story of their Venice adventure in *his* novel, *La Confession d'un enfant du siècle,* in which George was thinly veiled as Brigitte Pierson. Musset referred to himself as a "child" in the title.

One of the characteristics of writers of the Romantic Age, when the "subjective" approach was the literary fashion, was to use their most personal experiences—and those of their friends—as material for novels. Balzac and Sand did it without the slightest hesitation, and Musset's tale of Venice was published barely two years after he returned to Paris. One's love life, joys, and sufferings, and everyone else's, were a marvelous source of truly realistic inspiration. Imagination was hardly required.

Sand remained in Venice until July 1834. In her absence from France, Aurélien de Sèze, one of her first paramours, married the daughter of family friends. George wrote him with congratulations and a demand for the return of her love letters, but Aurélien, familiar with the literary scene, advised her that he had decided to burn them out of concern that "if you review them, some reminiscences might escape into some composition of yours."

Arriving in Paris, Sand had in tow the hapless Doctor Pagello, whom she had persuaded to share her life in France. It was one of her spur-of-the-moment and instant-gratification ideas, obviously impractical for both, and Pagello himself understood this reality, informing his father that he would take leave of George as soon as they reached Paris. "I love her beyond everything and I would confront thousands of difficulties rather than allow her to undertake alone such a long journey," he wrote in his diary.

Whether or not Pagello's presence in Paris really made sense to Sand, it certainly came as a powerful shock to Musset, who, the Venice nightmare notwithstanding, could not accept that his own liaison with Sand had ended. From Baden, in Germany, where he had gone in August in great rage, he wrote frantic letters to Nohant. George was there for the summer even though Doctor Pagello had turned down an invitation to join her out of respect for the institution of marriage; she was, after all, still married to Casimir Dudevant. In any event, Pagello soon tired of standing between Sand and Musset, and went home to Venice, where he got married and lived to be ninety-one.

But George and Musset were caught up in a vicious circle of breaking up and making up when they both returned to Paris, both growing more and more desperate. At one point, she cut her dark hair and sent it to Musset. Musset came back to her, then threatened to kill her. Finally, Sand concluded that the affair was over—for good. "My love is no more than pity," she wrote him. On March 9, 1835, George resumed her residence in Nohant. That same night she wrote twenty pages of a new novel.

Her next move was to obtain a divorce from Casimir, do away with the fiction of her marriage, and put some order in her family and financial affairs. George had therefore proposed that under a division of property, she would keep Nohant and Casimir be given the Paris town house on rue de la Harpe, which produced a respectable rental revenue. To handle the legal arrangements, Sand turned to a lawyer, recommended by friends, who would become the next "man in her life."

He was Louis-Chrystosome Michel from the town of Bourges south of the Loire Valley. He was known as "Michel de Bourges" and was famous both as a lawyer and as a fierce leader of the Republican opposition to the increasingly authoritarian monarchy of Louis-Philippe. Only thirty-seven, he struck George at first as an old man—short, bald, stooped, with a huge head. Lamartine, the Republican poet, once described him as a man hewn from granite. But Michel exuded charm, magnetism, and intelligence, and Sand fell in love with him almost instantly. He was the first man stronger than herself among those who ever attracted her. She did not even seem to mind when he called her "imbecile," impatient with her political backwardness, and when she found out that he was married.

Michel became George's lover as well as political mentor, turning her into a social revolutionary for the rest of her life. Through him, she entered political opposition circles along with her now firmly established friendships in the literary and artistic worlds. During the Age of Romanticism, in fact, the liberal political opposition to the growing rigidity of the Citizen King's regime was closely allied with the intellectuals, artists, and writers who had pioneered the new era. A number of the latter were actively engaged in politics. It was the birth in modern history of a powerful interaction between politics and culture, a phenomenon that would play an enormous role in the nineteenth and twentieth centuries.

At the same time, "women of ideas" were asserting themselves in the 1830s in an unprecedented fashion on the French intellectual, artistic, and political scene. Janis Bergman-Carton, an art historian, has written that the July Monarchy had brought about "the first era of revitalized female literary and political activity since the French Revolution. . . . [It] was, in part, a function of a shift in the power structure of the French literary community from the private area of salon culture to the public arena of mass media. Women of ideas flourished with the rapid growth of the popular press."

George Sand, as the most famous woman in France in the mid-1830s, was the symbol of literary Romanticism and political liberty. Much of her fiction was serialized in newspapers and magazines, and with over sixty percent of Parisian women fully literate, her exposure and her influence were immense through her "novels of the individual."

But she was not alone. Delphine de Girardin, the wife of a newspaper publisher, commanded much attention as well through her writings, along with Sophie Gay and Eugénie Foa. New women's magazines, such as the *Journal des femmes,* launched in 1832, provided valuable outlets for women authors. But many of them also presided over literary salons, including Delphine de Girardin and Marie d'Agoult, who wrote novels under the pseudonym Daniel Stern. Then there were the great artistic talents: the actress Marie Dorval and the singer Pauline Viardot, both active in literary and political circles, and both friends of George Sand. But at that moment, Sand was already the most politicized among the "women of ideas"—largely under the guidance of Michel, her Bourges divorce lawyer.

In April 1835, Michel took over the defense of Republican opposition leaders at the great Paris trial resulting from the past year's violent antigovernment riots in Lyons, where the king's soldiers killed hundreds of workers protesting oppressive new laws. With the advent of the industrial revolution in France, organized workers were the "army" of the Republicans, emerging for the first time as a significant political force (the 1789 revolution had, of course, a wholly different character). This was another phenomenon that would help to define future French and European history.

In Paris, Michel settled at Sand's quai Malaquais apartment, which became a radical political and artistic center with political strategy and social questions debated until the wee hours. George met men like Pierre Leroux, Alexandre Ledru-Rollin, and Hippolyte Carnot—the top leaders defended by Michel—and they remained her personal and political friends for life. Delacroix, who had painted her first portrait the year before, came often from his apartment a few blocks away. Liszt, whom

Musset had presented to George, was also a regular at the quai Malaquais reunions. Liszt, in turn, brought his friend Félicité de Lamennais, a Roman Catholic priest who believed himself destined to be the prophet of liberal, social, and democratic Catholicism he thought the church should promote. He, too, became a favorite friend of George Sand.

Sand was not unaware of Liszt, either. They admired each other's creativity, and she was especially attracted to his explosive personality and dramatic demeanor at the piano. Moreover he was six years younger than George. Paris was full of gossip that Liszt and Sand, both so famous, were lovers, but there is no evidence of it. In any case, Liszt was in love with Countess Marie d'Agoult (whom Sand had not met yet) and he was waiting for Marie to leave her husband, which she did that summer.

Though Liszt had already developed a firm friendship with Fryderyk Chopin, it never occurred to him to invite the Pole to the quai Malaquais brainstorming. Politics were not Chopin's milieu, at least at that stage, and he probably would have been bored and felt excluded. Sand, however, had Polish friends of her own, among them the poet Mickiewicz (a close friend of Chopin), with whom she maintained a lively correspondence. When Abbé Lamennais, the radical priest, published his *Paroles d'un croyant* ("Words of a Believer") with astonishing print runs approaching three hundred thousand copies, Sand arranged through Mickiewicz to have the book appear in a Polish translation as well. The Polish publisher in Paris was Aleksander Jełowicki, another friend of Chopin, who shortly thereafter took priestly orders and became Fryderyk's confidant. Thus, Sand had already entered Polish intellectual circles long before she met Chopin.

After Marie d'Agoult came to live with Liszt, they began to visit George, and the three became devoted friends even though the two women were very different and quietly critical of each other (Marie suspected that George had designs on Liszt). This rapport would lead to a most crucial event in George's life.

In May 1836, the court at La Châtre granted George the divorce from her husband, but Casimir appealed to a higher court in Bourges. There, Michel reappeared as Sand's lawyer after serving a short prison sentence for alleged political offenses (he had already resumed visiting her at the discreet *pavillion* off the highway in Nohant). At court, George was demure in a simple white dress and a flowery scarf as she listened to Michel's thundering oratory on her behalf. In the end, Casimir dropped the appeal. George was to keep Nohant and have custody of their daughter, Solange; Casimir was given the Paris town house and custody of their son, Maurice. At last, George Sand was a completely free woman in every sense.

Michel had helped her to win the divorce, but their liaison had run its spontaneous course. George, fatigued by his incessant political harangues even at their most intimate moments, concluded that he had turned into a "tyrant" and told him so. But, naturally, Sand could not be long without a man, and Michel was almost immediately replaced as lover by Charles Didier, a handsome and intelligent Swiss writer only one year younger. She had met him several years earlier. Now she moved to his apartment on rue du Regard in Paris, then he visited her in Nohant. However, Didier did not last long: He bored George. She wrote Liszt, who was in Geneva with Marie d'Agoult: "I am happier [now] than ever in my life. Old age comes. The need for great emotions is satisfied beyond all measure. . . . Saintly and durable affections are what is needed after thirty years of a life ravaged by all the dangers. . . . All that is far behind me."

George may have meant sincerely this renunciation of love and romance (and, presumably, sex), but she could not predict the future. In August 1836, with Michel and Didier seemingly forgotten, George and her children traveled to Switzerland to join Liszt and Marie d'Agoult. They spent two months together, then George returned to Paris early in October with an obscure young man named Gustave de Gévaudan. Liszt and Marie were to follow, abandoning once and for all their Swiss hideaway, when she decided that Geneva was no longer fun and he realized that he could not afford to stay away from Paris and retain his fame as a pianist. People like Chopin, Thalberg, Hiller, and Kalkbrenner were monopolizing Parisian attentions with their keyboard artistry.

Back in Paris, Sand, Liszt, and Marie took rooms at the Hôtel de France where George met and heard Fryderyk Chopin for the first time at the reception on October 24. Although Chopin entertained her twice before the end of the year, their encounter was not exactly a *coup de foudre* (love at first sight). George, her recent protestations notwithstanding, had not burned all her bridges. She still kept in touch by letter with Michel. Didier was invited to a party at the Hôtel de France in November, then allowed one night of disappointing lovemaking with George. In January 1837, Sand went to Nohant.

And Chopin himself was making no special effort to follow up on the nascent friendship with Sand despite his ecstatic diary entry that his "heart was captured" by her. Always cautious and noncommittal, he was not ready to rush into a serious new relationship. Besides, he was still fully expecting to spend the coming summer with Maria Wodzińska under the "gray hour" understanding with her mother concerning a possible announcement of an engagement. But there could be trouble ahead.

In a generally chatty letter from Dresden on October 2, Countess Wodzińska had accused Fryderyk of "lying" about keeping his promises to wear wool socks with his slippers and going to bed before eleven o'clock at night because he had not reconfirmed it in writing. Chopin probably did not take this warning too seriously since Maria had added a warm postscript: "*Adieu,* until May or June or later . . . Your very faithful secretary!" On November 1 (which was after meeting George Sand), he wrote the countess a cheerfully appeasing letter: "Why is it already midnight? At noon, there must be lessons until six o'clock, then dinner, and from dinner into the world for the evening [until eleven o'clock] . . . I am not lying and I think about my slippers and I play [the piano] during the Gray Hour."

Yet George, too, was on his mind. On December 13, he sent a note to a Polish friend, Józef Brzowski, that said: "Today I have a few people at home, among them Madame Sand, [and] Liszt will play, [and] Nourrit will sing. If this may be agreeable to Mister Brzowski, I shall expect him in the evening."

The year 1836 ended for Chopin with a touch of special emotion as he attended the wedding of his physician friend Jaś Matuszyński, who had shared with him the first apartment on Chaussée d'Antin. Now Fryderyk lived alone at his new lodgings, making travel plans for the new year, wondering about the prospects for his personal life, and spending long hours composing. He was working on the Ballade no. 2 in F major, Scherzo no. 2 in B-flat minor, Nocturne in B major, and Sonata no. 2 in B-flat minor, one of his most inspired works (the *Marche funèbre,* its third movement, had been written two years earlier). And he may have begun outlining his cycle of préludes.

The future was promising and exciting—if only his health and his strength held up.

Chapter 13

CHOPIN'S HEALTH, however, was not holding up adequately—with melancholy consequences for a romantic future with Maria Wodzińska; her parents feared a marriage to a man plunging deeper and deeper into illness and quite possibly facing an early death. Yet, at the same time, this attitude could be a blessing in disguise, a thought that had begun to occur to the thin-skinned Fryderyk.

His health had now entered an up-and-down cycle, with alternating better and worse periods, like a fever chart (and increasingly frequent mood swings), that would plague him for the rest of his life. It was an inexorable downward spiral. In February 1837, Chopin came down with an acute grippe with high fever and a frightful cough that made him spit blood. He again had hallucinations, hearing knocks on his door and "seeing death" there. Fryderyk had to spend two weeks in bed (this time without Dr. Matuszyński at the apartment to look after him around the clock), and the cough persisted even when he was back on his feet and at the piano. "Chopin coughs with unspeakable charm," Marie d'Agoult (who saw him almost every day) wrote to George Sand in Nohant.

But even before the onset of the grippe, Countess Wodzińska began to prepare him for the inevitable. On January 25, she told him in a letter from the family castle at the Służewo estate in Poland that while her older daughter, Józefa, in Dresden was expecting her there, "I don't know when I shall be able to go." Under the plan elaborated at their last summer's meeting in Dresden, all of them, including Fryderyk, were to gather again there. Maria would, of course, come with her mother, and, if all went well, the engagement would be formalized. But Madame Wodzińska's vagueness was a subtle warning—she alluded to no forthcoming encounters—and this was not lost on Chopin. And a postscript from Maria likewise failed to suggest that she expected to see him in any foreseeable future (she informed him only that she was reading *Germany* by Heine with great interest), unlike what she had indicated prior to the reunion the previous year.

The next warning signal was contained in a letter from his mother late in February, wishing Fryderyk a happy birthday, but also informing him that "Madame Wodzińska told me that you had promised her to go to sleep early, which made me very happy because it is so necessary for your health, but that you have not kept your word." A few days later, he received a short thank-you note from Maria for the "pretty copybook" he had sent her; it ended with the words, "*Adieu,* remember us!" No mention of any new meeting. As far as it is known, this was Maria's last communication to Fryderyk (he had sent a breviary to her sister, Józefa, with the request "Please, sigh for me, too").

Chopin must have realized at that point that he had not passed Madame Wodzińska's "test" concerning the care for his health and his behavior, and that, in effect, it was all over between him and Maria. He knew that she would never go against her parents' wishes (her brother Antoni had warned Fryderyk about it). In retrospect, it also appears that it had dawned on Chopin that Maria's feelings for him were no more than a girlish infatuation with a great artist.

It is possible that Countess Wodzińska had other motives, in addition to Chopin's health, in deciding to end his contacts with Maria. As one of Chopin's biographers suggests, the countess had "spies" in Paris—Polish women friends—who may have reported to her Fryderyk's social relations with "other women," such as George Sand and Marie d'Agoult, leading her to conclude that he was untrustworthy. In any event, such suspicions, combined with his apparent failure to look properly after his health (she may have had "spy" reports about Chopin's frequent attendance at social events and dinner parties), provided the pretext for the breakup.

Józefa, Maria's sister, wrote in her diaries that "the breakup happened . . . because shortly after our return to Służewo, news about Chopin and Madame Sand began to reach us, and . . . naturally the question of his marriage to Maria fell by itself." This, however, is a tendentious account because at that stage Chopin and Sand had seen each other only three times in the company of many friends late in 1836, and they would not meet again for fifteen months, when the Maria matter was long ended.

The pretext may have been necessary, however, to conceal what several early biographers believe to have been the real reason. According to this version, the Wodzińskis had concluded that Maria should marry a wealthy Polish aristocrat who would live with her in Poland rather than Chopin, the hand-to-mouth composer with an uncertain income, fragile health, and absolute unwillingness to settle in his homeland for good. Maria had written him once that she and the rest of the family never ceased "regretting that your name is not 'Chopiński,'" which would have had a Polish nobility sound. And, rather amusingly, the Marxist version of Chopin's life, appearing in Polish publications during the communist rule, depicts Fryderyk as the victim of "reactionary landowners" who would not allow their darling daughter to marry an impoverished genius, no matter how famous.

Be that as it may, Chopin's reaction, at least in the few surviving letters he wrote Madame Wodzińska after the rebuff, was quite restrained albeit with a touch of sentimentality. On April 2, he included a postscript in a letter to her from a Polish woman who was a mutual friend in Paris that he was expecting news from Antoni Wodziński, then fighting in a Polish unit of the French army in the Spanish civil war, but also added a quick reminiscence of Maria in Marienbad, and concluded that "there are days when I cannot help myself. . . . Today, I would rather be in Służewo than be writing to Służewo. I could have said more than I can write." He finished with his "respects" for Count Wodziński, Maria, and the other family members. In a long letter to the countess on June 18, Chopin wrote about Antoni's urgent need for funds following the defeat of the Polish legion in Spain, so that he could return to France (he added that he had immediately met some of these needs himself, "but it was a drop in the ocean"), then went on to describe great balls and festivals in Paris and Versailles, mindful of her burning interest in celebrities.

Fryderyk asked her in the letter not to be "angry" if the Pleyel piano he had bought and shipped to Służewo did not please her. Madame Wodzińska did not wish to have Chopin for a son-in-law, but she had no scruples about asking him for favors such as expediting a piano by sea and land to a remote rural estate in Poland and collecting autographs for her of famous people like Mickiewicz, Heine, and Liszt. Again, Chopin sent his "respects" for the count, Maria, and others.

Restrained in his responses to Służewo, Chopin was nevertheless at loose ends emotionally. He even attended a séance with the famous Parisian fortune-teller Marie-Anne-Adélaïde Lenormand, who counted Polish poets Mickiewicz and Słowacki among her clients and who assured him a "happy future," which he still took to mean a future with Maria. He reported the prophecy to his parents, but his mother commented that the fortune-teller probably promised happiness to all comers and begged him to stay away from Mademoiselle Lenormand. During that disconcerting spring of 1837, Chopin set to music poems by his friend Stefan Witwicki—in addition to a busy composing schedule of his own—including "Spring," a sad and hopeless song about a "tear" running down a cheek and a sparrow flying higher and higher, and vanishing in the clouds beyond the horizon.

What appeared on Chopin's horizon, instead, were expressions of exuberant interest in him on the part of George Sand. On March 28, Sand wrote Liszt, inviting him to join her and Marie d'Agoult in Nohant, adding: "Marie told me that one could expect Chopin [here]; tell him that I ask him to accompany you, that Marie cannot live without him, and I worship him!" Writing Marie d'Agoult, who had gone back to Paris, on April 5, Sand went even further: "Please tell Chopin, whom I worship and all the others whom you love and I love, that they will be welcome if you bring them along." She repeated these sentiments in two more letters to d'Agoult during April.

Sand, however, not only continued to exchange letters with Michel, but to receive him at the Nohant *pavillion* love nest simultaneously with her ardent invitations to Chopin; Marie d'Agoult, who loathed Michel, had told George that "in your place, I would love Chopin more."

Liszt and d'Agoult naturally passed all these invitations on to Chopin, but he chose not to respond. It is not likely that his winter illness had prevented him physically from going to Nohant or anywhere else, because on March 30 he was well enough to join five other pianists, including Liszt, at a charity concert for Italian political emigrants, commemorating Bellini's death two years earlier. Fryderyk played his own variations on a march from Bellini's opera *I Puritani*. It was a very exacting bravura performance. Each of the six pianists had to compose his own set of variations, the ensemble to be published as *Hexaméron,* a curiosity in music. Chopin seemed fine afterwards. More probably, this reluctant man had hesitated to accept Sand's invitation because he had not entirely given up on Maria Wodzińska, murky as the prospects were (Marie d'Agoult, his sharp-tongued friend, commented that Fryderyk was "an undecided man . . . he is consistent only about his cough").

Chopin, however, did not dismiss George from his thoughts altogether. In the margin of a short letter in May to Antoni Wodziński in Saragossa, he scribbled: "I may go for a few days to George Sand's" although he also told him: "I write and prepare manuscripts." It is hard to believe that Chopin had picked Maria's brother by sheer accident to mention so casually that he might visit Sand. He must have assumed that it would be passed on to Służewo to stir up jealousy or regret, if nothing else. In any event, he did not go to Nohant for nearly two years, but the idea of George Sand was now firmly planted in his mind, if not yet his heart.

Fryderyk was indeed quite busy writing and preparing manuscripts during the spring and early summer of 1837. He cited his work in his letter to Antoni Wodziński as the reason for declining an invitation from the Marquis de Custine, who was insistently behaving as Chopin's self-appointed guardian and protector, to travel with him to Ems, a spa on the upper Rhine, to build up his strength after the winter grippe.

Chopin turned down likewise at that time, but for very different reasons, the invitation extended by Count Charles Pozzo di Borgo, the Russian ambassador in Paris, to become the court pianist of Emperor Nicholas I in St. Petersburg. Speaking in the czar's name, the ambassador offered Fryderyk the title of *Premier pianiste de sa Majesté l'Empereur de Russie,* a most tempting proposal. He made it clear that, having left Warsaw before the 1830 uprising, Chopin was not considered a "political emigrant" and his failure to renew his Russian passport in Paris would not be held against him.

But, according to his nephew Antoni Jędrzejewicz, Fryderyk replied stiffly that although he had left before the uprising and his weak health had prevented him from returning and participating in the struggle for independence, he "shared the fervent hopes of his fighting compatriots . . . and therefore regarded himself as a [political] emigrant, and could not accept under any circumstances the honor offered him."

Independent-minded as he was, Chopin would not be likely, anyway, to become a ruler's employee—even as the czar's glorified musician—particularly so far away from the real center of the world's culture. That was why he left Warsaw in the first place. Like Mozart and Beethoven, among others, Chopin certainly sought support among powerful aristocrats of his day—Polish, French, and others—to make his way in the world, and many of his works are rather obviously dedicated to princes and princesses, counts and countesses. Snob or not, he also curried favor with the powerful upper-class bourgeoisie as the society evolved in the post-Empire era. This was vital to his success because music was still the domain of the elites, aristocratic or bourgeois. But there was a distinction between seeking elite backing and accepting employment as many composers in the past had done. Joseph Haydn, for example, earned his living as *Kapellmeister* to the Esterházy family. More recently, Chopin's friend Felix Mendelssohn served as town music director in Düsseldorf. Cherubini was director of the Paris Conservatory. Rossini was the head of the Paris opera. Fryderyk's Warsaw friend, Antoni Orłowski, was the conductor at the Rouen theater. Even Liszt had become music master to the German court of Saxe-Weimar. And so on.

During 1837, Chopin was completing some of his most interesting Polish-inspired works, the four mazurkas forming opus 30 (dedicated to Princess Maria Wirtemberg, a novelist and sister of Prince Adam Czartoryski). To Charles Rosen, "of all the short works of Chopin it is the mazurkas that capture the full range of his genius," with his "most brilliant innovations," "extraordinary fluidity," and the "wonderful continuity" from one mazurka to the next. To Tadeusz Zieliński, these mazurkas prove, more than ever before, that this genre is at the "very center of his artistic" creation and not a secondary track, and that it is "strongly connected to the soul of folklore." He observes that the Mazurka in C-sharp minor, op. 30, no. 4, has the "character of a poem" full of "violent changes in expression," from an amusing theme to a romantically obsessive melody over different tonalities.

But Chopin's Polishness, as expressed in the mazurkas and polonaises, ran parallel to other strains in his creativity. The poet Heine, a friend, wrote in the *Augsburg Gazette* that Chopin "belongs . . . to three nationalities: Poland gave him the soul of a knight and the memory of her suffering; France [gave him]charm; Germany [gave him] Romanticism. . . . He is not a Pole, nor a Frenchman, nor a German—his provenance is higher: His real homeland is the homeland of the Mozarts, Raphaels, Goethes, the land of dreams and poetic marvels. . . . Chopin is a genius musical poet."

Chopin also completed that year the twelve études of the second cycle (op. 25), dedicating it to his friend Marie d'Agoult, two new nocturnes, the splendid Scherzo no. 2 in B-flat minor, and the Impromptu in A-flat major. Aside from the new études, the Scherzo no. 2 is his most ambitious work at that stage of his life. It is rich in energy and extraordinary in diversity of humor, playfulness, sarcasm, and joy, although it also has its darker and more dramatic moments. The impromptu, however, was less admired, at least at the time. A critic in *La France musicale* ridiculed Chopin's style, charging that "he goes in quest of an idea, writes, modulates through all the twenty-four keys, and, if the idea fails to come, he does without it and concludes the little piece very nicely." Chopin, of course, was both furious and depressed.

But nothing seemed to distract him from his devotion to work. Despite the demanding schedule of lessons that took up much of the day at the Chaussée d'Antin apartment and his nocturnal sociability, Chopin composed almost daily in the morning, before the first pupil appeared, and often late at night. Composing came naturally to him— although not easily in terms of committing musical ideas to paper—and Fryderyk didn't need to wait for the Muses for inspiration. As Jon Newsom remarks, "We know that Chopin, the composer, was so ruthless in dealing with Chopin, the improviser, that however fertile his musical imagination, the act of shaping his ideas into a coherent and compelling musical composition was often a torment." His awful health and mood swings notwithstanding (both getting progressively worse), Chopin was so self-disciplined and professional that his creativity remained uninterrupted even at the worst of times, almost until the end.

Chopin's dedication to social life found steady encouragement from the Marquis de Custine, who flooded him with a cascade of invitations, which Fryderyk accepted more and more often. He evidently enjoyed the functions, attended by the artistic celebrities of Paris, at Custine's city town house or his country estate.

On March 18, Custine wrote Chopin to invite him to spend a number of days at his Saint-Gratien estate on Lake d'Enghien and tour together the region around Paris, stressing: "I think that such an excursion would be salutary for your health." Shortly thereafter he sent Fryderyk a curious, short letter, declaring in the opening sentence: "You have attained the heights of suffering and poetry: The melancholy of your creations invades hearts deeply; the listener is alone with you, even in a crowd." He went on to say that "the possibility of listening to you occasionally is a real consolation in the grave days threatening us; only art, as you feel it, may be able to unite people divided by the realistic side of life; people love and understand each other through Chopin. . . . Think about me; I can only think about you!"

This may have been in response to a letter from Fryderyk that "when heart's grief is transformed into illness, we are lost," which may, or may not, have been a reference to the rebuff by the Wodzińskis—Chopin was always extremely discreet about his private life and suffering—but now he seemed to trust Custine, accepting his friendship and hospitality. He visited the marquis fairly often during the spring of 1837 at the rue de La Rochefoucauld, performing for the other guests, who included his own friends and acquaintances like Berlioz and his English wife, Harriet, the tenor Gilbert Louis Duprez and his wife, Alexandrine, and the great Romantic novelist Chateaubriand. Custine never failed to thank Chopin for his latest visit and music when he invited him, always in writing, for the next soirée. During that time of emotional turmoil, Custine's homes, where all his wishes were instantly met, were something of a safe haven for Chopin. Notwithstanding Custine's homosexuality, there is nothing to suggest any such interest in him on Chopin's part as the friendship grew nor any indication that the marquis had ever attempted in any way to seduce him. Besides, Fryderyk's sexuality was extremely limited in every direction.

Custine, however, saw himself increasingly as Chopin's protector. In a lengthy letter late in April, he insisted that Fryderyk must look after his health, after explaining that he loved him so much that he did not fear annoying him with repeated advice. "You are sick," he wrote, "and, what is more, you may become considerably sicker. You are approaching the limit of the torture of your soul and suffering in your body. . . . You must let yourself be treated like a child and a sick person, and convince yourself that now you have only one objective: your health; the rest will return on its own."

Urging Chopin to spend a three-month vacation with him—a month at Saint-Gratien and two months at a spa on the Rhine—Custine told Fryderyk that if money was an obstacle, "I shall be able to lend it to you; you can repay it later . . . If you feel a lack of love, please allow at least friendship to function: Live for yourself and for us."

Fryderyk declined the long vacation, but in mid-May he accepted a weekend in Saint-Gratien, bringing his Polish cellist friend Józef Brzowski. Describing in his memoirs their journey from Paris in a cabriolet procured by Chopin, Brzowski noted that they were greeted on arrival by Custine and his two live-in lovers, the middle-aged Englishman St. Barbe and the boyish Polish Count Gurowski, and given a tour of the castle and the gardens. A Pleyel piano in the main salon and the adjoining Turkish parlor were the features, Brzowski recalled, that attracted their attention the most.

In the afternoon, Chopin, Brzowski, and Gurowski were driven in the cabriolet to the village of Montmorency, where many exiled Poles lived. Chopin led his companions to a country inn where they had a collation of milk (his favorite drink), fresh butter, and bread. Fryderyk felt so good that he proposed a jaunt to the Hérmitage in the Montmorency woods where Rousseau had once lived, to ride donkeys as he had done in the past. The donkeys were held on lead lines by two women, the younger one with Brzowski and the older one with Chopin, who was "very occupied with her, undoubtedly only in the poetic sense, and . . . joking with her." Suddenly hitting a tree with its head, Brzowski's donkey stopped abruptly, throwing him to the ground and running away as Chopin "was dying from laughter." At the Hérmitage, they inspected the small table on which Rousseau had written his novel *La Nouvelle Héloïse,* and a broken-down piano on which (fifty years later) the Belgian opera composer André Ernest Modeste Grétry had played while in retirement.

Returning to Montmorency on their donkeys (Brzowski's had been retrieved), they went by cabriolet to the village of Enghien, where they were to dine with Gurowski, who had forgone the donkey ride and rejoined them at the local restaurant. After a "luxurious" meal with much Bordeaux and Champagne, they raced back to Saint-Gratien where Custine and his guests awaited them.

The group, Brzowski recounts, was *la crème de la société parisienne,* and Chopin sat at the piano. First came two études and the beginning of the Ballade no. 2 in F major. Then, at the request of the audience, he played several mazurkas. Finally, Chopin improvised an inspired, fiery piece he described as an old song of uhlan regiments, saying to Brzowski, as the listeners applauded wildly, that "by tomorrow, they will have forgotten it." Supper was presently served, and after the meal María Santa Cruz de Merlin, a well-known soprano, performed Spanish songs, castanets in hand, with Chopin as accompanist. But Custine asked for more: Chopin readily agreed to play improvisations on the Spanish songs (which he had never heard before that evening), and it was well after midnight when he rose from the piano. It must have been nearly dawn before he was in bed—just the kind of behavior Countess Wodzińska had so dreaded.

A few weeks later, Chopin entertained Brzowski and a group of friends in a private upstairs dining room at a fashionable restaurant on the corner of rue Montmartre, then took them home and, "in good humor," played for hours, mixing serious music with musical jokes and farcical demeanor. Ignacy Gurowski, Custine's young lover, joined them at two o'clock in the morning, convincing Chopin to drive with him to Saint-Gratien. Chopin, to say the least, was not evidently worried about his health when having a good time.

In Nohant, George Sand, too, was having a good time, after a fashion. Having at long last broken with Michel in June after months of furtive meetings and bitter exchanges of letters, she was ready both to work and to embark upon new romances. And, as usual, Nohant was full of guests. If she thought about Chopin, she kept it to herself.

Over a two-month period late in the spring George produced a new novel, *Les Maîtres mosaïstes,* one of her best, as Liszt played the piano in the adjoining room and nightingales sang in the tall trees. It was her version of the Venice events with Musset (the title referred to the master stonecutters who worked on the mosaics in St. Mark's Square). Among the guests was Charles Didier, who had hoped to rekindle his affair with her—"she would have preferred *Zopin,*" in the words of Liszt, who often amused himself mispronouncing his friend's name—and George was not interested. She had *some* interest in Pierre-François Bocage, a handsome thirty-eight-year-old actor who had played opposite Marie Dorval in *Antony* (and urged George to write a play for him). They had a brief affair, and would remain friends.

More serious was the appearance on the Nohant scene of Félicien Malle-fille, a huge, bearded Martinique-born playwright, nine years younger than

Sand, whom she had appointed in July as her children's tutor and her latest lover. She had met him some years earlier and found him unpleasant; now she was taken with him. Her new intellectual—but Platonic—friend was the radical politician and writer Pierre Leroux, a man her age and a widower with a number of small children, whom she boundlessly admired (she had first met him through Michel in Paris)—and helped to support. He would be her principal political mentor over decades.

That same month of July, as George Sand in Nohant was busy reordering her life once more, Chopin traveled to London. It was a spur-of-the-moment decision, accepting the invitation from Camille Pleyel, the piano manufacturer and a close friend, to accompany him on a business trip to England. Whether Chopin was plainly bored during the Paris summer—Liszt and Marie d'Agoult had gone to Bellagio on Lake Como in Italy and many of his other friends were also away—or trying to forget Maria Wodzińska (which was less and less likely), the idea of London appealed to him. A few weeks there sounded more amusing than several months at a Rhine spa which Custine had proposed.

Chopin's only condition was that he would travel incognito and be introduced only as "Mr. Fritz" to avoid social or musical commitments and ensure that the London sojourn would be entirely a vacation. With his works regularly published in England, he was very well known and quite admired there, but he feared invasions of privacy. The purpose of Pleyel's trip was to discuss business ideas with John Broadwood, the head of Broadwood & Co., the leading English piano manufacturer, but it left much time for sight-seeing and relaxation.

Journeying by train from Paris to the Channel coast, they crossed over by ferry, arriving in London on July 7, and taking rooms at one of the best hotels. Chopin had at least two Polish friends in London—Stanisław Egbert Koźmian and Leon Ulrych—and, true to form, he did not wish to see anybody else. For one thing, he did not speak a word of English. He attended a concert by the pianist and composer Ignaz Moscheles, a Czech who lived in London, but evinced no interest in meeting him. Moscheles, who had long been anxious to make Chopin's acquaintance, had no idea that Fryderyk was in town, learning about it only after his departure. In his diary, Moscheles noted wistfully that "Chopin, who spent a few days in London, was the only one among visiting artists who not only did not call on anybody, but did not even wish to be visited because every conversation worsened his suffering." Mendelssohn, who was a friend, learned about Chopin's "unexpected" presence from Moscheles when he later came through London; he told Hiller in a letter that Chopin had been there, "but did not visit or meet anybody."

The only exception was a dinner at the home of John Broadwood on Bryanston Square, where Chopin agreed to come with Pleyel as "Mr. Fritz." At dinner, Chopin chatted volubly in French, then listened politely as several guests played the piano. When Pleyel mentioned that "Monsieur Fritz" also could play, he was asked to sit at the keyboard—and he instantly lost his incognito status. Marceli Antoni Szulc, a teacher, pianist, and Chopin's first serious biographer, describes the scene in his account published in Poland (but based on foreign sources) in 1873: "Immediately, he enchanted the listeners. In the course of his playing, people began to look at each other meaningfully, exchanging comments, and when the final chords died, there was an explosion of shouts of admiration and worship: 'Only Chopin can play like this!' it was exclaimed." J. W. Dawson, the editor of the periodical *Musical World*, was among the guests, and he wrote that "when Chopin visited our capital briefly, only a few had the joy of hearing him play or, rather, improvise, and those few will never lose this remembrance. . . . He is, in our opinion, the most enchanting of all the salon pianists."

Koźmian, a poet whom Chopin knew in Warsaw and who settled in London after the 1830 uprising, was Fryderyk and Pleyel's constant companion. He told his brother Jan in a letter how the visitors spent their time: "They came to amuse themselves in London. They are staying at one of the premier hotels, keep a carriage, simply looking for ways to spend money. One day we are in Windsor, the second day in Blackwell, the third in Richmond. . . . We often go to the opera. Pasta is marvelous in *Medea* and *Romeo.* I have not seen *Ildegonda* because Chopin does not want to hear boring music. . . . Moscheles played a long [Beethoven] concerto [at his performance]: Chopin says that his playing is terribly baroque."

London, however, did not make a great impression on Chopin. In a letter to a friend in Paris, he complained about mud in the streets, adding that "you can have a good time here—carefully—when you are here briefly." And he offered further impressions: "Great things!!—Great urinals!—But there is no place to pee. . . . But the Englishwomen, but the horses, but the palaces, but the carriages, but the wealth, but the luxury, but the space, but the trees—but everything, starting with soap and ending with razors, is extraordinary—everything is the same, everything overeducated, everything washed, but black like a nobleman's ass!" The vulgar Polish word for the backside is *dupa,* and Chopin, having discovered the existence of a company named Duppa et Co., reported that "here, they have Duppy [plural of *duppa*] spread all over signboards. Now you can praise London!!!"

Chopin and Pleyel returned to Paris on July 25, after a visit of nearly three weeks.

While in London, Chopin had received a letter from Countess Wodzińska. Its contents are unknown, but it appears that she was informing him of the family's decision not to go to Dresden that year.

Back in Paris, Fryderyk wrote her on August 14, after giving her news about Antoni Wodziński's health in Spain, that "your latest letter reached me in London where I had wasted a month. I thought that from there I would have gone to Germany through Holland. . . . I returned home, the day is waning, and surely it will wane completely in my room. I await from you a letter less sad than the last one. My next [letter] may be only an addition to a [letter] from Antoni."

Most probably, despite all the earlier warnings, Chopin still hoped to be invited to join the Wodzińskis in Dresden, as originally planned, and to see Maria. Judging from the travel plans he had apparently made in London, the trip to Dresden remained on his mind. Clearly, however, Madame Wodzińska had now put an end to these hopes. Chopin passively accepted the verdict. He was not a fighter over emotions.

This was the official finis of Chopin's romance with Maria and all the contacts with the Wodzińskis, although the countess wrote him once more in November to have him forward a letter to Antoni and again the following April. "Please accept the assurances of my most cordial feelings that I shall keep until my death," she said in that final missive. She was a resolute woman.

At his Paris apartment, Chopin gathered the letters from Maria and Madame Wodzińska along with a rose, now dried, that his quasi fiancée had given him in Dresden when they said farewell for the last time. He placed them in a big envelope on which he scribbled in large letters *Moja Bieda!* ("My Grief!") and tied it with a blue ribbon. He kept it until he died. Fryderyk, after all, was a sentimental man.

Chapter 14

CHOPIN'S GRIEF DID NOT LAST very long for, next, he was chosen lover and "child" by the most famous woman in France, if not in all of Europe. He submitted with enthusiasm and sentimentality to this choice, though it had taken some time to materialize. For both, it was a long-range proposition, not simply instant gratification.

Returning to Paris from Nohant in October 1837—three months after Fryderyk came back from London—George Sand took the initiative of reviving the contact they had established a year ago. Chopin had not accepted the invitations to Nohant in the spring (despite his hint to Antoni Wodziński that he might and his moonstruck diary entry), but she was determined to attract, if not capture, him sooner or later. She had written that Chopin was "created" for her by "Providence," and a friend had remarked mordantly that she planned to "annex" Fryderyk.

Sand's current affair with Mallefille, who remained behind in Nohant tutoring the children, was no obstacle for the time being in this endeavor. George had a big heart and she rarely turned her back on past lovers; she usually remained quite fond of them. Besides, she was not about to ditch Mallefille before acquiring Chopin. And, for once, she was patient.

This time, Sand approached Chopin through a mutual Polish friend, Count Wojciech Grzymała. The forty-four-year-old Grzymała was Fryderyk's best friend in Paris along with Julian Fontana and Jaś Matuszyński, but, presumably because he was so much older and more experienced, he was the most trusted in matters big and small. A bear of a man with a huge mustache and a booming voice, Grzymała (known to the French as "Albert" or "Adalbert" because his full name in Polish was unpronounceable to them) was the image of an old-fashioned Polish nobleman. Sand described him lovingly as "a fat, coquettish Pole . . . encased in a monstrous . . . pyramidal jacket"; she had met him through the poet Mickiewicz, and a warm relationship developed between them.

Grzymała had served in London as the delegate of the "National Government" during the 1830–1831 uprising, then settled in Paris where he was most active in the exiled community, founding the Polish Literary Society, of which Chopin was a member. He also made and lost great sums of money on the stock market and in other financial enterprises. And, above all, he was a most amusing, colorful, and convivial companion. At Grzymała's request, Sand helped out with a bazaar sale to benefit impoverished Polish political refugees (there were around ten thousand of them in France).

It is likely that through Grzymała, Chopin and Sand met one or more times, briefly or otherwise, that autumn. Maurois cites an admiring Chopin diary entry about George dated October 1837, but more probably it was written the year before. In any case, there is no record anywhere of their meetings in late 1837, possibly because relevant letters or diaries are missing.

Sand returned to Nohant before Christmas while Chopin busied himself with lessons, composing, and his social life. On the anniversary of the Warsaw uprising, he inscribed in the album of an unidentified Polish friend the trio passage from the Funeral March that would become part of his Sonata no. 2 in B-flat minor, op. 35.

The spring of 1838 was an upbeat time for Chopin in every way. On February 25, he played for King Louis-Philippe and the royal family at the Tuileries. On March 3, Fryderyk performed at a Paris concert one of the two-piano parts of the Allegretto and finale movements from Beethoven's Seventh Symphony, arranged by Charles-Henri-Valentin Alkan, a young pianist he liked very much, for eight hands, the other players being Alkan and Alkan's conservatory teacher, Pierre-Joseph Zimmermann, and Adolf Gutmann, his own favorite pupil. On March 12, Chopin was in Rouen, participating in a benefit concert organized by Antoni Orłowski, a Warsaw Conservatory colleague and now Rouen's theater music director. He played his Concerto no. 2 in F minor with the Rouen Orchestra conducted by Orłowski before an audience of five hundred. Two weeks later, the *Gazette musicale* published a review by Ernest Legouvé, a well-known writer and critic (and Chopin's friend), answering the question "Who is Europe's first pianist—Liszt or Thalberg?—let all the world reply . . . Chopin!" For Fryderyk to be willing to play publicly three times in the space of three weeks was most unusual— but it was an unusual time for him, perhaps one of premonitions.

While Chopin played for the king and others during the winter, Sand was host in Nohant to her friend Balzac (who had invited himself), although what he would write about this stay to his Polish mistress, Countess Eveline Hańska (later his wife), was brutally unfriendly. He referred to her as a literary "colleague," remarking that "she is a boy, she is an artist, she is great, genereous, devoted, chaste; she has the great traits of a man; ergo, she is not a woman. . . . I was speaking with a colleague. . . . A woman attracts, but she rejects, and, because I am so much a man and she has this effect on me, she must have it on men who are similar to me; she will always be unhappy." Whether or not Balzac had Chopin in mind—as less of a man than he—the novelist was right on the last point. Liszt, who liked her, commented in his book on Chopin that Sand "disdained men more than Don Juan disdained women." (Balzac may have, indeed, been "so much a man," but it is interesting to note that his first mistress was a few years older than his mother.)

Balzac also volunteered that George's comments on Liszt and Marie d'Agoult during their Nohant conversations had provided him with rich material for the drafts of the novels *Galériens* and *Amours forcés,* which he was writing at the time and became, in the end, *Béatrix ou les Amours forcés,* published the following year. Sand, of course, also appears in the novel, thinly disguised. She, too, would disguise friends and acquaintances in *her* novels.

In mid-April 1838, George Sand was again in residence in Paris, staying with her friends Manuel Marliani, the Spanish consul in Paris, and his French-born wife, Charlotte, at their spacious apartment at 7, rue de la Grange-Batelière. As it happened, the Marlianis also had many Polish friends, including Mickiewicz, Grzymała, and Chopin.

Chances are that it was on George's suggestion that Carlotta Marliani had invited Chopin to an evening reception at their home on April 25. But even if George and Fryderyk had met the previous October, nothing explains why they had no further contact until April; if they had not, fifteen months would have elapsed since the last time they had seen each other. Given their mutual personal attraction as well as Sand's invitations to Fryderyk to come to Nohant in the spring of 1837, it does not make a great deal of sense, certainly from her side. It introduces a major gap in their story. The version, recorded by some biographers, that it was Marie d'Agoult who had kept Chopin away from Sand to punish her for alleged flirtations with Liszt is not credible.

As for Chopin, he instantly accepted the Marliani invitation. Maria Wodzińska was now safely behind him; a short letter he received from her mother earlier in April confined its purpose to requesting that he arrange for a new edition of poems by Julian Ursyn Niemcewicz, an elderly Polish poet (and West Point graduate) who resided in Montmorency, and to provide music for them. Not a word about Maria or any future meetings to reawaken Fryderyk's interest.

On the eve of the Marliani reception, Chopin wrote an unidentified friend: "Please do not refuse dinner with Witwicki and Grzymała tomorrow, Thursday. I expect you at 5:45. If you have nothing better to do in the evening . . . allow me to introduce you at Madame Marliani's, where you will see several interesting persons." The evening of April 25 was the turning point in the Sand-Chopin romance. The next day, George sent him the famous note, "One adores you—George!" to which Marie Dorval added: "And me too! And me too! And me too!" Chopin pasted it in his album-diary.

Two days later, Sand wrote Delacroix that she was leaving Paris for Nohant the next dawn, but "to make you decide to come tonight, I shall tell you that Chopin is playing piano for us in a small group, elbows on the piano, and that is [when] he is really sublime. Come at midnight, if you are not a sleepyhead, and if you meet people of my acquaintance, do not tell them because Chopin has a terrible fear of strangers."

In Nohant, George lived through weeks of soul-searching about what could, or should, be her relationship with Chopin—and with Mallefille. She realized that this was the most important decision-making moment in her life, but it was unclear to her where exactly Fryderyk stood with Maria, and she agonized over whether she had the right to interpose herself. Chopin may have told her *something* about Maria when they saw each other in Paris, but, obviously, not that it was all over. He tended to be so discreet about himself as to become a cipher to his closest friends. For that matter, Sand might have heard vaguely about Maria from Grzymała, though, in all likelihood, he knew very little himself.

Grzymała nevertheless was the only person to whom she could turn to resolve her doubts. She often addressed him playfully as "my husband" and referred to Chopin as "our child" or "our little one" when she talked or wrote to Grzymała. Evidently, Sand had defined her attitude toward Fryderyk even before they had embarked on a liaison: She would mother him. On May 20, George penned an emotional, thirty-two-page letter to Grzymała, asking for his judgment and advice because "all my future behavior will depend upon your answer on this subject." It was the latest in a series of letters about Chopin that they had been exchanging on her initiative.

Not mentioning Maria or Fryderyk by name, George started out with this basic question: "Is this person, whom he wants or must or thinks he must love, the one proper to make his happiness, or must she augment his suffering and sadness? I do not ask whether he loves or is loved, whether it is more or less than me. I know more or less, because of what is happening with me, what must be happening with him. I ask to know which of us he must forget or abandon for his restfulness, for his happiness, for his life, which seems to me too uncertain and too fragile to resist great pain. I do not wish to play the role of the evil angel."

"If I knew," she continued, "that there is another link in the life of our child, a sentiment in his soul, I would have never leaned down to breathe a perfume reserved for another altar." Sand then went on to explain how she would handle Mallefille, whom she did not name, either, but described as "an excellent, perfect being . . . who, after nearly a year with me, had not once, not for a single minute, made me suffer through his fault." Yet, she wrote, "[he] is molding wax upon which I had placed my seal and, when I wish to change the seal, I shall succeed with some precaution and patience. But today, it is impossible and his happiness is sacred to me."

George covered page after page with different scenarios of life with or without Chopin, or life divided between him (much or little) and Mallefille—all depending on the "truths" she hoped to extract from Grzymała—but so bombastically unrealistic as to sound like the plot from one of her novels with all concerned living and loving together in angelic harmony. Returning to reality, Sand discussed the possibility of life with Chopin alone, acknowledging that in many ways "he is absolutely unknown to me. . . . I have only seen the side of his being that is lighted up by the sun," and begging for guidance "so that I know well his position in order to establish mine."

Quite insightful, George raised the question of whether Chopin could accept marriage, a daily relationship and "all that which, in a word, seems far from his nature and contrary to the inspirations of his muse." This, however, didn't need be an obstacle, and, next, Sand set forth a situation in which she and Chopin would respect each other's freedoms, tastes, and priorities. She appealed to Grzymała to convey her feelings and views to Fryderyk "to make him understand them . . . and to put his heart at ease." And she added: "I do not wish to steal anybody from anybody, except prisoners from their jailers and victims of executioners, and therefore Poland from Russia."

George also urged Grzymała to save Chopin—and "be firm" about it—from sacrificing himself because of a "sense of duty" to marriage to "a childhood friend . . . whom he no longer loves." The past, she wrote in full ignorance that Maria no longer remained in her way, "is an appreciable and limited thing; the future is infinity because it is unknown." It would also help, Sand suggested as she continued to outline her strategy, if Grzymała would explain to Chopin her attitude toward Mallefille so that Fryderyk does not feel that he has "some kind of duty to me that would . . . painfully fight another [duty]."

Finally, in a most revealing way, George raised with Grzymała the matter of having—or not having—sexual relations with Chopin. The crux of her long digression on this topic was that Fryderyk had disappointed her when he failed to try to make love to her the last time they were together in Paris, although she was ready to give herself to him. Incensed, Sand wrote that "to despise flesh may be wise and useful only with those who are no more than flesh; but with those one loves, it is not the word 'despise' but the word 'respect' that one must use when one abstains." Chopin had apparently told her on that unhappy night that "certain deeds could spoil the remembrance," and George found it to be a "stupidity," wondering whether "he had had a mistress unworthy of him. The poor angel!" She obviously knew nothing of his sexual history (or nonhistory), and, always insightful, she was hoping to defuse a future problem. Given her own awful sexual history, this was not surprising.

Sand ended the letter announcing: "This is my ultimatum: If he is happy or should be happy with her, let him do it. If he must be unhappy, prevent him [from it]."

Grzymała must have reassured George that Maria Wodzińska did not stand in her way and that Chopin was free to do as he pleased because she wrote him a note from Nohant that she would be back in Paris on June 6. "Come to see me," she asked, "and try to make sure that the little one does not know. We shall surprise him!" Grzymała, however, must have informed Chopin and asked him to act "surprised" because Fryderyk wrote back: "I cannot be 'surprised.' . . . I saw Marliani yesterday and he told me about her arrival. . . . God knows what will come of it. . . . Seriously, I am not well."

Twenty-eight-year-old Chopin and thirty-four-year-old Sand became lovers shortly after her return to Paris, launching what would be a nine-year relationship. Wisely, she did not press him for marriage and, not unexpectedly, he never proposed to her. George was willing to accept him on his terms, which, at that point, meant no commitments and absolute freedom for Fryderyk to pursue his composing, teaching, and after-hours social lifestyle. The only difference was that they now spent much time together, entertaining together and visiting friends together. Sand's writings leave no doubt that she and Fryderyk had a sex life, at least during their first years, but George abstained for a long time from discussing its quality, even in a disguised form in her novels. It must be presumed that Fryderyk entered into this liaison as a virgin (Teresa of venereal disease fame should not count), and that George must have conveyed a dash of experience to "our little one," overcoming some of his dislike of carnal contact. It must also be assumed that the thought of having children, even if she desired it with him, never crossed Chopin's mind.

They seemed very happy with this arrangement, and George was ecstatic, to judge from her letters to friends and her diary. She wrote in her memoirs that she saw Chopin, "whose genius and character I tenderly love," every day. She reported that they spent hours in "celestial embraces," whatever that meant. "This is absolute heaven," she informed Charlotte Marliani. Sand, naturally, had her moods, too, and Chopin said in a note to Grzymała during the summer of 1838 that "as for Aurora [sic]—yesterday was foggy; today I expect the sun."

Despite the heat and dust, Chopin and Sand spent the entire summer in Paris. Delacroix used the time to make the first sketches for their portrait together, having a Pleyel piano moved to his huge atelier on rue des Marais-Saint Germain on the Left Bank for the purpose. Then he began painting what became the famous unfinished "double" portrait of Fryderyk and George, with him seated at the piano and her standing behind, her arms crossed. The portrait was never fully completed, except for the faces, apparently because Chopin decided he did not like it (the two men often violently disagreed over visual arts without jeopardizing their friendship), and the canvas remained at the atelier until Delacroix's death in 1863. Between 1865 and 1873 (nobody is sure), an unidentified culprit slashed the portrait into two parts (the right side of the portrait, depicting Chopin, remains in Paris at the Louvre; the left side, with Sand, is at the Ordrupgaard Museum in Copenhagen).

One of the great joys of that summer was the visit of fifty-six-year-old Niccolò Paganini to Chopin's apartment. It was a surprise arranged by Fryderyk's pupil and friend Elise Peruzzi, the Russian-born wife of the ambassador of the Duke of Tuscany to France. She also was a friend of Paganini, the violinist Chopin had worshiped since childhood above all other living musicians. Madame Peruzzi recalled in her memoirs that "one morning we took Paganini to hear Chopin, and he was enchanted; they seemed to understand each other so well." Fryderyk, of course, had heard Paganini play, in Warsaw and then in Paris, and he was very familiar with the tall, thin Italian's violin concertos. Paganini would die two years later.

Though Madame Peruzzi does not mention it, George Sand was likely to have been at Chopin's apartment the day Paganini came to visit him; she often stopped there when he was giving lessons, listening quietly. George had a fine musical education and, as Maurois has pointed out, "she sustained [Chopin], herself a musician capable of appreciating, inspiring, and even advising."

Chopin and Sand maintained a busy, if unostentatious, social schedule throughout the summer. They thought it would be in poor taste to be seen in public together too soon. Fryderyk may have been somewhat concerned about the reactions of his conservative aristocratic Polish friends. But those they entertained at Chopin's apartment or met at the homes of friends often included George's former lovers: Michel, Didier, Bocage, and Mallefille. However, contrary to her expectations, Mallefille refused to "understand" the new state of affairs.

At first unaware of the truth, Mallefille wrote a poetic essay, *Les Exilés,* in honor of Chopin's "Polish" Ballade in G minor that was published in the *Gazette musicale,* preceded by a letter to the composer confessing that "hidden in the darkest corner of the room, I wept as I listened to the somber images evoked by your . . . Ballade." One evening, however, Mallefille realized that he had been replaced by Chopin in Sand's heart and bed, and he swore vengeance. He stalked George with a dagger as she left Fryderyk's Chaussée d'Antin apartment—where she went almost every evening—forcing her to flee for her life, then challenged Chopin to a duel. The idea of the slim, consumptive Fryderyk, who had never held a weapon in his life, dueling with the powerful Mallefille was absurd, and George instructed Grzymała and Pierre Leroux, her radical politician friend, to talk sense to him. In a note to Leroux before his meeting with Mallefille, she wrote: "When the question of women comes up, tell him that they do not belong to men by the right of brute force, and nothing is settled by slashing somebody's throat." Mallefille gave it up.

Chopin and Sand shared most of their time with friends like Delacroix, Heine, Pleyel, the cellist Franchomme, the Marlianis, Custine, the music publisher Schlesinger, the banker Léo, Grzymała, Mickiewicz, Fontana, and other assorted Poles. Liszt and Marie d'Agoult were in Italy that summer; besides Marie and George were not getting along well at all, indeed were exchanging nasty letters. Among Fryderyk's Polish friends, George's favorite, apart from Grzymała, was Mickiewicz. She admired his poetry and drama (much of it already translated into French), and helped to make him better known in France with her 1839 *Essay on Fantastic Drama: Goethe—Byron—Mickiewicz,* published in the very influential *Revue des deux mondes.*

When Mickiewicz was appointed professor of history of Slavic literature at the Collège de France (after teaching Roman literature in Lausanne), Sand dragged Chopin to his lectures. She also tried to learn Polish, not too seriously, and addressed short jocular notes in broken Polish to Grzymała, calling him "dear husband" and signing "your wife." Chopin himself became involved in seeking to arrange a new and better translation of Mickiewicz's huge epic drama *Dziady* ("The Forefathers' Eve")—he thought the original translation was inadequate—and proposed in a letter to Grzymała that Mickiewicz undertake it, with Sand improving the quality of the French-language version and providing her *Essay* as the introduction. Overoptimistic about the interest of French readers in Polish drama, he wrote that "everybody would be able to read it and many copies could be disposed of." In the end, nothing came of this ambitious project.

Chopin also had American friends and connections in Paris. He often dined at the home of the American banker Samuel Welles, where, in 1837, he first met Madame Peruzzi (Paganini's friend), whose father had served as the Russian consul general in the United States. She recalled that at the Welleses', "I, like everyone present, was enchanted listening to Chopin's mazurkas, waltzes, nocturnes, &c., which he played on a wretched square piano." Madame Peruzzi lived at the time at a pension "for ladies alone"—it was the year before she married the Tuscan ambassasor—"and I had a splendid American grand piano which was placed in the large drawing room . . . so that I felt quite at home, and there received Chopin, Liszt, and [Henri] Herz."

Fryderyk had known Paul Émile Johns of New Orleans since 1832, and had met James Fenimore Cooper through the Polish patriotic committees. Chopin's friend Julian Fontana had lived for a few years in New York before settling in Paris—and becoming his extraordinary helper and protector—and the aging poet Niemcewicz's background included Philadelphia and its Philosophical Society, in addition to West Point.

The new romance and association with George Sand in no way interfered with Chopin's dedication to composition. Composing for him was like breathing, and he worked at it in good and poor health, in good and bad humor, in happiness and in depression, in good and bad weather, in his Paris apartment, in the French countryside, and even in hostile foreign surroundings. He had amazing powers of concentration and immense inner resources, requiring no external stimuli to inspire him. George's company was not reflected in his music, one way or another.

Indeed, 1838 was as productive as the past year. And Chopin's creation between 1832 and the end of 1838—his first seven full years in Paris—added up to 106 individual pieces, from full-fledged compositions to half-finished or unfinished works (and even single-page manuscript scribbles). This brought his opus numbers to 34, from Opus 15, when he first arrived. Some of these works were published immediately, others with varying delays, some after his death, and some never. Naturally, musical output is measured by quality and not volume, but the scope of

Chopin's creativity over this period, to say nothing of its beauty and variety, demonstrates how busy this brooding perfectionist kept himself, day in and day out.

During 1838, Fryderyk completed two extraordinary polonaises, four new mazurkas,and three new waltzes. And he worked on the Twenty-four Préludes in all twenty-four sharp and flat key signatures (that is, all twelve keys, major and minor), and on what would emerge as the Sonata no. 2 in B-flat minor. All of them were supremely ambitious undertakings.

Chopin displayed his emotional and artistic range and diversity splendidly in the two polonaises forming Opus 40—no. 1 in A major and no. 2 in C minor. The first is the most famous of all his polonaises, known popularly as the "Military Polonaise" because of its optimistic martial drumbeat in a major key with fortissimo markings. The second, with its ominous bass phrase, introduces deep sadness, melancholy, and a sense of grave mourning.

Described by the musicologist Adrian Thomas in the *Cambridge Companion to Chopin* as a "single-minded call to arms," the A major Polonaise has captured the imaginations of generations of patriotic Poles. (Its opening bars were the theme of the Warsaw Radio before World War II and the farewell sound breaking into silence on the air-waves when the invading Nazis succeeded in smashing the capital's resis-tance in September 1939, almost exactly a century after Chopin had composed the defiant polonaise.) Tadeusz Zieliński has written that its tone is "heroic-solemn," sounding like a "lapidary military command," while the "pulsations of massive chords by both hands . . . trace the apotheosis of knightly bravery [and] the power and majesty of the nation." It is, Zieliński says, "the vision of a victorious and triumphant Poland."

The A major Polonaise would not be published until 1840, but Chopin played it, possibly for the first time in public, in October 1838, for the Marquis de Custine and his guests at the Saint-Gratien country manor. Custine wrote a friend that it was "an orgy of happiness." This polonaise would much later be scored for the orchestra, but it was an artistic error that would have made Chopin turn in his grave in horror: His piano alone offers all the sounds required to express his feelings; there is no need for brass or drum thumping.

Playing the A major Polonaise calls not only for enormous dexterity

198 ⌒ Chopin in Paris

and robust fingers, given the intricacy of the work, but extreme physical strength as well to be able to perform it fully and adequately: a strong back and strong arms, forearms, and hands. It is something of a mystery how the weak and sickly Fryderyk could muster the power and energy to play some of his own compositions, but summon them he did. Moreover he never compromised because of his health over what he regarded as the requirements of his composing originality, no matter how exhausting. In fact, Chopin's last polonaise—in A-flat major, op. 53, known as the "Heroic"—composed four years later, when he was thirty-two and his physical condition further deteriorated, is quite demanding physically, especially in the powerful left-hand staccato octaves. Liszt, who exacted equally exquisite pain in his own works, pronounced the final polonaise to be "a danger to health." This is perhaps why there were to be no more pure polonaises: the Polonaise-Fantaisie in 1846 was much gentler.

Charles Rosen, alluding to the études as well as to the polonaises, speaks of Chopin's "sadism," adding that "in most of his work actual pain is associated with emotional violence." Such a conclusion, presumably correct, inevitably opens whole new horizons—indeed, a Pandora's box—on Fryderyk's psychological and mental condition, and his behavior in personal relations away from the piano. Was he, for instance, a masochist, too, and did he seek to inflict pain, even subconsciously? He suffered, of course, from mood swings and, as a composer, relished contrasts in both style and theme. The two new polonaises in 1838 may have been a case in point—a violent and triumphant one followed by one of morbid quiet.

The Polonaise in C minor, op. 40, no. 2, is "the most tragic and somber of Chopin's polonaises," in Zieliński's words. "The steadily pounded chords of the right hand, like bells, become the backdrop for the melody . . . emanating from tomb-like, abysmal depths," he writes. "It is painful gravity, tortured dignity, tragic majesty." Why did Chopin compose two such diametrically opposed works as part of the same opus, one after another, the same year? Zieliński believes that the two polonaises "seem to reflect the duality of feelings aroused at the time—in the artist and his compatriots—by thoughts about Poland." If there is a better explanation—Was there "duality" in him beyond Polish patriotism?—only Chopin had it. But, as usual, he did not provide elucidations.

Chopin dedicated both Opus 40 Polonaises to his friend Julian Fontana.

The four mazurkas, op. 33, likewise completed during 1838, are widely regarded to be among Chopin's most important works, far more interesting than the four mazurkas, op. 30, he had composed two years earlier. The Mazurka in D major, op. 33, no. 2, for example, has led Rosen to remark that "it is music as an agent that acts directly on the nervous system, induces a kind of intoxication." Adrian Thomas thinks that the mazurkas are "the result of Chopin building on embodiments of a long-lived folk tradition and investing them with the individual imagination of an exile."

But, again, Chopin engages in an intriguing play of diversity—if not downright contradiction—within the same group of compositions. The first mazurka in Opus 33 conveys bitterness, frustration, and sadness. The second mazurka (the one Rosen found intoxicating) is a gay, care-free, and unpretentious folk dance, something like a Polish village oberek. The third one is modest and quiet, bearing out Chopin's notation of *semplice* ("simple"). The fourth is rich in texture, humor, ideas, and melodies, with a contrasting and colorful diversity of themes.

And there was new diversity in his life, too, that Chopin encountered before the end of that rich year, although it would soon turn into a nightmare.

At some point during the summer of 1838, George Sand had decided that her fifteen-year-old son, Maurice, who suffered from rheumatism, should spend the winter somewhere in the warm "south" and that she would accompany him along with his sister, Solange, who was ten. She also desired a "quiet retreat" to work on her new novel, *Spiridion,* and, in Maurois's words, "she experienced, as usual, the need to live conjugally with her new lover." Her first idea was to go to Italy, where she had traveled several times, but her Spanish friends—Consul General Marliani and the statesman Juan Alvarez y Mendizábal—counseled the island of Majorca, off Spain's eastern coast in the Mediterranean. So did Marquis Francisco Valldemosa, a native of Majorca and landowner there. Sand enthusiastically accepted the advice, sharing her thoughts with Chopin and expressing the hope that he would join the family.

Fryderyk resolved to travel with George and her children although, as was his custom, he agonized for many weeks over the decision. But it is safe to assume from available correspondence and diaries that Chopin, again wracked by spasms of coughing, had actually asked George to let him come. Liszt has written that Chopin's health was so alarming that he simply had to get away from the Paris winter. Grzymała, Fontana, Matuszyński, and Chopin's doctor, Paul Léon Gaubert, urged him to seek the sun. The argument, offered by several biographers, that Fryderyk chose to leave Paris to hide his relationship with George, a political radical, from the Czartoryskis and his other Polish aristocratic friends (and to prevent word of it from reaching his parents in Warsaw through them) makes little sense because he could not keep it a secret forever. It was one thing not to flaunt the relationship in public in Paris and quite another to run away. Nor is it true that the Sand liaison would make him lose pupils from the aristocracy: There was always a long waiting line to be taught by the maestro.

Still, it was not an easy decision for Chopin, a man well set in his ways, to accept being away from his Parisian home and its sense of security for long months. But Zieliński suggests that, in the end, Fryderyk *was* motivated by love: "He was willing to leave Paris during the season, including his lessons, friends, meetings with [Polish] emigrants, publishing matters, and his normal social life, even for a year or more, in order to be near his beloved." He is probably right about the love-starved Fryderyk. It was one of his very few emotional initiatives.

George, of course, was delighted. In a letter to Delacroix in September, she proclaimed that "if God were to send me to death in an hour, I would not complain because three months of uninterrupted ecstasy have elapsed. . . . I begin to believe that there are angels disguised as men who spend some time on earth to console and carry with them to heaven poor, tired, miserable souls, near perdition." But Delacroix, who was very fond of both and a great admirer of Chopin's music, had doubts regarding how long the bliss would last. He told her so.

In her memoirs, Sand recounts that in discussing the plan to take her son south, Chopin had told her that "if he were in Maurice's place, he would soon recover." She continued:

> I believed it, and I was mistaken. I did not put him in the place of Maurice on the journey, but beside Maurice. His friends had long urged him to go and spend some time in the south of Europe. People believed that he was consumptive. Gaubert examined him and declared that he was not. "You will save him, in fact," he said to me, "if you give him air, exercise, and rest." Others, knowing well that Chopin would never make up

his mind to leave the society and life of Paris without being carried off by a person whom he loved and who was devoted to him, urged me strongly not to oppose the desire he showed à propos and in quite unhoped-for way. . . . Chopin was just then in a state of health that reassured everybody. With the exception of Grzymała, who saw more clearly how matters stood, we were all hopeful. I nevertheless begged Chopin to consider well his moral strength, because for several years he had never contemplated without dread the idea of leaving Paris, his physician, his acquaintances, his room even, his piano. He was a man of imperious habits, and every change, however small it might be, was a terrible event in his life.

Having made up his mind, Chopin chose to confine the knowledge about the proposed Majorca trip, at least initially, to a small group of friends: Grzymała, Fontana, Matuszyński, and Gutmann. Because he needed money for the journey, Fryderyk informed Pleyel of his plans in order to sell him the Opus 28 Préludes for 2,000 francs, with a 500-franc advance (he expected to complete them in Majorca). Pleyel also promised him that a fine piano would be shipped to Majorca. Next, Chopin borrowed 1,000 francs from the banker Léo, and received an advance of 400 francs against a payment of 1,500 francs from the publisher Schlesinger for French and German rights to the four new mazurkas and three waltzes.

There seems no question that Fryderyk was enthusiastic about the Majorca expedition—out of love for George, a sense of romance, and the promise of quiet concentration on composing, without daily lessons and social activities. Ewa K. Kossak, a Polish scholar, has written that "the decision to spend the winter together was entirely Chopin's, with no insistence from his mistress." Sand was not "annexing" him, at least for the time being.

George and Fryderyk had agreed to depart separately from Paris to avoid inevitable gossip. A departure together would not have gone unnoticed. Sand left first, on October 18, with Maurice, Solange, her half brother, Hippolyte, and the maid, Amelia, stopping en route in Lyons, Avignon, and Nîmes. Fryderyk was to join them in Perpignan, near the Spanish frontier. Before leaving, George wrote him at midnight: "We are starting at dawn" and "I am sad that . . . you are having a bad night. Try to organize your time so that you can rest in Paris for at least three nights, and do not get too tired. . . . Love me, dear angel, my dearest happiness. I love you!"

Chopin, of course, did not believe in rest. Two days after George's departure, he spent the evening at Saint-Gratien with Custine and his friends. He played there the new Polonaise in A major as well as a short composition called "The Prayer of Poles," a largo based on a patriotic religious song (not published in his lifetime), and the Funeral March that would become part of the Sonata no. 2, op. 35. Fryderyk told Custine that he was on his way to Majorca with George Sand, a piece of news that greatly upset the marquis and led him to write Sophie Gay, a novelist friend, that "Chopin is leaving for Valencia, in Spain . . . for another world!"

Custine went on angrily: "You cannot imagine what Madame Sand was able to do with him in one summer. Consumption is reflected in his face, which looks like a soul without a body. . . . When I thought that I may never see him again, my heart bled. The unhappy person does not see that this woman loves like a vampire! He is following her to Spain. . . . He will never return from there. He did not have the courage to tell me that they will be together; he said only that he needed a mild climate and rest! Rest!—in the company of a vampire!"

On October 27, Chopin turned over the keys to his apartment to Julian Fontana and left Paris by coach with Mendizábal, the Spanish cabinet minister, who was returning home. Four days and nights later, on October 31, Fryderyk joined George in Perpignan. It was a comfortable journey, and Sand wrote Charlotte Marliani that Chopin looked "as fresh as a rose and as pink as a radish."

Their great and frightening adventure would start the following day.

Chapter 15

THE THREE MONTHS OR SO that Chopin and Sand spent in Majorca provided the initial test of living together and beginning a long, intimate mutual discovery. These were two people of immensely different and difficult temperaments. And the Majorca experience sowed the seeds of fundamental conflict. Fryderyk found himself exercising the totally unaccustomed, awkward, and confusing role of paterfamilias toward his mistress, whom he knew only superficially, and her children, whom he did not know at all.

What was astonishing was the impact on Chopin's health and his musical creation. Majorca turned out not to be the ideal spot for the winter; he had to work there under the most atrocious conditions imaginable, yet produced memorable compositions.

Fryderyk met the children, Maurice and Solange, for the first time when he arrived in Perpignan on October 31, 1838. From the outset, the rapport between him and the youngsters, especially Maurice, was uncomfortable, to say the least. George, of course, had never suggested that they regard him as their stepfather, but a de facto understanding had nevertheless developed. Even though Sand treated her new lover as if he were her third child, she taking charge of all the travel and living arrangements, Chopin still was the man in the household. Maurice and Solange had to cope emotionally with this reality.

Maurice, who had inherited some traits of George's character, was a sensitive adolescent of fifteen, who had considerable talent for making drawings and watercolors of people and landscapes. But he disliked

Chopin and detested his music. He also resented his mother's liaison with the composer. The lively, fun-filled Solange, then ten, played the piano (but lacked talent). She found Chopin charming and formed girl-ish romantic ideas about him, a mind-set that would lead to much grief later. She knew how to manipulate Chopin from the start.

On the morning of November 1, Chopin, George, her children, and the maid, Amelia, traveled by coach to the nearby Mediterranean port of Vendres, where they boarded the coastal steamer *Le Phénicien* for the sail to Barcelona (Hippolyte stayed behind in Perpignan). This was Chopin's first time aboard a seagoing vessel, which he seemed to enjoy, and his first trip to southern Europe. They landed in Barcelona the fol-lowing evening and took rooms at the Hotel de las Cuatro Naciónes on Capuchinos Rambla, one of the city's main boulevards.

Because George Sand was an indefatigable travel writer (on top of all her other writings), amateur historian, and amateur sociologist, the group stayed five days in the Catalonian capital, visiting the ancient cathedral, the old town and Inquisition dungeons, attending an opera performance at the Liceo (to please Chopin), being formally received aboard the French warship *Le Méléagre,* and making a sea excursion northeast of Barcelona. Sand's book *Un hiver à Majorque* is a blend of learned travelogue and an account of the "family's" travails on the island (she also mailed extensive articles on life in Majorca to the *Revue des deux mondes*).

On November 7, in the afternoon, the five of them went aboard *El Mallorquín,* a freighter propelled by a steam engine as well as sails (the funnel protruded between the main sail and the forestaysail) for the overnight crossing to Palma in Majorca. Chopin evidently was not trou-bled physically by the trip. They enjoyed perfect weather under a starry sky, and, according to biographer Niecks, the pleasantly monotonous sound of water slapping gently against the vessel's hull and the helms-man's song had inspired the Nocturne in G major, op. 37, no. 2. A. Coeuroy, a contemporary critic, has written that "it is almost a bar-carolle. . . . Chopin had found there the 'blue note' " (a "blue note" is a minor interval injected in a melody or harmony where a major would be expected, producing an effect that, to most ears, has a sad quality). True or not, Chopin did compose two nocturnes in Majorca; they would be published in 1840.

*   *   *

But the lovely crossing was a deceptive dream in the face of the reality they encountered upon arrival in Palma at 11:30 A.M. the next day. They welcomed the heat after the cold of Paris, but George and Fryderyk were shocked to discover that there were no hotels in Palma. It appeared for a while that they would have no place to spend the night and that, in effect, they were stranded—a horrible fate. Finally, thanks to introductions George had to the consul of France and a leading Majorcan banker, she was able to locate two tiny, dirty rooms on calle de la Marina, a slum street, above a barrelmaker's shop. The music Chopin heard those first days in Palma was the sound of hammers and saws downstairs.

Sand, who instantly acquired a lifetime disdain of all Majorcans, offered this description of their first day in Majorca:

> In Palma, one must be recommended and announced to the twenty most outstanding persons and be expected for several months to hope not to have to sleep in an open field. All that was possible for us to do was to secure two furnished, or rather unfurnished, little rooms in a rather bad location where foreigners are very happy to find a folding bed with a dirty hard mattress, straw-bottomed chair, and, by way of food, pepper and garlic without restraint. In less than an hour we convinced ourselves that if we did not appear to be enchanted by this reception, we should be receiving piercing looks as impertinent [people] and troublemakers, or, at least, be regarded with pity as though we were insane. . . . The slightest grimace you made upon finding vermin in your bed and scorpions in your soup would command the deepest contempt and raise universal indignation against you. We therefore refrained from complaining.

As for Chopin, he did not complain at first even to his best friends; in fact, he wrote a jubilant letter to Julian Fontana in Paris on November 15, after a week in the two cramped rooms in the town. As often happened, he was out of tune with George. Besides, it was the day they were moving to new lodgings.

"I am in Palma," Fryderyk wrote,

> among palm trees, cedars, cacti, olives, oranges, lemons, aloes, figs, pomegranates, etc. Everything that only the Jardin des Plantes [in Paris] has in its greenhouses. The sky is like turquoise, the sea like lapis lazuli, the mountains like emeralds, the air as in heaven. In daytime, it is the sun, everybody is lightly dressed and it is hot; at night, it is guitars and

singing at all hours. Balconies here are enormous, with grapes overhead; Moorish walls. Everything, like the city, looks toward Africa. In a word, it is a marvelous life.

But there was musical business on Chopin's mind, too: "Love me! Go and see Pleyel because the piano has not arrived yet. By what route did they send it? You will receive the Préludes soon. I shall probably live in a marvelous monastery, in the most beautiful spot in the world: the sea, the mountains, palm trees, a cemetery, a Crusaders' church, ruins of mosques, thousand-year-old olive trees. And I live a little more. . . . I am closer to what is most beautiful. I am a better [person]. . . . Tell Pleyel that he will soon receive the manuscripts. Say little about me to [my] acquaintances. . . . Tell [them] that I shall return after the winter." Writing directly to Pleyel on November 21, Fryderyk informed him: "I have arrived in Palma, a beautiful country—permanent spring—olive trees, orange trees, lemon trees, palm trees, etc. My health has improved; how do you feel?"

The "marvelous monastery" Chopin had mentioned was the abandoned medieval Carthusian monastery rising in the mountains above the village of Valldemosa and overlooking the sea, some three Spanish leagues (eight miles) from Palma. It had been abandoned by its handful of monks after Mendizábal, then Spanish prime minister at the head of a liberal and Masonic cabinet, had ordered all the convents and monasteries in the country closed by a decree signed on February 19, 1836, to free Spaniards from what he regarded as evil influences of the Roman Catholic Church (he was the friend who had persuaded Sand to spend the winter in Majorca).

Learning that Inácio Durán, an opposition politician, and his family, who inhabited several cells at the Valldemosa monastery, would be departing soon, George made Chopin and the children travel with her there in a two-wheel *birlocho* vehicle on November 13 to inspect the premises. They liked it greatly—it was beautiful, mysterious, and romantic in the autumn fog—and it turned out that three cells could be rented from Durán for the modest sum of thirty-five francs annually. It seemed like the perfect solution after the horrors of one month living in a villa just outside of Palma from which they would be evicted by the owner—and after the first week in the furnished rooms in town. The only problem was that the Duráns could not move until December 15.

The villa where George and her ménage stayed in the meantime was a small but comfortably furnished structure in Establiments, two leagues north of Palma. It was called *So'n Vent* (Catalan for "House of Winds") and it belonged to a local citizen known only as "Señor Goméz," who charged them fifty francs a month, a very expensive rental (certainly as compared with the monastery cells). As sketched by Maurice Sand, the villa was a whitewashed Mediterranean-style, one-story house with two dormer windows in the attic and a red-tile roof. Stone steps led from the street to the main door. A low wall surrounded the garden and the villa.

So'n Vent was the only place George had been able to find for them to live: The calle de la Marina rooms were obviously unbearable. For nearly a week, she had devoted most of her time looking for an apartment in Palma (though she also found time to visit the ancient cathedral and other historical monuments to gather material for her articles). Sand decided to rent the villa after she had utterly failed to locate an apartment in the city. As she put it in an article:

> It was impossible to find in the entire town even one habitable apartment. An apartment in Palma is composed of four absolutely naked walls, without doors or windows. In most bourgeois homes, glass windows are not used, and when one wishes to secure such a delicacy [*sic*], it has to be constructed. Each tenant therefore takes away with him, when he moves, the windows, the locks, and even doorjambs. His successor is forced to start by replacing them, unless he enjoys living in the wind, which is a taste greatly accepted in Palma.

At first, the Sand family was happy at the villa. It was on the day they settled at *So'n Vent*—November 15—that Chopin penned his delighted letter to Fontana. The weather was perfect for the first three weeks. They took long walks, George spent several hours a day tutoring the children and much of the night completing *Spiridion,* her "metaphysical-mystical" novel; she was able to send the last part of the book to her Paris publisher on November 20.

Chopin, however, was irritatingly idle because Pleyel's piano had not yet arrived, and only late in November was Sand able to borrow for him a second-rate instrument from the Ripoli family in Palma. But its sound was so awful that it only served to frustrate and upset him. In a note to Pleyel, Chopin wrote sadly: "I dream of music, but I do not play—

because there are no pianos here—it is a savage country in this regard." Still he managed to control his impatience, listening to the silences of the Majorcan night, the bells of the mules out to pasture, the sounds of guitars, and the singing of boleros, and, at dawn, the "wild cry" of the awakening pigs in the peasants' enclosures. Quite amazingly, in fact, Chopin was able to compose on that abominable piano during November his Mazurka in E minor, op. 41, no. 2, which he called *Palmejski* in Polish (for having been written in Palma) and which critics hailed for its "dramatic displays" and "poetic effect." Zieliński believes it is "one of the most beautiful and . . . saddest" of Fryderyk's mazurkas. Chopin seemed to create best when life around him was quiet, and the villa offered him absolute peace.

The *So'n Vent* idyll ended on December 6, when the rains came. In Sand's word, it was the "deluge." The villa's walls, she wrote in her memoirs, "were so thin that the lime with which our rooms were plastered swelled like a sponge. For my part I never suffered so much from cold, although in reality it was not very cold; but for us, who are accustomed to warm ourselves in winter, this house without a fireplace was like a mantle of ice on our shoulders, and I felt paralyzed. Chopin, delicate as he was and subject to violent irritations of the larynx, soon felt the effects of the damp. We could not accustom ourselves to the stifling odor of the braziers, and our invalid began to ail and to cough."

Actually, Chopin fell ill even before the rains. On December 3, he wrote Grzymała: "I'm coughing and hawking, [and] loving you. . . . This is a devilish country as far as postal service, people, and comforts are concerned. The sky is as beautiful as your soul; the earth is as black as my heart."

George added to the letter that "Chopin has been rather suffering in recent days. He is [now] considerably better, although he suffers from changes in temperature that are frequent here. . . . Let Providence guard us because there are no doctors nor remedies here. . . . The lack of the piano upsets me very much because of the little one. He rented a local one, which irritates rather than soothes him. He works despite all that. . . . We are not organized: We have no donkey, no servant, no water, no fire, and no sure way of sending out manuscripts. So I am busy with the kitchen instead of literature."

On the same day, Chopin wrote Fontana, bringing him up to date.

First, he asked him not to give up the lease on his Paris apartment, then informed him: "I cannot send you any manuscripts because I have not finished [them]. I was sick like a dog for the last two weeks: I caught a cold despite eighteen degrees (centigrade) of warmth [sixty-four degrees Fahrenheit], roses, oranges, palms, and figs."

In one of his most memorable—and amusingly ironic—epistolary passages, Chopin told Fontana that the island's three most famous physicians had examined him: "One smelled what I spat, the second one tapped me from where I spat, the third felt me and listened as I spat. One said that I died, the second one that I am dying, and the third that I will die." He wrote that he "barely" managed to dissuade the physicians from bleeding him.

Bleeding was an accepted treatment for phthisis at the time, and Sand also recalled that she fought to talk the doctors out of it, fearing that bleeding would dangerously weaken Fryderyk. Chopin went on to remark that Providence had saved him, but "this has had an impact on the Préludes, and God only knows when you will receive them. . . . Do not tell people that I was ill because they will turn it into a fable." Fontana noted on the letter that it had been a full month en route from Palma.

Meanwhile, word spread in Palma that Chopin was consumptive—and therefore represented a major danger to the population. George recounted that

> from this moment we became an object of dread and horror. . . . We were accused and convicted of pulmonary phthisis, which is equivalent to the plague in the prejudices regarding contagion entertained by Spanish physicians. A rich doctor, who for the "moderate" renumeration of forty-five francs deigned to come and pay us a visit, declared, nevertheless, that there was nothing the matter [with Chopin], and prescribed nothing. Another physician came obligingly to our assistance; but the pharmacy at Palma was in such a miserable state that we could only procure detestable drugs.

At this point, Señor Goméz, the landlord, dispatched a letter to Sand evicting them from the villa. "The fierce Goméz," George wrote, "declared, in the Spanish style, that we *held* a person who *held* a disease, which carried contagion into his house, and threatened prematurely the life of his family." He also demanded that she pay for disinfecting the villa, repainting the walls, and burning the bed and the bedclothes.

"This," Sand commented, "did not cause us much regret, for we could no longer stay there without fear of being drowned in our rooms." The problem, however, "was to know where to go, for the rumor of our phthisis had spread instantaneously, and we could no longer hope to find shelter anywhere, not even at a very high price for the night." In the end, Chopin, Sand, her children, and the faithful maid Amelia were saved by the French consul, Pierre Fleury, who invited them to stay at his Palma residence for four days and nights—from December 10, when they left *S'on Vent,* until December 15, when they were free to take over the cells at the monastery in Valldemosa.

In a letter to her friend Charlotte Marliani, Sand wrote on the day before they left the villa that "in short, our expedition here is, in many respects, a frightful fiasco." But, ever optimistic, she also expressed her determination to spend the rest of the winter at Valldemosa, "the most poetic residence on earth . . . This is the sole happiness of this country. I have never in my life met with nature as delicious as that of Majorca." George also spent one thousand francs, purchasing from the Duráns the furniture for the cells they would occupy at the monastery.

Valldemosa may well have been "the most poetic residence on earth," but Sand's insistence on staying in Majorca through the winter under the most appalling conditions was, pure and simple, an act of obstinate folly. The terrible rains never seemed to abate, and the monastery cells were damp and unheated. Chopin's health was getting steadily worse, the island doctors were clearly incompetent, the pharmacies had no adequate medicines, and Fryderyk could not stomach the local cuisine, based on dishes of pork cooked in oil—forcing George and the maid, Amelia, to improvise special meals for him from meager supplies available in the village below the monastery. Moreover, the Sand-Chopin contingent were regarded and treated as pariahs by Valldemosa peasants because of fear of "contagion" by his illness, their failure to attend church, George's (and Solange's) predilection for wearing masculine attire, and her habit of smoking cigars and cigarettes in public. It had never crossed Sand's mind that they were gratuitously defying the quasi-medieval way of life and customs of provincial Majorca.

Nor did George's awareness of Fryderyk's condition seem to affect her stubborn decision to overcome at all costs the challenge of Majorca—until it became truly unbearable. Chopin, it appears, had little or no say

in the family decision making—man of the house or not—and, in a
startling way, Sand was blaming him for distracting her and the children
from the wet wintry joys of Majorca.

She observed in her memoirs that her son, Maurice, "recovered perfect health" even as he faced the rain and the wind from morning until
evening. Neither she nor Solange "feared the flooded roads and the
downpours," George went on.

> We had found healthy and most picturesque lodgings in an abandoned
> and partly ruined monastery. I taught the children their lessons in the
> morning. They ran around the rest of the day while I worked; in the
> evening, we strolled together in the cloister under the moonlight or we
> read in our cells. Our existence would have been most agreeable in this
> romantic solitude, despite the wilderness of the country and the nasti-
> ness of the inhabitants, if the sad spectacle of the suffering of our com-
> panion and days of serious worry about his life had not, forcibly, taken
> away the whole pleasure and benefit of the voyage.

"The poor great artist," Sand related in the memoirs written long
after their separation,

> was a detestable patient. What I had feared, though not enough, unhap-
> pily did happen. He became completely demoralized. Accepting his suf-
> fering with fair courage, he could not vanquish the anxieties of his
> imagination. For him the cloister was full of terrors and phantoms, even
> when he felt well. He would not say it, and I had to guess it. Returning
> from nocturnal explorations of the ruins with my children, I would find
> him, at ten o'clock at night, pale at his piano, with haunted eyes, and hair
> standing on end. He needed several instants to recognize us. He then
> made an effort to laugh, and he played sublime things he had just com-
> posed or, better said, the terrible or heart-rending ideas that had cap-
> tured him, despite himself, in that hour of solitude, sadness, and fear.

In what sounds like a description of Chopin's manic-depressive crises,
complete with hallucinations—possibly for the first time since Stuttgart
seven years earlier—Sand recounted the evening when she and Maurice
had returned to the monastery from shopping in Palma, covering the
three leagues in six hours amidst catastrophic inundations on the way,
and found Fryderyk weeping as he played one of his new préludes.

"Seeing us enter," she wrote, "he stood up with a great cry, then told us in a lost fashion and a strange tone, 'Ah! I knew well that you were dead!'" Chopin told her later, George added, that "while awaiting us, he had seen all that in a dream, and, making no distinction anymore between this dream and reality, he became calm as he played the piano, persuaded that he was dead, too. He saw himself drowned in a lake; heavy, frozen water drops were falling on his chest." Sand recalled that she had pointed out to Fryderyk that he had been hearing raindrops falling on the roof of the cell, and "his composition [written] that evening was full of raindrops that resounded on the roof tiles, but were translated in his imagination and in his chant into tears falling on his heart from the sky."

This may have been the Prélude in D-flat major, op. 28, no. 15, and Zieliński writes that in it Chopin repeats "monotonously" in the accompaniment "a sound acting as raindrops falling continously." Chopin had himself jokingly referred to one of the Twenty-four Préludes as the "Raindrop Prélude." But the strange Majorca nights also produced on his battered old piano, which had been moved to the monastery, the Prélude in A minor, op. 28, no. 2, "written in depression and pessimism, with fatigue with life," in Zieliński's words.

In any case, George Sand's role in Majorca was rapidly being transformed from that of mistress to nurse and cook for Chopin. In the December letter to Charlotte Marliani, she complained: "If you knew what I have to do! I almost have to cook. Here, as another amenity, one cannot get served. The domestic is a brute: bigoted, lazy, and gluttonous; a veritable son of a monk (I think that all of them are that). . . . Happily, the maid whom I have brought with me from Paris is very devoted, and resigns herself to do the heavy work; but she is not strong, and I must help her. . . . Proper nourishment is difficult to get when the stomach cannot stand either rancid oil or pig's grease. I begin to get accustomed to it; but Chopin is ill every time we do not prepare his food ourselves."

The tone of their relationship was now set for years to come.

Chopin's own account of life at the monastery was consistent with his emotional and mental state as described by Sand. In a mid-December letter to Fontana, he wrote that in "[my] cell, you can envision me, uncoiffed, without white gloves, pale as ever. . . . The cell has the shape of a tall tomb. . . . Next to my bed, there is an old square table, barely adequate for me to write on, with a lead candlestick (a great luxury here) with a candle. . . . Bach . . . my scribblings . . . silence . . . one can shout . . . still quiet . . . I am writing to you from a strange place."

Turning to business, which was seldom away from his mind, hallucinations or not, Chopin told Fontana: "I cannot send you the Préludes because they are not finished; but I feel better and I shall hurry." He instructed him to pay the Chaussée d'Antin apartment rent, inquired about his Polish butler, and asked Fontana to give the building's porter twenty francs for New Year. "Today, the moon is most beautiful," Fryderyk mused. "It's never been like this, but, but . . . my manuscripts are asleep, but *I* cannot sleep. I just cough and am covered with adhesive plaster, awaiting spring—or something else." He requested Fontana not to tell the banker Léo about his illness "because he will worry about [his] one thousand [francs]."

Pleyel's piano had finally arrived from Marseilles, but it was being held in customs in Palma, awaiting the payment of an import tariff of four hundred francs. "Customs," Chopin wrote Fontana on December 28, "want a mountain of gold for this mess. . . . People [here] are thieves because they never see foreigners and do not know what to ask for things. Oranges are gratis, but a button for my pants cost a fortune. Yet, all this is a grain of sand compared to this sky, this poetry, this color of the most marvelous of places."

The piano reached the monastery during the first days of January 1839, and Chopin was able to complete his Twenty-four Préludes, op. 28, as well as the two Polonaises of Opus 40 (dedicated to Fontana), Ballade no. 2 in F major, op. 38, and the Scherzo no. 3 in C-sharp minor, op. 39.

Just when in Majorca Fryderyk finished all these works does remain a bit mysterious, however. His December 14 letter to Fontana says that his "manuscripts are asleep" and the December 28 letter tells of the piano being held in customs. But on January 22, Chopin wrote separately to Pleyel and Fontana to announce that the Préludes were ready; he advised Pleyel: "I am sending you at last the Préludia finished on your piano, which arrived in the best of conditions—it was not damaged by the sea, bad weather, or the Palma Customs Office." The only possible explanation is that Chopin, a notoriously slow composer most of the time, had already done much work on the Préludes before he left Paris, then continued composing on the borrowed piano, and "chiseled" them on the Pleyel instrument over a period of no more than two weeks.

214 — Chopin in Paris

Chopin's biographer Niecks has concluded that "internal evidence suggests that the Préludes consist—to a great extent at least—of pickings from the composer's portfolios, of pieces, sketches, and memoranda written at various times and kept to be utilized when occasion might offer." Niecks does not indicate what the "internal evidence" is, and modern scholars might disagree with his judgment.

Addressing Fontana, Chopin issued a series of instructions concerning collecting the moneys for the Préludes from his French and German publishers, and repaying the loan to Léo. Fryderyk also announced that he would return to Paris only in May "or later." He promised to send Fontana the ballade, the polonaises, and the scherzo "in a few weeks," which raises the same question about when, precisely, Chopin had started composing them. The letter to Pleyel listed the amounts he expected to receive for the Préludes from foreign publishers, and offered him the rights to the polonaises, the ballade, and the scherzo for rather high prices. In a postscript, Chopin said: "I have just realized that I have not thanked you yet for the piano and that I am writing only about money—decidedly, I am a man of business!"

Life at the monastery was most confining for its five occupants. Though what Chopin had described as his "cell" was actually a suite of three connecting rooms facing on beautiful gardens, his privacy was at premium. Fryderyk slept in the room where the piano was installed. The central room, in Sand's words, was "destined for reading." George and the children slept in the third room. The maid, Amelia, was given a bed elsewhere in the huge monastery. As the weather improved during January, Maurice and Solange spent much of their daytime hours outdoors, often with their mother, and studied with her the balance of the day. But the suffering and ill Fryderyk kept to his room almost constantly, working at the piano and his little table, often by candlelight. He was reasonably comfortable because George was able to procure feathers from a Frenchwoman in Palma to make pillows for him, and sheepskins covered the floor.

By February, however, the situation was becoming untenable. Sand wrote that "as the winter advanced, sadness more and more paralyzed my efforts at gaiety and cheerfulness . . . the state of our invalid grew always worse . . . we felt ourselves prisoners, far from all enlightened help and from all efficacious sympathy . . . death seemed to hover over our heads to seize one of us."

Grudgingly, she had to acknowledge that Chopin, apart from his illness, simply could not stand Majorca any longer. "With his exaggerated sense of detail," Sand recounted, "[his] horror of misery and [his] needs of refined well-being, he naturally regarded Majorca with horror after a few days of illness. . . . Except for me and my children, everything was antipathetic and revolting to him under the sky of Spain. He was dying from impatience to leave, more than from the inconveniences of the stay [in Majorca].

"Our stay at the Valldemosa monastery was therefore punishment for him and a torment for me," Sand wrote, summing up the Majorca experience. Deferring to his feverish demands to leave the island, George finally agreed to forgo seeing the Majorca spring.

On February 11, 1839, they left Valldemosa with all their belongings—including the Pleyel piano. French Consul Fleury put them up again at his Palma residence as they awaited the departure of *El Mallorquín* for Barcelona on her weekly sailing schedule two days later. Chopin suffered there "a frightening expectoration of blood," as Sand put it. At first, she failed to sell the piano because potential buyers feared the "contagion" of its owner; in the end, it was purchased by the wife of the Palma banker who looked after George's finances during the Majorca stay. And Sand's bitter farewell to the island was contained in a letter to Charlotte Marliani hours before departure: "We were pariahs on Majorca because of Chopin's cough, and also because we did not go to Mass. They threw stones at my children. They were saying that we are pagans."

El Mallorquín sailed at three o'clock in the afternoon of February 13. To add insult to injury—and another humiliation—Chopin, Sand, the children, and the maid traveled surrounded by a herd of pigs that were being transported to the mainland, exposed to suffocating stench. The captain had assigned them a small, hot cabin below the deck for the overnight crossing, forbidding them to step out because of Chopin's "contagion." Fryderyk spent a sleepless night and, as George reported in a letter to her lawyer friend François Rollinat, "he arrived at Barcelona, still spitting basins full of blood, and crawling along like a ghost." From *El Mallorquín,* they were transferred in Barcelona Bay to a French warship whose doctor, "an honest and worthy man, came at once to the assistance of the invalid, and stopped the hemorrhage of the lung within twenty-four hours."

It was nearly a miracle that Chopin, barely twenty-nine years old, was alive when he found himself back on the European mainland and closer to civilization. Once more he was able to summon reserves of energy to go on surviving and creating his music.

Chapter 16

INDEED, CHOPIN IMPROVED almost as miraculously the moment he set foot in Barcelona. "From that moment," George Sand wrote, "he got better and better." He rested for a week at the hotel where they had stayed the previous November, then George, Fryderyk, Maurice, Solange, and Amelia sailed for Marseilles. From there they were to proceed to Sand's Nohant safe haven, the first time Chopin had agreed to go. But they were not spared the final Spanish indignity. George recorded that "when we left the hotel in Barcelona, the manager wished to make us pay for the bed in which Chopin had slept, under the pretext that it had been infected, and that the police regulations obliged him to burn it."

Painful, humiliating, and horrifying as the Majorca experience had been for Chopin, he produced there some of his most magnificent music.

And George was equally creative despite the enormous pressures on her. She rewrote much of *Lélia* for a new edition, toning it down somewhat, and drafted the final part of her metaphysical novel *Spiridion*, which was based, as usual, on many of those close to her. Fryderyk was unquestionably the model for "Alexis," a Benedictine monk, whose health "was again altered in the humidity of the cloister." Barcelona and Majorca monasteries served as scenes for this thick and complex tale, largely inspired apparently by the "Christian socialist" ideas of her radical philosopher friend Pierre Leroux.

That Alexis dies in the end in the name of faith did not seem to disturb Chopin unduly (Sand read her novels aloud as she went along, almost every evening). He may have not made the association (as he would not do later in a much more personally dramatic context), in part because of his short attention span, except when it came to music, and in part because his interest in literature was extremely limited; he was not much of a reader or listener, except when it came to Polish poetry. Finally, his command of the French language was never perfect—and Sand's rich style demanded an absolute knowledge of it.

Spiridion (the name of the abbott who had founded the mythical monastery) was first published, as were most of Sand's novels, in serial form, in this case in the *Revue des deux mondes,* but reader reaction was so hostile—reaching boredom and confusion—that her publishers begged George to return to *Lélia*-like literature. Sand, who lived from enthusiasm to enthusiasm, could not understand this attitude, insisting that she would no longer work on "mediocre" sentimental subjects. The publishers, she complained to a friend, seemed to prefer, along with their readers, "little novels . . . that appeal equally to beautiful ladies and their maids. These gentlemen expect that I shall soon give them a novel à la Balzac."

While George's *Spiridion* has long been forgotten, Fryderyk's Majorca creations, especially the Préludes—with which she personally identified, perhaps more than with his other compositions—are among his memorable ones. The Préludes of Opus 28, short works, "small forms" or "miniatures," were self-sufficient poetical entities—forerunners in terms of the day's musical conventional wisdom, even though they follow the systematic order of Bach's Preludes in the *Well-Tempered Keyboard.*

The musicologist Jeffrey Kallberg suggests that "Chopin issued a kind of a challenge to his audiences in publishing the Préludes. . . . By asking listeners and performers to accept a transformed genre whereby individual préludes might serve both as introductions to other works and as self-standing concert pieces, he challenged the conservative notion that small forms were artistically suspect or negligible." His point was that "we need to perform and study the Préludes individually" and "stop reading the title 'Prélude' as an obfuscating irritant, and instead to see it as a highly significant clue that can lead to powerful interpretative insights."

Kallberg along with Zieliński and other modern scholars sees each of the Twenty-four Préludes as a completely individual and independent creation; Kallberg asks that "we finally remove the veil of aesthetic suspicion from smallness." Zieliński cautions nevertheless that while each Prélude is an individual work that can be played alone, the Préludes are "a unified cycle," presenting "an enormous display of emotions, psychic states, and their subtle variations." In a sense, the Préludes are a guide to Chopin's personality and moods, superior to the limited insights found in his letters and his diary—and to the opinions of contemporaries. To listen to the Préludes is to steal a glance into Chopin's soul.

This was what George Sand heard in the music of the Préludes. She wrote in the *Story of My Life* that they were Chopin's "masterpieces . . . the short pieces he modestly titled 'préludes.'" Many of them, she went on, "bring thoughts of visions of suffering monks . . . and of funeral chants that besieged him; others are melancholy and suave: They came to him during the hours of sun and health. . . . Still others are of gentle sadness which, while charming your ear, break your heart."

Long after Chopin's death, George told how over the nine years of their life together, she discovered every day "the secret of his inspiration or his musical meditation." His piano, she wrote, "revealed to me the concerns, the embarrassments, the victories, or the tortures of his thoughts. I thus understood him as he understood himself." Sand's biographer André Maurois agrees with this judgment, adding that "in listening to him play, she followed his inner life, his always secret life, of which music alone was the mysterious and vague expression." To the extent that anyone really understood Chopin, it surely was George Sand, even in the bitterness of their rupture.

In Marseilles, where the group arrived by ship from Barcelona on February 24, Chopin continued to recover. He had excellent medical care in the person of Dr. François Cauvière, a highly regarded physician and friend of the Marlianis, the weather was warmer and more pleasant, and the Marseilles hotel accommodations provided him with the creature comforts he lacked at the Valldemossa monastery. Moreover he could eat "decent" French food. Chopin had truly returned to civilization, and his moods as well as the aggressive management of his business affairs reflected it immediately.

Two days after they had reached Marseille, George Sand wrote Charlotte Marliani: "My sick man . . . is much, much better. He endured very well the thirty-six hours of the crossing of the Gulf of Lyons. . . . He no longer spits blood, sleeps well, coughs very little, and, above all, he is in France! He can sleep in a bed that will not be burned because of it. . . . No one draws back when he proffers his hand."

Dr. Cauvière, at whose home they stayed during their first two days in Marseilles, had initially diagnosed Chopin's condition as quite serious, but soon became more optimistic as he observed his patient's steady improvement. He prescribed a milk-rich diet to fatten him, but forbade wine and coffee. Sand informed Pierre Bocage, the actor and her former lover, in a long letter that as soon as Chopin "breathed the dry air of Provence, he began, thank God, to come back to life and now he is fairly well; he has even acquired relative corpulence—of your or Maurice's kind—he almost does not cough, and he is as happy as a bird."

Nevertheless Dr. Cauvière ordered Chopin to remain in the south of France for two or three months—not to risk a relapse in northern wintry weather—and the trip to Nohant was consequently postponed. Fryderyk appeared to be satisfied with this state of affairs, particularly when the family moved after a month to the more comfortable Hôtel Beauvau from the Hôtel de la Darze where they had first settled. George also decided that she no longer needed Amelia, dismissing her on the astonishing grounds of laziness.

Neither Fryderyk nor George found Marseille, a busy seaport, to be especially attractive, and they were probably right. Chopin wrote Grzymała that "Marseilles is ugly. . . . it bores us a bit." Sand confided in a letter to a friend that "as soon as I stick my nose out of the window [to look] on the street or the port, I feel that I am turning into a loaf of sugar, a soap box, or a pack of candles. . . . Fortunately, Chopin with his piano chases away the boredom and brings poetry to our hearth."

And they both kept quite busy. Chopin, working on a piano obtained for him by Dr. Cauvière, put the final touches on the new scherzo (he always fussed until the last moment). He also began sketching what would become the great Sonata no. 2 in B-flat minor, op. 35.

Sand, of course, was deep in her next novel; nothing ever stopped her from writing. Fryderyk noted in a letter to Grzymała: "My angel is finishing the new novel, *Gabriel*. She has been in bed all day today, writing. You know, you would love her even more if you knew her as I know her today." George felt the same about Chopin in these idyllic months of their life together, writing Charlotte Marliani that "this Chopin is an angel. His goodness, sensitivity, and patience worry me sometimes; it seems that this is too delicate, too unusual, and too perfect a creature to live long our heavy and hard life on earth. Being mortally ill, he created in Majorca music that irresistibly brought on thoughts of paradise."

Coincidentally, the sudden death of a dear friend came as a tremendous shock to Chopin when he learned that the thirty-seven-year-old Adolphe Nourrit, his favorite tenor, had committed suicide, jumping out of a window in Naples on March 8. Late in April, Nourrit's widow had brought his body to Marseilles, en route to Paris for the burial, and a requiem mass was celebrated at Notre-Dame-du-Mont Church there, with Chopin playing on the organ during the elevation Schubert's *Die Gestirne* ("The Constellation"), which Nourrit had sung for them so many times in happier days.

In the meantime, Sand was concerned over such mundane matters as keeping away "hordes" of Marseilles literature lovers demanding to see her and music lovers demanding to see Chopin. "For now," she wrote Marliani, "I pretend that he is dead, and, if this continues, we shall send everywhere letters announcing that we had both passed away so that [people] weep for us and leave us in peace."

Chopin, too, had mundane affairs on his mind, notably the money he was anxious to collect from his publishers. No sooner than he was breathing easier—literally—in Marseilles, than he began bombarding his friend Fontana with lengthy instructions on how to deal with publishers as well as on giving up one Paris apartment and finding a new one for his return later in the year. Though Fontana was a childhood friend, unconditionally devoted to Fryderyk, the demands piled upon him were extravagant by any normal standards. Copying Chopin's often almost illegible music manuscripts for submission to publishers was, for example, a regular occupation for him. However, using his charm, Chopin was an accomplished user of people, and Fontana never refused him. He may not have known that Fryderyk referred to him behind his back as "*totumfacki*," a rather derisive Polish word he had coined from the Latin expression "factotum," literally meaning "do everything" and employed to describe people who did every kind of work. But Chopin also dedicated his splendid polonaises, in A sharp, and C flat, op. 40, to Fontana. Such is the fabric of friendship. The Polonaise in A sharp was one of his greatest works.

Fryderyk's extensive and insistent correspondence with Fontana, Grzymała, and others—principally letters addressed to them—from Marseilles, Nohant, and elsewhere does away with the myth that he detested writing to people. He wrote quite a bit, if not regularly, to his family in Warsaw, and never hesitated to dispatch short or long notes to friends, acquaintances, and even strangers in Paris and abroad, if it served his purposes. Albeit the bulk of his letters to Poland have been lost, his overall surviving correspondence is far from negligible. But to avoid answering letters that bored or annoyed him, Chopin had developed the affectation of hating letter writing, remarking once that "the pen burned his fingers." In any event, letters from his pen cascaded to Fontana in the aftermath of Majorca, setting a new pattern.

In a letter on March 2, a week after reaching Marseilles, Chopin wrote him at length about payments due from his publishers for the préludes, the ballade, and the polonaises. Then he turned to the matter of Paris apartments:

> Now if, which I doubt, you succeeded in finding apartments for the next months, divide up my furniture amongst you three: Grzymała, Jaś [Matuszyński], and you. Jaś has the most room although not the most sense, judging from the childish letter he wrote me. For telling me that I should become a Camaldolite [a member of a discalced order of Benedictine monks], let him take all the shabby things. Do not overload Grzymała too much, and take to your house what you judge necessary and serviceable to you as I do not know whether I shall return to Paris in the summer (keep this to yourself). In any event, we shall always write one another, and if, as I expect, it will be necessary to keep my apartments until July, I beg you to look after them and pay the quarterly rent.

Fontana lived a few buildings away from Chopin on the Chaussée d'Antin.

"For your sincere and truly affectionate letter," Fryderyk continued,

> you have an answer in the second Polonaise [Opus 40, dedicated to Fontana]. It is not my fault that I am like a mushroom that poisons [you] when you unearth and taste it. I know I have never been of service to anyone in anything, but also not much to myself. . . . I thank you for the friendly help you give me—who am not strong. My love to Jaś; tell him that I did not allow them, or rather that they were not permitted, to bleed me; that I wear vesicants, that I am coughing very little in the morning, and that I am not yet at all looked upon as a consumptive person. I drink neither coffee nor wine, but milk. Lastly, I keep myself warm, and look like a young woman.

(Chopin signed his letters to Fontana "F.", or "F.Ch.," or sometimes "Fryc" as he did to his family and Grzymała. To others, he signed "Chopin," "Fr. Chopin," "F.Chopin," or "F.Ch.")

On March 6, four days later, Chopin informed Fontana: "My health is still improving; I begin to play, eat, walk, and speak, like other men; and when you receive these few words from me, you will see that I again write with ease. But once more to business . . ." This particular business was Chopin's desire that the Préludes be dedicated to Pleyel, the new ballade to Robert Schumann, and the polonaises to Fontana. But he added that "if Pleyel does not like to give up the dedication of the Ballade, you will dedicate the Préludes to Schumann."

On March 10, Chopin's letter to Fontana took the form of an attack on his friend and publisher Camille Pleyel, starting with the remark: "I did not expect Jewish tricks from Pleyel." Concerning the amounts of payments for the ballade and the polonaises for publication in France and elsewhere in Europe, Chopin instructed Fontana to take them to Adolf Schlesinger, "should Pleyel make the least difficulties." He wrote that "Schlesinger used to cheat me, he gained enough from me, and he will not reject new profit—only be polite to him. Though a Jew, he nevertheless wishes to pass for something better. . . . Dear me! This Pleyel who is such an admirer of mine! He thinks, perhaps, that I shall never return to Paris alive. I shall come back and shall pay him a visit."

Two days later, however, Chopin sent Pleyel an astonishing letter to express his "regrets" that "Fontana had disturbed you with my problems." He wrote that "I thought I was authorized to direct him to you because you had proposed to publish my compositions. I am writing him today not to trouble you anymore." And Fryderyk added that he was saddened upon hearing from Fontana that Pleyel had been ill.

Scheming intricate strategies to play one publisher against another—though all of them were his friends (or thought they were), and hurling ugly epithets—this was Chopin at his most unattractive, a facet of his personality noted by very few. In a March 17 letter to Fontana, he called Pleyel "a scoundrel," and announced that "I prefer to deal with a real Jew. . . . I prefer being submissive to one Jew to being so to three [Jews]. Therefore go to Schlesinger, but perhaps you have [already] settled with Pleyel." In his next letter, Chopin ordered: "As they are such Jews, keep everything until my return," but, most confusedly, also advised Fontana that he had sold the Préludes to Pleyel, and that the ballade and the polonaises should not, after all, be sold to Schlesinger. A few weeks later, Fryderyk instructed Fontana to "hide my manuscripts (so) that they may not appear in print before time. If the Préludes are printed, that is Pleyel's trick.

But I do not care. Mischevious Germans, rascally Jews. . . ! Finish the litany, for you know them as well as I do."

At that stage, Chopin appeared to have turned entirely irrational in his relationships with his friends, the publishers. Urgently needing money, Fryderyk repeatedly asked Grzymała to advance him five hundred francs, and this anxiety may have accounted in part for his behavior. But he poured sarcasm and bitterness on other friends, too, including Antoni Wodziński, the brother of his erstwhile fiancée Maria, who had been fighting in the Spanish civil war (as many Poles did) and borrowing money from Fryderyk. Writing Fontana, he remarked, apropos of nothing, that "it is not likely that we shall have news soon from Antoni. Why should he write? Perhaps to pay his debts? But this is not customary in Poland."

Yet, Chopin showed care and concern for still other friends. He wrote about his sadness upon learning in April that Jaś Matuszyński had become gravely ill and was spitting blood. Familiar with the symptoms, Fryderyk concluded that Jaś, a physician, was suffering from consumption as well; they had often discussed the disease when they shared the first apartment on the Chaussée d'Antin.

Chopin's own health, however, had improved to the point where Dr. Cauvière approved the plan proposed by George Sand for a short visit to Genoa. Despite his intense interest in Italian music and things Italian—he once wrote a letter to George in excellent Italian—Fryderyk had never visited Italy, and he was anxious to make the trip.

On May 3, Chopin, Sand, and her son, Maurice, sailed from Marseilles to Genoa on a remarkably beautiful day. For George, it was something of a sentimental journey. She had gone there with Musset five years earlier on their way to Venice, and now it was another romantic foray—with her latest beloved. They spent twelve days in Genoa, with George as the cicerone, and with Fryderyk attending opera at least once—and filling his ears with Italian street music.

The return crossing to Marseilles was another adventure for Chopin. As Sand wrote Charlotte Marliani, "we have just arrived from Genoa in a terrible storm. The bad weather kept us on the sea double the ordinary time; forty hours of rolling such as I have not seen for a long time." Fryderyk suffered from seasickness, but George reported to Grzymała that "our little one gave proof of courage and I think he should demand a medal."

Portrait of Ludwika Chopin, Chopin's older
sister, painted in 1829 by Ambrozy
Mieroszewski, before her marriage to
Kalasanty Jędrzejewicz. Oil on canvas.

(Collection of Fryderyk Chopin Society, Warsaw)

Portrait of Izabela Chopin,
Chopin's younger sister, painted in 1820
by Ambrozy Mieroszewski. Oil on canvas.

(Collection of Fryderyk Chopin Society, Warsaw)

Portrait of Emilia Chopin,
Chopin's youngest sister, who died
as a child. Aquarelle and gouache
miniature on ivory by unknown artist.

(Collection of Fryderyk Chopin Society, Warsaw)

Portrait of Fryderyk Chopin painted
in Vienna in 1831 (when Chopin
was twenty-one) by an unknown artist
of the Waldmüller School.
(Collection of Fryderyk Chopin Society, Warsaw)

Lithograph of Ferenc Liszt by R. Weiss,
from drawing by Ary Scheffer.
(Collection of Fryderyk Chopin Society, Warsaw)

Three pages from Chopin's "Diary," written in Stuttgart in September 1831 upon learning of the fall of Warsaw to the Russians. This is the first documented example of Chopin's hallucinations. These consecutive pages are also known as the "Stuttgart Diary." The diary was destroyed in Warsaw during World War II. Reproductions have survived. (Collection of Fryderyk Chopin Society, Warsaw)

Portrait of Justyna Chopin, Chopin's mother.
Reconstruction of 1829 oil on canvas
painting by Ambrozy Mieroszewski.
(Collection of Fryderyk Chopin Society, Warsaw)

Portrait of Mikołaj Chopin, Chopin's father.
Reconstruction of 1829 oil on canvas
painting by Ambrozy Mieroszewski.
(Collection of Fryderyk Chopin Society, Warsaw)

Portrait of Maria Wodzińska. Miniature
by Anna Chamiec, according to pencil
self-drawing by Maria Wodzińska.
(Collection of Fryderyk Chopin Society, Warsaw)

Mezzotint of George Sand in 1839
by N. E.-J. Desmadril, according to
oil painting by A. Charpentier.
(Collection of Fryderyk Chopin Society, Warsaw)

Drawing of George Sand's children,
Solange and Maurice, by Nancy Merienne.
(Collection of Musées de la Ville de Paris)

Fryderyk Chopin photographed
during the final years of his life
(1847–1849?) by L. A. Bisson.
This is the only known photograph
of Chopin extant. (Collection of
Fryderyk Chopin Society, Warsaw)

First page of Chopin's Polonaise in G minor, composed when he was seven years old; probably his first composition. It was first published in Warsaw in 1817 by I. J. Cybulski. It was republished in 1990 by the Fryderyk Chopin Society of Warsaw and Green Peace Publishers in Tokyo. This is a virtually unknown composition, never before published in the U.S.

(Collection of Fryderyk Chopin Society, Warsaw)

Second page of the Polonaise in G minor.

(Collection of Fryderyk Chopin Society, Warsaw)

Photograph of Julian Fontana, circa 1850.
Fontana was one of Chopin's closest Polish
friends, copyist of his musical manuscripts,
and publisher of his posthumous works.
(Collection of Fryderyk Chopin Society, Warsaw)

Lithograph of portrait of Wojciech
Grzymała, Chopin's close friend in Paris,
by F. Villain from drawing by Ch. L. Bazin.
(Collection of Jagiellonian Library,
Jagiellonian University, Krakow, Poland)

Miniature portrait of Jane W. Stirling
by Anne Chamiec from the 1842
lithograph by J. J. M.-Deveri.
(Collection of Fryderyk Chopin Society, Warsaw)

George Sand half of the Sand-Chopin
portrait by Eugène Delacroix.
Oil on canvas, painted in 1838.
(Collection of Ordrupgaard, Copenhagen)

Fryderyk Chopin half of
the Sand-Chopin portrait
by Eugène Delacroix.
(Collection of the Louvre)

Chapter 17

ON MAY 22, after three months in Marseilles, Chopin, Sand, and her children left for Nohant on a slow journey during which, as George put it, "we would sleep at the inns like good bourgeois." Traveling by stages, they first sailed aboard a barge up the Rhône to Arles, the town in Provence the Romans had first made into a civilized settlement. After two days in Arles, the four of them, now joined by Jules Boucoiran, the children's tutor and George's old friend (and probably occasional lover), continued by carriage for a full week before reaching the Berry region. It was June 1, 1839, when Chopin finally saw Nohant.

Berry is as old as France itself, a countryside in its very heart that has not changed meaningfully over the centuries. The village of Nohant dates back to the start of the first millennium. Farming there began in the days when the Romans held that part of Gaul. The frescoes in Nohant's tiny Romanesque church are from the twelfth century. A castle near Sand's house was built by Guy III de Chauvigny in the fifteenth century; most of the numerous old castles dotting Berry were erected in the fourteenth and fifteenth centuries. George's home, called perhaps a bit grandly a château, was constructed in the eighteenth century atop ancient ruins.

The Berry landscape is mainly flat and rather desolate. It dips to form what Sand described as the "Black Valley"—it turns "violet and almost black on stormy days"—where Nohant is located. She had written about "the immensity of this abyss of dark greenery, delineated on the horizon by the blue mountains of La Marche." The entire valley, George said, could be seen "in one glance" from the roofs of Nohant's thatched huts. The Indre flows just south of Nohant and the Creuse meanders to the north (one of Berry's curiosities in her day was the Atlantic salmon that could be caught and eaten there, so far inland, having swum up the Loire and then the Creuse from the ocean).

Quite remarkably, the Berry country resembles very much the monotonous countryside around Żelazowa Wola in central Poland where Chopin was born. No wonder Fryderyk felt at home, serene and secure in Nohant from the first moment.

The *Berrichons,* the peasants and the small nobility of Berry, also reminded him of the people of Mazovia, the land of the mazurka. "Berry," Sand wrote, "is not endowed with a nature of *éclat*"—brilliancy. "Neither the landscape nor the inhabitants jump to the eye for their picturesque side [and] a trenchant character. It is the motherland of calm and *sang-froid.* Men and plants, everything there is tranquil, patient, slow to ripen. Do not look there for great effects nor great passions. . . . In many places [there is] great repugnance toward progress. . . . In Berry, prudence becomes suspicion." Again, Berry reminded Chopin of Mazovia.

At the same time, Berry had a profound sense of its own identity—almost local patriotism for what the French call "La Petite Patrie"—both among the peasants and the gentry. The farmers were quietly proud. The gentry and, especially, the jeunesse dorée of Berry knew how to assert their presence at home and beyond. Most of Sand's friends lived in the old castles between Sainte-Sévère in the south and Châteauroux in the north (she had met Jules Sandeau at the château of Coudray). Many made their homes in the town of La Châtre, some eight miles south of Nohant, where George galloped on her white mare almost every day. La Châtre was the center of social activity for her set of young, affluent, and sometimes talented friends. They all visited one another often for meals, drinking, dancing, conversation, and discreet lovemaking, and Sand's most devoted lifetime friendships came from Berry. When she first alighted in Paris, she found in the Club des Berrichons de Paris her unquestioning support group. The Berry gentry, Chopin soon discovered, was not all that different from the Polish gentry.

George used both the people and the locales of Berry as themes for her novels. Thus Mers-sur-Indre served as a backdrop for *La Mare au diable,* Montipouret appeared in *François le Champi* and *Le Meunier d'Angibault,* Briantes was the château in *Les Beaux Messieurs de Bois-Doré,* Pouligny-Saint-Martin and Sainte-Sévère were the scene for *Mauprat,* and Crevant was the village depicted in *Nanon*. Given Sand's amazing literary output, she was always looking voraciously for descriptive material, and Berry was a natural and marvelous source of research for her.

George Sand's Nohant "château," a graceful two-story house across a small cobblestone square from the village's Romanesque church, was the nearest thing to a family home Chopin had enjoyed since he left Warsaw almost nine years earlier. And it was the first time he had ever lived with a woman in a situation of virtual marriage under fairly normal circumstances; their stay together in Majorca and in Barcelona and Marseilles hotels hardly qualified as normal. Besides, George and Fryderyk were fully accepted by the Berrichon society (she made him acceptable), and no longer the "pariahs" of the Majorcan days. Only Chopin's relations with Maurice remained difficult—the boy, perhaps still thinking of his father far away at his Guillery domain in Gascony, went on resisting Fryderyk. But Solange was already developing a girlish crush on her "stepfather."

Chopin had never been as comfortable as an adult as he now was in Nohant. His big, bright bedroom on the second floor, facing the south, gave him a lovely view of the park, full of plants and flowers, in the back of the house and the fields beyond it. (Liszt once had that room.) George's own bedroom was also on the second floor; their rooms were separated by a library with interconnecting doors. A large sitting room, the dining room, the children's rooms, the guest rooms, and the kitchen were on the ground floor. The servants lived in the two attic rooms. The front entrance to the house faced a large yard planted with trees and protected by a wall. A grillwork portal opened to let carriages, horses, and people in and out of the property. The road leading southeast to La Châtre and northwest to Châteauroux ran behind the park (George's love-nest *pavillion* was at the edge of the park, just off the highway).

Fryderyk was absolutely free to do what and as he pleased: His only obligation was to join the family—and frequent guests—for dinner at five o'clock in the afternoon. George had arranged beforehand to have a Pleyel piano placed in his bedroom (there was another piano and a harpsichord in the sitting room), and Chopin kept his own schedule, which meant spending most of the time daily working upstairs. George's preference was to stay up writing all night, and the two often did not see each other at all until dinner, although she was busy much of the daytime with the running of the house and teaching Maurice and Solange (she had let Boucoiran go).

In this environment, Chopin's health was getting better and better every day and in every way. Dr. Gustave Papet, an outstanding young physician and friend of Sand, had agreed to look after Fryderyk full-time. Extremely wealthy, the twenty-seven-year-old Papet lived at d'Ars castle, less than two miles from Nohant, and was a frequent and watchful visitor (he practiced medicine for the sake of helping people, not to earn a living). Examining Chopin immediately after his arrival in Nohant, Dr. Papet pronounced him free of consumption—he found his "breast" to be "intact"—and concluded that Fryderyk's continuing weakness and cough were caused by bronchial illness that was incurable, but could be remedied through "successful medication." Dr. Papet expressed the belief that his patient would recover in time "nearly good health," and noted that, in the meantime, Chopin "falls asleep at the same time as Maurice and Solange" after their dinner.

At first, Fryderyk was in a great mood. He wrote Grzymała on June 2, the day after he reached Nohant, that "the countryside is beautiful; nightingales, swallows—only you, bird, are missing," and urged him to visit them "for at least a while . . . Pick a time when all are healthy and able to dedicate themselves to you as befits one's fellow man. Let us embrace, and I shall give you delicious milk [and] pills. You shall have my piano at your disposal. You will not go for want of anything."

Chopin spent the next five weeks repeating his invitation to Grzymała, but also, increasingly, charging him with errands. He asked Grzymała to bring with him silverware from his Chaussée d'Antin apartment, then to remember to bring him shoes, and to tell Fontana "to give you Weber's book for four hands from *Pièces faciles.*" In a July letter, Chopin reminded Grzymała to "command Jaś [Matuszyński] to give you two or three pair of my shoes from the big wardrobe." George had also invited Matuszyński to come to Nohant to see how her "thin man" was convalescing, but the Polish doctor was already too ill himself to travel.

But Chopin's most urgent instructions to Grzymała were to mail his letters to his family in Warsaw from Paris and to see whether any letters had arrived for him from Poland at Matuszyński's address. Chopin could not bring himself to inform his parents about his life with George Sand, sending letters from Majorca, Marseilles, and then Nohant to Grzymała in Paris to be mailed to Warsaw. Whether out of fear of commitment or to avoid censure for living out of wedlock with a woman or for some other reason, Chopin maintained this deception for at least three years.

Content and comfortable as he seemed to be in Nohant, Fryderyk was soon becoming impatient and relapsing into violent mood swings. His impatience took the form of the stream of invitations to Grzymała—and all the instructions that went with them—and Chopin's obsessive craving for the companionship of Poles and the sound of the Polish language around him. Except for a brief visit in Majorca in February by Karol Dębowski, an acquaintance, Fryderyk had not seen or heard a Pole since he left Paris late in October, obviously a major deprivation.

In July, he was saved from the around-the-clock siege of French by a short visit by his old friend, the poet Stefan Witwicki, whose poems he had often set, helping to create memorable patriotic and sentimental songs. Fryderyk no longer set Witwicki's verses, but now dedicated to him the mazurkas he had produced in Majorca. Grzymała turned up at long last in mid-August, and Chopin regained a bit of his good disposition. But when Tytus Woyciechowski, the most beloved of his friends, wrote that he had built a sugar refinery on his Poturzyn estate—and urged him to compose an oratorio—Chopin reacted with considerable irritation. Even though Tytus had just named his second son, Fryderyk, after him, Chopin sarcastically asked his parents in Warsaw "why he set up a sugar factory and not a convent for Camaldolese fathers or Dominican sisters. . . . Poor Tytus still holds on to his lyceum dreams, which does not keep me from loving him just as I did at the lyceum."

George Sand began to worry about Chopin's "melancholy," which to her meant depression, mentioning it in a letter to Grzymała a month before his arrival in Nohant. She also wondered whether Fryderyk "was not in need of a little less of the calm, solitude, and regularity that life in Nohant imposes." This, of course, contradicted her belief in Majorca—which she had initially regarded as the "promised land" as well—that what Chopin needed was peace and quiet, and good food. But, inevitably, Sand was reflecting Fryderyk's moods, his ever-growing impatience and inability to accept any manner of permanence in his life. He always seemed driven by dark, inner forces—even in the sunshine of Nohant and the love of the woman he persisted in calling "Aurora," and never "Aurore" or "George." Perhaps he could not accept love.

Certainly, Chopin could not accept what he felt fell short of perfection in his music. Listening to him struggle hour after hour and day after day with the chords of Scherzo no. 3, which he had first sketched in Valldemossa, Sand confessed her amazement over "this obstinate battle with the language of incommunicability. . . . It was a sequence of efforts, irresolutions, and impatience to recapture certain details of the theme of his composition." She deplored that Chopin would not keep intact "that which he had conceived as a whole." While understanding much of the essence of his music, George could not comprehend his total perfectionism.

Occupied as she was with Chopin, her children, and Nohant, George, too, craved Parisian visitors. Liszt and Marie d'Agoult no longer came to see her because the two women had allowed their friendship to fray over mutual suspicions, jealousies, and recriminations. But that summer Emmanuel Arago, one of Sand's political friends, came down to Nohant at the same time as Grzymała. François Buloz, director of the Théâtre Français and the editor of the *Revue des deux mondes,* which published Sand's articles and novels in serial form, dropped in with his wife for a few days (and, George noted, got drunk on "the worst possible wine").

Sand believed, as she had written another friend, that the voyage from Paris to Nohant was "simple" and "not tiring," but it was a thirty-hour expedition. The post coach left Paris at seven o'clock in the evening, traveled all night for a six o'clock breakfast in Orléans on the Loire, and stopped for a four o'clock dinner at Vierzon. An hour later, another carriage took passengers to Châteauroux, arriving there at nine o'clock in the evening. Finally, a smaller carriage delivered the visitors to Nohant four hours later.

In any case, Grzymała and Arago, both quite corpulent, survived the trip, enjoying Nohant hospitality for two weeks. Chopin and Grzymała spent hours on end chatting in Polish to the great amusement of Maurice and Solange, who vainly tried to imitate the rolling *rrr* of Polish words. The two men were gone by the end of August, and Fryderyk and George again had to face life alone. Apart from Dr. Papet, Chopin's only real Berry friend was, improbably, the hard-drinking, foul-mouthed Hippolyte Châtiron, George's half brother and a neighbor. He adored Hippolyte's scandalous storytelling.

It is impossible to know how their emotional and sexual relationship was developing that first summer in Nohant. George had inscribed the date "19 June 1839" on the wall of her bedroom, and biographers have speculated that it marked the night of their first lovemaking at her ancestral home. But such clues could be misleading. Chopin wrote in his diary two days after they left Nohant for Paris in October:

> the eyes of Aurora are veiled; they shine only when I play, and then the world is clear and beautiful. My fingers glide softly over the keyboard, her pen flies over the paper. She can write while listening to music . . . the music of Chopin, sweet but as clear as words of love. For you, Aurora, I would lie on the ground. Nothing would be too much for me, I shall give you all! A glance, a caress from you, a smile from you when I am tired. I do not want to live except for you: For you, I want to play sweet melodies. Will you not be too cruel, darling, with your veiled eyes?

Even in a diary, this was unusually emotional language for Chopin, who preferred to express his sentiments through music. But it may have been no more than Platonic language. André Maurois goes even further in his interpretation. He writes that Chopin's accusation of "cruelty" against her related to her efforts to encourage him to engage in sex. "The experience of Majorca," Maurois goes on, "and [Chopin's] relapse, so grave, that followed it, had proved to George that Chopin was not made for pleasures of love. Always ill, he could not stand them, and, despite her supplications, 'Aurora' very soon adopted a moderation that subsequently became total abstention." Maurois obviously assumed that Chopin and Sand had at least one sexual experience in Majorca.

After they broke up in 1847, Sand would write Grzymała that "for seven years I have lived like a virgin with him and with others. I have aged before time. . . . If a woman on earth should have inspired absolute confidence in him, it was me, and he never understood it. . . . He complains to me that I have killed him through deprivation while I had the certitude of killing him if I had acted differently."

As the autumn approached, Chopin's impatience in Nohant grew apace. Sand observed that "he always wanted Nohant and he never accepted Nohant. . . . His countryside desires were quickly satisfied. He strolled a little, installed himself under a tree, or picked some flowers. Then he went back to lock himself in his room."

Fryderyk's mind was now firmly centered on Paris, and he submitted faithful Fontana and Grzymała to fusillades of missives concerning apartments for himself and George and her children. Not only was he getting restless in Nohant, but he was anxious to resume giving piano lessons in Paris to start earning more money again; the payments by the publishers were nowhere adequate to finance Chopin's lifestyle.

In a letter to Fontana on August 8, Chopin confined himself to bringing him up to date on his composing, a subject he rarely mentioned, except when it involved his strategies for dealing with publishers. "I am composing here the Sonata in B-flat minor," he wrote, "in which will be the [Funeral] March that you already know. There is an Allegro, then Scherzo in E-flat minor, the March and a little Finale, perhaps three of my pages; the left hand *unisono* and the right [hand] are chatting after the March."

Chopin also told Fontana: "I have a new *Notturno* in G major, which will go together with the [Nocturne] in G minor, if you remember." The G minor had been written when Fryderyk first came to live in Paris, and he included the four opening bars in the letter to refresh Fontana's memory. The G major was one of Chopin's great nocturnes as well as a most complicated experiment with a three-bar period (instead of the usual four-bar period), the left hand running ahead of the right and producing the effect of a fluid motion that enhances a barcarolle character. It is a composition in compound double or quadruple time. Chopin, of course, loved to experiment and innovate.

He informed Fontana: "As you know, I have four new mazurkas, one from Palma in E minor, three from here—B major, A-flat major, and C-sharp minor." They formed the Four Mazurkas Opus 41, and Fryderyk added: "It seems to me that they are pretty, as the youngest children usually are when the parents grow old."

Chopin had received in Nohant a new piano from Pleyel, a better one than the instrument he had found on arrival, and he amused himself correcting the Parisian edition of Bach's works, "not only the errors of the engravers, but also the accepted errors of those who supposedly understood Bach—not pretending that I understand better, but from the conviction that, sometimes, I can guess. . . . So I have bragged to you."

Chopin urgently raised the matter of Paris apartments in late August and September letters to Fontana and Grzymała, after he and Sand had decided that, at least for a time, they should live separately. Thus Fontana and Grzymała were charged with finding two sets of lodgings. On September 20, Fryderyk asked Grzymała to rent a small apartment for him, "but if it is too late, take a large one." Concerning housing for Sand and the children, Chopin instructed him not to exceed the rent she was prepared to pay (he remarked that he could not convince her that it is better to pay a bit more than "to have many tenants in the house").

Sand added a postscript, suggesting that, after all, they may live together: "It is not necessary for all the rooms to be big and beautiful . . . the children's rooms, for example, could be small, provided they have fireplaces, and the rooms for adults should face south. . . . This is very important for the little one and because of my rheumatism. Besides, I do not need an excessively big or beautiful salon as I never receive more than twelve persons."

The following day, Chopin authorized Fontana to rent for him an apartment at 5, rue Tronchet, a few hundred yards from the new St. Madeleine's church on the Right Bank. He wrote that he had liked very much Fontana's description of it; the two men were exchanging letters almost daily, but most of Fontana's have disappeared. Three days later, Fryderyk asked Fontana to select wallpaper for the new apartment that would resemble the dove-colored wallpaper he had at the Chaussée d'Antin, but brighter and glossier for the two rooms (presumably bed-room and parlor), with a dark green stripe for the top. For the ante-room, Chopin wanted something different, but "respectable." However, he told Fontana that he should get "more beautiful and fashionable wallpaper, if you like it—and you know what I would like."

Devoted to comfort, beauty, and detail, Fryderyk went on to thank Fontana for finding an apartment that had a room for a servant, then turned to furniture, proposing that his bed and writing desk be sent to a cabinetmaker to restore them. He announced that he was requesting Grzymała to pay for the moving of the furniture to the new apartment, and asked Fontana to "smell out a servant, some decent, orderly Pole." Chopin also wished the "elastic" mattress of his bed be repaired, "if it is not too expensive," and to have the chairs "beaten" for cleanliness.

A letter on September 29 told Grzymała that Sand was worried that he had "forgotten" about *her* apartment, and that "if Fontana can be helpful in providing any service, errands, or running around, use him!" On the same day, Chopin explained to Fontana where, in the new apart-ment, he should hang the drapes from his old home, fitting muslin cur-tains under the bedroom drapes. In what was a full-fledged interior decorator's set of marching orders, Fryderyk suggested placing a cabinet between the windows in the parlor, and recovering in white fabric the red sofa from the dining room and installing it in the parlor. In one of his habitual attempts at playful bonhomie with his exhausted friend, he ended this particular letter by urging Fontana to "take a bath in a whale's infusion to rest from all the errands I impose on you because I know that, if time permits, you will gladly run [errands] for me, as I would gladly do for you when you get married."

Fontana and Grzymała finally secured the rue Tronchet apartment for Chopin. But now he and Sand came up with the notion that she and the children should live in an elegant *pavillon,* or villa, with a garden or a large courtyard. She was willing to pay 2,500 francs or more monthly, and Fontana was charged with finding just such a place. Chopin had also written Grzymała and Arago about it. In a letter on October 1, Fryderyk said that he would prefer if Sand's lodgings were near his apartment. In a most detailed request for a house with three bedrooms, a parlor, dining room, servants' room, and a basement, Chopin, the perfectionist, enclosed a diagram to show how they wished the rooms to be arranged in the villa. Parquet floors had to be new, staircases "decent," and the house absolutely had to have southern exposure. It had to be a quiet neighborhood: "no blacksmiths, no young women, if you know what I mean . . . no smells . . . no smoke."

On October 3, Chopin advised Fontana that they would be arriving in Paris the following week, adding that among all the other errands, he had forgotten to ask him to order a hat from his hatmaker Dupont, who "has my measurements and knows how light [a hat] I need. . . . Let him make it according to this year's fashion, without exaggeration, because I no longer know how you all now dress." Next, Fontana was to order gray trousers for Chopin from his tailor Dautremont, on the main boulevard, who "will be happy to learn that I am arriving." The tailor was also to make a "black, modest, velour vest." The servant, Fryderyk wrote, should charge less than eighty francs monthly, "perhaps sixty." Chopin closed the letter asking, "in the name of God, do not tell the Polish community, or any Jewess [Madame Léo], that I am coming so soon. . . . I am counting on finding the apartment when I arrive."

Fontana had to be a true magician because he was able to find for Sand two *pavillons* at the far end of a garden behind the apartment building on 16, rue Pigalle in the Montmartre section of the Right Bank, not far from the Chaussée d'Antin. One of the *pavillons* was to serve as a painter's studio for Maurice. Chopin thanked Fontana effusively, adding that Sand "considers you my most logical, best . . . most splenetic English-Polish beloved friend." Fontana had once lived in London, New York, and Havana; his London stay made George think of him as "English."

Fryderyk, however, always needed more attention. On October 8, again displaying his obsessive orderliness, he wrote Fontana to make sure that the new servant, a Frenchman named Tineau (no Pole could be found for the moment), would await him at rue Tronchet on Friday, the day he was to arrive, exactly at noon. He also wanted to be sure that the tailor would have the gray trousers and the vest ready on Friday and have them delivered to rue Tronchet "so that I can change [clothes] immediately." He promised Fontana that, in gratitude, he would keep rewriting "until my death" the polonaise he had dedicated to him: "You may not like yesterday's version, although I forced my brain for some eighty seconds."

Chopin, Sand, and her children reached Paris on October 11, after spending a night at Orléans. He went directly to rue Tronchet, but George, Maurice, and Solange had to stay with the Marlianis and other friends until the rue Pigalle *pavillons* were ready. Once George and the children moved into the *pavillons,* early in 1840, Fryderyk began spending most of his time there, including nights, and even receiving his students on rue Pigalle. Some of his aristocratic women students had refused at first to come for lessons to a middle-class neighborhood, but Chopin, as usual, had his haughty way. George Sand recalled his answer: "Ladies, I give much better lessons in my own room on my own piano for twenty francs than I do for thirty at my pupils' homes, and, besides, you have to send your carriages to fetch me. So take your choice!"

Chapter 18

THAT THE STUDENTS—the aristocratic daughters from Faubourg St. Honoré and Faubourg St. Germain, and young Polish emigrés—chose to come to Chopin for their lessons when he returned to Paris was no great surprise. Having taught the piano there for eight years, he had now attained the pinnacle of recognition as one of the greatest pianists and teachers of his time, as well as an enormously admired composer. Only Liszt could claim comparable artistry in all three realms, but in truth he did not possess Chopin's extraordinary pedagogic gifts—and he knew it. Yet, curiously, he succeeded better than Chopin in molding pupils into famous virtuosos. "Chopin was unfortunate in his pupils," Liszt, his friendly rival, once remarked. "None of them has become a player of any importance."

Though teaching was Fryderyk's principal source of revenue, far exceeding the income from his published compositions, he was extremely selective in accepting pupils. He far preferred "professional" pianists and very advanced students (for what today would be called master classes), albeit he took on highly talented "amateurs," and fellow Poles enjoyed priorities. Children were excluded as a matter of principle, but there were two striking exceptions: Carl Filtsch, a German-Hungarian music prodigy, whom Chopin agreed to teach when the boy was eleven—he sensed genius and saw himself in Carl—but the boy died from consumption at fifteen; and Adolf Gutmann, whom he regarded as his favorite pupil and started instructing when he arrived from his native Germany at fifteen. In general, Chopin was partial to female candidates for pupils.

To be Chopin's pupil was a mark of distinction, and Fryderyk was generous enough not to embarrass those who claimed, falsely, to have received his tutelage. "I have not given him any lessons," Chopin said about an unnamed person, "but if it may be useful to him to pass for my pupil, leave him in peace."

Jean-Jacques Eigeldinger, a leading Chopin scholar, estimates that between 1832 and 1849, the years spanning his Parisian period and his death, Fryderyk probably had around 150 students, "if by pupil one understands every person who has benefited from his advice," although "this number is certainly below reality." Chopin kept no records, and the only surviving trace of his lessons is a page from his pocket notebook listing students over six days of his London stay in 1848, a year before he died. There also exists a list of twenty pupils and their parents, obviously very far from complete, made by his Scottish student, friend, and sponsor Jane Wilhelmina Stirling sometime in the late 1840s.

The most helpful aid in reconstructing Chopin's teaching years, however, is the rich repository of remembrances by his students contained in volumes of memoirs and correspondence, ranging from Princess Marcelina Czartoryska to Wilhelm von Lenz, his most faithful interpreters in his lifetime. Their accounts, on the whole, are remarkably consistent in praising Chopin's teaching methods and recounting his occasionally strange behavior. But they also record his collapsing health. Friedrike Müller Streicher, who studied with him on rue Tronchet in 1839, remembered: "Alas! he suffered greatly. Feeble, pale, coughing much, he often took opium drops in sugar and gum-water, rubbed his forehead with eau de cologne, and nevertheless he taught with a patience, perseverance, and zeal which were admirable."

Teaching usually between October or November and May (students tended to be away from Paris during the warm months), Chopin received on the average five pupils daily at twenty francs per hour, according to Eigeldinger, although it must have been greatly reduced in the closing years of his life, when he taught reclining on a sofa, no longer able to stand or pace the room. Still, numbers do not tell the whole story of Chopin's teaching activities.

A handful of outstanding pupils, such as Princess Czartoryska, Gutmann, or Filtsch, worked with Chopin over periods as long as four or five years. But there also was the "lady from Liverpool," who rushed to London when he was there to be taught piano virtuosity in a week. The total of what Eigeldinger calls "professionals"—accomplished pianists such as Karol Mikuli or Madame Camille O'Meara Dubois—did not exceed twenty over the sixteen years of Chopin's professorship. Normally, he received a pupil once a week, and even Filtsch, the boy prodigy, was limited to three lessons weekly. But carried away by a particularly favored pupil or his good disposition on a given day, Fryderyk often allowed a lesson to run for many hours (the normal duration was between forty-five minutes and one hour), especially on Sundays. Then, he would play for or with his students, sometimes improvising.

Dividing his time fairly equally between teaching and composing after the return from Majorca—he called this schedule a "mill" to describe his "lucrative" hours—Chopin rose early to devote the entire morning and the first part of the afternoon to his pupils. Composing came later in the afternoon and at night, even if he went out for the evening, which was still frequent. This was an extremely heavy load, particularly as his health kept deteriorating, and by 1845, most of his composing was accomplished during the summers in Nohant. Chopin wrote from Nohant at one point: "It is impossible for me to compose during the winter," because it was too difficult in Paris, what with his teaching duties, bad weather, and social life. But he had no alternatives after his rupture with George Sand two years later.

Both as teacher and as composer, Chopin was a perfectionist and a firm believer in classical methods. Perhaps because his own musical education as a child and as a teenager appears to have been haphazard, Fryderyk was determined to give his pupils the most profound and superb education at the keyboard—the hard way. Chopin, of course, was widely believed to have been essentially self-taught at the piano, his mother being an amateur and his first music teacher, Żywny, a violinist. However, Zieliński, does not believe it possible that "a pianist-technician of such promise like young Chopin, soon to compete with the greatest virtuosi of his era, could have been self-taught, not guided by anyone and not taking advantage of anybody's experience." Zieliński's theory is that Fryderyk was actually taught by Wilhelm Wacław Würfel, a Czech-born musician of distinction who had settled in Warsaw and become a friend of the Chopin family. Würfel, according to Zieliński, had taught Fryderyk to play the organ in the latter's adolescence, but there is nothing to document the suggestion that earlier he had instructed him on the piano.

Zielinski acknowledges that there is nothing beyond a vague reference to Chopin as "Würfel's student" in an article in *Allgemeine Musikalische Zeitung* in 1829, when Fryderyk was nineteen, but he is convinced that Würfel was his teacher.

As a teacher himself, Chopin first had his students exercise with piano studies by earlier great teachers, especially Muzio Clementi (who had taught Field and Kalkbrenner, among other stars of the day), whose *Gradus ad Parnassum* was well known to pianists, and Johann Baptist Cramer, whose études remain among the acclaimed piano studies. And, of course, Chopin had his pupils practice preludes and fugues by Bach, whom he so deeply admired and whose works he played himself almost every day.

It is a mystery, however, why he never had his pupils play works by Mozart, the other figure he venerated, during their lessons. None of his students who have described their experiences with Chopin in letters and memoirs mention playing Mozart for him. He had them perform compositions by musicians of the contemporary era—Beethoven, Weber, Field, and Moscheles—but only rarely, and only with very special pupils, did Chopin encourage the playing of his own creations; when he did, he usually chose nocturnes.

Chopin followed all the classic precepts in teaching, but he had innovative ideas of his own as well. Enamored of the sound of the human voice (Eigeldinger writes that for Fryderyk "singing constitutes the *alpha* and *omega* of music"), he urged his pupils to listen as often as possible to the great opera singers. Chopin went as far as to tell Vera de Kologrivof Rubio that "you must sing if you wish to play," and made her take singing lessons. Conversely, he kept repeating tirelessly, "You must sing with your fingers!" as recalled by Émilie von Timm Gretsch, a young Latvian whom Fryderyk liked very much (she received thirty-three lessons, including some lasting several hours, hearing virtually all his compositions).

Chopin was a teacher totally involved with his students and, as long as he could move with relative ease in his apartment, he sat at a small upright "pianino" (the English called it a "cottage piano"), playing together with the pupil sitting next to him at the Pleyel grand, or playing passages alone to demonstrate whatever musical point he had in mind. Mikuli, who graduated from Chopin's pupil to become a teacher himself and then a Chopin scholar, wrote that "it was with veritable joy that he devoted all his strength to teaching several hours a day. . . . His demands, so difficult to satisfy, the feverish passion with which the Maestro tried to raise his disciples to his level, the obstinacy he used to make a passage repeated until it was understood, were proof of how much he took to heart the progress of a student. . . . A holy artistic zeal burned in him, and every word from his lips was stimulating and a source of enthusiasm."

Although the normally mild-mannered Chopin was prone to savage outbursts of irritation and anger when a pupil displeased him—these were the "stormy lessons"—Mikuli remembered that "he acted [most] efficiently, playing [for the students] not only isolated passages, but playing and replaying for them entire pieces, with scruples and perfection and a quality of inspiration that would be difficult to find to the same degree when he played at a concert."

Eigeldinger makes the crucial point that "unlike a Clementi, a Hummel, a Kalkbrenner, or a Czerny, Chopin had not created a school or instituted a pedagogic tradition. . . . It was not in his nature to impose his personality on his pupils in the sense that Liszt marked his disciples with his lion's claws. Too much of an aristocrat and poet to be a leader, Chopin was content to suggest and imply, winning devotion without any attempt to convince."

To Chopin, music was a language—in the same way that Goethe proclaimed it "the language of the inexpressible"—but he also knew how to use language to explain and explore music. As George Sand noted, "Chopin speaks little and rarely about his art, but when he does speak about it, it is with admirable clarity and certainty of judgment." In fact, he often employed the expression "*speaking* a piece of music" to describe what he was conveying through music. Chopin wrote in a preliminary essay on piano teaching that "the difficulty of playing . . . great masters is an abstract difficulty, a new kind of acrobatics," and he often told students, "Play as you feel," "Put all your soul into it," and "Easily, easily!" When a pupil played a Clementi passage carelessly, Chopin leaped out of his armchair demanding shrilly, "What is that? Is it a dog that has just barked?"

During the Paris years, Fryderyk made notes in pocket notebooks (they were found only after his death) for what he planned to be his piano "Method." Assembled subsequently and published as his "Project of a Method," the notes define his fundamental concept of music, thought, and language as "the expression of thought by sounds; the manifestation of our sentiments by sounds; the art of expressing thoughts by sounds; the expression of our perceptions by sounds; man's undefined word *is* sound; one uses sounds to make music as one uses words to make a language; indefinite language [is] music; an abstract sound does not make music just as a word does not make a language."

Chopin has spelled out these linkages of language and music with clarity and insight. Because the existence of these notes was unknown during his lifetime, only posthumously—and surprisingly to some—he would emerge as a mature musical *thinker*, although this is what he had been striving to preach all his adult life. And underscoring the importance of broad cultural interaction, so powerful at the time of the Romantic Revolution, it is more than likely that Chopin, the musician, was stimulated in his thinking by his frequent conversations about art with George Sand, the writer, and Eugène Delacroix, the painter.

Delacroix, for whom music was his second love after painting (and who played the violin as a child), recalls in his *Journal* the day when he went for a carriage drive with a very ill Chopin down the Champs-Élysées and "he talked music with me, and that gave him new animation." He writes: "I asked him what established logic in music," and Chopin "made me feel what counterpoint and harmony are; how the fugue is like pure logic in music."

Musical and mathematical aptitudes often come together. Although Chopin is not known to have had any specific interest in mathematics, or knowledge of it, his emphasis on logic in music and on science in general suggests that his mind was as orderly as a mathematician's. Such a notion had not been grasped in the early part of the nineteenth century, but Chopin was an intellectual pioneer in his own fashion as well as an inspired man. He was heir to the tradition of Leonardo da Vinci and Galileo, who saw music as the bridge between mathematics and philosophy and therefore between the sciences and the humanities. Chopin's fascination with science and its practical applications—he kept reporting the latest inventions in his letters to the family in Warsaw—were part of it. And, of course, music was a theme of philosophical speculation by Aristotle and St. Augustine (as it would later be for Hegel, Kierkegaard, Schopenhauer, and Heidegger; it is worth noting that, for example, Albert Einstein was a youthful violin virtuoso).

And Delacroix continues:

That feeling gave me an idea of the pleasure in science that is experienced by philosophers worthy of the name. . . . Science, looked upon in the way I mean, demonstrated by a man like Chopin, is art itself, and, obversely, art is no longer what the vulgar think it to be, that is, some sort of inspiration which comes from nowhere, which proceeds by chance, and presents no more than the picturesque externals of things. It is reason itself, adorned by genius, but following a necessary course and encompassed by higher laws. This brings me to the difference between Mozart and Beethoven. As [Chopin] said to me, "Where the latter is obscure and seems lacking in unity, the cause is not to be sought in what people look upon as a rather wild originality, the thing they honor him for; the reason is that he turns his back on eternal principles; Mozart never. Each of the parts has its own movement which, while still according with the others, keeps on with its own song and follows it perfectly; there is your counterpoint, *punto contrapunto.*" He told me that the custom was to learn the harmonies before coming to the counterpoint, that is to say, the succession of notes which leads to the harmonies. The harmonies in the music of Berlioz are laid on as a veneer; he fills in the intervals as best he can.

On another occasion, Delacroix spent the evening with Chopin and Grzymała, "talking music." Chopin thinks that "Beethoven was tormented by the idea of Bach. He based his work on Bach a great deal." Discussing Haydn's quartets with Chopin, the painter was told that "experience gives it that perfection which we admire. . . . Mozart did not need experience; science, with him, was always on the level of inspiration. The *Rudolphe* "Archduke" Trio, op. 97, by Beethoven [has] commonplace passages together with sublime beauties."

In terms of actual physical piano playing—a notion that for him comes ahead of complex technique proper—Chopin's foremost advice to his students was to maintain a "maximum of suppleness," relaxation, and sensitivity of hearing and touch. He also believed that there are "as many different sounds as there are fingers," and he did much to launch revolutionary fingering. He proclaimed that a pianist's whole arm must be engaged in the playing, not simply the fingers and the wrists, thereby breaking more classical rules. He insisted that the elbow be level with the white keys, "the hand turned neither to the left nor to the right." "Find the right position for the hand," Chopin wrote in his Method notes. "The long fingers will occupy the high [black] keys, and the short fingers the low [white] keys. . . . A supple hand, the wrist, the forearm, the arm, everything will follow the hand *in the right order.*"

Then he summed up: "One needs only to study a certain positioning of the hand in relation to the keys to obtain with ease the most beautiful quality of sound, to know how to play long notes and short notes and [attain] unlimited dexterity. . . . A well-formed technique, it seems to me, [is one] that can control and vary a beautiful sound quality."

Von Lenz had this recollection of Chopin's teaching piano technique: " 'The left hand,' I often heard him say, 'is the choirmaster (Kapellmeister): it mustn't relent or bend. It's a clock. Do with the right hand what you want and can.' "

Finally, Chopin warned against working piano pupils into a "stupor"; he told them never to practice more than three hours a day.

Chopin had agreed to write three études (they became known as the "Three New Etudes" to differentiate them from the earlier Opus 10 and Opus 25 Études) for the third edition of a "Piano Playing School" manual published by Moscheles, the pianist and composer, and Fétis, the music critic and publisher. Moscheles, who finally met Chopin in Paris late in October 1839 (and with whom he played before the royal family at the Tuileries Palace a few weeks later), had asked Fryderyk for the études. Chopin had rapidly developed a friendship and admiration for Moscheles (whom he once criticized) after hearing his Sonata, and Moscheles was among the first to hear Fryderyk play his Préludes Opus 28, at an evening at the home of the banker Léo. Now he obliged Moscheles by delivering the three études after two weeks, an incredible feat of speed for Chopin—études regarded as highly as those in the previous sets. It is, of course, conceivable that Fryderyk had these pieces of music lying around for a long time, waiting to be given final shape, but Moscheles and Fétis were told nothing of the sort (and Chopin sold publication rights to the first two études to Schlesinger for, respectively, two hundred and five hundred francs).

As pianist and composer, Chopin contributed to nineteenth-century music the controversial concept and technique of *tempo rubato* (literally, "stolen time") that had first emerged in the early 1720s, then dropped from sight and hearing. As defined by Eigeldinger, the Chopin scholar, rubato is "a compensatory system that consists of lengthening or shortening the value of a note to the detriment or the benefit of the next one." Rubato shifted from Italian bel canto to instrumental music, and even

Mozart became aware of it in the 1770s. The musicologist Richard Hudson observes that there were two main types of rubato: "an earlier one in which note values in a melody are altered while the accompaniment keeps strict time, and a later . . . in which the tempo of the entire musical substance fluctuates." Chopin brought back this exceedingly difficult style, practicing and teaching it in its traditional manner, producing the most extraordinary sound effects. He may have been the first to apply the earlier style of rubato, which involved two performers, to the solo piano. And he was certainly one of the few musicians in history who could do it effectively. He was much criticized for *tempo rubato* at the time, chiefly by musicians who were unable to perform it themselves.

As Chopin burst on the musical scene in the first half of the nineteenth century, he was fortunate that pianos, too, had been subject to the kind of innovations that made his music relatively easier to play. In 1821, for example, the French piano manufacturer Sébastien Erard had perfected the so-called double escapement action, which, according to Cyril Ehrlich, enabled notes to be repeated quickly without the key having to return to the full height—level with the keyboard—before restriking. Ehrlich, a scholar of the history of the piano, writes that double escapement extended the "performer's vocabulary" and made many virtuoso compositions "unthinkable without Erard."

The Erard piano, as Ehrlich observes, improved the pianist's ability to execute "certain kinds of *bravura* passages," but Chopin, much given to *bravura,* held the Pleyel piano in higher esteem (presumably not only because Camille Pleyel was a friend). Both pianos offered performers a full seven octaves on the keyboard, but Eigeldinger points out that the Erard resulted in a heavier touch. Pleyel, on the other hand, had the hammers covered with a soft and elastic skin and introduced laminated soundboards, providing "a particularly satisfying quality," in the words of a contemporary piano technician. Chopin expressed his preferences, explaining that "when I feel out of sorts, I play on an Erard piano where I easily find a ready-made tone. But when I feel in good form and strong enough to find my own individual sound, then I need a Pleyel piano." Liszt preferred the Erard.

Chopin's hands were relatively small and the "velvet" fingertips flat, but they were so "flexible" that they "expanded," in Stephen Heller's words, to cover "a third of the keyboard." Niecks, the biographer, writes that "the startingly widespread chords, *arpeggios,* &c., which constantly occur in his compositions . . . seemed to offer him no difficulty, for he executed them not only without any visible effort, but with a pleasing ease and freedom. . . . It was like the opening of the mouth of a serpent which is going to swallow a rabbit whole."

Fryderyk Chopin turned thirty on March 1, 1840. By the standards of the time, this was solid middle age, and he was fully established on the European musical scene as a great composer and pianist. Much of his best work was already behind him, but his creativeness remained power-ful—and he still had much more to say musically. He had found relative stability in his relationship with George Sand, spending more and more time at her rue Pigalle *pavillons,* particularly when he felt ill, letting the rue Tronchet apartment stand empty for days and nights on end— which he did for two more years, never eager to make major decisions. Polish scholar Tomaszewski has called this period of Chopin's life with Sand in Paris and Nohant the "Years of Asylum."

At thirty, however, Chopin's health was in steady decline despite peri-odic "good" stretches. On April 1, Dr. Paul-Léon-Marie Gaubert sent George Sand a detailed list of instructions on the care of "our sick per-son" and named her to be his "representative" in carrying them out. This is what Fryderyk had to do: In the morning, before getting up, he was to drink a cup of sugared infusion with a drop of syrup; next, he had to have his chest rubbed with a special pomade; before going to sleep, he had to drink a herbal potion; he had to dress warmly, but without "suf-focating"; he was allowed to drink his favorite Bordeaux wine, but diluted in water at a one to three ratio; and "as much as possible, all excessively lively emotions must be kept away . . . for at least a time." Dr. Gaubert became Chopin's personal physician after Fryderyk returned from Majorca, replacing his brother, Dr. Pierre-Marcel Gaubert, who died when the patient was away.

Witwicki, Chopin's poet friend, visited him early in April, then addressed him in a letter on April 17 as "my dear, little, so very pale *Szopenek,*" but urged him to make time in his schedule for piano lessons for the daughter of a Polish friend. On one occasion, Chopin dispatched a note to his pupil Gutmann, summoning him to come to play his new Scherzo in C-sharp minor for Moscheles, due to visit that afternoon, because "I am unfortunately too weak to play my things for him; so you must play."

For her part, George Sand was again concerned about Chopin's mental state and the new onset of hallucinations. He was seeing, she wrote, "a cohort of phantoms," and "as a Pole he lived in a nightmare of legends" born from "all the superstitious memories of Slav poetry. . . . The phantoms called him, embraced him . . . and he pushed away their skeletal faces away from his [face] and fought under their icy hands."

It was at that stage that Sand realized that she would have to look after Chopin probably forever, the Majorca experience having been no more than a prelude, and that therefore she had to bring him under her roof permanently (Dr. Gaubert's instructions were a compelling reason). She wrote in the *Story of My Life:* "He again began to cough alarmingly, and I saw myself forced either to submit my resignation as nurse or to pass my life in impossible journeying to and fro. He, in order to spare me, came every day to tell me with a troubled face and a feeble voice that he was wonderfully well. He asked if he might dine with us, and he went away in the evening, shivering in his cab. Seeing how he took to heart his exclusion from our family life, I offered to let him one of the *pavillons,* a part of which I could give to him. He joyfully accepted. He had his room there, received his friends there, and gave his lessons there without incommoding me. Maurice had the room above his; I occupied the other *pavillon* with my daughter."

From the very outset of the Chopin-Sand liaison, in the course of it, and long after both were dead, controversy raged among their friends and acquaintances—and later total strangers and biographers—as to its real nature. After their rupture, friends and biographers divided as to who had been the guilty party—and who had damaged whom. Frederick Niecks, Chopin's best biographer and a Chopin partisan in this historical debate, provides an excellent example of the clashing views in his sarcastic comment on Sand's decision to have Fryderyk move to rue Pigalle: ". . . the saintly woman, the sister of mercy, took, after some time, pity upon her suffering worshiper, and once more sacrificed herself." It would seem, however, that regardless of any deeper, conscious or subconscious motivations on George's part, the fact remains that she was there for Chopin when he so obviously needed help—and had no alternatives.

Chopin and Sand spent the whole year 1840 in Paris, in part because of his health even though she believed that Nohant would do him a world of good. Because she could move to rue Pigalle only in January, George was also busy with decorating her *pavillons*. She favored antique furniture, as did Fryderyk, and Gutmann described after a visit the brown carpet covering the whole floor of her bedroom and the walls "hung with a dark brown ribbed cloth." Her large square bed, rising "but a little above the floor," was covered with a Persian rug. There were "fine paintings" on the walls. In the salon, Gutmann recounted, George received guests seated on an ottoman, smoking a cigarette.

Rue Pigalle soon became part of Sand and Chopin's active social life although she was working on her play *Cosima* and starting on *Horace*, a novel based on her romance with Musset, while he labored with his daily lessons and his composing. In November 1839, within weeks of their return from Nohant, the Marquis de Custine, too, was back in Paris and back in their circle, again sending ardent invitations to Chopin. Early in June of that year, Custine, then forty-nine, had traveled to Russia, where he spent just under three months, gathering impressions and material for what would become his masterpiece, *La Russie en 1839* (known in English as *Empire of the Czar*). In it, Custine did for Russia what his fellow French traveler, Tocqueville, did for the United States several years earlier with *Democracy in America*. More than a century and a half later, both remain classics about the two great nations.

In his November 15 letter to Chopin, Custine failed, however, to mention his travels, except to say that "I am returning from the end of the world, but you (are returning) from even farther away because one travels farther with heart and imagination than by post coach." Noting that he was resting at his country mansion "after wanderings in Siberia," Custine announced that he was sending Chopin a ticket for a forthcoming performance at the Italian Opera and would attend it himself for the pleasure of seeing him there. Whether or not they met at the opera, Chopin played shortly thereafter for Custine at Saint-Gratien, causing the marquis to write of his "sleepless night" after hearing him at the piano and finding him "more superb, greater."

Early December brought another invitation from Custine and at the end of the month a lengthy missive about the meaning of friendship and words of "regret" that Chopin does not "fulfill the obligation of giving a bit of yourself to him who appreciates and understands you." He called Fryderyk an "inconstant sylph." As for Chopin, he seemed genuinely to like Custine, visiting and entertaining him on many occasions.

In June 1840, he played at Saint-Gratien, and in July, Chopin, Sand, Grzymała, and Delacroix traveled there to see him.

Chopin and Delacroix, the latter twelve years his senior, were seeing more and more of each other, spending hours discussing art—and disagreeing most of the time (except about music) in the friendliest of ways. Over and over, Chopin argued that to him eighteenth-century Classicism in painting remained superior to Delacroix's color-charged, heroic, and Romantic works. Romanticism, evidently, often meant different things to different artists who were part of the same broad cultural movement. In January 1840, Delacroix amused himself drawing the famous caricature of Chopin, then made more sketches for the Sand-Chopin "double portrait." He also began to visualize Fryderyk's angelic face as a model for Dante—in the context of his *Divine Comedy*—as part of the ceiling of the library of the Luxembourg Palace he had been commissioned to paint. In the final oeuvre, Dante is being presented to Homer by Virgil (Chopin would be able to see "himself" when Delacroix took him and Sand to see it completed on April 1, 1847, one of the last things the couple did together).

Starting it in Nohant during the summer of 1839, and completing it in Paris sometime during the winter, Chopin created the Impromptu in F-sharp major, op. 36, that Zieliński regards as his "most outstanding and most original composition" aesthetically, and a "fantasy . . . with acutely differentiated parts, forming a musical tale of deep and somewhat mysterious meaning." Chopin himself, however, was less sure about the impromptu, writing Fontana that "maybe it is mediocre; I don't know myself because it is too fresh. . . . We shall see later."

Apart from the impromptu, 1840 was not a particularly fertile year for Chopin. He wrote the *Grande Valse* in A-flat major, op. 42, a mazurka, and began sketching a new polonaise. His failing health bothered him considerably; despite Dr. Gaubert's assurances, he was now convinced that he was consumptive, coughing and spitting blood in increasingly frequent episodes. His physician friend Jaś Matuszyński, himself in the final stages of consumption, believed that they shared the same lethal illness.

Political tensions in Paris also served to distract Chopin, especially in view of Sand's deepening involvement with radical movements. Striking workers rioted during much of August, and on September 4, the king's police attacked them with exceptional brutality. Sand wrote that "these gentlemen murdered [people] left and right in order to remain in practice." Fryderyk usually paid little attention to politics—and he usually disagreed with her opinions—but this time, Sand noted, "Chopin, who doesn't believe anything, has finally acquired certainty and proof."

Actually, the apolitical Chopin abhorred all extremes. He took a generally dim view of George's "Christian socialist" radicalism, inspired by Leroux, her philosophical mentor. In November 1841, she had founded *La Revue independente* with Leroux as editor and proletarian artists from all over France (a bricklayer poet from Toulon—her favorite—and a shoemaker, weaver, locksmith, coiffeur, and baker poets) as contributors. The *Revue* published their poetry along with Sand's own novel *Le Compagnon du Tour de France* (which Buloz, her regular publisher, had refused to print because it sounded too much like "communism," a term then being discovered and feared by the bourgeoisie). She also gave the *Revue* her next novel, *Horace,* in which a magnanimous and heroic jewelry worker clashes with an egotistic, lazy bourgeois intellectual (modeled after Musset) during the bloody June 1832 riots (the mistreated mistress, Marthe, is George); the worker exhorts proletarians to unite to establish a new social order (which put George well ahead of Karl Marx, whom she did not know at the time, in urging proletarian unity).

Horace, started by Sand in Nohant, is still well remembered; the shrill *Le Compagnon* is not. (But it took 155 years befor someone decided to translate *Horace* into English). Next, she unveiled in the *Revue* the novel *Consuelo,* destined to be famous. Her avowed objective was the creation of "people's literature," which made her a pioneer among cultural revolutionaries. But not satisfied with the *Revue* alone, George also founded an opposition newspaper in Berry, naming it *L'Éclaireur de l'Indre du Cher et de la Creuse* and making Leroux its editor as well. As for Chopin, skeptical as he was about her *"beau geste"* enterprises (his words), he contributed fifty francs to the newspaper. All her "patriot" friends were "taxed" to finance it; Fryderyk's contribution was his beau geste toward Sand.

But Chopin was even more impatient with Polish religious and patriotic messianism, making no contributions to that cause. It was a movement launched by a Polish-Lithuanian visionary named Andrzej Towiański, who had turned up in Paris in the early 1840s and persuaded a number of Polish emigrés, including Chopin's poet friend Adam Mickiewicz, to join his crusade for ending the exile and resurrecting Poland. He preached that Poland was the "Messiah of Nations" whose suffering would save the world (as Christ had), and he proclaimed himself the prophet of the crusade. Chopin's reaction was that Towiański's movement was "insanity," and he wrote Fontana from Nohant that "Mickiewicz will end up badly, unless he is mocking you."

On April 26, 1841, Chopin gave his first public concert in six years, playing at the Pleyel auditorium to extraordinary applause from the audience, which included Sand, Liszt, Berlioz, Kalkbrenner, Heine, Delacroix, and Mickiewicz. He treated them to the Préludes, his new Ballade, and the new Scherzo, in addition to études, mazurkas, and nocturnes. The concert was a major social event in Paris, and, as Liszt wrote in the *Gazette musicale,* "carriages brought the most elegant ladies, elegantly dressed young men, the most famous artists, the wealthiest financiers, personalities from the highest levels—in a word, the whole social elite, the aristocracy of birth, of fortune, of talent, of beauty."

Chopin had agreed to appear publicly under the greatest pressure from his friends (including Liszt, whose all-Beethoven concert he had attended the previous evening), but he fought against it until the last moment. Sand described it as a "Chopinesque nightmare," adding that "so many things terrified him that I proposed to him to play without candles, without an audience, and on a mute piano." In his review, Liszt noted that Chopin's music reflected "his constant, suffocated pain, his unwillingness to communicate with the outside world, melancholy that he disguises behind appearances of gaiety."

Both Chopin and Sand were under intense social pressure, taxing especially Fryderyk's fragile nervous system. Elizabeth Barrett Browning, the poet, who knew them well and saw George as her role model, described with horror an evening at George's: "Mobs of ill-bred men adore her on their knees, between clouds of smoke and jets of saliva. . . . A Greek called her by her first name, embracing her. . . . A man of the theater, of incredible vulgarity, threw himself at her feet, calling her sublime!" André Maurois writes that while this milieu amused Sand, "it exasperated Chopin." He could no longer stand Paris.

On June 18, Chopin, Sand, and Maurice went to Nohant for the summer after an absence of twenty months (Solange stayed behind at her Paris boarding school, planning to join them in August). The April concert had brought Fryderyk six thousand francs (the equivalent of three hundred lessons), and now he could afford to be in the countryside "in unemployment the whole summer." Sand, however, had made up her mind that they were spending too much, and she instituted a variety of savings in the daily management of the house. Still, she ordered country outfits in flowered percale and Scottish fabrics from her Paris dressmaker. Chopin asked Pleyel to send him still another piano. And, of course, they could not enjoy Nohant without visits from their friends.

Among them were George's beloved Viardots. Louis Viardot was the thirty-nine-year-old former director of the Théâtre Italien in Paris and nineteen-year-old Pauline Viardot-García, already one of Europe's most famous opera singers, was his wife. Pauline was the younger sister of María Malibrán, an earlier star of the opera. She was one of Chopin's favorite piano pupils, and Maurice Sand sketched a caricature of them during a lesson, showing a distraught Pauline at the keyboard of an upright piano and a stern Fryderyk, a finger pointing at her and a shock of hair wildly over his forehead, exclaiming, "That's the [way to] play Listz [*sic*]! It's not wanted for accompanying the voice." Pauline had initially studied with Liszt, but Chopin had acquired by then a pronounced dislike for him as a person and a musician, and he lost no opportunity in showing it.

Fryderyk regarded Pauline as living proof of his belief that the human voice and the sound of the piano complemented each other. Chopin and Sand had become close friends of the Viardots—Louis and Pauline had first met at their rue Pigalle home—and now Fryderyk enjoyed the presence of a fellow musician. Sand wrote that "Pauline and Chopin read entire scores at the piano," playing parts from Mozart's opera *Don Giovanni* and works by composers ranging from Handel to Glück and Haydn. Though Pauline was pregnant, she sang entire Italian operas to Fryderyk's accompaniment at the piano. Sand also took practical advantage of Pauline's presence in Nohant: She used her as a model for the central person in a new novel, *Consuelo,* which reflected many of Chopin's views on music's evocative powers (and became one of her most successful books). In time, the Viardots would bring along their Russian novelist friend, Ivan Turgenev, when visiting Nohant. And Louis Viardot was made to help finance George's *Revue.*

In August, Grzymała joined the group, and Chopin again had an opportunity to speak Polish to his heart's content. The ever faithful Fontana strangely was never invited, as if he really were nothing more than Fryderyk's "totumfacki."

Through a bizarre coincidence of timing, the Wodziński family once again entered Chopin's life. First, Antoni Wodziński, the brother of Maria and Fryderyk's childhood friend, had embarked on a complicated love affair with Countess Marie de Rozières, seven or more years older than he. Once Chopin's pupil, she claimed that he and Sand approved of her plans to marry Antoni, who had shown no interest in the idea whatsoever. Fryderyk became so furious with de Rozières, an old friend of George's, that he forcefully opposed the invitation to her to come to Nohant. This was the first serious dispute between Chopin and Sand.

To Fontana, he wrote that de Rozières was "an insupportable pig who dug into my [garden] lot in some strange way, and sniffs with her snout for truffles among roses. . . . In a word, she is an old spinster. We, old bachelors, are much better!"

About the same time, word reached Chopin that, on July 24, Maria Wodzińska had married Józef Skarbek, the wealthy son of Fryderyk Skarbek after whom Chopin had been named. The Skarbeks owned the Żelazowa Wola domain where Chopin was born when his father tutored their children. Actually, Chopin had learned of their intention to marry as far back as January in an indignant letter from his adoring sister Ludwika in Warsaw. She had written on January 9 that the wedding would most likely take place in May, adding that "everybody is astonished" by it, and wondering "what does Antoni think about it?" Ludwika felt that Maria was betraying Fryderyk.

There is nothing to indicate that Chopin had reacted at all, or how, to Ludwika's news or to the marriage of Maria, whom he had not seen in five years. He never mentioned her in his many comments about Antoni Wodziński—and the money Antoni still owed him—in letters to Fontana. Pride, of course, would have been a perfectly plausible explanation for such silence. But it is much more probable that Fryderyk had simply expunged her from memory—and that he had never really loved her in the first place.

Antoni Wodziński wrote subsequently in his book *The Three Romances of Frédéric Chopin* that his sister Maria—whose marriage to Skarbek had been annulled, a second one ending in widowhood—remembered Fryderyk in her old age "as her fingers . . . played works of the immortal musician." Wodziński then asked rhetorically whether Chopin had forgotten Maria, answering: "Undoubtedly so . . . All regrets, true as they may be, have the fragility of colors that are erased with time." This naturally applied to Konstancja Gładkowska, as well, supposedly Chopin's first love.

George Sand, the third of Chopin's "romances," wrote many years later that his mother "was the only woman whom Chopin had really loved," and she was surely right. Even so, he never attempted to see her after the meeting with his parents in Karlsbad in 1835—and never saw her again. Perhaps love was an abstraction in his life: As he had noted in his essays for the piano Method, "playing great masters is an abstract difficulty," and, presumably, so is love. But love to Fryderyk could also be "pure logic," just as, in his own words, the fugue was "pure logic in music."

In a letter to Fontana three weeks after Maria's wedding, Chopin asked him, out of the blue, "not to dream that I died, but to dream that I am being born, or something similar. . . . In fact, I am becoming as gentle as a child in diapers. . . . And now I daydream." The central paradox in Chopin was that his self-assurance as a musician was streaked with recurrent self-pity as a person.

On November 2, 1841, Chopin, Sand, and Solange were back home at rue Pigalle (Maurice had returned earlier). For Fryderyk, it was back to his daily piano lessons and the pursuit of composing that had occupied him in Nohant.

The Nohant summer had been fabulous in terms of Chopin's creativity, although he spent much time with his friends, started an amateur theater, began to teach piano to Solange, tried to play billiards (but kept dropping cue sticks), rode a donkey in Berry fields, and kept up a barrage of instructions to Fontana. He also kept sending him music manuscripts as soon as he had them ready to be copied before being submitted to publishers; his originals tended to be unclear, full of changes and erasures, and Fontana may have been the only person able to decipher them. Chopin had completed compositions that summer at record speed, hardly agonizing over every bar as was his custom, to judge from the tempo and volume of deliveries to Paris. And there is no sign that the news of Maria Wodzińska's marriage had the slightest effect on what and how Fryderyk composed. She was the past.

The present were the works still published in 1841 or the following year. There was the Polonaise in F-sharp minor, op. 44, with "the greatest military passage in Chopin's Polonaises," as Charles Rosen has observed, with "the effect . . . as purely percussive as any composer of the time had dared to write." This was the most "brutal" of Chopin's music. Then came the Tarantella, op. 43, which may have been inspired by Italian opera he heard in Paris or by the street music of Genoa. Next Chopin dispatched to Fontana Ballade no. 3 in A-flat major, op. 47, a magnificent, tour de force of composition that led Rosen to comment that "Chopin was unique among the composers of his generation . . . in his ability to vary rhythmic textures and to make them correspond to long-range harmonic movement." At Schlesinger's request, Fryderyk composed a new prélude (op. 45), bearing no resemblance to the Majorca cycle of Twenty-four Préludes, and standing by itself, in Zieliński's description, as a gem of sentimental and intellectual "refinement." There were two more nocturnes (op. 48), the *Allegro de concert* (op. 46), a work for the piano whose elements Chopin began assembling almost a decade earlier with the idea of writing a third concerto for piano and orchestra, and, finally, the Fantaisie in F minor, op. 49, a serious work, reminiscent of the ballades.

No common denominator of any kind exists in this impressive output—there is, in fact, probably more variety and diversity in it than in any group of works during a similar period—and nothing may be found to suggest influences stemming from Chopin's awareness of Maria Wodzińska's marriage. If anything, the Nohant summer of 1841, may have been one of the happiest times for Fryderyk.

But no sooner had he reached Nohant in June than Chopin drowned Fontana in incessant requests and errands. First, he instructed him to pay his Paris rent, the concierge, and the "flower lady." In a single June letter, he asked Fontana to buy at Houbigan Chardin on Faubourg St. Honoré and send on to him "Benjoin" soap, two pairs of Swedish gloves, and flacons of patchouli and *bouquet de Chantilly,* an elephant ivory "hand" on a black stick for "head scratching" (from a specialty shop in the Palais Royal gallery), two of his busts by the sculptor Jean-Pierre Dantan, available in gypsum and in bronze, a flannel-covered metal water bottle "for hot water on the belly," a traveling pillow—and a copy of Cherubini's treatise on counterpoint.

The next letter sent Fontana racing back to the Palais Royal shopping gallery for three blouses for the country that Chopin meticulously described (he also enclosed a sketch of the shopping gallery with its entrances and passages, presumably to make sure that his friend would waste no time looking for the stores). In July, it was a request to Pleyel to send a better piano to Nohant "because this one is no good." In August, Chopin directed Fontana to call on a Dr. Roth on rue de Mont-Blanc to arrange to have a case of Tokay wine sent to Marseilles (no explanation). In September, he announced that he had bet Strasbourg pâté de foie gras and lost (no explanation of the bet), and needed Fontana to go to Chevet at the Palais Royal gallery to buy a large pâté in a round wooden box for thirty or forty francs and rush it to Nohant. He added: "I am furious that so much money is required for the pâté, especially when it is needed for other things."

In October, Chopin instructed Fontana to move all his furniture from rue Tronchet to rue Pigalle, ending the fiction of living apart from George Sand. A last-moment request was to order from Dupont, the hatmaker, a hat "for Monday . . . but absolutely for Monday." But Chopin's maniacal correspondence with Fontana also had gentle touches: One day in October, he wrote that "today I have finished [the] Fantasia—and the sky is beautiful, my heart is sad, but it does not matter. Otherwise, my existence might not be useful to anybody."

Back in Paris, Chopin resumed active social contacts with his Polish and French friends. On December 2, he played for the second time for the royal family at the Tuileries, a crowning event to end a successful year. And he was very much at home in the *pavillon* at rue Pigalle.

As 1842 began, Chopin, still feeling well in the aftermath of Nohant, agreed to another public concert at the Pleyel auditorium. It took place on February 21, and he was joined on the program by Pauline Viardot-García and the cellist Franchomme. He played four nocturnes, three mazurkas, three études from Opus 25, the new ballade, and passages from the impromptu, and a polonaise. It was quite an ambitious undertaking, but the house was full, applause deafening, and the concert brought Chopin over five thousand francs. Michel de Bourges, the political lawyer and George's former lover, praised Chopin in a long review in *Revue et Gazette musicale,* concluding that his music was "poetry . . . beautifully translated into sounds."

But death, always haunting Chopin, again invaded his life. Wojciech Żywny, his first music teacher, died in Warsaw on the day of the Pleyel concert. And on April 20, Jaś Matuszyński died of consumption in Fryderyk's arms in his rue de Verneuil apartment. He was thirty-two years old, exactly the same age as Chopin. George Sand, who also was present, recalled that Matuszyński died "after long and terrible agony, which poor Chopin endured almost as if it had been his own. . . . He was surprisingly strong, courageous, and devoted for such a fragile being. But then he broke down."

Chapter 19

"HAVE YOU SEEN LISZT . . . and are you still on the right footing with him?" Mikołaj Chopin asked his son in a letter from Warsaw on December 30, 1841. "In conversations here, I am often asked if I know whether, as [people] are saying, he is coming here with Madame Sand; I could only answer that you have not mentioned it in your letters. If he does come, I hope that he will visit us."

That three years after Chopin had traveled to Majorca with George Sand and more than two years after he had spent the summer in Nohant and, in effect, began living permanently with her in Paris, his father could ask such a disconcerting question was not merely glaring proof of his absolute ignorance of Fryderyk's life. It was, indeed, astonishing that the family, notwithstanding frequent visits to Paris by their many well-connected friends, had no idea about the fairly public Sand-Chopin liaison and believed, instead, the extraordinary bit of Polish gossip that *Liszt* was George's lover.

But much more significant and disturbing was the extent and duration of Fryderyk's monumental deception of his profoundly caring and loving parents and sisters (and their husbands) about his relationship with Sand. It raises again the fundamental question about his ability to love and trust, even his mother whom, to believe Sand, he loved above all other women, and about his honesty in dealing with his family and others close to him. His secretiveness was obsessive.

Chances are that Chopin had ignored the inquiry about Liszt and Sand in his letter to the family on February 25, 1842, the first one in three months, according to Mikołaj's missive to him on March 21, because his sister Ludwika returned to a gossipy question about Sand on the same date, clearly unaware of George's ties to Fryderyk. Ludwika's curiosity about Sand, as a famous person, arose from the mention in a Paris newspaper review of Chopin's February concert that George had attended it with her "two daughters" and she remarked indignantly that "it is not right that they do not know in Paris how many daughters George S. has." Ludwika evidently knew from reading in the press that Sand had only one daughter—Solange; she had no way of knowing that the other girl at the concert with George was Augustine Brault, a young cousin she had adopted.

Chopin's letter of February 25, written four days after the concert, has vanished, but he may have referred to the presence of Sand and the girls because he was a name-dropper in his correspondence home (and Sand was a "big name"). He was not yet ready, however, to reveal his "secret" about George. Writing on March 21, Mikołaj acknowledged Fryderyk's letter along with newspaper clippings of the concert's reviews, as he congratulated him on his success.

Actually, Chopin had dropped a hint of a new personal situation in a letter to the family just before Christmas of 1840. Mikołaj caught it instantly, responding in January that "we are enormously happy that someone is caring for you, as you tell us, but we are consumed by curiosity to learn something more about this relationship." (The editors of a Polish-language collection of Chopin's correspondence with his family suggest in a note that "surely it has to do with George Sand. It turns out that this 'relationship' of several years had not found thus far more space in Chopin's correspondence with his family.") Obviously, Chopin never explained the allusion to this "someone," and as late as May 1842, when he was back in Nohant for another summer, he still had Grzymała post his letters to the family from Paris.

Reconstructing Chopin's life is rendered extremely difficult by the yawning gaps in his correspondence with the family and with others, and, often, facts emerge—as they do in Leonardo da Vinci's inverted writing—from comments and responses by his parents and sisters to events related in his vanished letters. For example, no letters from Chopin to his family during 1840, 1841, and 1842 are known to have survived although he had written several. Likewise, all the letters from Mikołaj to Fryderyk between 1836 and 1840 are missing, and none exist between 1842 and the father's death in 1844. Under the circumstances, it is impossible to determine who knew what and when, and what, if anything, had been done about various matters.

A case in point is a rather surprising request by Justyna Chopin to Fryderyk for a secret loan. She made it in a letter on March 21, 1842 (sent in the same envelope with letters from Mikołaj and Ludwika), the second of three letters Justyna ever wrote her son. After observing that a "good and sincere child" should honestly answer "yes" or "no" concerning a loan, depending on his ability to make it, she wrote: "This is the thing: I owe three thousand Polish zlotys; Father does not know about it; and if he knew, he would be very saddened; and, naturally, it has to be paid back; so, if you could send it in the course of the year, not all together, but in installments, write me in care of Barciński" (Antoni Feliks Barciński was the husband of her daughter Izabela). The request was surprising inasmuch as it was the family that had been sending money to Fryderyk in Paris for years, until he began to earn enough to live comfortably, but it is unknown whether Chopin obliged his mother.

By the same token, there is no known response to a question from Ludwika in a letter of December 29, 1841, whether it was true that "next spring you would like to see [our] parents," as she had heard from a friend returning from Paris. In the event, no such meeting ever occurred, and Chopin has given no sign that he desired it or thought about it. Nobody ever considered the possibility of a visit to Warsaw by Chopin, the permanent Polish exile.

On May 5, 1842, two weeks after Jaś Matuszyński's death, George Sand and Chopin left for Nohant to help him recover in the peace and quiet of Berry from the shock of losing his friend and to restore his health. Impatient as Fryderyk had been in the autumn, now he was impatient to return there. Maurice and Solange came with them.

The combination of emotional and physical exhaustion of the recent months had taken a toll on Chopin. He had been ill before and after the February concert, keeping to his bed even as Matuszyński was on death's threshold. He complained in a note to Grzymała that "I have to lie in bed the whole day because my snout and my glands hurt so much." And Matuszyński's demise had brought back all the nightmarish visions of his own death; Fryderyk remembered that Mozart had died at the age of thirty-four, and now, having himself turned thirty-two, he mused about having perhaps only three years to live. He was so weakened by the time of the departure for Nohant that he had to be helped down the stairs at the rue Pigalle *pavillon* and into the carriage.

And, once more, Nohant seemed to give Fryderyk a new lease on life. He felt at peace in his large, second-floor bedroom, with its Chinese-style blue and red wallpaper, and the thick carpet. Flowers were in their May bloom in the garden below his window. Every morning, Jean Alaphilippe, the house servant, lit the fire in the bedroom, then brought Chopin his morning chocolate. Soon, Fryderyk was at the Pleyel, fine-tuned according to his detailed instructions, composing again, while George next door feverishly penned her new novel. Having promised Leroux to complete the final section of *Consuelo* by May 22, in time for the forthcoming issue of the *Revue,* she wrote eleven chapters in ten days, sustained by cigarettes and coffee, and suffering from atrocious migraines and eyestrain (she told Balzac in a letter: "I write novels at night, I ride my horse in daytime, and I play billiards in the evening").

Though Dr. Papet had found his chest in good condition, Fryderyk still felt "mucosities" in his lungs that gave him the sensation of "suffocating." By the end of May, however, Chopin had recovered sufficiently to come down to the garden in the evening to join the indefatigable George and Maurice and Solange in their games. His relations with Maurice and Solange had finally improved, especially with the boy, although he had to be immensely careful in terms of the children's own very delicate relationship with their mother. The quiet and artistic Maurice, now nineteen, was Sand's favorite (she called him "Bouli"), and she was sharply critical much of the time of the ebullient, but often lazy and sassy fourteen-year-old Solange, often called "Sol." Solange, naturally jealous of Maurice, had turned to Chopin for affection, radiating warmth and coquetry. As soon as they had reached Nohant, Solange presented Fryderyk with a bouquet of the first lilacs of the year. He resumed teaching her piano, having become very fond of the girl—but no more than that. He quickly realized that in the Sand family, he lived in an emotional minefield.

Fryderyk forgave at the same time Marie de Rozières (that "insufferable swine") after Antoni Wodziński, his great friend, had dumped the thirty-seven-year-old spinster piano teacher following an ardent love affair that she had hoped would lead to marriage—and incensed Fryderyk by demanding his and George's support for her plans. The Wodzińskis had quite a way of treating those (more or less) in love with them, and Fryderyk must have felt empathy for Marie. He welcomed her to Nohant, not failing to take advantage of her trip to ask her to bring a fine wool shawl for Françoise Caillaud, George's oldest servant, for whom he had developed great affection. Sand charged Marie with inquiring from a gardener on rue Saint-Lazare about the price of hot-houses for the Nohant flowers and purchasing four billiard balls (two white, one red, and one blue) to replace those gnawed by the château rats to the point they seemed "marked by smallpox." George also required special paper to roll her cigarettes as well as little cigars.

Sand had assigned Marie a small room on the ground floor because Stefan Witwicki, Fryderyk's Polish poet friend, was occupying one of the best guest rooms. But Marie was happy in Nohant. She wrote a friend about daydreaming under an old birch tree when "the sound of Chopin's piano barely reached me, so deeply was I absorbed in remem-brances. . . . Later, I strolled at length with Chopin along the longest alley in the woods, chatting about Poland." She then recounted how Sand "had stayed in bed yesterday until dinner. . . . You had to see Chopin in the role of a nurse, dedicated, thoughtful, faithful. . . . We went upstairs, but she would not let us come [into the bedroom] so, awaiting her permission, we played the 'Invitation to a Waltz.' " Throughout Marie's stay in Nohant that summer, she and Chopin often played piano pieces for four hands together (when Marie first met Chopin, she hoped to become his pupil, but could not afford his twenty-franc hourly rates; hearing her play, however, he offered Marie a free lesson for every free lesson she gave Solange).

Much as they cared for each other—or loved each other—there is lit-tle reason to think that Sand and Chopin had resumed (or started) sex-ual relations during that third summer in Nohant, or at any other time. They had apparently concluded, as George would later tell Grzymała, that erotic activity threatened Fryderyk's health and even life and that therefore Sand, now thirty-eight, had categorically ruled it out. There exists, however, a different version, according to which Chopin was so keen on sex and "desperate" over George's abstinence that he took a Nohant peasant girl as mistress. This most unconvincing story is cited by Ferdynand Hoesick, not the most reliable of Chopin's early biogra-phers, who reports that it had first been mentioned by Solange Sand Clésinger (not very reliable, either) to a Samuel Rocheblave after her mother's death. Rocheblave, in turn, repeated the story in conversations and lectures.

What occupied Chopin and Sand—and their friends and neighbors—during many Nohant evenings was amateur theater that Fryderyk directed from the piano and their puppet theater with 120 puppets, all dressed by George. She recounts in "Le Théâtre des marionettes de Nohant" that "these performances were similar to so-called charades," but "everything started with pantomime, which was Chopin's invention, [and] he improvised at the piano while the young people performed different scenes together with comical dances. . . . The artist carried them on the wings of fantasy as far as he wished, from joke to solemnity, from caricature to majesty, from joy to passion. . . . As soon as Chopin noticed a performer, he immediately, and with incredible skill, adapted to his role the content and the form of music." Other times, he would vanish and reappear behind the piano in a stunning comical imitation of an old Polish Jew, the emperor of Austria, or King Frederick the Great of Prussia. Balzac was so impressed by Fryderyk's mimicry that he wrote of a character in his novel *Un Homme d'affaires* that "he is endowed with the same talent for imitating people which Chopin possesses in so high a degree; he represents a person instantly and with astounding truth." Liszt found that Chopin displayed in pantomime "an inexhaustible *verve drolâtique.*"

The great event of the Nohant summer in 1842 was the long-awaited visit on June 4, by Eugène Delacroix, one of Chopin's two or three true French friends and his favorite conversation partner. Awaiting the painter, Sand wrote him that her "Chopinet" was "agitated" about what to plan to amuse him, where to go for walks, what to give him to eat. Her half brother, Hippolyte, she promised, would make eighteen of his most beautiful cows pose for him, and a Berry peasant ball would soon be held. She set up a studio with the best possible light on the premises for him to paint.

Delacroix had been ill with acute laryngitis before leaving Paris, and the heat and dust of the diligence journey made him feel even worse, but George installed him in the best guest room and Fryderyk brought him his favorite Chinese tea. Within three days, Delacroix was ready to start working on a painting for the tiny Nohant church, assisted by Maurice, who had been an apprentice at his Paris atelier for a year. Looking around the village, Delacroix discovered in the faces of women servants and women peasants "a sweetness . . . only seen in the paintings of old masters," and he was inspired to paint what he would call the "Education of the Virgin." He selected Françoise Caillaud, George's servant, to be the model for St. Anne and her daughter Luce for the young Virgin. George wrote later that whenever she faltered at work and looked at them, she found that St. Anne and "my little Virgin" are "so true, so naive, so pure that I can resume work with beautiful characters and fresh ideas."

The Viardots had been invited for the summer, as usual, but Pauline was on a singing tour of Spain, and they could not come before Delacroix's departure. Wistfully, he exclaimed, "to be in the country between Pauline and Chopin, that *is* something!" He had to settle for listening, together with Chopin, to George reading aloud the manuscript of *Consuelo,* the story of a Spanish singer modeled exactly after Pauline (who thought that the novel should be made into an opera in which she would appear).

But Delacroix and Chopin had plenty of time for their conversations about art. Sand wrote Charlotte Marliani that Delacroix talked "with all his heart, without remembering his sore throat." The two men continued in Nohant their running Paris argument about the relation "between the tones of painting and the sounds of music," emphasizing the role of "reflections" and "shadows." Again, they produced much profound intellectual analysis about the nature of art, possibly more and better than most of their Romantic era contemporaries.

In almost all other cases, musicians discussed music with other musicians, and writers debated literature with other writers—more often than not savagely attacking one another, as did, for example, Balzac and Sainte-Beuve. Sainte-Beuve, once Sand's mentor, wrote that she had "a beautiful soul and a fat ass" and that "she devours her lovers, but instead of throwing them later in the river, she beds them in her novels." On the intellectual plane, Fryderyk discussed aesthetics of music in exchanges of letters with his Warsaw teacher, Józef Elsner. But apart from Chopin and Delacroix, the only artist of their generation to bridge genres of art was Heinrich Heine, the poet who knew and loved music (Goethe, who died in 1832, belonged to an earlier generation of music lovers).

Delacroix, the "complete artist," also bridged painting and literature; he knew and venerated Byron and Shakespeare, who had inspired much of his art. When Byron died, Delacroix wrote in his *Journal* that "the future, in its justice, will number him among those men whom passions and an excess of activity have condemned to unhappiness, through the gift of genius. One would say that he wanted to paint himself in his verses; misfortune, that is the lot of such great men." He used the example of Shakespeare three hundred years earlier to explain the meaning of Romanticism of his age: "They really have a soul, passion, tastes. Consider Shakespeare, who makes his Jew say: 'Has not a Jew hands, eyes, etc.', and there you have exactly the claim of the Romantics."

Sylvie Delaigue-Moins, a modern chronicler of the Nohant summers, observes quite accurately that Delacroix was "immediately fascinated by the mélange of spontaneous inspiration and controlled force in Chopin's improvisations." Delacroix himself wrote his friend J. B. Pierret in Paris the day he arrived in Nohant that "through the half-opened window on the garden, you capture in some instants the music of Chopin who is working on his side [of the house]; it blends with the song of the nightingale and the fragrance of rosebushes." Two weeks later, he wrote Pierret: "I am having tête-à-têtes with Chopin . . . whom I like very much, and who is a man of rare distinction; he is the truest artist I have ever met. He is one of the few whom one can admire and esteem."

Writing Sand after his return to Paris early in July, Delacroix reminisced about the joys of Nohant, asking sadly, "and my tête-à-têtes with Chopin, where shall I find them again? . . . So take care of yourself, take care of Chopin. Perhaps he will work now that I do not interrupt him so much; I am sure that he had neglected his work many times to keep me company." A few days later, Delacroix informed Sand that his wife, Jenny, noticed that he had left behind in Nohant a pair of his underwear.

And it was in Nohant, Delacroix acknowledged subsequently, that he had conceived the idea of using Chopin's face as a model for Dante's for the ceiling of the Luxembourg Palace. It was in Nohant that Delacroix inspired Chopin. As Sand recalls it in her *Impressions et souvenirs,*

Chopin . . . improvises as if haphazardly. He stops. "*Eh bien, eh bien,*" exclaims Delacroix, "*ce n'est pas fini!*" "It hasn't begun [Chopin says]. Nothing is coming to me . . . nothing but reflections, shadows, reliefs that will not settle. I am looking for the color, but I cannot even find the outline." "You will not find one without the other," responds Delacroix, "and you are going to find them both." "But if I find only the moonlight?" [Chopin asks]. . . . "You will have found the reflection of a reflection," answers Maurice. This idea pleases the divine artist. . . . And then the *note bleue* resonates and there we are, in the azure of the transparent night. . . . We dream of a summer night: We await the nightingale. A sublime melody arises.

Many years after Chopin's death, Delacroix noted in his *Journal* that he had been talking about him with Grzymała, who "was telling me that Chopin's improvisations were far bolder than his finished compositions. It was evidently something like comparing the sketch of a painting to the finished product." And as Tovey pointed out nearly a century later, Beethoven had said "that no artist deserved the title of 'virtuoso' unless his extemporizations could pass for written compositions." Tovey added that "by all accounts, Beethoven's actual extemporizations, which he could extend to as much as an hour, were overwhelmingly impressive, and probably owed but little of their impressiveness to the trivial detail reported in the statement that Beethoven extemporized passages far more difficult than any he had published." Judging from the testimony of his contemporaries who heard him improvise, this was equally true of Chopin. Fontana, who published much of Chopin's work posthumously, wrote that "from his earliest youth, the richness of his improvisation was astonishing. . . . Chopin's most beautiful finished compositions are merely reflections and echoes of his improvisations." Balzac recalled that Chopin "found sublime themes on which he embroidered caprices."

George Sand had invited to Nohant that summer other guests who pleased Chopin considerably less than Delacroix. Specifically, they were her former lovers, the lawyer Michel de Bourges in June and the actor Pierre Bocage in July. It is hard to imagine what had possessed George to summon them, with Fryderyk sharing her life full-time at that stage. It is conceivable that at thirty-eight her vanity required the rekindling of old loves, even momentarily, and that, by the same token, she wished to spark the fire of jealousy in Fryderyk.

If this was what she really had in mind, George did succeed in the latter endeavor though it was difficult to distinguish between jealousy and simple irritation in Chopin. Michel stayed at Nohant for only a day or so because his pomposity now annoyed George—as did his obvious dislike of Chopin. He was not asked to remain longer. The case of Bocage, who was as handsome as monkey-faced Michel was ugly, brought more complications. Sand had told Chopin about her brief fling with the actor, and he reacted most angrily. He locked himself in his upstairs bedroom, and refused to join the rest of the family at a performance given by Bocage at the La Châtre theater that evening. George had made Fryderyk feel ridiculous and, he feared, look ridiculous.

Neither Michel nor Bocage appeared again at Nohant for the balance of Chopin's life with Sand. When Paul Gaimard, a naturalist about whose work on fossils in Oceania Sand had read, turned up as a guest, Chopin excused himself after the conversation turned to "Christian socialism" and Leroux. This time, Fryderyk was plainly bored.

Meanwhile, a new problem faced Sand and Chopin in Paris. They were increasingly dissatisfied with their rue Pigalle quarters because of difficult access to the *pavillons* through the courtyard and also the noise, and they were determined to find new lodgings. Trusty Julian Fontana, however, was temporarily in London, and they had to depend for help on other friends. Toward the end of July, Charlotte Marliani wrote that she might have found just what George and Fryderyk needed, but she insisted that they come to Paris to decide for themselves. They departed on July 28, leaving Nohant—and Solange—in the care of Marie de Rozières.

What Charlotte had proposed to Sand and Chopin were separate apartments in square d'Orléans, a luxurious enclave, just below Montmartre, where the Marlianis themselves now lived as did many figures of arts and culture. The square, not visible from the outside, is a private court with nine four-story white stone structures, each containing two or three spacious apartments, and the courtyard itself is a tree-lined garden. It is an L-shaped compound formed by rue Saint-Lazare, which runs east–west, and rue Taitbout, which rises uphill toward Montmartre. The square's main entrance, for carriages and pedestrians, is through a porte cochere at 80, rue Taitbout, but in the 1840s, the entryway was at 34, rue Saint-Lazare. It is below rue Pigalle.

The square was built by a seventeenth-century royal court lawyer, Magny de Maisonneuve, who named it the Cité des Trois Frères ("City of Three Brothers"), and it is still occasionally called Cité d'Orléans. In 1822, a Mademoiselle Mars had purchased it from the Maisonneuve family for 250,000 gold francs, and in 1829, the square was sold to a British architect named Gresy, who reconstructed it along more modern lines. (The square today looks almost exactly as it did in 1842, when Chopin and Sand established residences there, and it still is very exclusive.) George and Fryderyk fell in love with the square, and on August 5, they signed leases for their respective apartments.

George took two apartments at No. 5, square d'Orléans, and Fryderyk an apartment at No. 9. It seemed like a perfect solution: They were across the court from each other and could be together as often and as long as they desired while each maintained individual privacy. George had a large apartment on the ground floor and one on the fourth floor for Maurice's bedroom and painter's studio and for Solange's bedroom. Fryderyk took a smaller ground-floor apartment with a foyer, a bedroom, and a sitting room looking out on the garden and its fountain. Chopin's new servant, Jan, a Pole recruited by Grzymała from the Polish Club in Paris (the one who massacred the French language), lived in a garret. The annual rent was six hundred francs (the equivalent of thirty piano lesson fees), while George paid three thousand francs for her ampler lodgings. The Marlianis lived at No. 7, and, at Sand's suggestion, they shared meals there, dividing the expense. She wrote her friend Charles Duvernet: "We have invented having one *marmite* [a cooking pot] together at the Marlianis, which is much more economical and much more enjoyable than each [eating] at one's own place." Then, they spent the rest of the evenings there, often with invited friends. Of course, there was music almost every evening.

For Sand, it was a dream come true, a "phalanstery" of common living of friends as advocated in Count de Saint-Simon, Pierre-Joseph Proudhon, and Charles Fournier's early "socialism" teachings; but it also had the advantage of being a *luxury* phalanstery. She rented a billiard table, and "in the evening . . . friends would visit one another like good neighbors in the countryside" over the sand-topped garden paths. And, aside from the Marlianis, other friends lived at the square: Pierre-Joseph Zimmermann, the conservatory professor, and his daughter and son-in-law, Charles Gounod, the composer; Louis and Pauline Viardot; the pianist Kalkbrenner; the writer Alexandre Dumas *père;* the writer Louis Enault (later the author of a minor biography of Chopin); the sculptor Jean-Pierre Dantan, who did Chopin's bust; the comedian Antonin Marmontel (whose father, the composer Antoine-François Marmontel, owned the Chopin portrait painted by Delacroix); and the composer Charles-Valentin Alkan. Sand had tried to find a studio for Delacroix in the square compound so that all the friends could be as near to one another as possible, but failed. The square became known as the "Little

Athens," as the Chaussée d'Antin area was called earlier. (Today, the square houses the French National Guild of Authors and Musical Composers along with upscale tenant families.)

It was at the square d'Orléans apartment that Wilhelm von Lenz, pianist and counselor of state to the Russian Imperial Court, first met Chopin when he called on him in October 1842. He had taken lessons with Liszt, who, in turn, recommended him as a pupil to Chopin. Lenz recalls in his memoirs that "Chopin came to greet me—a young man of medium height, slender, lanky, his face worn and expressive and his dress of the greatest Paris refinement. Never since have I encountered a spectacle of such natural, seductive elegance. Chopin did not invite me to sit down and I remained standing, as in the presence of a sovereign."

Lenz writes that Chopin then asked him, "What can I do for you? Are you a pupil of Liszt? An artist?" to which Lenz replied, "A friend of Liszt— may I be allowed the happiness of studying your Mazurkas, which I treat like a Bible, under your guidance? I have worked on a few of them with Liszt," adding that "I realized, too late, that I had blundered."

Chopin, however, invited Lenz to play "what [he had] worked on with Liszt, I still have a few minutes." When Lenz finished, "Chopin courteously whispered: 'This run isn't yours, is it?—*He* showed it to you—he has to put his stamp on everything; well, he may . . . he plays for *thousands* of people and I rarely play for *one*! All right, I'll give you lessons, but only twice a week, that's my maximum; it will be hard for me to find three quarters of an hour.'" Next, Chopin asked, "And what do you *read,* how do you spend your time in general?" For this question, Lenz says, he was "well prepared," answering "I prefer George Sand and Jean-Jacques [Rousseau] above all other writers." Chopin "smiled and was a beautiful sight at that moment . . . [and] said: 'So Liszt has prompted you; I see you are initiated, so much the better. Be punctual, my house is like a dovecote and my time is planned by the minute. I can see already that we shall become better acquainted; a recommendation from Liszt says something, and you're the first student he has sent me; from mere acquaintances, we are now friends!'"

Lenz became in time one of Chopin's leading pupils, a Chopin scholar, and the author of a study entitled *Great Virtuosi,* in which he concentrated on Chopin and Liszt.

Lenz was not the only person to feel that Chopin sometimes acted like "a sovereign." Following Chopin's concert in February 1842, Berlioz, who disliked him as much as he was disliked by Fryderyk, wrote in the *Journal des débats*:

> Chopin always remains on the sidelines: One does not see him at the theater nor at concerts. One could say that he seems to be afraid of music and of musicians. He comes down from the clouds once a year and allows himself to be heard in Pleyel's *salons,* and only then the public and the artists can admire his magnificent talent. The rest of the year—unless one is a prince, minister, or ambassador—it is difficult to dream about the joy of hearing him. . . . His playing is . . . full of capricious charm, it is distinguished by the highest subtlety and originality, and his new creations are not beneath the earlier ones from the viewpoint of courage, harmony, and charm of the melody.

Having rented the square d'Orléans apartments, George and Fryderyk returned to Nohant for the balance of the summer, arriving there on the evening of August 9. Their only visitors during this stay were the Viardots with their baby daughter, Louisette, in September, after Pauline's triumphant singing *tournée* of Spain. Solange celebrated her fourteenth birthday on September 13, and dancing went on until one o'clock in the morning, with Chopin providing some of the music. It was then that the adolescent Maurice made his first feeble attempt to court (or seduce) Pauline.

George took to her bed again, and Marie de Rozières commented on Chopin's solicitude toward his mistress; she also noted the change in his attitude toward her: "Chopin . . . tries to compose and we all are good friends." Soon it was time to go back to Paris and move into the new square d'Orléans lodgings. Madame Leblanc, George's new Paris servant, was instructed to have "coffee, bouillon, eggs, butter, and cream" ready at the apartments for their arrival on the morning of September 28.

Sand wrote a friend on October 10 that "the apartment is very beautiful and very comfortable" and that "for his part, the maestro prepares a magnificent *salon* to receive his magnificent countesses and his delicious marquises. . . . Solange returned on Sunday to her boarding school without tears or fury. . . . Maurice is hammering nails and attaching his plaster boards to the walls. We are all working like Negroes."

But, of course, there was time to make music and listen to music.

Chopin organized frequent musical evenings at his apartment, playing himself and encouraging friends like Pauline Viardot and the tenor Louis Lablache to perform. At the end of November, thirteen-year-old Charles Filtsch, Chopin's pride and joy as a student, played at his apartment for the first time before an audience; Fryderyk, on a second piano, joined him in his Concerto no. 2 in F minor. The elegantly attired boy, slim and serious, was like a miniature of the maestro. Filtsch played again the following January before several hundred guests at the home of Baron Nathaniel de Rothschild, with Chopin beaming happily, and in April made his first public appearance at the Erard Hall, a concert that Fryderyk had helped to arrange.

Fontana was back in Paris early in 1843, and Chopin attended his concert on March 17. Fryderyk also resumed his patronage of the Italian Opera in the new season, applauding Pauline Viardot in Rossini's *Semiramide.* He helped to organize performances at the Théâtre Italien by the Polish dancers Roman and Konstancja Turczynowicz, at the request of mutual Warsaw friends. He tried to recruit in Paris a harp player for the Warsaw Opera Orchestra, but the project failed because the orchestra could not pay the required salary and expenses.

Chopin was busier than ever during the winter of 1842–1843, with his social life, his lessons, and his composing. His health was holding up reasonably well and his mood was unusually good. The novelty, the comforts, and the enjoyment of life at square d'Orléans helped to make it so. But, as usual, this was an up-and-down cycle, and the "good" period did not last very long. Sand wrote Charles Duvernet that "Chopin has been suffering at the first signs of cold [weather]," and in February Fryderyk sent a note to Pleyel saying, "I wanted to come to see you . . . but I feel very weak and I am going to lie down. . . . I love you more and more, if that is possible." A few days later, Chopin dispatched a message to his physician, Dr. Jean Molin: "Be so kind as to come to see me today; I am suffering!" George sent another note to Molin: "Chopin is suffering very much. Perhaps you could come tonight. The patient has severe neuralgia, which manifests itself painfully . . . to which you could put an end, making it possible for him to spend a quiet night." Subsequently, Sand wrote a friend that Chopin was not "doing too badly," and that he was undergoing a "homeopathic treatment that is successful."

*　　　*　　　*

Ill and well, on and off, Chopin produced in Nohant and in Paris a remarkable body of new music during 1842 and the first months of 1843.

The most outstanding in this group of compositions was the Ballade no. 4 in F minor, op. 52, that Zieliński describes as the opening of "the last period of creativity." He writes that it is "the most lyrical and the most thoughtful of all the Ballades . . . As all [the ballades] it presents a certain musical tale, which, this time, is associated with some [kind of] subjective history, played out deep in his soul." To Charles Rosen, both the introduction and main theme of Ballade no. 4 "come back with a display of counterpoint and coloristic transformation which is one of the most moving pages in all nineteenth-century music." The opening, he writes, is "Chopin's masterpiece of elegiac style" and the main theme is "one of Chopin's most original inventions." Chopin had started the F minor Ballade in Nohant and completed it at square d'Orléans in Paris, dedicating it to Baroness Charlotte de Rothschild, one of his best pupils and the wife of Nathaniel de Rothschild. Chop in and the Rothschilds had become very close friends at that time, and later he also dedicated to her the Waltz in C-sharp minor, op. 64. (This waltz was one of three he composed as Opus 64 during the summer of 1846, when he felt relaxed, happy, and playful, perhaps for the last time.)

The first of the three was written in D-flat major, and it became known among friends as the *Valse au petit chien* ("The Little Dog Waltz"), but it is also famliar as the "Minute Waltz." It was dedicated to Chopin's old friend, the beautiful Countess Delfina Potocka. The story, as related by Niecks, the biographer, and others in varying detail, is that one evening, as George and Fryderyk watched their little dog Marquis on the garden terrace going round and round trying to catch his tail, she said, "If I had your talent, I would compose a pianoforte piece for this dog." Chopin, the story goes, rushed to the piano to write. In another version, Fryderyk improvised it "when the little dog was playing with a ball of wool." Either way, his sense of humor was still intact despite the ravages of illness. He played the *Petit chien* Waltz, among other works, at his last concert in Paris in 1848, when he was barely alive; it had been published the previous year. The third of these waltzes was in A-flat major.

During that period Chopin also completed his Scherzo no. 4 in E major, op. 54; the famous Polonaise in A-flat major, op. 53, popularly known as the "Heroic"; and the three Mazurkas of Opus 50. It is impossible to establish when, precisely, Chopin had actually finished any of these pieces—he was in the habit of starting a work, then stopping, starting something else, going back to the first one, and so on—and it is not certain whether the sequential opus numbers reflect the order of completion.

Chopin's creativity in 1842 emphasizes again how free he was of patterns or distinct "creative periods" that might have reflected any particular mood or psychological condition. One finds, instead, extraordinary variety, ranging from the powerful patriotic chords of the A-flat major Polonaise and the nostalgia for Poland in the Mazurka in C-sharp minor, op. 50, no. 3, to the lyricism and poetry of the Scherzo no. 4. This last mazurka, for example, is a patriotic manifesto par excellence; it was dedicated to Leon Szmitkowski, an officer in the rebel Polish army in the 1830 uprising against the Russians. Zieliński thinks that it had "to bring tears to the eyes of every Pole in exile, and the composer himself surely wrote it in a state of strong emotion."

The dedication of two of his important works to Baroness Charlotte de Rothschild throws interesting light on Chopin's special personal connections with the financial powers of France under the July Monarchy simultaneously with his—and George Sand's—friendships with artists and radical politicians of the day. It brought the world of music and the world of business and money together in an unprecedented fashion, and, significantly, in relationships that went far beyond the traditional confines of musicians-for-hire at the beck and call of rich patrons.

Baron Nathaniel de Rothschild, at whose home Chopin and Filtsch had performed, was the son of James Rothschild, the representative in Paris of the Rothschild financial empire. James, in turn, was the youngest of the five sons of Meyer Amschel Rothschild of Frankfurt, who had established the great dynasty, placing a son in each key European financial center (London, Paris, Vienna, Naples, and hometown Frankfurt). Meyer Amschel died in 1812, after playing a crucial role in finanacing various European governments in wars that spanned the eighteenth and nineteenth centuries, and creating in the process the fantastic family fortune. James secured the family's power in France when he opened the Maison Rothschild, a merchant bank, in Paris in 1815.

As French historian Jean Tulard has noted, the 1830 July revolution opened "the way to power to the banks" (he also cites Karl Marx's comment that the "financial aristocracy, which ruled under the July Monarchy, had its Episcopal Church in the banks"). The banker Jacques Lafitte was King Louis-Philippe's first prime minister, and Maison Rothschild acquired a "quasi monopoly" on all the treasury borrowing and lending. It was the engine in financing the start and the rise of the industrial revolution in France.

At that stage, James Rothschild was probably the richest man in France, with his annual income estimated at one hundred million francs, or more. And it was at that stage that Chopin met him, starting a lifetime friendship with the Rothschild family. He most likely never thought of them as being Jewish. James and his wife, Betty, had sophisticated cultural tastes apart from his dedication to moneymaking. He was a friend of Heinrich Heine, the German-Jewish poet self-exiled in Paris, who was Chopin's close friend as well.

Chopin met James Rothschild through Heine and through his Polish aristocracy connections (the Rothschilds and the Czartoryskis were friends) shortly after he came to Paris. In any event, Betty Rothschild became one of Chopin's first pupils, late in 1832. Subsequently, Chopin's Rothschild friendship extended to James's son Nathaniel (who had been granted a baronetcy by King Louis-Philippe) and his wife, Charlotte. Biographer Niecks relates that the cellist Franchomme "told me that his friend [Chopin] loved the house of Rothschild and this house loved him, and that, more especially, Madame Nathaniel [de] Rothschild preserved a touching remembrance of him." In fact, as Chopin lay dying, Charlotte de Rothschild lovingly embroidered a cushion for him.

In a fascinating and probably unique manner, Chopin and Sand brought together at their square d'Orléans phalanstery a most improbable combination of guests, crossing normal political, social, financial, and artistic lines quite strictly observed elsewhere in the Parisian society. They were not trying to prove a point: They knew a great many people in many circles who were attracted to them and their genius (with a touch of snobbery among both hosts and guests, primarily artistic and intellectual snobbery).

Chopin's guests were the bankers—the Rothschilds, the Léos, and the Welleses (the American banker Samuel Welles and his wife were Fryderyk's frequent dinner hosts); and the Czartoryskis, Radziwiłłs, Potockis, and others of the Polish high aristocracy; the royal aide-de-camp Count de Perthuis, Custine, and other French aristocrats, and his special Polish friends like Mickiewicz, Fontana, and Grzymała; and his musician friends, chiefly Franchomme, Hiller, and Alkan.

Cigar-smoking Sand attracted her leftist political friends, principally Pierre Leroux, Louis Blanc, Emmanuel Arago, and Father Lamennais, and literary figures, from Hugo to Balzac and Sainte-Beuve; and personages like Lamartine, who was a poet as well as militant politician. Finally, the "regulars" included their common friends: Delacroix, Heine, Fétis, Marie Dorval, the Viardots, and the Marlianis (Liszt and Marie d'Agoult were not among square d'Orléans guests; Liszt and Chopin's friendship had cooled off, and Marie and George had become sworn enemies). There was nothing quite like it in Paris when it came to talent in all the arts, intellectual power, political position, aristocratic tradition, and enormous wealth. It was the elite of France. And it showed Chopin's personal standing in a multitude of otherwise unrelated Parisian milieux.

In another dimension, though certainly not intended as such in any planned fashion, the Chopin-Sand soirées played a remarkably important long-range role in French and European political evolution near the midpoint of the nineteenth century. Yet, they have gone almost entirely unnoticed and ignored in this sense—or underestimated—by historians and biographers more attentive to the elegant and titled high society and musical aspects of the *salon* informally conducted by George and Fryderyk.

In the rapidly changing France of the post-Napoleonic age and the inexorable march of the industrial revolution with its impact on political organization and the nation's social dynamics, the square d'Orléans phalanstery was one of the few places, if not the only one, where those in power, economically and politically, had the opportunity to meet, converse, and become acquainted with those in radical opposition and, conceivably, learn something from them—and vice-versa. Even François Guizot, the ultra-conservative historian and prime minister after 1840 (he championed "a monarchy limited by a limited number of bourgeois"), appeared occasionally under the Sand-Chopin roof. These soirées were a most civilized convergence of culture and politics, and arguably an important element in the broad process of shaping the century.

Apart from political philosophers turning up at the square d'Orléans, like Leroux and Blanc, many of the artists were political activists or holders of strongly expressed opinions. George Sand, Lamartine, Hugo,

Delacroix, and Heine were the most obvious examples. And these evenings had an international political flavor as well. Poles of all persuasions, even the aristocrats, preached the Polish independence cause, thereby defying the authoritarian rulers of Europe. Princess Cristina di Belgiojoso-Trivulzio, a close friend of Chopin and Sand, was the voice of Italian independence fighters then led by Giuseppe Mazzini (whom Thomas Carlyle, the great English historian, described as "a man of genius and virtue"). Lamartine and Mazzini would soon lead "Spring of the People" revolutions in their countries. And Heine spoke in this Paris circle of German freedom and liberalism aspirations.

It was Heine who introduced George Sand to twenty-five-year-old Karl Marx, the German-Jewish admirer of Saint-Simon, when he came to live in Paris in 1843, just as she inaugurated her phalanstery. Several of Heine's poems were suggested by Marx; Heine, of course, had introduced Chopin to James Rothschild.

There is no evidence that Marx ever came to the square d'Orléans, but he soon joined Sand as a contributor to *La Réforme,* a radical daily newspaper that her friends Leroux, Arago, and Ledru-Rollin had founded two years earlier, writing for it until his expulsion from France in 1845. Sand and Marx corresponded with each other in the ensuing years. If Chopin ever met Marx, there is no mention of it anywhere. But it was in Paris that Marx encountered the visiting German philosopher Friedrich Engels for the first time. Their collaboration, leading to the *Communist Manifesto,* began during those Parisian days.

Young Marx's exposure to the French social radicals—George Sand's friends—who drew their inspiration from Saint-Simon and Proudhon, was crucial in his ideological development. French historian Régine Pernoud has written that Marx was "a direct heir of Saint-Simon," who died in 1825, and that Europe of the late nineteenth century and the beginning of the twentieth "could be qualified . . . as Saint-Simonian." Ironically, Sand and her "Christian socialist" colleagues belonged to the affluent bourgeois middle class—as did Chopin. Marx, who knew them so well, did not hesitate to declare in the *Communist Manifesto* that "the bourgeoisie, historically, has played a most revolutionary part. . . . It has torn away from the family its sentimental veil."

Whether or not Chopin actually met Marx, he was surely, and very directly, present at the creation of modern history.

Chapter 20

ON SUNDAY, OCTOBER 16, 1842, Mikołaj Chopin wrote his son, as usual in his meticulous French, what is his last known letter to him. He commented on the news contained in Fryderyk's most recent letter to the family (probably written in Nohant, but dispatched from Paris) that "the air in the countryside has fortified your health and that you expect to spend a good winter, that you have new lodgings inasmuch as you were too cold." Then he asked: "But will you not be isolated if other persons do not change [lodgings]?"

Since Fryderyk's letter to which the elder Chopin was replying has disappeared, it remains a mystery what and how much he had finally told the family about the "other persons"—and whether at long last he had identified George Sand to them. Having mentioned spending the summer in the healthy air of the countryside, he most likely did not name Nohant—he still insisted on his letters to Warsaw being mailed from Paris—presumably not to be linked with George as far as his family was concerned. The Chopins, knowing about Sand and her fame, would instantly have connected Nohant with her.

And one must be curious to learn what in Fryderyk's letter would have led the perspicacious Mikołaj to wonder whether "other persons" were changing homes as well. Had Fryderyk hinted that he was living with such "other persons"? In his rather maddening reticence—or confusion—Chopin had also failed to give his father his new Paris address though he must already have known that it would be square d'Orléans. This forced Mikołaj to write to the rue Tronchet address (apparently

Chopin had never informed the family about having moved to the rue Pigalle *pavillon*).

The rest of Mikołaj's letter was devoted to chatty comments about Fryderyk's social and professional life in Paris, praising him for having dined with Liszt ("you have been friends, [and] it is well to be rivals with delicacy"), and bringing him up to date on the doings of the Wodziński family. Then, at the end, the seventy-one-year-old schoolmaster broke the bad news to his son: "To speak of us, I shall tell you that if it were not for my cough, which is becoming more insupportable every day, I would be doing passably [well]. I go out very little, except to our little garden where we have had different kinds of fruit, among them a few bunches of grapes that I had nurtured and that have ripened perfectly. . . . Be well, my dear child, your mother and we embrace you tenderly, pressing you against our heart with all the strength that we have left."

Chopin's reaction to the news of his father's "insupportable" cough is unknown. The next preserved letter from him to the family is dated almost two years later, but this is meaningless in terms of how he might have reacted because most of his correspondence to Warsaw has disappeared. Likewise it is unclear whether Chopin knew about the severity of Mikołaj's cough. Writing Fryderyk on the same day (the family usually placed all their individual letters in the same envelope), his sister Ludwika reported having just returned from three months in the Polish countryside with her children, "I have found everybody here healthy." In *her* letter, his sister Izabela also told him "We are all healthy," although she added that "Papa . . . coughs as usual . . . [and] when he has company, he regains his good humor and forgets about the annoying cough."

The question obviously arises whether Mikołaj's cough, apparently chronic, judging from Izabela's remark, indicated that he, too, was consumptive. If so, it becomes possible that Chopin's tuberculosis was of a hereditary nature (or genetically transmitted); his little sister, after all, had died of what appeared to be consumption. In any case, Mikołaj's health or cough are not mentioned in the extensive Polish and French medical literature on Chopin. Fryderyk received his father's letter in November as he lay in bed at the square d'Orléans the apartment, "suffering quite a lot."

The year 1843 marked the advent of Chopin's long "*vie mourante*"—the gradual waning of life, as George Sand put it many years later—and more and more visits of death upon those dearest to him. Death always haunted him.

Meanwhile, his health was betraying him again. February had brought "suffering" and "neuralgia," and the urgent appeals to Dr. Molin. And word of his condition was spreading. On February 19, *Kurier Warszawski* back home reported that Chopin's "strength was weakening." It was astounding how relatively well and how long Fryderyk was able to function in his deplorable physical state.

Still, he began to enfeeble discernibly despite surges of activity and good humor. After the opening months of 1843, when he became ill once more, his creativity diminished in an unaccustomed way. With most composers, the volume of creativity in a given year is meaningless, considering individual inspiration, health, personal problems, or other distractions. Normally composers have no self-imposed quotas—art cannot be scientifically planned—but the amazingly self-disciplined and (so it would seem) permanently inspired Chopin had been producing amazing works at a steady rate for the past fifteen years or so. Only Mozart, for example, composed great quantity, quality, and diversity year in and year out until he died. Chopin's 1843 slowdown was therefore meaningful, particularly when seen in perspective.

Winter and spring in Paris were essentially uneventful for Chopin. He was waiting to hear from Leipzig publishers Breitkopf & Härtel about his offer to sell the new scherzo for six hundred francs, the ballade for six hundred francs, and the polonaise for five hundred francs for the German and Central European market. And he went on with his lessons, sometimes as many as eight a day, despite his fatigue, and the Sand-directed rich social life. As the spring brought warm weather, it was time to leave Paris. They left for Nohant on May 22.

In the meantime, Liszt arrived in Poland on a concert tour. He first played in Kraków late in March, raising toasts to Chopin and Mickiewicz at a dinner in his honor. On April 1, Liszt was in Warsaw, where he gave three concerts, performing Chopin's études and mazurkas at the second concert and the Mozart *Don Giovanni* variations at the third. *Gazeta Warszawska* commented that "in Chopin's Mazurkas, Liszt spoke to us in our language, he spoke with our emotions."

Liszt also called on the Chopins, delivering tickets for his concerts. Although Liszt's and Fryderyk's friendship had cooled off in recent years, they had made up to some degree, dining together the previous autumn. Actually, it had been Chopin who chose to distance himself from Liszt—rightly or wrongly, he envied his talent at the piano—while the Hungarian, notwithstanding occasional cutting remarks about Fryderyk, remained a faithful admirer. In Poznań, in western Poland, he met the Berlin music critic Ludwig Rellstab, who in the early 1830s wrote savagely denouncing Chopin's innovations, but had now changed his mind, asking Liszt for a letter of introduction to Fryderyk. Liszt obliged, telling Chopin in a simultaneous "dear old friend" letter that he and Rellstab would surely get along because the critic was "a man of great culture . . . and you are well brought up." And Liszt added: "I want to take this opportunity to repeat once more, even if you consider me boring, that my friendship and admiration for you will always remain the same, and you can dispose of me as a friend under any circumstances." It is unknown whether and how Chopin responded.

Chopin and Sand's fourth summer in Nohant began to show the strains of their life together. For the first time in their liaison, George found it trying "to be alone" with Fryderyk, the absence of friends during the first months in the country making it worse. At the square d'Orléans, she was surrounded by friends all her (nonwriting) waking hours while Chopin spent the entire day in his apartment giving lessons. In Nohant, on the other hand, they lived on the same floor in the same house, forced to spend the after-hours together—alone. Inevitably, they were getting on each other's nerves, accentuating Fryderyk's normal irritability. In fact, many of their friends, including some of Chopin's Polish friends, concluded that he was at fault, with his endless demands, egoism, and mood swings. Mickiewicz, for example, was reported to have said that Fryderyk was "the evil genie of George Sand, her moral vampire, her cross . . . who might end up killing her." Madame Juste Olivier, an acquaintance who had once dined with them in Nohant, wrote in her diary that Chopin was "a man of intelligence and talent, charming . . . but heart, I don't think he has."

That year, Chopin and Sand had arrived only with his Polish servant, Jan (whom George resented for being paid more than her *Revue* editors) and her Paris cook. Maurice had gone to visit his father at Guillery in the southwest and Solange was still at her Paris boarding school. Of Berry friends, Dr. Papet and his wife were in Paris. Hippolyte, Sand's half brother, was unnerving Chopin (who at the outset had enjoyed his company) with his drinking and ribaldry. And Fryderyk was not interested in his daughter Léontine and her husband Théophile Simonet; they bored him.

The only saving grace was eighteen-month-old Louisette Viardot, whose mother, Pauline, was away at a series of recitals in Vienna and had sent her to Nohant for the summer with her nursemaid Jeanette. Both George, whom she called *maman,* and Fryderyk fell absolutely in love with the baby. As Sand wrote Pauline, Louisette "says *Chopinek* in a way that would disarm all the Chopins of the world. . . . Chopin venerates her and spends his time kissing her hands. . . . She converses with Chopin in Polish." Perhaps a touch of exaggeration, but this was probably the only time Fryderyk was seized with stirrings of fatherhood.

But George was angry with Jan, his servant, for courting (or whatever) Jeanette, and she was unhappy in general. She wrote Pierre Bocage that Nohant "has changed a lot since you saw games and laughter reign here. My approaching forty years are making me serious. . . . The sad health of our friend has created among us a great habit of melancholy or, at least, has retrenched our habits."

Hoping to improve his health through exposure to fresh air, George encouraged Fryderyk to accompany her on walks in the Berry countryside. Because he had trouble actually walking, she procured a donkey named Margot for him to ride in a velvet saddle behind her. "When an enterprising 'reproducer' donkey went after [Margot's] virtue," Sand wrote Maurice, "she fought back with strong kicks, like a true Lucretia. Chopin shouted and laughed, and I treated [him] with my umbrella. In the end, we all emerged healthy from this terrible adventure, and [Margot] did not have to kill herself with a stiletto."

Everybody's mood soared when Delacroix arrived in Nohant on July 17. It was an especially memorable occasion because he was able to travel by train from Paris to Orléans and go on by diligence only from there. The Paris–Orléans railroad, one of the first long-distance lines in France, had been inaugurated that spring by the Compagnie du Nord, largely financed by the Maison Rothschild. For Delacroix, suffering from rheumatism, this was a godsend. And reaching Nohant, he resumed at once what he called his "convent life."

Chopin and Sand told Grzymała in a joint letter that "the country serves [Delacroix] well . . . he paints, sketches the countryside, rides a donkey, plays billiards, absorbs fresh air as much as possible." Chopin also had advice for Grzymała in the Parisian summer heat: "Don't get tired. . . . Don't walk on scaffoldings . . . Take baths in the Seine. . . . Don't lose your watch . . . and think sometimes about the old musician who unnecessarily lingers on in this world." The signature was "Chop." Fryderyk had written him separately with assurances that George was not the author of "gossip" supposedly spread by their friend Charlotte Marliani about a singer named Agathe with whom Grzymała was said to be in love.

Delacroix's presence chased away Chopin's fatigue. The two men spent long hours sitting under a tree or strolling in the woods, chatting about art, people, and everything else. Delacroix always addressed Fryderyk as "my dear Chopin." In the evening, George joined them for more conversation, listening to Delacroix's criticism of the singer María Malibrán, Pauline's sister (he thought she tried too hard to appear "noble" on the stage) and to both men condemning Berlioz for pitching trombones against flutes, "an easy artifice," in his *Requiem*. But all were in agreement in praising Mozart to whom Delacroix compared Chopin in his "deep originality" and "perfection of composition." Then, Delacroix and Sand, both smoking cigars, listened to Chopin's music that, he said, "God makes descend . . . on [his] divine fingers." And George was happy that Maurice, still an apprentice with Delacroix, had arrived in Nohant.

But Delacroix had to leave ten days later, and within days Sand complained in a letter to him (while thanking him for cigars and a lighter he had sent her) of the "monotonous life" she now shared with Chopin and Maurice. She would continue, she promised, her "moral support" for Maurice to help him become a painter and for her other "little one . . . Chopin of the suffering health and resignation." George then added that she had "voluntarily" committed "suicide" three years earlier to avoid a "ridiculous agony," presumably a reference to her decision on sexual abstinence.

Sand's maternal sentiment for Chopin rose again when he left for Paris on Sunday, August 13, to discuss with Schlesinger the publication of his new works and to bring Solange to Nohant from her boarding school. It was the first time in years that he traveled alone, but the tiring trip was now so much easier with the Paris–Orléans railroad. And Sand had written Charlotte Marliani to make sure that the concierge at the square d'Orléans aired Chopin's apartment, brought hot water for his toilette, and was available to run errands. She assumed that Charlotte would provide Fryderyk with meals during his short stay.

George wrote Charlotte: "Here is my little Chopin; I entrust you with him; take care of him, in spite of himself. He looks badly after himself when I am not there, and he has a good but stupid servant. I am not concerned about his dinners because he will be invited from all sides. . . . But, in the morning, I fear that he might forget to swallow a cup of chocolate or bouillon, which I force on him when I am there. . . . Chopin is well now; he needs only to eat and sleep like everybody else."

Chopin used well every moment he had in Paris. He attended a performance of *Oedipe à Colonne,* the masterpiece of the eighteenth-century Italian opera composer Antonio Sacchini, saw a few friends, fetched Solange at Madame Bascan's boarding school, and with her took the train to Orléans on the evening of August 16. They were in Nohant at midnight of August 17. Chopin had been gone for five days.

Back in the country, Solange resumed her piano lessons with Chopin, a practice that would lead in time to new problems between him and Sand. That Solange, now fifteen, had a case of puppy love for Chopin—or even was seriously in love with him—was a fact that George, experienced woman that she was, could not have missed. And that she clearly favored Maurice over Solange, and often threatened her with punishment for supposed "nonchalance" and imposed a rigorous schedule on her, inevitably pushed the girl toward Chopin, the other adult in the household—who also was a charming genius. Solange, to be sure, was temperamental and as stubborn and hardheaded as her mother. Chopin was quite fond of her and declared himself pleased with Solange's piano accomplishments as did Sand, complimenting Marie de Rozières, who taught the girl in Paris, on her "admirably posed" hand and "charming touch" at the keyboard. But there are no indications that Chopin encouraged in any way the girl's amorous feelings toward him.

The Viardots and Pauline's mother arrived in Nohant on September 1, delighting almost everyone there. Baby Louisette was happy to see her parents. Fryderyk and George were just as happy to see Pauline and Louis: Pauline was Chopin's favorite opera singer and pupil, and Sand loved her so much she called her "my *fifille*" (a diminutive of daughter). Maurice was enchanted because he was in love with Pauline. Only Solange was in distress. She resented her mother's attitude toward Pauline and Chopin's admiration for the diva. She was even impatient with Maurice's rather noticeable crush on Pauline. In brief, Solange found herself wholly ignored while Pauline was the worshiped female center of attention in Nohant. Her only consolation was that Sand was too busy with the Viardots to criticize her and make her account for every hour of her time.

Louis Viardot had to return to Paris on September 8, but the women stayed another week, with Maurice extremely pleased that he had Pauline to "himself" for that short period, including a great traditional Berry wedding they all attended. It was the marriage of Sand's widowed servant Françoise Caillaud to Jean Aucante, a local farmer, and George had invited friends from all over Berry to the three-day feast at the Nohant mansion. Sixty guests dined and drank at tables set up on the lawn after the wedding ceremony. Then, there was dancing for three nights in a row. Solange, whose fifteenth birthday coincided with Françoise's marriage, did not miss a single dance. Maurice kept following Pauline. And Chopin heard for the first time the sound of Berry bagpipers playing the "Marsillat bourrée," the ancient regional dance, and discovering the "savage dissonance" of the natural F note instead of the F sharp that bagpipes cannot produce. The following summer, he may have composed two bourrées of his own; Hanna Wróblewska-Straus, the curator of the Fryderyk Chopin Society in Warsaw, says these bourrées, mentioned in contemporary accounts, and occasionally heard today, may, at the very least, be attributed to him.

The day after the feast, Maurice escorted Louisette, her mother, and grandmother to Orléans to take the train to Paris. The family was alone again, but the restless Sand came up, as usual, with ideas to keep them amused. At the end of September, she organized a three-day excursion along the Creuse, east of Nohant, as far as the ruins of the château in Crozant. There were nine of them: Sand, Maurice, Solange, Hippolyte, and his wife on horseback; Chopin on his donkey; and three servants in charge of carriages with food, drink, blankets, and clothes. It was the wildest part of the otherwise flat Berry and they moved slowly through gorges in the mountains that, George wrote, were "small, but more inaccessible than the Alps," with uncharted tracks and abysses. Chopin, she added, climbed everywhere on his donkey, slept on hay on the ground, and never felt better than among these dangers and fatigue." Sand swam in the river and sunned herself, acquiring an Indian-like dark tan. Maurice sketched the Crozant castle.

October in Nohant was spent by Sand on her latest social justice battle, this time fighting government censors to be able to publish in her *Revue indépendante* an exposé of the atrocious treatment of a fifteen-year-old girl named Fanchette, who was expelled from a convent shelter and abandoned along a highway because her pregnancy was embarrassing to the institution. After the scandal broke out—Sand and her friends had come upon the story in July—local authorities embarked on a cover-up. Fanchette was placed back in the convent where, Sand feared, the nuns would try to make her "expiate the shame of *their* behavior." Now George was determined to have the girl released, and this was the goal of the exposé article she had written. She prevailed in the end and the article was published, freeing her to start *Jeanne,* a novel based on the life of a peasant girl—obviously Fanchette's.

With his essentially conservative views, Chopin usually stayed out of Sand's social crusades, but on this occasion he is said to have been moved by Fanchette's fate and fully encouraged George in the battle, according to Sylvie Delaigue-Moins, the historian of Nohant.

On October 28, Chopin and Maurice left for Paris, leaving behind George, who wanted time and solitude to work on *Jeanne* and concentrate on the progress of the *Éclaireur de l'Indre, du Cher et de la Creuse,* the opposition newspaper she had founded with Pierre Leroux (and an initial financial contribution from Fryderyk). Chopin was anxious to return to Paris to resume his lessons and his earnings; George agreed because of the onset of bad weather and "the devil's cold" in the big rooms of the Nohant mansion. Maurice wanted to be back at Delacroix's atelier.

George was to return on November 29, and this was the first time in five years, since they began living together on Majorca, that they were separated for a whole month. But Sand was watching over him from afar. Again, she instructed Marie de Rozières to make sure that "my poor little child" eats well, to keep an eye on him, and summon Dr. Molin, if needed. She wrote to her: "Look after him, even against his will. . . . Nothing is easier for this Pole [Fryderyk's servant] than to prepare a bouillon and a cutlet. But he [Chopin] will not order it himself, and may even forbid it. So you must deliver a sermon to him." Even before Chopin's departure, George had written Grzymała that she counted on him to "inform me about everything openly and sincerely. . . . I shall be with you probably at the end of November, but I shall come on a day's notice if my little one [should] become ill."

Actually, Chopin was quite ill even before he left Nohant: He felt weak and his long-rotting teeth hurt him. Sand asked Maurice in a letter a few days after their departure to "tell me if Chopin is ill; his letters are short and sad. Take care of him if he is ailing. Take my place a little. He would take my place with as much zeal if you were ill." On November 4, she wrote Fryderyk at square d'Orléans: "Good morning, my Chip Chip. Chase away your [bloody] flux, which worries me. Discuss it with Dr. Molin and do what he tells you. Maurice says that you feel neither well nor poorly. This does not console me. Isn't he hiding one-half [of the truth] from me, and aren't you feeling rather badly rather than well? Are you at least busy enough to tear yourself away from your sufferings? Are you seeing people who amuse you? Do you sleep nights? I would like to know this before all else, but you are not telling me. I kiss you just as I love you."

By November 10, Chopin was seriously ill: He had pains in his chest, coughed, and spat blood. Dr. Molin came to see him daily, insisting on his homeopathic treatments, and after a few days Chopin had improved to the point of being up and about—though still forbidden from going out in the street. Maurice had informed his mother that during the day Fryderyk did not feel badly, but at night "he coughs, suffocates, spits." But despite her promise to Grzymała, she was not rushing to Paris on "a day's notice." She wrote Grzymała that, according to Charlotte Marliani and Marie de Rozières, Chopin was better, there was nothing to worry about, and the two women had urged her to remain in Nohant.

George explained that she was following this advice not only because she had "important affairs" to wind up, but because she feared that if Fryderyk saw her unexpectedly, ahead of scheduled time, "he would feel shamed in the delicacy of his heart, seeing that I abandoned important occupations to sit with him like a nurse . . . although I am happy to be [a nurse]. Poor angel! I shall never disenchant him, you can be certain, and my life belongs to him forever." Sand actually believed what she said and did at every given moment. Life to her was a fantasy, a romantic novel—with a touch of self-serving righteousness.

Chopin, at the same time, wished to convey his concern for George, sick as he was. In a pathetically cheerful letter he sent her at Nohant on November 26, he begged her not to get too tired—and to bring good weather "because here rain is falling all the time." He wrote that he was resting at home because it was Sunday, adding, most untruthfully, that "illness remains far from me, I only see happiness ahead [and] I never had more hope as [I do] thinking about the coming week." Fryderyk related that "we went to a good dinner at Madame Marliani's. Afterwards, some went to an evening reception, others busied themselves sketching, and still others went to bed. I slept in my bed, like you [do] in your chair, tired like after a heavy effort. . . . Do not stop thinking about your old, very old acquaintances who, obviously, think about nothing but you. . . . Four more days!"

Finally, after shipping Chopin's piano and packing jam jars, George and Solange left on November 29 for Paris where Sand was so anxious to see "my two male children."

During his fourth Nohant summer, Chopin composed less than in previous years—for whatever combination of reasons—but the quality never faltered. It was so with the two Opus 55 Nocturnes, in F minor and E-flat major; the three Opus 56 Mazurkas, in B major, C major, and C minor; and the Berceuse in D-flat major, op. 57.

The two nocturnes, very sentimental in style, were dedicated to Jane Wilhelmina Stirling, a wealthy Scottish noblewoman, one of the daughters of an Edinburgh banker, who became Chopin's pupil probably early in 1843, falling (and remaining) in unreciprocated love with him until his death. Not exactly beautiful, the tall, slim, pale Jane was six years older than Fryderyk. First, in January 1844, Chopin autographed for her the score of his Nocturne in E-flat major, op. 9, no. 2, written around 1831, and this was little more than a courtesy. But the actual dedication of two very important nocturnes to Miss Stirling, when they were published late in 1844, was a rather uncommon act of friendship, endearment, or indebtedness, especially when Chopin had known her for such a short time.

The three Opus 56 Mazurkas, written in 1843 (the C minor is the longest of all his mazurkas), were dedicated to Catherine Maberly, a friend of Stirling and likewise a Chopin student. Though Chopin had dedicated works to very close friends, like Fontana, Princess Czartoryska, and Countess Delfina Potocka, or fellow composers like Liszt and Schumann, he curiously never dedicated a composition to George Sand (nor to Konstancja Gładkowska or Maria Wodzińska). It was always very difficult to know which among Fryderyk's actions of this kind were motivated by principle, eccentricity, friendship, or business advantage; love, if he ever really felt it, was not a consideration.

In any event, this was the first time that Jane Stirling's name appeared in connection with Chopin (apart from the autograph earlier in 1844), marking the start of an astonishing relationship of vital importance to him. A Stirling biographer, Audrey Evelyn Bone, suggests that they met as early as 1832, but there is no evidence to support it. Lindsay Sloper, an English pianist and Chopin's pupil, has told Niecks, the Chopin biographer, that he had introduced Stirling to him because she desired to become a student, too. Chopin agreed and, according to another biographer, assured her that "you will play very, very well one day."

The Berceuse, op. 57, the only one he ever wrote, may have been inspired by little Louisette Viardot on whom he doted that Nohant summer. "The work is pure tone color," in the words of Charles Rosen, and it was Chopin's celebration of parenthood he had never wished for himself. In December, he offered the new nocturnes and mazurkas to Breitkopf & Härtel in Leipzig for six hundred francs each; it was back to business reality.

The new year—1844—brought Chopin more illness and suffering. His health was now in steady decline despite occasional, temporary upswings. He tried his best to keep up with his work, obligations, and pleasures, but it was tough going: He could hardly breathe. January was simply awful, with a touch of the grippe, constant cough, and what Sand described in a note to Dr. Molin as "great nervous oppression" and asked the physician to visit Fryderyk (she asked Dr. Molin at the same time to receive her friend Louis Blanc, the radical historian, to "cure him of nervous depression from which he has suffered for a long time").

When Zofia Rozengardt, Chopin's twenty-year-old Polish pupil and fiancée of his close friend Bohdan Zaleski, the poet, invited him to come to listen to her play, Fryderyk sent her a brief note that because of his "breathlessness" he would not "have the pleasure of listening to you tomorrow morning." But a few days later, he advised her that "if a quarter to one [o'clock] suits you, I shall be able to listen to you. All the best." On the afternoon of February 2, he played at the square d'Orléans apartment for his Polish friends, including Zaleski and Witwicki. Zaleski noted that Chopin was "pale, miserable, but in good humor and inspired . . . and he ended with an improvisation on 'Poland Is Not Yet Lost' in every manner, from warlike to sounds of children and angels. . . . He had first played the splendid Préludes, then the Berceuse, then a Mazurka." Early in March, Chopin attended the funeral of the mother of Camille Pleyel, one of his music publishers, and *La France musicale* reported that he was "very ill." The bad health prevailed throughout the early spring.

George Sand was at his side all the time, looking after his condition, comfort, and needs. But the personal relationship had changed markedly since the start of the liaison. Marie de Rozières spoke in a letter that winter of "mutual tenderness" between George and Fryderyk and of their respect for each other as creative artists. But she concluded that "love is no longer here, at least from one side [that of Sand]. . . . There is tenderness and devotion mixed, according to the day, with regrets, sadness, boredom." And, obviously, they fought. Zofia Rozengardt wrote her parents in Poland about lessons with Chopin: "He is as capricious as a spoilt child, scolds his pupils, treats his friends coldly. This happens most on days when he is ill, physically ill, or has argued with Madame Sand." But George and Fryderyk continued to be seen together in public. On April 28, they joined Liszt and Dumas *père* at a concert by Alkan. On May 11, they went with Victor Hugo to the Odéon Theater for the première of a new production of *Antigone* by Sophocles with music by Mendelssohn, and with Pierre Bocage (Sand's former lover) in the lead role of Creon.

Returning home from the theater, Chopin found a letter (it is unknown from whom) informing him that his father had died in Warsaw on May 3. Mikołaj was seventy-three; Fryderyk was thirty-four, a grown man. His immediate reaction was extreme shock and a plunge into deep depression; he locked himself in his bedroom for days, refusing to see anyone, including George. For twelve and a half years since Fryderyk left Warsaw, his father wrote him frequently and faithfully to express his and the family's love, pride, and support; offered fatherly advice about his health, management of money (he kept urging him to save some for a "rainy hour"), career steps, relations with friends and critics; and passed on Warsaw news and gossip.

Mikołaj commented on Fryderyk's descriptions of his life and work in Paris; he was the confidant of his son, who opened up to him more than to anyone else (if not always fully). And now he was gone, and Fry-

deryk entered his years of true loneliness—he would never reveal as
much of himself to Sand, Grzymała, or Fontana as he had to his father.
Chopin's depression persisted, and on May 12, George wrote Auguste
Franchomme, his cellist friend, that "our poor Chopin has learned a little while ago about the death of his father. He locked himself up in his
room, but I beg you to visit him tomorrow because you are one of the
few people who could have a calming effect on him. I suffer because of
his grief; I am unable to console him." On the same day, she wrote Dr.
Molin to come to see her "at one o'clock. . . . Chopin has learned about
his father's death. He is broken, and I, indirectly, too." Sand's letters,
dated May 12, show that the news about his father had reached Chopin
on *May 11*—and not on May 25, as reported by his biographers. It is
improbable that it would have taken a letter over three weeks to reach
Paris from Warsaw (surely it was sent as soon as Mikołaj died), but it
could have taken a week or so.

Chopin's father was buried on May 6, at Warsaw's Powązki Cemetery,
with the city's entire cultural, artistic, and scientific elite in attendance;
he was very well known and respected. The priest delivering the prayer
at the gravesite mentioned Mikołaj's son's "European fame" and the
Kurier Warszawski published a poem proclaiming that although "the
good Chopin" had passed away, "he left us a son whose great talent . . .
brings pride to our motherland."

Antoni Barciński, Chopin's brother-in-law (Izabela's husband), wrote
him in June (no exact date appears on the letter) that Mikołaj had died
after "not a long illness" and that his age, after a lifetime of hard work,
was "his real and final illness. . . . During his weakness, which was not
manifested by bodily suffering, but by slowly ebbing strength, he was
always calm, conversing, and even gay." While Chopin's biographers
have ascribed Mikołaj's death to heart and lung illness, Barciński offers
no evidence of it. Nevertheless, Mikołaj himself had written his son
about his "insupportable" cough. The fact that he and his wife had
moved from their own apartment to the Barcińskis' earlier that year suggests that the "final illness" was much longer than acknowledged. It may
well have been tuberculosis.

Barciński's very lengthy missive was in response to a request from
Chopin (in a letter that has vanished) for a detailed account of his
father's illness and death. He told Fryderyk that Mikołaj "mentioned
you often, and in his last days on this earth he instructed me to encour-

age you, to accept [in his name] . . . the blow with resignation."
Chopin's letter to Barciński must have finally revealed to the family that
he lived with George Sand, if he had not done it earlier in lost letters to
his father (who had inquired about the "other persons" in his communication of October 1842). This is quite probable because Sand wrote his
mother, Justyna, on May 29, that "there is nothing [better] to console
the best mother of my beloved Fryderyk than to assure you of the [mas-
culine] strength and self-control of this admirable child. . . . You know
how deep is his pain and how his soul suffers, but, thank God, he is not
ill, and in a few hours we are leaving for the country where, finally, he
will rest after this terrible event."

In what sounds like a letter from mother to mother, George told
Justyna that she need not worry that

> he is without care. . . . I cannot remove his suffering, but I can look after
> his health and provide attachment and dedication as you would have
> done. This is a most pleasant obligation, [and] I am happy that I can take
> it upon myself, [and] I shall never fail him. . . . Advising you that I shall
> sacrifice my days for your son and that I regard him as my own son, I
> know that, at least in this respect, I can calm your soul."

Justyna replied in French on June 13:

> Your moving words . . . calmed somewhat my poor being, tortured by
> sadness and anxiety . . . [and] my anxiety about Fryderyk was limitless.
> After the blow I had suffered, I kept thinking that this dear child, alone
> in a faraway country, with such fragile health and such a loving heart,
> will surely be shattered by this most cruel of news. . . . I suffered that in
> this terrible moment I cannot embrace this most beloved son and help to
> lift him out of despair. . . . My soul did not have a moment of peace. You
> understood well what was happening to me; a mother's heart was needed
> to feel it and to breathe real consolation into my heart. Thus Fryderyk's
> mother thanks you sincerely and entrusts her beloved child to your
> motherly tenderness. Be his guardian angel as you were my consoling
> angel.

In his letter to Chopin, Barciński begged him to "think about yourself, about your health . . . do listen to the saving counsel, based on wisdom and heart, of your guardian angel whom, knowing only from her
writings, I venerate, respect, and worship, and if I could ever see you, I

would drop at her feet and flood her with tears of gratitude for the tender and maternal care she offers you." His wife, Izabela, sent words of "gratitude" to "your protectress for the tenderness for you and her feelings for us. Her few words have calmed Mother and us about your health." But Izabela also inquired as to where Nohant was located: "People ask me and I don't know."

George Sand was now formally accepted as Chopin's friend and protector—if nothing else. They were aware of her fame and perhaps had even read her novels. And Fryderyk's mother and the rest of the family thought of her as a surrogate mother.

Chopin, Sand, Maurice, and Solange arrived in Nohant on May 30. But rather than recover from the shock of his father's death, Fryderyk came down immediately with an acute dental infection, his teeth having been decaying since adolescence. He was in bed with a high fever for a week and, as George recalled, he hallucinated in his sleeplessness about the ghosts of his father and Jaś Matuszyński, often confusing them. As it had in childhood and adolescence, in Vienna and in Stuttgart, death was haunting and stalking Chopin again. Sand spent days and nights at his bedside.

But responding as it always did to psychological stimuli, Fryderyk's overall health improved rapidly (his dental infection also went away) when his older sister Ludwika and her husband Kalasanty Jędrzejewicz announced their plans to visit Paris in July. He had not seen Ludwika since he left Warsaw twelve and a half years ago; Kalasanty was still a bachelor when Chopin had last seen him.

Sand invited the Jędrzejewiczes to stay at her square d'Orléans apartment, and Chopin went to Paris on July 13 to await their arrival the following day. It made sense for them to use George's apartment, which was larger and more comfortable than Fryderyk's. Moreover Sand had decided to stay behind because her new newspaper publisher, Louis Véron of *Le Constitutionnel,* insisted on a new novel from her as soon as possible after Eugène Sue, also a well-known writer whose own novel was to appear in forthcoming issues, became suddenly ill. George had such a reputation for churning out novels, virtually on request, that she was the logical choice for Véron to make, and she did not disappoint him: The latest instant novel was *Le Meunier d'Angibault,* one of the forgotten ones.

Thoughtful as she could be, George found time to rush a letter to Ludwika in Warsaw delicately warning her about the changes in

Chopin's health, appearance, and habits since they had last seen each other. She did not want the sister to be shocked or taken aback, explaining that, generally speaking, his health was not too bad, although he looked "miserable," and that the Jędrzejewiczes should not be alarmed by his explosive morning coughing fits. His lungs were healthy, Sand added. She also remembered to tell Ludwika, lest she be surprised, that many friends referred to the great musician as "little Chopin." And she invited the couple to Nohant, after Paris, but not until Fryderyk rested for the long trip to Berry.

Fryderyk, Ludwika, and Kalasanty had a marvelous time together. Chopin enjoyed being their Parisian cicerone, taking them to the botanical gardens, museums, and theaters, introducing them to his Polish friends (Grzymała was in town, but Fontana was in New York) and to the Marlianis, the Franchommes, and the Léos. He arranged a reception at his apartment. The three of them went to Père Lachaise Cemetery to place flowers on the grave of Jaś Matuszyński. And Fryderyk exchanged short messages with George several times a week.

Less than two weeks later, however, Chopin suddenly bolted back to the countryside, leaving the Jędrzejewiczes to continue discovering Paris on their own. Forewarned, Sand met him in Châteauroux with a diligence on July 25 to bring him home to Nohant. Chopin attributed his sudden departure to the need to complete the Sonata in B minor on which he had been working, on and off, since the previous year. He did not say what was the hurry.

His sister and brother-in-law did not seem to mind. Kalasanty, an engineer, was particularly interested in learning more about French industrial technology to see how it could be applied in Poland. But Sand may have been right when she wrote Charlotte Marliani that Fryderyk simply had had enough of social activity in Paris, especially upon hearing that Ludwika and Kalasanty were hoping to watch the celebrations of the anniversary of the July revolution the following week, repelled by the idea of having to spend hours in the middle of a crowd watching fireworks. Chopin could have asked Gryzmała, who had all the right contacts, to arrange for all of them to watch from windows of the Tuileries palace on the Seine, but he failed to mention it to him when they spent an evening together. Besides, Grzymała was preoccupied by his losses on the stock market and the pain in his coccyx, acquired when he fell down the stairs. But Fryderyk did write Grzymała from Nohant asking for "a piece of the window" at the Tuileries for his relatives. Still, it was very much like Chopin to run away from discomfort at the first sign (Sand added a note to the letter to Grzymała that "my little Chopin's health is returning, but he is saddened by your aching *derrière*").

Ludwika and Kalasanty arrived in Nohant on August 9, for a visit of nearly three weeks, a much more relaxed experience than Paris. Sand remembered this brief interlude later as one of the happiest periods in her life with Chopin. And she instantly developed a warm friendship with Ludwika whom she would describe as being "entirely superior to her time and her country, with an angelic character." Fryderyk strolled with the Jędrzejewiczes through the Nohant park, proudly showing them George's gardens and the spot where he planned to erect a hothouse. The brother and the sister spent the mornings over hot chocolate in the sitting room, reminiscing about their childhood while Kalasanty and Dr. Papet went hunting. Often, Fryderyk and Ludwika played piano four-hands, as they had as children in Warsaw, remembering old airs and melodies. In the evening, Chopin improvised at length to the joy of his listeners. On one occasion, Solange, now sixteen and a demure young woman, played a Beethoven sonata Fryderyk had taught her. On another, Fryderyk and Solange played together his Berry bourrées. And George read from her new *Meunier d'Angibault* novel for Ludwika, who savored the distinction of listening to one of Europe's most celebrated writers.

But the Jędrzejewiczes, with their children in Warsaw, had a schedule to keep. Fryderyk went with them by diligence to Orléans on August 28, and on to Paris by railroad, a novelty for Kalasanty (Chopin carried with him the finished chapters of *Meunier* for Véron). In Paris, Fryderyk took his guests to the Comédie Française and the Vaudeville Theater; their last evening was spent at the Franchommes', with the cellist and Chopin playing together far into the night. That was the last time Ludwika heard her brother at the piano. The Jędrzejewiczes left for Warsaw on September 3, but Ludwika received before their departure a farewell letter from George assuring her that "you are in my heart next to Fryderyk." Chopin returned to Nohant on September 4.

With Fontana away in New York, Chopin had turned to Franchomme to act as his agent and negotiator with music publishers. Writing from Nohant on August 1, he apologized for troubling him, adding, "I love you and I turn to you as to a brother. I kiss your children. Cordial regards for your wife." What Chopin wanted was to prevent Schlesinger from delaying the publication of a particular work, but also to have Franchomme play Schlesinger against another publisher concerning the price of that piece (not identified in his letter, but in a letter from Schlesinger that Fryderyk had sent on to Franchomme). The following day, Chopin dispatched a lengthy and highly confusing set of instructions to Franchomme concerning strategies for negotiating payments with Schlesinger and three other publishers, suggesting amounts varying from three hundred to one thousand francs for one composition or a group of them.

Franchomme must have been as gifted a businessman as he was a cellist because Chopin wrote him on August 5, thanking him for settling the matter with Schlesinger. But Chopin must have been strapped for money at that stage—perhaps because his illness in the winter had forced him to cut back on lessons and reduced his income—and he had to borrow five hundred francs from Franchomme. Sand was having at the same time problems collecting from Véron for *Meunier*.

Marie de Rozières also soon found herself running errands for Chopin. From Nohant, he asked her to deliver letters to Ludwika, who was still in Paris in mid-August, before coming to the country. Early in September, he wrote that if a Monsieur Franck, who lived above him on square d'Orléans, had not returned "the Encyclopedia and *L'Humanité,* please remind him." A week later, he asked Marie to dispatch a letter to Ludwika, who had stopped in Vienna en route home, enclosing songs his sister had heard in Nohant, with the music transcribed by him and the lyrics by Solange. Then, Marie was requested to send to Ludwika in Warsaw a letter from Sand saying: "You are the best doctor Fryderyk ever had because it is enough to start talking about you for him to regain his will to live."

It seemed as if Fryderyk spent much of his time, particularly when he was in Nohant, thinking up things he could ask his many devoted friends to do for him. His obsessive preoccupation with detail and his perfectionism had turned him at a young age into a pedantic man, often insufferable. It worsened with age. In mid-September, it was again Franchomme's turn to be helpful to Fryderyk. Chopin asked him to collect six hundred francs from Schlesinger, keeping five hundred francs for himself as repayment of the money the cellist had loaned him during the summer. If Schlesinger failed to pay, Chopin said, he would write his banker friend Léo to borrow five hundred francs to pay back Franchomme. Fryderyk was always afraid that if his publishers were "clever tradesmen," they might "cheat [him] like honest people." And something must have gone wrong because Chopin went to Paris on September 22 to meet with Schlesinger.

He saw the publisher immediately, apparently resolving the dispute, and, as he told Sand in a brief letter, he had lunch with Marie de Rozières and went on to visit Delacroix who was sick at home. "For two and a half hours," he wrote, "we talked about music, painting, and especially about you." Chopin must have felt well that week because he also played his new Sonata for cello and piano in G minor, op. 65, with Franchomme, called on Grzymała and Léo, and accepted an invitation from Princess Czartoryska at Hôtel Lambert on Île St. Louis. He was back in Nohant on September 27.

October in the countryside was quiet and relaxed, if increasingly chilly. George was busy preparing forty pounds of prune confiture, a task calming for the nerves, but absorbing all her energy. Fryderyk was "chiseling" the Sonata in B minor, but his mind was again on business matters. On October 22, he wrote Marie de Rozières: "If you see Franchomme, please ask him to write me" whether he has received a letter from Léo. He ended with a touch of badinage, begging her to "accept all the usual salutations placed at the end of a letter when one can take advantage of owning a handbook on correspondence." Fryderyk had developed the habit of sweetening his errand requests to friends with this sort of light banter. A week later, he asked Marie to inform the concierge at his square d'Orléans apartment that he expected to be in Paris in a few days and to order "smooth" muslin curtains for his sitting room if the old ones were worn. Marie was to check on it. The badinage du jour was: "Please amuse yourself with Bach in my place" (she should play Bach in his absence).

On October 31, Chopin wrote his sister Ludwika (via Marie in Paris, whom he used for a post office because no mail to foreign countries could be sent directly from Berry) with casual Nohant news about plans to expand the lawn and break open a door from the mansion to the hothouse that was being built next to it. He mentioned that Solange "is a bit weak today and sits in my room" and that Maurice was planning to visit his father soon. In the first open criticism of one of George's children, he added that Maurice, "in whose nature there is no courtesy," had not asked to forward thanks for a small cigar-making machine that Kalasanty had sent him. Next, he related extensively the deaths of a woman of Sand's acquaintance in a village near Nohant and of an old friend of her parents in Paris, neither of whom Ludwika had ever met. Always fascinated by the subject of death, Fryderyk concluded that "in a word, there has been more sadness than happiness since seeing you," a gross and wholly unnecessary exaggeration.

During November, Chopin kept alerting Marie de Rozières about his imminent return to Paris, asking to have the fireplaces lighted in his apartment before his arrival the following Sunday and have Madame Durand, the cleaning woman, "make an exception for me on Sunday and come to see me after one o'clock." Several days later, he advised that he was delaying his trip until Monday or Tuesday. Although Sand was planning to remain in Nohant until early December, Fryderyk was anxious to get back to Paris. He was getting bored in the country, was worried about problems with his music publishers, and anxious to resume the cash flow from piano lessons. On November 28, George and Dr. Papet drove him to Châteauroux from where he continued on to Orléans and Paris.

Impatiently awaiting Sand, Chopin wrote her at least twice during the first week of December. He was alone but, apparently, in good humor. It was snowing in Paris, and he told George that her garden "looks like sugar, [like] a swan, cream cheese, the hands of Solange, the teeth of Maurice." Fryderyk had fires lighted in her apartment and his servant, Jan, put flowers in her kitchen. He informed George that he had personally chosen a black "levantine" fabric for the dress she had asked him to order and took it to the dressmaker (he noted that the fabric cost nine francs a meter, "so it is of the best kind"). He also dined at the Franchommes' and visited the Marlianis (who suffered from a cold), but decided not to make "unnecessary visits" because "I lack adequate apparel." And, Chopin wrote, "the lessons have not yet started in earnest. *Primo,* I have received only one piano. *Secondo,* few people know that I have returned, and only today I had visits from a few interested persons. It will come slowly, I am not worried."

The problems with Schlesinger continued, however, to worry Fryderyk. In a short note in mid-December, he had offered the publisher the new Sonata in B minor and "Variations" (the note failed to clarify which Variations he had in mind) for 1,200 francs, adding that "I would have come to see you, but I don't feel well." In the end, Schlesinger turned him down after they disagreed about publication dates, and the Sonata was purchased by Joseph Meissonnier.

George Sand reached Paris on December 12, with Maurice and Solange. But, in the meantime, Chopin showed signs of unexplained interest in Jane Stirling, his Scottish pupil since the previous year. He had already dedicated the two nocturnes to her, and now he wrote Franchomme, inviting him to come to see him at his apartment, because "Miss Stirling, who would like to discuss her lessons with you, is here." This was bizarre because Franchomme was a cellist and Jane Stirling presumably had not developed a sudden interest in cello lessons. Chopin, who must have been aware that she was in love with him, subsequently sent regards for her through Franchomme, even before his rupture with Sand.

Chopin's eccentricities took many forms, but one of the most startling ones was his response to a very special request from Felix Mendelssohn. The German composer had written him from Berlin on November 3, asking whether "you could be so kind, as my old friend, as to write a few bars of music and to note at the bottom that you wrote them for my wife [Cecilia]." He explained that since they had last met, in Frankfurt, when he and Cecilia were engaged, "every time I want to please my wife greatly, I must play for her something from your music; she has a special fondness for everything you compose."

It was a most gracious request, and easy to meet, but weeks and months elapsed without a reply from Chopin. Mendelssohn must have concluded that either the letter had never reached Fryderyk or that he simply chose to ignore it.

Then, more than eleven months later, Mendelssohn received a letter from Chopin, written on October 8, 1845. It said: "My dear! With a little bit of goodwill, please imagine that I am writing this letter immediately after receiving the mail that had brought me pleasant news from you. Because my heart has nothing to do with this delay—please accept these words as if they had arrived on time. If the page enclosed with this letter is not excessively wrinkled, and if an opportunity presents itself, please hand it to Madame Mendelssohn from me. Allow me, also, to remind you that even if you have friends and admirers closer to you and more deserving, you do not have one who is more devoted. Always yours with all my heart. Chopin."

The "page" for Cecilia Mendelssohn was a full-fledged composition, an extraordinary present. Chopin regarded it as a purely private matter and did not wish the work to be published. Mendelssohn respected the privacy, and the work remains a mystery, for the manuscript has disappeared. But, then, Fryderyk believed in the mysterious—more and more as he aged and felt the end approaching, step by step.

Chapter 21

ON MAY 11, 1845, Carl Filtsch died in Venice at the age of fifteen, in the course of a European concert tour. Death had come again to claim a life among those closest to Chopin. Filtsch was his best and most promising pupil, one of the rare musicians whose playing brought tears to Fryderyk's eyes. He died as Chopin was recovering from his latest winter and early spring bout with lung-tearing cough, asthma, and fever.

On Easter Sunday, Chopin, always worried about his friends, had written an equally ailing Stefan Witwicki in Freiwald, Germany: "I miss you very much. . . . With you, I could have wept a lot."

For Chopin, there was no pianist as divinely inspired as the slight, intense boy from Transylvania who had come humbly to his door three and a half years earlier with a letter of introduction from a mutual friend and a plea to be accepted as a student. Carl had arrived in Paris with his brother Joseph, also a child pianist, on November 29, 1841, and called immediately on Chopin with a letter from Countess Fredericque Müller Streicher, a Czech who was his pupil between 1839 and 1841 (when she expressed her admiration one morning after Fryderyk had played from memory fourteen Bach preludes and fugues, he answered, "This, one never forgets!"). Normally, Chopin did not accept children as pupils, but he must have been immensely impressed by Filtsch because he began teaching him the following month at the average rate of three weekly lessons until April 1843, and arranged his first public appearances.

Wilhelm von Lenz described in an article in the *Berliner Musikzeitung* how Chopin taught Filtsch his Concerto no. 2 in F minor, op. 21:

Chopin wanted the pianist to take pains to render all the runs in cantabile style. This was the way he taught Filtsch, the beloved of his heart, to understand the first movement (Allegro Maestoso). . . . It was never a question of the second and third movements. Chopin insisted that each solo be studied separately; during the lessons, Filtsch was never permitted to play the movement through. This would have emotionally upset Chopin who believed . . . that the power of the entire movement is contained within each solo [section]. . . . When Filtsch finally received permission to play the whole movement, for which he had prepared himself by fasting and prayers of the Roman [Catholic] Church as well as by reading the work under Chopin's direction (who had forbidden him to practice), the maestro said: "Now this movement is sufficiently established for us to perform it publicly; I shall be your orchestra." With his incomparable range of accompaniment skills, Chopin evoked all the ingenious and elusive [qualities] of the instrumentation. He played from memory. I had never before heard anything comparable to the first tutti as he played it himself at the piano. As for the little one [Filtsch], he worked marvels. The ensemble left you with an impression for a lifetime.

This particular performance was held, according to Lenz, in the presence of a group of ladies, including George Sand. After Chopin and Filtsch had played together, Fryderyk said, "You have played this well, my boy, I must try it myself. . . . Yours is a beautiful artistic nature, you will become a great artist," whereupon little Carl burst into tears. At that point, Chopin dismissed the ladies—only Sand was allowed to embrace Filtsch—and told Carl and his brother that they would now take a walk. They strolled over to Schlesinger's music shop, where Chopin presented the boy with the score of Beethoven's *Fidelio,* saying, "I am in your debt, you have given me much pleasure today!"

Joseph Filtsch, Carl's brother, wrote their parents on March 8, 1842, that "the fact that he is Chopin's favorite pupil has a very great significance for his career. Besides, George Sand, who lives with Chopin, has a lively interest in Carl, and the influence on him by this intelligent, nice, and still charming woman is great. The maestro calls Carl his 'little urchin,' who knows everything, repeats everything and plays everything." Joseph recalled that when Carl was playing a Chopin nocturne, "he came over to me and whispered, 'nobody in the world will play it like him . . . except me.'" And when Carl was asked why he did not play the nocturne like his brother or like Chopin, he replied: "I cannot play according to the feelings of others." Chopin, Joseph wrote, was "very pleased."

Letters home from both boys described how Chopin and Sand looked after them, taking them to glittering Paris dinners and receptions. They listened together to Pauline Viardot at square d'Orléans, dined at the Kalkbrenners' and met the Rothschilds, Meyerbeer, the ambassadors of Saxony and Hanover, and "their ambassador," Count Apponyi, the Austrian envoy to Paris (Hungary was part of the Dual Monarchy). Little Filtsch was the darling of Parisian high society, the toast of the town—it was chic to adore him. Telling their parents about a reception at Chopin's apartment when Carl played for invited diplomats, aristocrats, and bankers, Joseph concluded, "It was a great day and you can appreciate the progress Carl is making and the high position enjoyed by Chopin."

And he summed it all up in a letter at the end of November: "I have never seen Chopin so moved as at the latest lesson. Carl was playing Chopin's Concerto in F minor, a work requiring equally superb technique and interpretation. He finished the first part, played the Larghetto, and next attacked the finale in such excellent execution, so intellectual, that I was astonished at the silence of the maestro, and I really became worried. I was ready to accuse him simply of being capricious, but I saw my error: He was really crying and he could not speak. He took my hand, and said one word, 'Unbelievable!' When he recovered, he turned to Carl and said: 'Very good, my boy, some things are magnificent, others not as good . . . !'"

Ferdinand Denis, a professional world travel writer who often visited the square d'Orléans, reported in an article in Vienna's *Der Humorist* in February 1843 that on one occasion, after listening to Filtsch, Chopin explained: "My God! What a child! Nobody has ever understood me as this child has. . . . It is not imitation, it is the same sentiment, an instinct that makes him play without thinking as if it could not have been any other way. He plays almost all my compositions without having heard me [play them], without being shown the smallest thing—not exactly like me [because he has his own cachet], but certainly not less well."

After completing lessons with Chopin in the spring of 1843, Filtsch began to play all over Europe on concert tours (he also began composing). In May 1845, he reached Venice after triumphant concerts in Paris, London, and Vienna. He died there a few days later from unknown causes. Obviously, Chopin must have been apprised very quickly of Carl's death. But there is no recorded reaction on his part.

Two other Chopin student-prodigies died young: Caroline Hartmann, a German who began playing publicly at the age of eight and to whom Chopin dedicated his Rondo in E-flat major, op. 16, just before she passed away at twenty-six in 1834; and a youth named Paul Gunsberg. The only child prodigy of that generation to survive and soar into greatness was Anton Rubinstein, *not* a Chopin pupil.

Chopin was slowing down perceptibly. The year 1845 brought only three mazurkas and the settings of two poems by Bohdan Zaleski—the first one a sad, quiet "Ukrainian School" song and the other, somber, about a Cossack and his girl who died far away from each other. Various unrelated reasons accounted for Chopin's reduced productivity. He was finding it harder to compose during the winter in Paris. In Nohant, as Fryderyk wrote in a midyear letter to the family, "I am not playing much because my piano is out of tune," but also: "I am, as usual, in a strange dimension . . . those *espaces imaginaires,* but I am not ashamed of it." He added, rather confusingly, "not seeing very far ahead, I wrote three new mazurkas . . . without thinking." They had been requested, Fryderyk explained, by a Berlin acquaintance whose father was about to open a music shop, Stern & Co.

All three of the Mazurkas, op. 63, composed in Nohant, were major works and Stern & Co. published them early in 1846. While it was very rare for Fryderyk to compose a whole opus only to please an "acquaintance," the request may have acted as an incentive to help him overcome a period of acute depression and high nervous tension caused by the winter illness and, quite possibly, by Filtsch's death. In contrast with almost all his other works of that period, the mazurkas for Stern carried no dedication.

Actually, Fryderyk was less idle in 1845 than his correspondence alleged. He began writing the Barcarolle in F-sharp major, op. 60, and the very important Polonaise-Fantaisie in A-flat major, op. 61, and planning several nocturnes and mazurkas. And that was the year when the Sonata no. 3 in B minor, op. 58—dedicated to Countess Emilie de Perthuis, a friend and wife of the royal aide-de-camp—and the Berceuse were published to great critical and public acclaim. The Third Piano Sonata, the last of this genre, represented, in the words of musicologist

Anatole Leikin, Chopin's reconsideration "not only of sonata form, but of the sonata genre as well" because "his sonatas, like his mazurkas or nocturnes, are marked by a special musical idiom." Zieliński believes that the Sonata no. 3 is Chopin's "deepest" work.

Most of the winter of 1845 was a time of acute illness for Fryderyk. George Sand wrote Stefan Witwicki in Freiwald (Germany) late in March that between Chopin's "coughing fits and his lessons, it is difficult to find a moment of peace and silence." About the same time she informed Ludwika in Warsaw that "our dear little one was greatly tired by the severe winter . . . but since the weather improved, he has been completely rejuvenated and revived. Two weeks of warmth helped him more than all the medicines."

Noting that Chopin's health was defined by weather, George came up with an idea of how to shelter him from the Paris winters:

> If I succeed in earning a lot of money this summer to travel with the family, I am thinking seriously about taking him away for the three worst months of the winter and [taking him] to the south. If he could be protected for a full year from the cold, he would have, together with the next summer, eighteen months of rest to be cured of his cough. I shall have to insist because, regardless of what he says, he loves Paris. But not to make him suffer excessively and keep away for too long from his pupils, he could be allowed to spend September, October, and November here, then return in March and give him additional time until May, before returning to Nohant.

Meanwhile, feeling better, Chopin tried to go on enjoying Paris, including a written exchange with Delacroix about shoes. First, Delacroix asked Fryderyk for a letter intervening with the shoemaker, Monsieur Brown, who had ignored the painter's direct letters, to agree to make boots for him. He wanted Brown to come to his home at 54, rue de Notre-Dame-de-Lorette, at nine o'clock in the morning. He also complained that "it is said that life elapses and we do not see each other. I love you sincerely, venerate you, and consider you as one of those who bring glory to our unhappy kind." Brown evidently still went on ignoring Delacroix who, having found another shoemaker—Rapp at 19, rue Feydeau—was now inquiring what "form of tips" Chopin wished for *his* shoes: "He makes rounded tips, like the English wear . . . [and] order winter boots [for yourself]."

At about that time, Chopin seems to have declined an invitation by Charles-Valentin Alkan to join him, Pixis, and Zimmermann in a performance for eight hands of the adagio and finale of Beethoven's Symphony No. 7 in A major. There is no record of Chopin's participation nor of a reply to Alkan's letter of March 1, asking him to play with them. But Fryderyk and George went to the conservatory on March 21 to hear Mozart's *Requiem,* a work he loved. Two days later, Delacroix went with them to a performance of Haydn's *Creation;* in the late evening, Chopin listened to Stefan Grotkowski, a Polish baritone, sing several of his songs. On March 24, he attended an Easter Sunday feast at the Czartoryski Hôtel Lambert, where he publicly criticized the poet Mickiewicz for submitting himself to the "servitude" of Andrzej Towiański, the mystic from Lithuania. It was one of the rare occasions when Chopin spoke ill of a friend in front of strangers, but this was a matter about which he felt strongly; despite his own mystical penchants (or because of them), he resented "professional" mystics.

Still during the spring, Chopin, Sand, Maurice, and Solange saw Bocage and Marie Dorval at the Odéon and admired the celebrated English actor William Macready in *Macbeth* and *Hamlet* at the Ventadour Theater. Fryderyk, whose own character was so Hamletlike in its endless indecisions, had first seen Shakespeare's play in Warsaw and was mightily impressed by it. (He wrote Tytus Woyciechowski on August 21, 1830, "Tonight [it is] to *Hamlet,* I am going!"). Jan Kleczyński, a student and biographer of Chopin, who knew him well, has written that Fryderyk had initially marked the manuscript of his Nocturne in G minor, op. 15, no. 3, composed in 1830, with the words: "After a Performance of *Hamlet,*" but then scratched them out, remarking, "Let them guess themselves." Sand had written Macready an admiring letter after the Ventadour performances, and the actor visited her and Chopin at square d'Orléans with his famous American world traveler friend George Sumner. The hosts sat all evening fascinated by Macready's and Sumner's discussions of Shakespeare.

On another level of cultural discovery, Chopin, Sand, and the children rushed to see a group of Americans purporting to be Indians from Iowa visiting Paris. Referring to them as *les sauvages indiens* (Indian savages) and "Joways," Fryderyk wrote his family that the wife of one of the Indians, "whose name in Indian was Oke-wi-mi and in French, 'Female Bear Who Rides on the Back of Another One,' had died of nostalgia for her homeland, and was buried at Montmartre Cemetery where Jasio [Matuszyński] is buried. Before her death, she was baptized and the funeral was held at the Madeleine Church." Sand, Chopin, and the children also received at her apartment Tom Thumb, the Barnum Circus midget, then performing in Paris as a celebrity.

By mid-May, heat in Paris became oppressive, and George and Fryderyk began to think about moving to Nohant for the summer. George had started on a new novel, *Isidora,* and hoped to complete it in peaceful Berry. Chopin, too, was ready to go, purchasing a calèche, a vehicle with a folding top, to make their journey more private and pleasant than by diligences. But Dr. Papet warned them that a typhus epidemic had broken out in the region and urged a delay. Finally, they left Paris on June 12, with Pauline Viardot, just back from a Russian *tournée,* joining them in Nohant a few days later.

Within days of their arrival, all of Berry was struck by the worst floods of the century, cutting roads and highways, inundating fields and houses, and washing away Sand's garden and lawns around the mansion. Berry's isolation from the outside world was total. Louis Viardot, trying to come to fetch his wife, was turned back. But after the flood receded and Pauline was able to leave on July 3, Sand, Chopin, and the children found themselves alone—without guests—and tensions in Nohant rose unpleasantly.

Sand was completing *Isidora* and corresponding with publishers in Paris about future novel and newspaper serialization contracts (two of them, Anténor Joly and Charles Lesseps, had come to Nohant on brief separate visits to discuss new projects), and George was in high spirits over being so much in demand. Fryderyk, however, was at loose ends— tense, nervous, and irritable. He refused to drink his morning hot chocolate because it reminded him of sharing it the previous summer with his sister Ludwika, whom he seemed to miss greatly. Working on and off, Chopin composed the three mazurkas and sketched other works over the course of the summer, but was dissatisfied with himself.

Moreover, his Polish servant, Jan, and Sand's cook Suzanne were at swords' points, fighting all the time. Jan, using his very limited French, told her that she had "a mouth like a backside" and was "as ugly as a swine," while Suzanne complained, accurately, that Chopin was paying him excessively high wages, much above what other Nohant servants were earning. Each threatened to quit if the other stayed, but their respective employers wanted them both to remain: Chopin insisted on keeping Jan as someone who spoke Polish (he disliked all change, anyway), and George thought Suzanne was a better cook than the aging Françoise. Inevitably, the servants' tug-of-war became another argument between Chopin and Sand, further raising the tensions.

A much more basic and ever deepening difference of opinion concerned Solange, now a sensual and independent-minded seventeen-year-old, whom George never tired of criticizing, often with reason, for her devil-may-care attitudes (obviously inherited from her mother), her lack of orderliness and profound laziness, the latter largely stemming from Nohant boredom after the excitement of Paris. Fryderyk naturally abstained from making any comments on the subject to George. But Solange was seeking his company more and more—visiting him in his room upstairs, bringing him flowers, and playing piano with him—in part because she liked and admired him, and in part to find an emotional antidote to Sand's stern treatment of her and, of course, to annoy her mother. Ironically, Sand, who had been complaining about Chopin's fits of jealousy over Pierre Bocage and her other men friends, was now jealous of the relationship between Fryderyk and Solange, much as she sought to conceal it. She may even have seen Solange as a rival, although she had no serious basis for this.

Then there was the problem of the twenty-two-year-old Maurice, who demanded that, as the "real man of the house," he should be accepted as the head of the family and the sole decision maker. As Maurice and Chopin continued to dislike each other, with the young man still resenting Fryderyk's liaison with his mother, Chopin's position was increasingly difficult. For some of the summer, however, Maurice had the company of Eugène Lambert, a fellow painter's apprentice, and the two spent much time together sketching in the countryside, which obviated excessive self-assertion.

It may have been his sense of loneliness that led Chopin, normally not a very reliable or frequent letter writer, to devote himself to unusually long letters to his family in Warsaw during the summer of 1845. Some were written at one sitting, others over a period of days, just as he wrote some of his musical compositions. This installment-plan letter-writing, as one of his biographers has remarked, was reminiscent of a diary that he sent home in "chapters" of unequal length. Very Chopinesque, the letters were often disjointed, confusing precursors of the stream-of-consciousness style.

In a letter dated "18–20 July 1845," Chopin described the June floods in Berry, then noted, "I was not made for the countryside, but I am enjoying the fresh air." He wrote that he kept looking into the guest room where Ludwika and Kalasanty stayed the previous year, "but there is no one there . . . sometimes an acquaintance, arriving here for a few days, occupies it." Fryderyk reported that he no longer had hot chocolate, and that he had moved the piano in the sitting room to the wall "where there was a little sofa with a table where Ludwika often embroidered my slippers" and Sand worked "on something else." He went on to tell about his three new mazurkas and an invitation he had received to attend the unveiling of a monument to Beethoven in Bonn the following year, adding that "if you should be somewhere near there, perhaps I would go."

Meanwhile, he continued, Princess Natalia Obreskov, a friend and mother of one of his pupils, would visit Warsaw en route to St. Petersburg and on her way back to Paris in the spring and would be glad to bring "our Mameczka" in her carriage. In such an event, "it would be necessary for all of you, sisters, brothers-in-law, and grandchildren to come, too," he added. Pauline Viardot would also visit Warsaw and "she promised me that she would sing for you" a Spanish song she had composed in Vienna: "I like it very much and I doubt that anything more beautiful of this kind can be heard or imagined. This song will unite you with me—I always hear it with great emotion."

Next, Chopin recounted Paris gossip, including the fact that Victor Hugo had seduced the wife of a painter named Billard ("he is ugly, his wife was pretty"). The Billards became legally separated, he continued, "but Hugo suddenly left on a trip for several months, and Madame Hugo (so generous) took Madame Billard under her protection." Accompanying Hugo was "Juliette, an actress from the Porte de St. Martin Theater for the last ten years, whom Hugo has kept for a long time despite Madame Hugo and their children. . . . Parisian tongues are happy to have something to talk about, and it is an amusing story, with Hugo . . . always presenting himself to the world at every opportunity as a greatly serious and superior [person]." Chopin also reported that Donizetti had arrived in Paris and would be composing a new opera, while Lamartine and his wife were taking waters a half day's distance from Nohant.

"I hope that I am providing you with news," Fryderyk wrote, devoting a full page—incomprehensibly—to the description of how "electro-magnetic telegraph between Baltimore and Washington produces extraordinary results," making it possible for merchandise ordered from Baltimore at 1 P.M. to leave Washington at 4 P.M., "a distance of seventy-five English miles." From the telegraph, which might have interested his brother-in-law Kalasanty, an engineer, Chopin immediately turned his attention to Solange, saying "that if my letter does not hang together, it is because I write a sentence a day. . . . Yesterday, Solange interrupted me to ask to play with her four-hands. Today (I am interrupting the letter) to watch a tree being cut down in the garden, near the road. This tree has been frozen, so it has to be cut down."

Then, an account of letters he had received from Franchomme and Marie de Rozières, informing him that François-Antoine Habeneck, the French violinist and composer (who, as a conductor, had first introduced Beethoven's symphonies in France), was going to Bonn for the unveiling of Beethoven's monument, and that Liszt had written a cantata. "Speaking of monuments," Chopin told his family, one would be erected in Abbeville in honor of Jean-François Lesueur, the composer, and another one, on the place de Louvre in Paris, in memory of the Prince d'Orléans, "the one who killed himself, jumping out of his carriage." Carrying on with non sequiturs, he followed with the news that after heavy rains had swept the Champs-de-Mars area in Paris, workers discovered there a Greek marble statue of Hercules catching the goat of Amalthea among the ruins ("the goat is gone, only the horns remain—it is a very interesting subject"). Fryderyk added that the statue was placed in the Palais des Beaux-Arts "where, last year, I took the Jędrze-jewiczes."

Chopin also was an accomplished multilingual punster, writing in Polish that "Godfroi de Bouillon was named that way because he was the most *consommé* captain of his time" (Bouillon had led a crusade to the Holy Land).

"This is the fourth time I am sitting down and I expect to finish the letter this time," Chopin announced on a new page, devoting most of it to plans for the approaching anniversary of the July Revolution in Paris, Ludwika and Kalasanty having watched a similar celebration the previous year. Then there was a section on the fights between Jan and Suzanne, the servants, and Fryderyk remarked that "for the sake of peace, I may have to let him go, which I would hate."

A letter to Warsaw, dated "Nohant, Beginning of August 1845," started with the comment that "it is stupid always to finish [a letter] on another day than it was started. This letter is being written for five days now." Next, on to a string of more Chopinian non sequiturs, interesting in that they showed what Fryderyk thought and did, from great achievements to trivia; they are revealing insights into his complicated and so little understood mind. They also provide insights into his attitudes toward people around him.

Concerning Marie de Rozières, for example, Chopin noted that he would forward to her a letter from Ludwika that he had just received in a packet from Warsaw, remarking that "she will surely reply because she likes to write, although she often has nothing to write about, but this is a pleasant vice and I regret that I am not in her category." Of Pierre Leroux, now the editor of Sand's local opposition newspaper, *L'Éclaireur,* Fryderyk wrote the family at great length that his problem is that "he starts [something], but does not quite finish. If he throws out a great idea, it is enough for him. It is so with the new [printing] machine, which he did not quite finish. It works, but not exactly enough. This has already cost him and his close friends tens of thousands [francs]; twice as much is needed in addition to goodwill and determination."

On another page, Chopin provided news about Berry events, royal doings in Europe, and some name-dropping: "Madame Viardot has gone to the Rhine where Meyerbeer invited her in the name of the King of Prussia along with Liszt. . . . The royal family will receive there the queen of England, who has already left for Germany with her husband, Prince Albert. Mendelssohn in Cologne is also busy with musical preparations for his king because Queen Victoria will be received in Stolzenfels. In Bonn, Liszt demands shouts of *Er lebe!* [Long Live!]. . . . In Bonn, they are selling cigars: *Véritables cigares à la Beethoven,* who only smoked Viennese pipes. They have sold so much furniture, old desks, old shelves after Beethoven that the poor composer of the *Symphonie pastorale* would have had a huge furniture business. . . . Professor Blanqui, an acquaintance of Kalasanty, has received an order from the young Spanish queen on his return from Madrid, where he was sent by the manufacturers of the famous d'Aubusson carpets."

And about himself: "Oh, time flies! I do not know how it happens, but I cannot do anything decent although I am not lazy. . . . But I must complete several manuscripts before leaving here because I cannot compose in the winter. After your departure, I wrote only that sonata. Now, except for the new mazurkas, I have nothing ready to be printed although it is necessary. . . . I hear diligences! They are driving past the garden: Will one of them stop for you to alight?"

The balance of the letter was a long compendium of news, comments, and observations on a score of totally unrelated subjects, a free association of ideas. For example: "I came back from a drive with Sol [Solange], who mightily drove me around in a cabriolet, in the company of Jacques." Jacques was "a huge dog of fine pedigree," and Chopin described it and its background over lengthy paragraphs.

Significantly, Chopin noted the death from consumption of the Belgian violinist Alexandre Artôt, an acquaintance, at the age of thirty, an event that hit close to home. He wrote: "[He] was so strong. . . . Nobody who had seen us together would have guessed that he would be the first to die, and from consumption. . . . I must shave because I have a big beard so, again, I set this letter aside. . . . I have already shaved, which is why I do not look fatter, although they tell me I am gaining weight. . . . I shall soon write again that I love you cordially. I would like to write very much, but I do not know from which end to start, if we are to have a written chat, like when we really chatted over hot chocolate in the morning in your room next door."

This was followed by a postscript: "Monsieur Brunel, the French engineer who invented [the idea of] a tunnel under the Thames in London . . . has now invented a new locomotive with which it will be possible to cover fifty English miles in an hour. . . . Sol, who has brought me hot chocolate for a snack, asks me to write that she embraces Ludwika. She has a very good heart."

When Solange was a child, Sand shared this view, writing her on one occasion that "you have a good heart, but too much violence in your character." Now, however, she had concluded that there really was nothing good about her daughter. In a letter to Marie de Rozières, George discussed Solange's ways: "She dresses, she undresses, she gets on a horse and gets off, she rises and she lies down, she scratches herself, she yawns, she opens a book and closes it, she combs her hair. . . ." When Sand arranged to have Marie de Rozières send Solange piano studies by Moscheles, the girl thought they were too difficult and had no desire to make an effort to "decipher" them.

By now, the Nohant Quartet—Sand, Chopin, Maurice, and Solange—lived in growing dissonance, each more or less at odds with the other. Angry with Solange, Sand was also increasingly disenchanted with Chopin whose own conflicts with Maurice, her beloved "Bouli," complicated matters even further. She wrote Marie de Rozières about Chopin that "on sunny days, he is gayer, but on long, rainy days he becomes somber and is lethally bored. He is not amused by anything that occupies and pleases me in the country. At such times, I would love to transport him to Paris by waving a magic wand. But, on the other hand, I know that he will be bored there without me. I would willingly sacrifice for him my attachment to the country, but Maurice is of another opinion, and if I listened to Chopin more than to Maurice, there would be cries of indignation. This is how things go in the closest knit families."

Now, Maurice had his way most of the time. When George proposed a trip with Chopin to Italy during the approaching winter to help him overcome his cough, Maurice vetoed it—much as Fryderyk was willing to "give a few years of my life for a few hours in the sun." And Chopin, as he knew he would do, fired his Polish servant, Jan, under pressure from Maurice; the new man was a Frenchman named Pierre.

Maurice had gone on a short visit to Paris on September 1, taking along the first two volumes of his mother's new three-volume novel, *Le Péché de Monsieur Antoine* (which she described as "arch-socialist and communist," but which would bring her twelve thousand francs). Returning to Nohant, Maurice accompanied Augustine Brault, George's twenty-one-year-old second cousin whom she had adopted a few years earlier. Augustine was the daughter of Adelaïde Philbert Brault, a cousin of George's mother, and a hard-drinking textile worker named Joseph Brault, and Sand had concluded that the girl was not being brought up in an adequate environment. She was reputed to have made a cash payment for the girl to the Braults. Sand placed Augustine at the Paris Conservatory to study voice, and she often came to rue Pigalle where she met Solange and Maurice as well as Chopin, and had attended concerts with them. Now, George decided that it was time to "enlarge" the family—it was unclear why—and Maurice was instructed to escort her to Nohant (and bring with him pearl gray fabric, chosen by Marie de Rozières, for a new dress for Solange).

By all accounts, Augustine was a pleasant young woman, but her arrival served to aggravate Nohant tensions. Though they had known each other for years, Solange and Augustine concluded, shortly after the latter's appearance, that they shared a mutual and cordial dislike. Chopin thought that it was a "stupid" mistake for Sand to have Augustine join the family permanently, and he said so; but his views no longer carried much weight. Solange suspected her mother of inviting Augustine to be her "second daughter" and to prepare her to marry Maurice (Sand, in fact, had mentioned such a possibility in a letter to the Braults). Maurice, apparently forgetting his passion for Pauline Viardot, was falling in love with his thrice-removed cousin. In the end, Sand unwittingly succeeded in creating two rival alliances within the family: Chopin and Solange on one side, and Maurice and Augustine on the other. George found herself in the middle, probably increasingly leaning toward Maurice and Augustine. After nearly seven years with George, since the start of their Majorca enterprise, Chopin began to feel like an outsider.

Chopin spent the first week of October in Paris, meeting with music publishers and old friends, apparently feeling quite well for a change (it was during that week that he answered Mendelssohn's letter from the year before and sent the composition for his wife). Sand wrote Ludwika in Warsaw that "our dear Fryderyk is not doing badly; we have a beautiful autumn after an awful summer, which he endured rather well." Dr. Papet had just examined Chopin, finding all his organs to be "perfectly healthy," and telling her that Fryderyk is given to "hypochondria," likely to persist until he reached the age of forty when "his nerves will have lost their excessive sensitivity." Chopin was approaching thirty-six at that point, and was becoming concerned over his ability to concentrate—and therefore to compose. He had begun work on a sonata for piano and cello, to be played with Franchomme, and what would be the Polonaise-Fantaisie, but it was slow and hard going.

Sand, meanwhile, had established a new speed record by completing her latest novel, *La Mare au diable,* in four days and four nights. It was a fairly short novel and she was able to read the entire manuscript aloud to Chopin and the three young people in the course of one evening. George dedicated the novel, one of her best, to Fryderyk, calling it "a modest story, placed among humble landscapes." A few evenings later, Solange defeated Chopin at chess eight times in a row.

Chopin returned to Paris for the winter on November 29, and Sand and the children arrived on December 9. They found the city appalling, "darker, sadder than ever," as George put it, and colder each day. Sand and Solange took to their beds, and Chopin "coughed more than anybody." Fryderyk warned Grzymała that he could not visit him too early in the morning "because it is already ten o'clock when I am done coughing."

On December 12, Chopin began writing a letter to his Warsaw family, completing it on December 26. First, he described in great detail the firing of the servant Jan and the hiring of Pierre, including his past employment. Next, several pages were devoted to Sand's visit to her cousins, the de Villeneuves, at their castle in Chenonceaux, near Tours, that was built during the reign of Francis I. George discovered there letters written by her grandmother, Madame Dupin.

Turning to his life back in Paris, Chopin wrote: "I am starting my mill. Today, I gave only one lesson, to Madame de Rothschild, but I cancelled two others because I had something else to do. . . . Now I would like to complete the sonata with the cello, the Barcarolle, and something else that I do not know how to call, but I doubt that I shall have time because the rush is starting." He was being asked, he reported, whether he would give a public concert, "but I doubt it." Liszt and Meyerbeer had also returned to Paris, Fryderyk noted, "and I found [Liszt's] card at home today." Chopin and Sand were busy all the month attending ballet, opera, and the theater, the latter to see a play with Marie Dorval in the lead role as *Marie Jeanne* about a peasant girl with a child abandoned by her husband. "A marvelous scene," Chopin wrote. "Everybody is weeping; all you hear in the theater is people blowing their noses."

Continuing the letter on Christmas Eve, Fryderyk wrote that "the doorbell does not stop ringing, and everybody here has a cold. That I cough intolerably is nothing strange, but the Lady of the House [Sand] has a sore throat and she cannot go out, which makes her impatient . . . the more good health one normally has, the less patience with physical suffering. There is no medicine in the world for that—even common sense does not help."

Chopin did find time to practice the new sonata with Franchomme, "and it went well. I do not know whether I shall have time to print it this year." He also learned from Franchomme about the death of the young wife of the painter Paul Delaroche, remarking in the letter: "I have survived so many people younger and stronger than I that I think I am eternal."

Chapter 22

FOR CHOPIN, AS A PATRIOT, the year 1846 was overshadowed by the failed bloody pro-independence uprising in Kraków, the ancient royal city in southern Poland. In personal terms, it marked the beginning of the end of the most important and secure period in his life, punctuated by the complex amours of Solange and the publication by Sand of an extraordinary novel of which Fryderyk may or may not have been the model for its despicable hero. In fact, thereby hangs the tale.

Actually, the year started for Chopin on an upbeat note although the winter, as usual, had brought dizzying coughing fits, fever, and general weakening. Still, with Sand, Solange, and Augustine, on February 20, he attended a carnival fund-raiser for needy Polish emigrants at the Czartoryskis' Hôtel Lambert, as ever the most imposing private residence in Paris. Over 3,500 guests filled the huge mansion on Île St. Louis in the Seine to dance, drink, and eat. Contemporary accounts emphasize that Solange and Augustine shone at the ball: It was like a coming-out occasion for them before the best of Parisian society.

The Kraków uprising began in earnest the next day, February 21. It is improbable that Prince Czartoryski and his fellow exiled Polish aristocrats and politicians—and, for that matter, Chopin—were wholly unaware of the unfolding drama in Poland as they danced and made merry at Hôtel Lambert at the start of carnival. There had been massive arrests and severe clashes throughout the country for nearly a week. Austrian forces had entered Kraków on February 18, two days before the Czartoryski ball, and Poles there were resisting. Word of the spreading unrest must already have reached Paris, although news of Kraków fighting may not have; communications still were quite slow. In any case, Polish hosts and guests at the ball were in a cheerful and optimistic mood about the happenings at home.

The initial plan was for simultaneous uprisings in all three parts of Poland under foreign occupiers—Austria, Prussia, and Russia—with the goal of preserving the relatively autonomous status of the "Kraków Republic," formed by the city of Kraków and its surrounding area. This "republic" had been created by the 1815 Congress of Vienna and given local freedoms, although it was administered and controlled by the three occupying powers. When Polish underground movements learned that the Kraków Republic was to be abolished altogether, they decided on launching armed uprisings to save it. Naturally, there had been no hope of actually expelling the occupants from Polish soil. In any event, Prussian security agents discovered the conspiracy in mid-February, arresting in Poznań the military chief of the movement, a young historian named Ludwik Mierosławski, and Austrian forces seized Kraków to disarm the plotters there.

The uprising on February 21 succeeded in ousting the Austrians—the first act of armed Polish resistance since 1831, except for a brief rebellion in the Galicja province around Kraków in 1836—and a National Government of the Polish Republic was formed, appealing to the rest of the country to join in the independence struggle. The battle for Kraków went on for two weeks, until the uprising was smashed on March 5, and Austrian and Russian troops captured the city. Presently, the Kraków Republic was dissolved, and Kraków itself incorporated into the Austro-Hungarian Empire as part of the province of Galicia ruled by Vienna since 1815.

Notwithstanding his close ties with the Polish emigré community in Paris, Chopin had no advance notice of the uprisings. Neither did his hosts at the Hôtel Lambert carnival ball. It was not an accident.

Poles exiled in France and elsewhere in Western Europe had all along been sharply divided between a politically conservative faction, headed by Prince Czartoryski and devoted essentially to the preservation of the Polish culture and spirit of national identity, and strongly liberal and more confrontational organizations advocating both independence and a democratic political system in Poland. These differences again became an issue at the time of the Kraków uprising. The aging prince, who had briefly headed the rebel anti-Russian provisional government toward the end of the 1830–1831 Warsaw uprising, had learned his lesson about the realities of power in post-Napoleonic Europe and was not about to challenge it again. The French government was most grateful to Czartoryski for not entangling it in Polish civil wars. And his influence in Paris was so great that the august Collège de France sought his endorsement of poet Adam Mickiewicz before offering him the prestigious Slavonic Literature chair.

The new uprisings were the work of radically minded antioccupation groups, represented in Paris by the Democratic Society, very much at odds ideologically with the Czartoryski faction. The society, in fact, was directly engaged in planning the 1846 rebellions, most of its members being veterans of the Warsaw rebellion. Its manifesto declared that Poland must rely on its own forces and resources to regain independence—not on foreign powers—and that to protect this independence it must be democratic and progressive: "Europe is alive with new conceptions of the social order. It is being organized on new foundations [and] in order to live in Europe, Poland must do the same."

Chopin, not politically active but patriotically inspired, had ties with both camps. He had powerful patrons, indeed friends, among the Czartoryskis and other Polish aristocratic families in Paris because of his social tastes. Fryderyk gravitated toward the powerful nobility in exile because it also assured him of access to French high society under the July Monarchy, which, in turn, was his entrée to broad spheres of social distinction—and profitable piano lessons that, among other advantages, accrued to him. At least one half of his pupils were titled.

However, Chopin also had close friends among the "Democrats," many of whom were exiled Polish writers, poets, and musicians—and these were artists' friendships. Chief among them were the poets Bohdan Zaleski and Stefan Witwicki (whose poems he often set to music), friends from their common Warsaw adolescence. A pleasant poetic acquaintance from the Dziurka coffeehouse days, but not an intimate friend, was Seweryn Goszczyński, nine years older than Fryderyk, who had fought in the 1830 uprising, then emigrated to France after years of underground conspiracies (for which he was sentenced to death in absentia by the Russians) and participation in the abortive 1836 Galicja uprising. In Paris, Goszczyński was a leading activist in preparing the 1846 rebellions.

Those militant writers formed the core of the "anti-aristocratic" political program fighting the Czartoryski faction, but Chopin was never affected personally by the struggles among his Polish friends. He was so greatly admired as an artist, regarded by all as a true Polish patriot, and loved by many that his politics—if any—did not really matter. Goszczyński, for example, would never have shared conspiracy secrets with Fryderyk (it would have been, anyway, a highly implausible proposition), but thought the world of him. Zaleski and Witwicki adored him, and the three men were in permanent contact (Chopin even found time to write Witwicki when the poet, then seriously ill, went to live at a German health resort in the early 1840s). And Chopin kept pretty much to himself his doubts about the success of the armed struggle in Poland (he confided them only to Sand).

Word of Kraków's fall on March 5 (Fryderyk's saint's day) had not yet been received in Paris, and Zaleski had sent a note of congratulations to the square d'Orléans apartment, expressing his hope that his next saint's day would be celebrated "in free and independent Poland. Things in Kraków look wonderful." There is no record of Chopin's reaction to this latest Polish tragedy, but he must have taken it almost as hard as the fall of Warsaw fifteen years earlier. George Sand unquestionably conveyed his sentiments when she wrote a relative a few days later, asking her to pray for "this poor Poland, which desires to regain its name, its language, nationality, and religion!" She added that "for several days, I have been so deeply moved and touched that I cannot sleep. . . . Polish existence is at stake."

But sleep or not, Sand and, presumably, Chopin helped Solange, Augustine, and Maurice to dress up for a Mardi Gras costume ball while the fighting still went on in Kraków. Augustine was dressed as Charlotte Corday, the murderess of Marat during the French Revolution (perhaps a political message in those conservative days). Solange was in a regal costume of the Louis XIV era. Life had to go on in Paris, at least for the new generation.

The young people attended a brilliant musical soirée Chopin held at his square d'Orléans apartment on April 30, shortly before the family moved to Nohant for the summer. *Tout Paris* was present: the Czartoryskis and the Sapiehas (another Polish royal family), Delacroix, the Viardots, and all the "phalanstery" regulars. Earlier, Sand had written Ludwika in Warsaw that her brother "isn't doing badly although March this year was very cold and sad. . . . However, our dear Fryc is not ill and he works, too much in my opinion, on his lessons. On the other hand, idleness does not agree with his restless and nervous character. Soon, however, I am stealing him away from his adoring [female] pupils and taking him to Nohant where he will have to eat a lot, sleep a lot, and compose a little."

Fryderyk, for his part, received a delayed response from his mother regarding his suggestion the previous summer that she might visit him in Paris, a suggestion that probably he did not mean too seriously. Justyna, in the third letter she had written him over all these years, had herself concluded that it was not a good idea. Princess Obreskow had called on Madame Chopin and, indeed, offered to take her to Paris in the autumn. "Perhaps her plans will change," Justyna wrote, "which would satisfy me because going with her I would have to spend the whole winter with you, and what would you, poor thing, do with me? I would upset you, because knowing your heart [I know] that you would be restless, you would think that I am bored, that I do not have enough comfort, and so on. No, my dear child, I shall not do that, especially because there are persons with you who care for you tenderly [and] for which I am very grateful to them. Perhaps God will permit me to see you again; I do not lose hope because I have faith in His mercy." Chopin apparently did not insist.

In mid-April, Fryderyk joined Franchomme for a week or so at the home of the cellist's relatives in Côteau, near Tours, to keep consulting with him on the composition of the Sonata in G minor for cello and piano on which he had been working for a long time. They had been practicing passages together for the past year, but Chopin still was not satisfied. Besides, he was tense, nervous, and continuously irritated, possibly the toll from the winter and the February uprising in Kraków. His bad humor, if we believe Sand, was now affecting all those around him. She wrote Maurice, then visiting his father in the southwest, that Fryderyk had returned from Côteau "more annoying than ever and more than ever he looks [for faults]. It amuses me, reduces Mademoiselle de Rozières to tears, [but] Solange fights the attacks of the claws with teeth bites [of her own]." With George complaining to her son in this fashion about Chopin, the erosion of their relationship was deepening inexorably.

*   *   *

Sand, Solange, and Augustine left for Nohant on May 5, and Chopin followed on the twenty-seventh, for his seventh summer at the Berry mansion. George met him in Châteauroux with a carriage to make the drive home more comfortable. Nohant that year was very much *en beauté,* and so was the house itself, where, to Fryderyk's surprise, Sand had the dining room repainted in pearl gray. And she told him of plans to redecorate the mansion extensively as soon as she received payment for the novel she was busy completing. It was called *Lucrezia Floriani,* and George worked on it seven days a week from seven in the morning until five in the afternoon, with a short lunch break. She had received a three-thousand-franc advance from the publisher of *Le Courrier français,* which planned to serialize the novel, and would get five thousand francs more on delivery of the manuscript on or about June 15.

But June also brought an unusual heat wave to Berry, making Chopin suffer grievously. And Sand showed little sympathy for him when she wrote Marie de Rozières that

> Chopin is completely astonished by [the fact] of *sweat.* He is unhappy, and he claims that he keeps washing himself, [but] he stinks. It makes us laugh to the point of tears to see such an ethereal being not consenting to sweat like everybody else. . . . He smells of eau de cologne, but we tell him he smells like Pierre Bonnin, the carpenter, and he flees to his room as if he were pursued by his own smell. . . . I embrace you. Chopin, not— he stinks!

But Fryderyk also had trouble composing. He wrote Franchomme on July 8: "I do everything in my power to work—but, somehow, it just doesn't come to me—and if it continues like this, my creations will resemble neither the chirping of birds nor the sound of porcelain being smashed. I have to accept it." Perhaps to find inspiration, he had asked Marie de Rozières to send him, from his Paris apartment, the pocket score of Mozart's *Requiem.*

As he often did, however, Chopin was exaggerating his state of mind: It was his habit of self-pity. The following evening, July 9, he was in a fine mood as Pauline Viardot, briefly visiting Nohant, sang well into the night and Fryderyk improvised music and impersonations until the small hours magnificently. Elisa Fournier, a friend from La Rochelle, who had stayed at the mansion on earlier occasions, was bowled over with admiration for Chopin's performance, writing her mother that his "genius" for imitations ranged from a Bellini opera aria to the prayer of Poles in distress, and from variations on Berry "bourrées" to the sound of a broken-down calliope.

Even Sand, so familiar with Fryderyk's mood swings, welcomed this change for the better in his behavior though she took full credit for it. She wrote Marie de Rozières on August 8 that "he is very nice this year. . . . I did well to show some of my anger, which gave me a bit of courage to tell him some truths and to threaten him that I might get tired [of it]. From that moment, he has been sane, and you know how good, excellent he is when he is not crazy."

Having complained to Franchomme that he was unable to compose, Chopin sent him five weeks later, on August 30, three manuscripts for which publishers in Paris and Leipzig were to pay 1,500 francs ("Do not deliver the manuscripts without receiving payment," he enjoined Franchomme). Even the short covering letter had been written in two sittings, with Fryderyk explaining: "I would chat with you endlessly, but I have no time to start this letter anew because Eug. Delacroix, who is kind enough to take these few words with him, is leaving instantly. He is an artist deserving of the greatest admiration—I spent beautiful moments with him. He venerates Mozart—he knows all his operas by heart."

Delacroix had delighted the household, as usual, by spending the last two weeks of August in Nohant, enjoying himself hugely. He wrote a friend: "I am incredibly lazy, I am not doing anything, barely reading, but the days are passing too quickly. . . . Chopin played Beethoven marvelously for me; it is worth more than all the theories." Arriving in Paris, Delacroix wrote Sand that he had delivered the three Chopin manuscripts to Franchomme, having worried about bandits on his trip back with the music "more than about my money."

Chopin had not identified in any letters the manuscripts Delacroix had taken to Paris, but he is known to have completed during 1846 the Polonaise-Fantaisie in A-flat major, op. 61, considered one of his greatest works; two Nocturnes (in B major and E major, op. 62, nos. 1 and 2); three Mazurkas (in B major, F minor, and C-sharp minor, op. 63, nos. 1–3); and the Barcarolle in F-sharp major, op. 60, he had started in the autumn of 1845. Delacroix must have carried some of them. The Sonata in G minor for cello and piano was not yet ready. Writing the family in October, Chopin remarked: "About my Sonata with the cello, sometimes I am satisfied, other times not. I throw it into a corner, then I pick it up again. I have three new mazurkas . . . but time is necessary to judge them well. When one writes it, it seems good, otherwise nothing could be written. Only afterwards reflection comes, and rejects or accepts it. Time is the best censor and patience the best teacher."

The Polonaise-Fantaisie was dedicated to his pupil Anne Veyret almost as an afterthought. He instructed Franchomme to do so in a postscript to a letter two weeks after sending the manuscripts with Delacroix, which confirms that this work had been in the batch from Nohant (the same postscript included regards for Jane Stirling). The reason for the dedication was unclear, as so often with him, but Madame Veyret was the wife of Charles Veyret, a rich industrialist and honorary consul of Ecuador, who was a friend of both Chopin and Sand; he often extended long-term loans to George. The Polonaise-Fantaisie was, after all, a very important work and a highly innovative one. Chopin's first major biographer, Marceli Antoni Szulc, commented in 1869 that "his masterly . . . modulation" leads from "a tearful, sweet remembrance" to the main motive with "strings ringing like brass trumpets." Fryderyk, who seldom did anything without a reason, may have decided at the last moment to dedicate the Polonaise-Fantaisie to Madame Veyret for materialistic considerations, never alien to him, as well as for pure friendship.

But pure friendship must have dictated the dedication of the three mazurkas to the beautiful Countess Laura Czosnowska, a friend of the Chopin family whose husband had shot himself dead out of jealousy in her presence. Fryderyk had always been very fond of her, and he had persuaded Sand to invite her to Nohant that summer along with Grzymała,. While Chopin was happy to have friends with whom he could speak Polish, George had developed an instant dislike for Laura—perhaps jealousy as well—sparing no nasty comments behind her back. The countess, she said, had "too many baubles on her robes" and her talk caused "migraines." Her presence turned Sand angrily against Fryderyk as well. Whenever Ludwika was mentioned in conversation, George would sing her praises, emphasizing that she was "worth a hundred times" more than her brother. Sand even criticized Laura's little dog Lili, claiming it had "bad breath." Maurice and Augustine made cruel jokes about Laura after her departure, which led to a shouting clash between them and an indignant Chopin. In the end, Fryderyk's response may have been to dedicate the mazurkas to the countess—to get even with Sand. Clearly, this was not a happy summer for them.

Solange and her amours were another feature of the summer of 1846. The story could have been taken from the libretto of an Italian opera or (equally beloved by Chopin) Mozart's *Marriage of Figaro,* from a Molière comedy, or even from a romantic novel by George Sand. In the first place, of course, was Solange, her character and her relationship with her mother, her brother, her cousin Augustine, and Chopin, creating resentments, misunderstandings, intrigues, and imbroglios on a colossal scale. The mounting conflict between Chopin and Maurice, and its effect on Sand's attitudes, made difficult human matters even worse—further complicating the situation involving George and Fryderyk. And, finally, there were Augustine's designs on Maurice, who was not entirely certain what he desired for himself, and Sand's indecision about her plans for him. There was not one cool head in this breathlessly and absurdly emotional household.

At eighteen, Solange was "a beauty," in André Maurois's words, resembling her remarkable and stunning great-grandmother, Aurore de Saxe. But she was "naturally cold and bizarre," he writes, "always ready to do anything because of her spirit of contradiction. . . . A bit crazy, she had her mother's toughness without having her genius. . . . Solange was a rebel. The mother did not tolerate in the daughter the independence she had once demanded for herself." Respecting nothing and nobody, Solange did as she pleased, to Sand's constant fury, and manipulated all those around her as best she could. Maurois writes that Solange "fascinated" Chopin because she was the only one in the household who did not treat him like "a spoiled child." Sometimes "she mocked Chopin [or] played the coquette with him." She was friends with Augustine when it suited her—and otherwise treated her like an enemy.

The frustrated Sand had put Marie de Rozières in charge of Solange's education, but she remained determined to control her upbringing, particularly when it came to relations with men, a subject with which she was eminently familiar. "Not a word, even indifferent, about the masculine sex. . . . This is prudence I recommend to you," George wrote Marie concerning themes she could discuss with the adolescent Solange. But the girl did not need Sand's advice, dealing with men in her own fashion.

The first serious opportunity presented itself when George Sand took

Solange and Augustine with her to the Berry estate of Count Stanislas de Lancosme-Brèves at Mézières-en-Brenne for four days of steeple-chase races. The count raised Thoroughbreds and Sand was the secretary of the Berry riding club, and they were friends. Chopin, naturally, had no desire to travel fifteen leagues in exhaustingly hot weather to watch horse races, so the three women went alone on June 7. Solange and Augustine filled their trunks with elegant clothes and Louis XIII–style hats. A contemporary sketch shows Solange at Mézières-en-Brenne as a self-assured young woman wearing a high-neck, long-sleeved tight bodice with peplum, a many-petticoated full skirt, and a large tilted hat with a side veil over her jet-black hair.

It was at the steeplechase that Solange met Viscount Fernand de Préaulx, a twenty-four-year-old relative of Count de Lancosme-Brèves. Sand described him as "tall, thin, strong, a superb head, great hair, blue eyes, black eyebrows, clear complexion, a hoarse voice, an open, frank, naïve, and affectionate attitude, somewhat better put together than a peasant, rides a horse like a Cossack, obliging, gentle as a lamb, but always ready to tear down the reins of a miscreant who looks at a lady critically." De Préaulx came off this word portrait as not being very bright, with the additional caveat that "one would like a little bit of a fortune," suggesting that he was not particularly rich. Having made it obvious that he had fallen in love with Solange and "being attentive to her slightest desire," Sand indicated that she would be willing to accept him as a son-in-law despite his drawbacks in intelligence and wealth. However, she remarked with apparent concern that Solange was "capricious, changeable." It seemed as if George was anxious to see Solange married and gone from her life.

De Préaulx and Count de Lancosme-Brèves visited Nohant during the last week of July, presumably to expose the young man to the rest of the Sand household and to have more time with Solange. George had concluded at that point that her daughter "liked" de Préaulx and she made it clear that she would favor their marriage even though she privately described him as "a peasant gentleman, very naïve, very round, very simple. . . . He shows no intelligence, especially in words. . . . As for me, I love him from all my heart. But he is not a man [who would] shine in Paris. He knows nothing about modern civilization; he has spent his life in the woods, with horses, boars, and wolves whose heads he smashes with the handle of his whip."

Sometime in September, Solange announced that she was engaged to de Préaulx. Chopin, whose opinion at that stage may not have been sought by anyone in Nohant, approved of the marriage because, according to Maurois, "this aristocratic pretender meets [Fryderyk's] prejudices." But now Sand decided that the wedding should be delayed because she thought that Solange ought to wait at least six months to determine whether de Préaulx "is as perfect as he seems." Reminding her daughter how "little happy" she had been in her own marriage, George expressed doubts whether Solange understood love: "She is a little child whose senses do not speak out at all and who does not feel that instinctive attraction or repulsion do give strength to inclinations and antipathies." And she wrote Charlotte Marliani: "My belief is that Solange would not mind being called Madame." As for Chopin, he took it upon himself to side with Solange in her desire for a wedding soon. He and Sand quarreled, but, in the end, she relented and agreed to a wedding early in 1847.

Next, Chopin found himself in the midst of another family crisis. This one concerned Maurice and Augustine. It appeared that while Maurice had at first encouraged Augustine, who was ready to wed him, he presently changed his mind in what George later described as a "rather cruel act," reminiscent of his father's behavior toward women. At that point, Solange's detestation of Augustine, plus a strong penchant for intrigue, led her to convince Chopin that the cousin was Maurice's secret mistress. Fryderyk, both gullible and prudish, and always disposed to believe Solange, turned on both Maurice and Augustine, denouncing him to his face in violent words and treating her with "frightening bitterness." As it happened, Chopin was just then in the midst of one of his rages against the world.

The charge was unjustified, but Fryderyk's attack on Maurice represented to Solange a most gratifying attack on her mother. Maurice responded with threats of leaving Nohant for good, a thought that horrified Sand. Not surprisingly, she reacted by chastising Chopin. As she wrote in *Story of My Life,* "This could not and should not be [allowed to happen]. . . . Chopin could not stand my legitimate and necessary intervention. He lowered his head and declared that I did not love him anymore. What blasphemy after these eight years of maternal devotion! But the poor aching heart had no consciousness of his delirium."

Writing his family from Nohant on October 11, Chopin complained for the first time about Sand and her household. Fryderyk reported that he had wanted to invite to Nohant his composer friend Józef Nowakowski, who had left his card at the square d'Orléans apartment after arriving in Paris, but "they do not want him here." George and Maurice had joined in vetoing the invitation. Chopin told of "little jokes, then grosseries" by "the cousin [and] the son" directed at Laura Czosnowska after her departure and of Sand's remarks in her presence about his sister Ludwika being "worth a hundred times more than you," to which "I replied, 'I think so.' " Chopin mentioned that Solange's and Maurice's marriages were both "in the works," expressing the hope that they would take place soon so that, in effect, George's attitude toward him would improve. As an example, he cited Maurice's successful opposition to Sand's plans for spending the past winter in Italy, writing that after the marriages "these views . . . would change."

The balance of this extremely long letter—Chopin was increasingly developing the habit of penning lengthy missives home when he was unhappy—was given to the fact that their little dog, Marquis, refused to eat from gold-leafed dishes, to news of discoveries of new planets and calculations of their orbits, and the invention in London of an "automaton called *Eufonia* that pronounces quite clearly . . . long phrases and sings an aria of Haydn and 'God Save the Queen.' " Fryderyk observed that "if opera directors could have such androids, they would not need choirs that cost a lot and cause a lot of problems." He certainly possessed an endlessly curious mind.

Parallel with all the real life events surrounding Chopin was the imaginary *Lucrezia Floriani,* which soon acquired a rather dramatic existence of its own. *Lucrezia* was George Sand's new novel, a steamy, bodice-ripper roman à clef that created instant sensation when its first serialization installment appeared in the Paris newspaper *Le Courrier français* on June 25.

This is the Sandesque boilerplate plot of the novel: Lucrezia is a great Italian actress who retires from the stage at the young age of thirty to her home on Italy's Lake Iseo to devote herself to the education of her four children and writing successful plays. She has had numerous love affairs, but does not consider herself a courtesan because she had always "given" to her lovers and never received anything, even from friends. As André Maurois sums up Lucrezia: "She had loved much, but never without a sincere desire for a shared life and eternal fidelity. She had passions of eight days and even of one hour, but each time she believed she was devoting her whole life to it."

Lucrezia then meets twenty-four-year-old Prince Karol de Roswald (six years her junior!), an aristocrat from central or eastern Europe, who is adorable, gentle, sensitive, exquisite, "an angel [with] a beautiful face, like a great sad woman." They fall in love and, naturally, Lucrezia looks after him as she does after her children. Soon, however, Karol's true selfish character is revealed: He becomes jealous, intolerant, and [Maurois adds] intolerable. "One day," Sand writes, "Karol was jealous of a parish priest who came for a donation. On another day, he was jealous of a beggar whom he took for a disguised lover. Still another day, he was jealous of a servant . . . who had answered [him] with harshness that did not seem natural to him. Then it was a salesman, then the physician. . . . Karol was even jealous of children . . . especially of children. These, indeed, were the only rivals he had, the only beings about whom Floriani thought as much as about him."

Karol displayed his irritation and fury through icy politeness and "that is when he was veritably insupportable . . . [to] torture those who loved him." This constant battle destroys the "unhappy Lucrezia," she loses her beauty, she becomes yellow and wrinkled, she suffers from having been condemned to premature old age by the mistreatment of a lover who no longer respects her. And she no longer loves Karol. One morning, she suddenly dies.

Inevitably, it was assumed by a great many readers, particularly among artists and Fryderyk and George's friends (and enemies), that *Lucrezia Floriani* was a thinly veiled version of their life together, Chopin being the model for Prince Karol and Sand for Lucrezia. It became the subject of major Paris gossip, and it would later be a controversy involving different Chopin and Sand biographers. It has been cited, at the time and subsequently, as the ultimate cause of the rupture between the lovers. Such characterization, however, is inaccurate. *Lucrezia* probably, but not necessarily, was *a* factor in the breakup; there were other factors, possibly much more important. Still, the novel was part of the destructive emotional climate that had come to prevail in the Sand-Chopin household by 1846.

To be sure, Lucrezia and Karol resembled George and Fryderyk enough to warrant the widespread belief that Sand had, maliciously, copied reality. It is not out of the question, on the other hand, to suggest that she thoughtlessly followed her professional custom of modeling characters on real people, creating composites based on those she knew. If nothing else, this method was less taxing on her imagination; indeed, other authors of her generation—notably Balzac—often employed it. But it does become a matter of intent, the question being whether Sand—to hurt, punish, or embarrass Chopin—had deliberately depicted him as the despicable Karol. For example, Marie d'Agoult, writing under her own pen name of Daniel Stern, had clearly done it to Liszt in her novel *Nélida* after they broke up as lovers.

Sand herself forcefully denied the charge, although it raises another interesting question—whether under all the pressures on her during 1846, when she wrote the novel at her usual breakneck speed, George had not lost her critical faculties to the point of ignoring the harm she might be inflicting on the object of her maternal feelings. Or, finally, were the accusations partially true? Had Sand been carried away by too much coffee and the momentum of her narrative? For his part, Chopin was not the easiest and most unselfish of creatures, genius notwithstanding.

In *Story of My Life,* Sand claims:

> It has been pretended that . . . I have painted his character with a great exactness of analysis. People were mistaken when they thought they recognized some of his traits. . . . Proceeding by this system, I have traced in Prince Karol the character of a man determined in his nature, exclusive in his sentiments, exclusive in his exigencies. Chopin was not such [a man]. Nature does not design like art, however realistic it may be. . . . Chopin was a résumé of these magnificent inconsequences, which God alone can allow Himself to create. . . . He was modest on principle, gentle by habit, but he was imperious by instinct and full of a legitimate pride, which was not unconscious of itself. . . . Moreover, Prince Karol is not an artist. He is a dreamer, and nothing more; having no genius, he has not the rights of genius. He is, therefore, a personage more true than amiable. . . . This story is so little ours! It was the reverse of it. There were between us neither the same raptures nor the same sufferings. Our story had nothing of a novel; its foundations were too simple and too serious for us ever to have had occasion to quarrel with each other, apropos of each other.

Responding to criticism by the writer Hortense Allart, Sand wrote: "I am neither so great, nor so mad, nor so good, because if I were united with Prince Karol, I confess that I would not have allowed myself to be killed. . . . I would never think of sending away a friend whose eight years of mutual devotion had rendered him inappreciable." She added: "If I had given Karol the talent of Chopin, I would have also given him his heart and wisdom, and then he would cease being Prince Karol."

At best, Sand had exaggerated the figure of Chopin—if he *was* to be Prince Karol, which suggests common literary license in creating composites. Apart from the fact that Karol was not presented as an artist, or anything else for that matter, Chopin was not as obsessively and pathologically jealous although he had shown considerable jealousy—under the provocation of George inviting former lovers and potential future lovers, even for "passions of one hour." Still, she had written a friend as far back as 1843 that "Chopin's friendship has the character of an exclusive and jealous passion." In the emotional complexities and turbulence of life in the Sand household, Fryderyk probably was jealous to some extent of Maurice as a rival for her maternal loyalties, but certainly not to the extent attributed to the fictional Karol.

There is no question that Sand was becoming increasingly impatient with Chopin's moods and his constant illness as she nursed him over the years. She had made it plain in letters to friends long before she wrote *Lucrezia;* all these pent-up resentments may have exploded in the novel. Liszt wrote many years later that "they had only survived [together] with the one by a violent effort of respect for the ideal which he had gilded with its fatal brilliancy; [and] with the other by a false shame which was predicated on the pretense of preserving constancy in fidelity. The time came when this fictitious existence . . . dried up under the eyes of the spirtualistic artist. . . . It seemed to him to surpass what honor permitted him not to perceive."

Chopin's nineteenth-century biographers tend to blame Sand for accelerating the rupture through *Lucrezia.* Maurycy Karasowski, highly unreliable when it came to facts, wrote that "the depressed invalid now became a burden to her. At first, her somber mien at times and her shorter visits to the sickroom showed him that her sympathy for him was on the decrease; Chopin felt it painfully, but he said nothing." Whatever Sand's "mien," Fryderyk never lived in a "sickroom" and was up and about long after their rupture, and this account makes the rest of Karasowski's views rather doubtful:

The complaints of Madame Sand that the nursing of the invalid exhausted her strength, complaints to which she often gave expression in his presence, hurt him. He entreated her to leave him alone, to take walks in the fresh air; he implored her not to give up her amusements for his sake, but to frequent the theater, to give parties, &c.; he would be contented in quietness and solitude if he only knew that she was happy. At last, when the invalid still failed to think of a separation from her, she chose a heroic means.

The "heroic means," of course, was the decision to create *Lucrezia*—Karasowski's implausible idea. Sand did things on the spur of the moment, not out of premeditation, and Karasowski's version makes little sense. But she did write novels on the spur of the moment, as a way of life to the degree that any writer can do it, and the criticism of Sand's subsequent attitude by Frederick Niecks, Chopin's highly competent early biographer, merits attention.

"The arguments advanced by George Sand are anything but convincing," Niecks writes.

> In fact, her defense is extremely weak. She does not even tell us that she did not make use of Chopin as a model. That she drew a caricature and not a portrait will hardly be accepted as an excuse, nay, is sure to be regarded as the very head and front of her offending. But George Sand had extraordinarily naïve notions on this subject. . . . If impudence can silence the voice of truth and humanity, George Sand has gained her case. In her account of the *Lucrezia Floriani* incident George Sand proceeds as usual when she is attacked and does not find it more convenient simply to declare that she will not condescend to defend herself—namely, she envelops the whole matter in a mist of beautiful words and sentiments out of which issues . . . her own saintly self in celestial radiance.

The most puzzling aspect of this entire episode is that Chopin did not appear to take umbrage at *Lucrezia,* at least at the outset, and, instead, was quite complimentary about it. Sand says in *Story of My Life* that

> the portrait is so little that of a great artist that Chopin, in reading the manuscript every day on my writing desk, had not the slightest inclination to deceive himself, he who, nevertheless, was so suspicious. And yet, afterwards, by reaction, he imagined, I am told, that this was the case. Enemies . . . made him believe that this romance [novel] was a revelation of his character. At that time, his memory was no doubt enfeebled; he had forgotten the book, why did he not reread it!

In the letter to Hortense Allart, written in June 1847, Sand wondered "how is it possible that I composed this novel under his eyes and that I read it to him, chapter by chapter, when I was doing it, listening to his observations, or rejecting them, as it always happens when we work under each other's eyes, and that he had never thought of recognizing himself, nor me, in these lovers of Lake Iseo?"

That Sand read *Lucrezia* to Chopin is borne out by Delacroix, who recalled in a subsequent letter to Caroline Jaubert, a friend, that during his August 1846 stay in Nohant she had done so one evening in his presence. "I was in a state of torture during the reading," Delacroix wrote. "The executioner and the victim equally astonished me. Madame Sand appeared entirely relaxed and Chopin did not cease to admire the story. At midnight we left together. Chopin wanted to accompany me, and I took advantage of this opportunity to sound out his impressions. Was he playing a role toward me? No, really; he had not understood it. And the musician persisted in his enthusiastic praise for the novel." Delacroix had earlier complimented George upon hearing that she had dedicated a short new novel, *La Mare au diable,* to Chopin: "You had a good idea," he wrote her. It was the only book she had ever dedicated to Chopin, the composer who had never dedicated anything to her.

How does one explain Chopin's reaction to *Lucrezia?* It is hard to believe that he "had not understood it," considering his command of French, which he used every day for fifteen years, and his basic intelligence. Given his short attention span, except for music, it is conceivable that he simply was not listening to Sand when she read (though she refers to his "observations") and applauded out of politeness. André Maurois's comment is that Chopin's "extreme decency made him pretend impassibility."

None of the above is convincing. The publication of the novel's installments in *Le Courrier français* was completed on August 19, while Delacroix was still in Nohant. There is nothing to indicate that Chopin had changed his mind about admiring *Lucrezia* on the basis of criticisms that may have reached him from Paris during that time; Delacroix would have noticed it. Chopin moreover made no references to the novel in his October letter to the family in Warsaw, in which he had complained about the Sand household's unfriendly attitude toward his Polish friends. In retrospect, it is clear that *Lucrezia* was not an issue, one way or another, between Chopin and Sand during the balance of his time in Nohant that year.

Chopin left Nohant on Wednesday, November 11, in the normal course of events, to resume his Paris teaching commitments as he did every year. This was nearly two months after the end of the *Lucrezia* serial in the *Courrier*. Obviously, Fryderyk's departure was not precipitated by this or any other event although the tensions involving him and George and Maurice remained high. Sand was to join him in Paris later in the year or early in 1847, and, in the meantime, they kept up normal correspondence.

Yet, this was Chopin's farewell to Nohant. He would never again return there, to the house and the countryside where he had composed some of his most magnificent music during the seven extraordinary summers he had spent with George Sand. Nearly one half of his lifetime's musical creation was born in Nohant: thirty out of his sixty-eight opus numbers.

Within days of his arrival in Paris, Chopin composed two brief works, one a *Veni Creator* prayer that he played on the organ during Mass at St. Roch, the "Polish church," where he was the witness at the wedding on November 28 of his poet friend Bohdan Zaleski and his former pupil Zofia Rosengardt. The second one was never identified and neither of these works have survived. They were the only compositions under the heading of "religious" that Fryderyk is known to have written, perhaps because of his indifference to organized religion. He was, of course, a Roman Catholic in good standing, but he shied away from excessive devotion, criticizing Adam Mickiewicz for falling under the spell of the mystic Towiański.

Chopin had, however, a good friend in Aleksander Jełowicki, who held a doctorate in philosophy from Warsaw University and became in Paris exile a publisher of Polish-language books and periodicals, including the *Annuary of Polish Emigration,* as well as a militant politician and a deeply religious man. In the mid-1840s, the mustached Jełowicki entered a theological seminary in Versailles and soon took religious vows. Chopin and Father Jełowicki remained in contact in the ensuing years, and the priest exercised a discreet spiritual influence on Fryderyk, particularly as the composer approached his demise.

Fryderyk appeared to be in good spirits after his return to Paris. He played the piano together with the bride at the Zaleskis' wedding reception. He was a frequent guest at the Czartoryskis' Hôtel Lambert—he had a written invitation for every Saturday evening—and spent much time visiting with Delacroix and Franchomme. And, to judge from their correspondence, Fryderyk and George were again on warm, pleasant terms. Writing to her on November 25, he expressed the hope that her migraines were gone and that she "feel better than ever," and his satisfaction that "the whole group" was back in Nohant. This was a reference to Maurice's return from a trip and the arrival, two days after Chopin's departure, of Fernand de Préaulx, presumably to pursue the courtship and keep his fiancée company. Fryderyk informed Sand that a professor named Aubertin had admiringly read *La Mare au diable* as an "example of fine style." He promised to forward George's fur coat to Nohant the following day (it was growing bitterly cold there), and advised that the cost of a new piano for her would be nine hundred francs. He also asked George to thank Marquis, the dog, for "sniffing at my door." He wrote her again briefly on December 12, 15, and 30 about mundane matters, friends, and the weather. The December 30 letter, he said, "should reach you on New Year's Day together with traditional candy, *stracchino*, and *Cold Cream de Mme de Bonne Chose*." It was cold in Paris, Chopin added, and he and Grzymała were on their way to Hôtel Lambert "wearing all possible overcoats." The letter he had received from her the previous day "gave [him] much happiness."

It did not seem at that point that they were on the verge of breaking up, neither apparently having a motive for it. Chopin celebrated New Year's Eve with the Czartoryskis, writing Sand at least two chatty letters during January. He congratulated her on starting to write dramatic plays—she had already completed yet another novel, *Le Piccinino*—and remarked that people claimed to know him well: "If this continues, I shall start to believe that I am an important personality." On January 18, he played at a reception at the home of his old friend Countess Delfina Potocka. Thus far the year 1847 was shaping up well for him although, as he remarked in a mid-January letter to George, "illness follows illness here."

Arriving in Paris on February 6, with Solange and de Préaulx to start preparing their wedding, Sand resumed her normal social activities together with Chopin at square d'Orléans. The publication that month by Desessert of *Lucrezia Floriani* in book form had no impact on their relationship (in an April letter to his family, Fryderyk remarked in passing that his sister Ludwika will probably like *Le Piccinino* better than *Lucrezia,* "which had excited less interest here than the other novels").

He may, after all, have misunderstood the tale of Lucrezia and Karol and the effect it had on the reading public.

On February 17, Ash Wednesday, Chopin and Franchomme played the Sonata in G minor for cello and piano, op. 65, which Fryderyk had finally completed; he dedicated it to Franchomme. This première of the sonata was held at Chopin's apartment with Sand, Solange, Grzymała, Delacroix, and Arago the only ones invited to hear it. On March 23, Chopin and Franchomme played it again at Fryderyk's apartment at a reception in honor of Countess Potocka, in the presence of Sand, Prince and Princess Czartoryski, and Prince and Princess Wirtemberg. On April 1, Delacroix took Chopin and Sand to the Luxembourg Palace to show them their images on the ceiling: Chopin as Dante and Sand as Aspasia. On April 6, George and Solange fled Paris for Nohant after a dramatic shift in the girl's marriage plans.

And on April 9, Chopin suffered another great blow in his life: Stefan Witwicki, his poet friend, died after a long illness. Antoni Wodziński (Maria's brother) had died the year before. Now, as Fryderyk wrote Fontana in New York, "we are both Polish orphans"; all their other childhood friends had been "taken away." The only other one left from Warsaw lyceum days was Tytus Woyciechowski, but they had drifted apart. Shortly after receiving word of Witwicki's death, Chopin became gravely ill.

The sudden change in Solange's matrimonial intentions—and her mother's reactions—were events that, indeed, could have come from George's fertile imagination and pen. Almost overnight, Viscount Fernand de Préaulx was unceremoniously dropped in favor of Jean-Baptiste Clésinger, a thirty-three-year-old bearded sculptor, quite talented, but far from being a genius. Deservedly or not, in the Paris artistic community Clésinger had the reputation of being riddled with debts, drinking too much, and having seduced a young woman whom he then abandoned as his mistress after beating her with ferocious regularity.

Clésinger entered the Sand family picture the previous year when he had written George, whom he had never met, a letter full of orthography errors (according to Maurois), requesting permission to "engrave on eternal marble the touching title of *Consuelo*." Sand agreed, and Clésinger thanked her for "the happiness you have afforded a poor young man; he will proclaim it highly because, in his creations, he hopes always to remember George Sand to whom he owes what he is."

What happened next is not entirely clear, except that Clésinger was determined to "owe" Sand much more than permission to engrave book titles. When George and Solange arrived in Paris in February 1847, he was introduced to them by a mutual acquaintance, a former army captain named Stanislas d'Arpentigny. Having requested the introduction, Clésinger now demanded the "honor" of sculpting their busts in "eternal marble." No biographers explain how it all came about (Sylvie Delaigue-Moins, in her book, speaks vaguely of a meeting "the past year"), but on February 18, the day after Chopin and Franchomme played the Sonata in G minor for them and their friends for the first time, George and Solange went to pose for Clésinger at his atelier. He sculptured Solange as a huntress, nostrils flaring, bare shoulders, hair flying in the wind. In the course of the daily sessions, Clésinger completed Solange's flattering, romantic bust, and she fell in love with him, casting de Préaulx aside and calling off their engagement. Moreover, she insisted on marrying the sculptor as soon as possible. The viscount, she said, was too much "plaster" and she preferred "marble."

Sand at first attempted to dissuade Solange from marrying Clésinger, taking her back to Nohant. But the sculptor turned up at La Châtre, called on George and, in Maurois's words, "wrenched" the consent for marriage from her. She seemed herself fascinated by Clésinger's violence and brutality, and all she had to say about the rejected viscount was that "the poor abandoned one was a noble child who showed himself to be a true French knight." In Paris, Maurice was told in a letter from his mother that the marriage "will happen because this man wants it, does everything he wants the very hour, the very minute, without needing to sleep or eat. In the three days he has been here, he has not slept two hours and he behaves well. This tension of will, without fatigue or failure, astonishes and pleases me. . . . I see in it the certain salvation of the restless soul of your sister. She will march straight with him."

Chopin, who was no longer consulted by Sand about family matters, was informed that Solange had broken off with de Préaulx, and commented in a letter home: "I am sorry for the young man because he is very dignified and in love." He was kept in the dark, however, about Solange's decision to marry Clésinger, at least for the time being. "Not a word of any of this to Chopin," Sand instructed Maurice in a letter on April 16, the day she had given the sculptor her consent. "It does not concern him, and when the Rubicon has been crossed, the 'ifs' and the 'buts' can only do harm." Wasting no time, Maurice took Clésinger to Guillery to ask for Solange's father's consent, which was given freely.

Even though Fryderyk was not to be told anything, it did not take him long to realize what was happening. Sand had told Marie de Rozières that she could not and would not make him the family's "chief and adviser," adding that "the good, excellent Chopin does not understand anything of what is occurring." But in a letter to Warsaw, started on March 28 and completed on April 19, Fryderyk was able to report that Solange had changed her mind when time came to sign the marriage contracts, observing: "Better it happen before than after the wedding." He urged the family to remember the Clésinger name because "I will probably write you often about him . . . he was presented to Madame Sand," and mentioned that Clésinger had sculpted the busts of both women.

Still, there was nothing to suggest to Chopin that the pattern of his life with Sand might change because of the family situation and the way he was being kept out if it; *Lucrezia Floriani* obviously was not on his mind. In his letter to Warsaw, immediately after referring to the end of Solange's engagement to de Préaulx, Fryderyk wrote: "You ask me what I will do with myself in the summer; nothing different from what I always do: I shall go to Nohant as soon as the warm weather starts, and, in the meantime, I shall stay here to give many little tiring lessons, as usual." Actually, Sand had invited him again to Nohant when she left Paris in April.

But Chopin was blind to reality. Liszt, who was in Russia, inquired in a letter to Marie d'Agoult on February 10 whether "Chopin's rupture with Madame Sand is final? And for what reason?" Liszt may have drawn this conclusion from various friends and informants, including Marie de Rozières, who was abreast of all the developments, or he just guessed. Moreover Sand told different things to different people about her relations with Chopin, and Liszt might have been forewarned by her as early as February—or heard about *Lucrezia.* In any event, two weeks after Sand had set the date for Solange's marriage to Clésinger, it remained a secret from Fryderyk, suggesting that he was not to be trusted. He was not invited to the wedding. Then it all became moot.

Around May 1, Chopin became seriously ill again, his condition deteriorating apace following Witwicki's death, coincidence or no. The illness was described by Fryderyk as a "strong asthma attack," but he coughed, spat blood, and nearly suffocated, and his lungs—and possibly his heart—were clearly affected as well. So was his most fragile nervous system. George Sand was immediately informed of Chopin's illness, but chose not to come back to Paris—because she was busy with wedding preparations or for obscure reasons related to their faltering relationship. Marie de Rozières and Adolf Gutmann, Chopin's best student, looked after him full-time. George explained to Marie that she could not leave Nohant and, in turn, Solange and Clésinger alone—Maurice was still away—thus "avoiding scandal." She also complained that news of Fryderyk's illness had given her frightful migraines.

Sand, of course, was masterful at manipulation, including who should be told what and when. On May 6, she happily advised Charlotte Marliani that "in a fortnight Solange marries Clésinger, the sculptor, a man of great talent, who is making much money, and can give her the brilliant existence which, I believe, is to her taste." On May 8, George told Marie de Rozières that she "dares not" write Chopin because "I am afraid that he is against Sol's marriage and that . . . if I mention it, he will suffer an unpleasant shock." This was disingenuous: Chopin had said nothing in opposition to Solange marrying the sculptor; he was not supposed to know about it. On May 10, when Chopin began to recover, Sand wrote Grzymała that though "he was saved once more, his future . . . seems bleak."

Straight-facedly, George went on to tell him that Chopin must have suffered from not knowing about Solange's forthcoming marriage and being unable to offer advice. But, she declared,

his advice in matters of real life is difficult to consider. He never properly saw the facts nor understood human nature. . . . If any woman in the world should have awakened absolute trust in him, it is obvious that it was me, but . . . he never understood that. I know that many people accuse me, some that I weakened his health with the violence of my senses, others that I drove him to despair with my excesses. . . . He complains to me that I killed him behaving differently. . . . I became a martyr, but heaven is merciless toward me, as if I had to expiate some great crimes; despite so many of my efforts and sacrifices, the one whom I love with absolute, clean, and maternal love, is dying as the victim of senseless attachment to me.

Whatever she really had in mind, Sand took a different tack in her next letter to Grzymała two days later, on May 12:

> I still do not know whether my daughter will be married here in eight days or in Paris in fifteen [days]. In any case, I shall be in Paris for several days at the end of the month, and if Chopin is transportable, I shall bring him here. . . . His soul is all poetry and all music, and he cannot stand what is different from him. . . . His influence in the matters of my family would be, for me, the loss of all dignity and all love toward and from my children. . . . Talk to him and try to make him understand, in a general way, that he must abstain from concerning himself with them. . . . All this is difficult and delicate, and I know of no way of calming . . . a sick soul who is irritated by efforts made to heal him. The illness that eats this poor being, morally and physically, has been killing me for a long time, and I see him going away without ever being able to do him good because the restless, jealous, and somber affection he has for me is the principal cause of his sadness.

If Sand meant what she wrote about seeing Chopin "go away" at that point, it would seem obvious that she had made up her mind to break with him even before Solange's wedding and its resulting impact on their relationship. In this sense, George appears to have acted in a fully premeditated fashion, not in her usual spur-of-the-moment way. But, at the same time, she was not forcing the rupture. In a letter to Gutmann, also on May 12, Sand wrote: "It is a great misfortune for me" that Chopin's illness was occurring "at a moment like that in which I find myself. Truly, this is too much anxiety at one time! I would have gone mad, I believe, if I had learned the gravity of his illness before hearing that the danger was past. . . . Do not tell him that I write to you, and that for twenty-four hours I have suffered terribly."

Notwithstanding her protestations on May 8 of not daring to write Chopin about Solange's wedding, George did so a few days later. Fryderyk responded most cordially on May 15 that "none of your friends . . . wishes your child happiness more sincerely than I." He still thought they were on excellent terms: Nothing had happened of a grave nature to make him believe differently. In retrospect, Chopin does appear quite naïve.

Solange Dudevant Sand and Auguste Clésinger were married in Nohant on May 19, 1847. George Sand told Joseph Mazzini, a politician friend, in a letter on May 22 that "I have just married . . . my daughter to an artist of powerful inspiration and will. I had for her but one ambition— namely, that she should love and be loved; my wish is realized."

Chopin, of course, was not among the guests; not because he was not "transportable," but because Sand chose not to invite him. Interestingly, Solange, so fond of him, is not known to have made the slightest effort to have him invited. Sand sent him a formal announcement, which was not equal to an actual invitation. In any case, Fryderyk was quite trans- portable and felt well enough to travel on May 21, two days after the wedding, to visit his friend Thomas Albrecht and his goddaughter Thérèse in Ville-d'Avray, near Paris. He went there again on May 28. Chopin kept publicly silent on the subject of Solange's wedding, but in a letter to Warsaw on June 8, he gave free vent to his bitterness about the circumstances surrounding it, after mentioning that an asthma attack had kept him home for two weeks.

"The wedding took place in the country during my weakness— frankly I am not upset about it [the weakness] because I do not know what impression I would have made," Chopin wrote. But he, too, was less than honest, perhaps out of pride. It was not "weakness" that pre- vented him from attending the wedding, but the lack of an invitation, a fact he omitted in this account. And no weakness kept him away from the Albrechts two days after the Nohant ceremony.

"The groom," Fryderyk went on,

> comes from the devil-knows-what family. He was introduced here, but nobody had dreamed . . . that it would end up like this. . . . I did not like it right away when the mother [Sand] praised him to the heavens . . . [when] they drove to his atelier almost every day to pose for busts . . . they received every day flowers and various other novelties, little dogs, etc. The mother is a darling, but she has no practical sense worth a penny, and she invited him to the country; that was all he wanted; he went there, and [was] so clever that they had no time to look at him, and that is how it all ended.

Solange liked Clésinger, Chopin continued, because he was

> supposedly a second Michelangelo, he rides a horse superbly (he was a cavalryman, so no wonder). Maurice was also for him because he could not suffer de Préaulx. . . . Adding to it the secret the mother made of it,

they had about him only the information that he was pleased to give. . . . Meanwhile, all the friends here—Marliani and Delacroix and Arago and I—had [the information], how indebted he was, how brutal he was, and how he beat his mistress whom he now dropped, pregnant, as he got married . . . how he drinks (we have all seen it, but it goes on the account of genius). In one word, all the artists . . . are astounded that Madame Sand chose him as son-in-law. . . . So far, everybody is very content: He, as polite as he can be; she is happy with her new status—she is dressed in cashmere and rides her horse . . . But I do not give them a year after the first child—and the mother will have to pay for a long time. . . . The son came out the best from it, not only because he has a brother-in-law without a head in some respects, and of whom he can take advantage, but his father, the eminent Monsieur Dudevant, gave Sol nothing as dowry, not even a pin, so he will receive more.

Chopin, who managed to be quite well informed even at a distance, next related that Augustine, whom Maurice was going to marry, was now about to wed Théodore Rousseau, the famous landscape painter, who lived in the same house as Clésinger. "This," Fryderyk wrote, "is the smartest, in my opinion, because it removes all the problems from the heads of Madame Sand and her son, and they both gained very much: she with the obligation [she had] of supporting the whole family until the girls were married, and he with a promised marriage for which he had no desire."

All of them were in Paris, Chopin said, to make wedding arrangements for Augustine at the Notre-Dame-de-Lorette Church and at city hall, and planned to return to the country together. In a way left unexplained in his letter, Fryderyk saw the whole family during that time, saying that Solange "was polite with me, as usual, he [was] most polite, and I as usual, but I am sad in my soul." According to Chopin, none of Sand's old friends had been invited to Solange's wedding, and "in the Parisian world, this marriage has made a bad impression," because a statue by Clésinger shown at an exhibition was that of a naked woman "in the most indecent position." Turning slightly incoherent, Fryderyk wrote that "people wonder how a young person like Sol could be so passionate about a fraud who presents such voluptuous, not to say shameless, works. But in art, there is nothing truly shameless—and the generous belly and breasts are very nicely modeled—and I guarantee that at the next exhibition the public will glean the belly and the breasts of his wife in the form of a new statue . . . he will sculpt Sol's backside from white marble."

The whole marriage affair, Chopin insisted, "was a moment of folly that hardly lasted a month, and there was nobody to pour cold water on it." He wrote that the first letter he received from Sand about the wedding was on May 1, remarking that

it was too bad about the marriage—or very well, considering that Madame S. always functions exceptionally [well] and that everything always turns out well for her, even what seems improbable at the first glance. I tell her that she has a star that guides her, consoling her when black thoughts come. . . . She turned her misery with her husband into good results. The children, whom she loves above all things, were always with her—she brought them up in health and happiness. She is healthy herself despite her enormous work [and] her eyes do not falter after writing so many volumes [over ninety or so]. Everybody adores her. . . . Instead of a wedding party for her daughter, she gave one thousand francs to the poor of her parish.

But the most amazing thing about Chopin's reaction to the whole situation, including the way he was treated by the family in the context of the marriage, was that he fully expected to remain welcome in Nohant. After referring to the family's presence in Paris to prepare Augustine's wedding and their plans to return to the country, Fryderyk added: "I do not know whether I shall go with them—frankly, I do not feel like it because, in addition to the lady of the household, the son and the daughter, I would have to become accustomed to new figures, and I have enough of it . . . there are five new servants." And, just as interestingly, Chopin explained that he had gone to see the Albrechts after Solange's wedding to "renew myself a bit" before Sand's arrival in Paris. Incredibly, he still lived in a dream world.

Notwithstanding his obsession with Solange's marriage—his furious denunciations of all concerned added up to one of the longest letters he had ever written to Warsaw—Chopin kept up his busy social life in Paris. He posed for his portrait by Ary Scheffer, one of the best painters of his time, although Delacroix had already painted him several times. Then, he sat for sketches by Franz Winterhalter and another artist named Lehmann on commissions from wealthy friends. The new sonata and the mazurkas were being printed. Franchomme, Fryderyk wrote, visited him every day

and "my door never closes with various visitors I must receive." He continued to give lessons, remarking that "you cannot imagine how polite my
[lady] students are. . . . Yesterday, young [Madame] de Rothschild sent me
a beautiful *verre d'eau* with a gold-leafed tray and a spoon, and a crystal
wineglass with a base in gold-leafed silver in a charming case." He was not
satisfied with the quality of the opera, however, what with Pauline Viardot and other great singers away elsewhere.

Having chosen not to go to Nohant—and quite possibly not even having been invited by Sand in the aftermath of Solange's wedding—
Chopin remained in Paris in the midst of his occupations. On July 1, for
example, Delacroix and Grzymała came to his apartment to listen to
him performing with Franchomme his Trio in G minor for piano, violin, and cello, op. 8 (the identity of the violinist was not recorded).
Above all, Chopin was blissfully unaware of the storm brewing in
Nohant—not suspecting that it was about to engulf him.

After visiting his family, Clésinger and Solange returned to Nohant at
the end of June, and quarrels erupted immediately. According to most
versions, Solange touched them off by telling Rousseau (as she once told
Chopin) that Maurice and Augustine were having an affair. It continued
her warfare against her brother and her cousin—and through them with
her mother. The painter believed the story and turned his back on
Augustine. Sand went after Solange with vengeance. Then, it was a free-
for-all in Nohant. On July 11, as Sand tells it, Maurice and Clésinger
began fighting and the sculptor raised a hammer to hit his brother-in-
law. George slapped Clésinger in the face and he countered by shoving
his fist into her breast. Maurice ran to fetch a pistol to shoot Clésinger,
but a priest who happened to be visiting the mansion succeeded in
breaking up the brawl.

Sand, fuming, ordered Clésinger out of the house, forbidding him
ever to return. Solange chastised him for raising his hand against her
mother, but followed Clésinger, announcing that she would never come
back. George informed her that the square d'Orléans apartment in Paris
was closed to them, too. As they were leaving, Solange tried to borrow
the carriage Chopin always kept in Nohant to take them comfortably to
Paris, but Sand refused. From La Châtre, where they were taken by a
servant, Solange dispatched a letter to Chopin on July 18 that triggered
the final crisis.

She wrote him that she was ill and asked for his carriage for the journey to Paris, requesting an immediate reply and that she awaited in La Châtre "where I suffer from discomfort." Solange, aware of how much Chopin liked her, assumed that he would not refuse help. "I left Nohant forever," she told him, "after the most horrible scenes on the part of my mother. Please wait for me before leaving Paris; I want very much to see you immediately. I was categorically denied your carriage. So, if you wish for me to use it, please send a word of permission, which I will send to Nohant, to order [the carriage] to be sent over."

Chopin replied on July 21: "I learned with regret that you are ill. I hasten to place my carriage at your disposal. I wrote your mother about it. Please take care of yourself." He signed it: "Your old friend. Ch."

Solange saw Chopin in Paris that same week, giving her side of the Nohant events, but Sand wrote him about the same time with her account and views. That letter has disappeared, leading biographers to confusion concerning the sequence of what would be the final exchange between George and Fryderyk. In reply, Chopin wrote Sand on July 24, his last letter to her:

> It is not my place to tell you about Monsieur C[lésinger]. I became familiar with his name only when you gave your daughter away to him. As for her, I cannot be indifferent. As you probably remember, I intervened with you on behalf of your children without taking sides, whenever there was an occasion, being convinced that it was always your destiny to love them—because these are the only feelings that do not change. Disgrace may hide them, but cannot destroy them. This sense of disgrace is evidently very powerful because it caused your heart not to wish to hear about your daughter at a time when her future is in balance and when her physical condition requires maternal tenderness more than ever. In the face of such serious events, which must wound your most sacred feelings, I shall not speak of myself. Time will heal. I shall wait—always the same. Your devoted. Ch. (Regards for Maurice).

Sand had been impatiently awaiting Chopin's answer to her letter—the vanished one—writing Marie de Rozières on the morning of July 25: "I am worried, frightened. I have no news from Chopin in several days. . . . He was going to leave and, suddenly, he does not come, he does not write. . . . I would have already left [Nohant] without fear of passing him on the way and without the [sense of] horror I have in going to expose myself in Paris to the hatred of her [Solange] whom you judge to be so good. . . . Sometimes, to reassure myself, I think that Chopin loves her much more than me . . . and takes her side."

Fryderyk's letter arrived later that day, and Sand added to her missive to Marie: "I see that, as usual, my stupid heart has been duped, and while I spent six white nights tormenting myself about his health, he was busy speaking and thinking ill of me with the Clésingers. . . . His letter is of laughable dignity and the sermons of this good father of the family will serve as a lesson for me. . . . There are many things I can guess, and I know of what my daughter is capable in terms of credulity. . . . But, finally, I can see clearly! I shall act consistently; I shall no longer give my flesh and blood in exchange for ingratitude and perversity."

On July 28, George Sand wrote her last letter to Chopin:

I had requested yesterday post-coach horses and I was going to leave in a cabriolet, in this awful weather, very ill myself; I was going to spend a day in Paris to learn your news. Your silence had made me concerned about your health. During that time, *you* were taking your time to reflect and your answer is quite calm. That is well, my friend. Do what your heart dictates to you now and do take its instinct for the voice of your conscience. I understand perfectly. As to my daughter . . . she would be ungracious to say that she needs the love of a mother whom she detests and calumniates [and] whose most sacred actions and whose home she dirties with atrocious statements! It pleases you to hear all that and per-haps to believe it. I shall not engage in combat of this kind; it horrifies me. I like better to see you go over to the enemy than to defend myself from an enemy issued from my breast and nourished with my milk. Take care of her because it is to her that you believe you must devote yourself. I shall not resent you, but you will understand that I retrench myself in my role of outraged mother. . . . It is enough to be duped and be a victim. I forgive you and I shall not henceforth address any reproaches to you because your confession is sincere. It astonished me a little; but if you feel freer and more at ease this way, I shall not suffer from this bizarre betrayal. Farewell, my friend! May you be healed quickly of all your ailments, and I hope for it now (I have my reasons for that), and I shall thank God for this bizarre denouement of nine years of exclusive friendship. Give me your news occasionally. It is useless ever to return to the rest.

Delacroix, a friend of both, pronounced Sand's letter to be "inhuman," remarking that "one can see in it terrible feelings, long pent-up ill will."

Frederick Niecks, the fine and honest biographer, described the rupture between Chopin and Sand as "the catastrophe of Chopin's life."

Coda
1847—1849

Chapter 23

THE RUPTURE WAS, INDEED, a catastrophe for Chopin and a tragedy for both him and George Sand. Much has been written apportioning the blame—and each has provided diametrically opposed, heartbreakingly bitter accounts of what happened. But the truth remains elusive. A reconstruction of the events of spring and summer 1847, based on incomplete correspondence between the principals (numerous letters were lost or destroyed); the correspondence of their more or less well-informed and more or less tendentious friends; and various memoirs, suggest that the ultimate breakup resulted from a sequence of stunning misunderstandings—and too much anger and pride. Intrigues within the Sand household and by Solange and her husband made matters even worse. Arguably, neither George nor Fryderyk really desired a rupture, notwithstanding what each said about it afterward.

As André Maurois has sagely observed, "A quarrel between two beings who had loved each other much is a sad and silly thing. Most often, there is nothing really grave. . . . From resentment or pride, the one who has been calumniated refuses to explain him or herself. A silence that becomes prolonged makes one die for the other. This is how affections are broken. The stronger the sentiment had been, the more a sort of hatred is created by deception." So it may have been with Chopin and Sand who, in the end, lost all perspective on their life together.

George has offered her versions of the rupture in letters to friends and in her memoirs. The more restrained Fryderyk produced only one. Her first version was a dramatic seventy-one-page cri de coeur to her friend

Emmanuel Arago on July 26, the day after she had received Chopin's last letter. It was probably the longest missive (of a sustained emotional tenor) she is known to have written.

Chopin, George wrote, had changed completely in relation to her—"he no longer dies from [his] deadly love, which I could not reciprocate." Instead, "he simply tells me that I am a bad mother and that Solange is completely right, that he will not abandon her, etc.," she continued. "This friend, so loyal and blindly devoted (as he told me himself, and others told me), moves against me, hangs on Solange's skirt, and conspires with my son-in-law, knowing that he had raised his hand against me and that he should not see him at this time without risking his honor in my eyes, because for nine years I nursed him night and day."

Now George revealed what upset her the most about Chopin: her belief—not just suspicion—that he was in love with Solange. Delusionary as it may have been, it transformed Sand from victim of ingratitude on the part of her beloved "invalid" to a jealousy-consumed woman; jealous, without real proof, of her own daughter, after constantly accusing Chopin of *his* obsessive jealousy. And it turned her into a snarling, ugly person, a very different George Sand. She told Arago:

> To be able to see HER, he dares everything and tears everything down with dignified calm. He has a perfectly clean soul, I vouch for it, and he is too ill for his love not to be exclusively Platonic. Surely, SHE does not treat him like a man, and she never thought about him other than as someone like a *papa*. But if he, radiating this great, exclusive, and unbreakable passion . . . which he has accustomed himself to display, now makes this sudden shift, it must be caused by passion for another [woman], or I have no idea about such things. . . . What a relief for me! What oppressive ties have been torn! For nine years, my unflinching opposition against his narrow and despotic way of thinking competed with attachment, pity, and fear of him dying from grief. For nine years, feeling full of life, I was tied to a corpse, under a constant, visible . . . menace of his opinion. . . . What a beautiful future dawns before me after this past filled with suffering, boredom, frequent deep indignation because I had never seen in my life anything as insulting as his sick jealousy. . . . Thank God, it will not be me who will kill him, and, finally, I can start a new life after these nine years of slow torture with needle pinpricks. . . . I always told him that a skillful coquette would be more con-

venient for him than a sincere, loyal, and devoted friend. So he has been granted [it]. She will not give him what he does not ask her [for]; besides, in his condition he would have achieved it [only] with his last breath.

George followed it up less than two weeks later, on August 9, with a broadside addressed to her friend Charles Poncy, the stonemason poet, telling of her extreme bitterness and adding: "I had hoped, at least for the old age upon which I was entering, the recompense of great sacrifices, of much work, fatigue, and a whole life of devotion and abnegation. . . . I asked for nothing but to render happy the objects of my affection. Well, I have been repaid with ingratitude, and evil has got the upper hand in a soul which I wished to make the sanctuary and the hearth of the beautiful and the good. At present, I struggle against myself in order not to let myself die."

On August 27, Sand was at it again, as furiously as before, denouncing Solange and her husband in another letter to Poncy. Having first, in one of her easy enthusiasms, pushed for their engagement and quick marriage, George turned against them with vengeance within weeks of the wedding, probably at the start of June, as a result of violent "scenes" and disagreements she never quite explained (apart from the occasion when Clésinger hit her in the chest). She told Poncy of Solange:

> Barely married, she stomped on everything, she threw her mask away. She turned her husband, who has an ardent, weak head, against me, against Maurice, against Augustine, whom she hates mortally and who had no fault save being too good and devoted to her. It is she who forced the failure of the marriage of this poor Augustine, and made Rousseau temporarily insane, telling him an atrocious calumny about Maurice and her [Augustine]. . . . She tries to make quarrel with my friends. . . . She poses as the victim of my [supposedly] unjust preference for her brother and her cousin. She fouls her own nest. . . . She neither spares me, who have lived like a nun.

Writing Marie de Rozières, Sand reported that "this diabolical couple left last night, weighed down with debts, triumphant in their impudence, and leaving a scandal they will never be able to live down. . . . I never want to see them again, they will never again set foot in my home. . . . My God, I have not done anything to merit having such a daughter."

On November 2, five months after the scenes at Nohant, Sand

informed Charlotte Marliani that "Chopin has openly taken her [Solange's] side against me, without knowing anything of the truth, which proves a great need for [displaying] ingratitude toward me and a bizarre attraction to her. . . . I assume that to have turned to him in this fashion, she has exploited his jealous and suspicious character." George then accused Solange of fabricating "this absurd calumny of *love* or of exclusive friendship for the young man who has been mentioned to you." This was a reference to Victor Borie, an editor of the provincial newspaper she had founded with Leroux, and who, indeed, had been spending much time in Nohant. Ten years or more younger than Sand, he may well have been her occasional lover; George had earlier angrily charged Chopin with jealousy about Borie.

It sounded again like a tale from the pages of a Sand best-selling novel: George was jealous of Fryderyk's supposed love for Solange just as she was accusing him of being jealous of her alleged affair with the young Borie (Chopin having actually been jealous of Borie before he left Nohant the previous autumn). Solange's claim to Rousseau, the painter, that Augustine was having an affair with Maurice, which may have been accurate, added to the confusion reigning in the Sand household. Whatever Chopin's own lapses of judgment or behavior may have been at that stage, he also appeared to be a highly confused victim of the situation in which he allowed himself to be caught.

But to Sand, he was the enemy and the traitor. In her November letter to Marliani, she wrote that "Chopin's character grew more bitter from day to day; he made displays of contempt, bad humor, and jealousy in the presence of all my friends and my children! Solange took advantage of it with astuteness that is proper to her. Maurice began to be indignant toward him. Knowing and seeing the chastity of our relations, he also saw that this poor, sick spirit posed, perhaps without wanting to and without being able to prevent it, a peril as lover, as husband, as owner of my thoughts and my acts. He [Maurice] was on the verge of exploding and telling him to his face that he was making me, at the age of forty-three, play a ridiculous role and abusing my kindness."

Sand told Marliani:

> we have not written a word to each other in three months, and I do not know what the outcome of this coldness will be. I shall do nothing either to make it worse or to make it cease because I am not at fault. . . . [And]

I cannot, I must not and want not to fall again under his occult tyranny [that] wished, through continuous and often deep needle pricks, to deprive me even of my right to breathe. . . . The poor child did not know any more how to maintain this external decorum of which he was, of course, a slave in his principles and habits. Men, women, old people, children—everything was for him an object of horror and furious, senseless jealousy. . . . I could not stand him anymore. I am convinced that his entourage will judge it differently. They will make a victim of him and it will be nicer to suppose that at my age, I had chased him away to take a lover.

Writing Marie de Rozières on November 22, George declared that she was aware of "confidences" Chopin was making to his friends and that "I see that he is no longer in mastery of himself. . . . I had always anticipated that his friendship for me would turn to aversion because he does nothing by halves."

But what did really happen between Chopin and Sand? Were they both at fault and did they have a monstrous misunderstanding, feeding more and more on itself, that led to the impossibility of reconciliation?

Most biographers and contemporaries tend to blame Sand for the "catastrophe." Marceli Antoni Szulc wrote that "if blame . . . hangs over anyone, it certainly is not over Chopin." Niecks, the German-born music professor at Edinburgh University who had conversed and corresponded with many of Chopin's contemporaries, says flatly in his 1888 biography that "whatever circumstances may have been the ostensible cause of the rupture, in reality it was only a pretext. . . . George Sand was tired of Chopin, and as he did not leave her voluntarily, the separation had to be forced upon him." Delacroix had described her last letter to Fryderyk as "inhuman." Charles Baudelaire, the poet, who hated Sand for artistic, political, and aesthetic reasons, wrote that she was "stupid," adding that "she is heavy . . . she has in her moral ideas the same depth of judgment and the same delicacy of sentiment as the concierges and kept women. . . . That some men could have fallen in love with this latrine is proof of how lowly are the men of this century."

Sand, to be sure, was carried away by her suspicions that Chopin was in love with Solange, suspicions that quickly became obsessive and colored her whole attitude toward him. Short of mistaking friendship for a

young girl whom he had known from childhood, for erotic love for a
woman, there is nothing to corroborate George's dark accusations. It is
quite likely, however, that the very manipulative Solange had gone out
of her way to make her mother believe that Chopin was in love with her.
She was not a very nice person—and Fryderyk was very naïve.

It is necessary to see how Chopin perceived this crisis and how he
acted in response, wisely or not. Niecks provides a significant clue,
quoting at length from a letter to him from Franchomme, one of Fryderyk's closest friends: "The rupture between Chopin and Madame
Sand came about in this way. In June 1847, Chopin was making ready to
start for Nohant when he received a letter from Madame Sand to the
effect that she had just turned out her daughter and her son-in-law, and
that if he received them in his house, all would be over between them
[i.e., between George Sand and Chopin]. I was with Chopin at the time
the letter arrived, and he said to me, 'They have only me, and should I
close my door upon them? No, I shall not do it,' and he did not do it,
and yet he knew that this creature whom he adored would not forgive
him for it. Poor friend, how I have seen him suffer!"

Franchomme's reference was unquestionably to Sand's "missing letter," the one to which Chopin had replied on July 24, declaring that
Solange's welfare could not be a matter of indifference to him because
he had always stood up for both of George's children. The letter from
Sand must have been quite fierce to push Chopin into writing what
would be his farewell missive to her. George, in turn, responded with
her farewell letter on July 28. His request to make his Nohant carriage
available to Solange, who had asked for it, must have added insult to
injury in Sand's eyes, confirming her suspicion that he was in love with
her daughter. When she learned subsequently that Chopin had received
Solange and Clésinger at his Paris apartment despite her warnings,
George must have felt completely vindicated in her suspicion that Fryderyk had betrayed her. Chopin, for his part, clearly felt justified in
receiving the young couple because, as he told Franchomme, "they have
only me."

This sequence of events would seem to bear out Niecks's conclusion
that Chopin had every intention of returning to Nohant for the summer of 1847 until he received Sand's June letter. He evidently was not
bothered by not having been invited to Solange's wedding—or chose
not to be bothered. But it is less clear that Sand had been actually look-

ing for "pretexts" to get rid of Chopin. Writing Grzymała on May 12, a week after Solange's marriage, she did say that if "Chopin is transportable," she would bring him from Paris to Nohant. On July 25, hours before receiving Fryderyk's coldly negative response to her demand that he cut all contacts with the Clésingers, George complained to Marie de Rozières that she was "worried, frightened" in the absence of news from him: "He does not come, he does not write." Even in her agitated letter to Poncy on August 9, after the rupture, Sand wrote that "Chopin is in Paris . . . his health has not yet permitted him to make the journey"; she had to be referring to a journey to Nohant. And in the letter to Charlotte Marliani on November 2, she still seemed to keep the door open to a reconciliation, saying: "I do not know what the outcome of this coldness will be."

It sounded as if George was waiting for Fryderyk to take the initiative, notwithstanding her vituperations against him and vows not to be victimized again by his "tyranny." Even granting that Sand's overheated emotions had led her to the irrational suspicions of Chopin's love for Solange and the extreme and self-defeating act of serving him with an ultimatum about seeing the Clésingers, it is still far from evident that she desired the breakup because she "was tired of Chopin," as Niecks suggests. Finally, it is entirely plausible, and in character, that she was not quite sure what she wanted—and that she might have been amenable to a reconciliation if Fryderyk had taken the first step. She might even have accepted his mood swings, selfishness, and cruelties.

What, on the other hand, did Chopin desire? His farewell letter to Sand and Franchomme's recollections in his letter to Niecks establish that, as a matter of principle, he rejected George's ultimatum about the Clésingers, and this, too, would have been in character. Short of that, however, there is no hard evidence to indicate that it was Fryderyk who sought a rupture. For one thing, it would have made little sense, considering his own admission that Nohant was where he composed the most and the best—and where he had maternal care around the clock. Chopin was, after all, an egoist. His quarrels with Maurice did not seem to disturb him too much: He was planning on going to Nohant for the balance of the summer until that fatal exchange of farewell letters late in July. In the absence of evidence to the contrary, it is a fair assumption that Chopin would have been happy to preserve the status quo, especially as his health was deteriorating steadily, if Sand had not faced him with the ultimatum. If pride is a sin, it can also often be foolishness, and Chopin chose to exercise it in this situation. Maurois had it right when he concluded that "from resentment or pride, the one who has been calumniated refuses to explain him or herself." This was how the affection between Chopin and Sand was broken.

Chopin's subsequent behavior and his version of the events is another matter. He was through with Sand and he went to the other extreme of virtually adopting the Clésingers. Despite his tirade against the sculptor in his early June letter to Warsaw and his bitter prediction that the marriage would not last and that they would drown in debt, Chopin suddenly discovered a companion in the bearded Clésinger. When Solange was in Guillery visiting her father, Fryderyk dined with him. Having guessed correctly about the couple's debts, he loaned Clésinger five hundred francs (which was repaid). He obviously realized that his behavior ruled out reconciliation with George forever, and it must have suited him fine. Other women in Paris, old friends, were ready to replace Sand in caring for him and worrying about his health. It was just too bad about Nohant.

Though Chopin considered his relationship with George finished for good, he encouraged Solange to renew her contacts with her mother despite a less than fortuitous visit she had paid to Nohant in November. Sand no longer insisted that the "diabolical couple" could never set foot in the mansion, and she had sent word to Solange, then stopping at La Châtre, to come to visit. She offered her the use of the square d'Orléans apartment. But Solange was disappointed, writing Chopin that she had found her mother "as cold as ice, even unpleasant," and that Sand had told her that she could live in Nohant only if she abandoned her husband. Solange also found that her bedroom had been "completely emptied of furniture; the curtains had been removed, the bed taken away, and the room had been divided into two parts—one serves as an auditorium and the other as the stage; comedies are performed there. . . . Who could imagine it! Mother sets up a theater in the room where her beloved daughter had spent her wedding night!"

Chopin replied that he regretted the results of Solange's visit home, "but the first step has been taken: You showed your heart and a certain rapprochement has occurred; you were asked to write. Time will do the rest. You know well that one should not take literally what is being said." In another letter to Solange in Guillery, Chopin informed her that Sand's new novel, *François le Champi,* would soon appear serialized in a Paris newspaper.

But none of it served to change Chopin's attitude toward Sand. Ferdynand Hoesick, the early if not always fully reliable Polish biographer, has written that Sand was in "despair" after the rupture and that "it was a pity that Chopin did not feel it. . . . If he had known that Madame Sand suffers because of him, just as he suffered because of her, he might have tried to restore the broken ties, perhaps might have written to Nohant, to which he would certainly have received a welcome reply." He may have been right and, indeed, some of Sand's friends attempted to correct her view of Fryderyk's position. Thus, Pauline Viardot wrote to her in November denying that Chopin was "part of a faction of Solange . . . which denigrates you. . . . This is absolutely false, I swear, at least as far as he is concerned. On the contrary, this dear and excellent friend is preoccupied and afflicted by only one thought: the hurt that this unhappy affair must have caused you. I have found no change in him—he is always as good and as devoted as ever, adoring you as ever. . . . In the name of Heaven, do not always believe officious friends who come to tell you gossip."

Apparently, Chopin, too, had such friends. Hoesick writes that Fryderyk's friends' resentments against Sand—including many ladies of the Polish aristocracy in Paris—"began to have an effect on Chopin, who, morally depressed, turned out to be a fertile recipient." According to Hoesick, Chopin's "most sincere friends" sought to convince him that "Madame Sand was his vampire, his evil genius, that tired of his illness, she had had enough of the trying role of nurse . . . that she wanted to be rid of him at any price, and when other methods failed, she wrote *Lucrezia Floriani* . . . so that he would understand how he burdened his friends and would let go of her. Such insinuations, which had all the traits of emigré intrigues and gossip, had their destructive effect, and falling upon Chopin's oversensitive soul, achieved their goal. In the end, Chopin believed everything he was told about Madame Sand in relation to him. He even came to believe that Prince Karol in *Lucrezia Floriani* was his malevolent caricature, and from that time on, whenever he spoke of Madame Sand, he called her *Lucrezia* . . . including in a letter to Grzymała." Inevitably, Sand would hear about it.

Because most of Chopin's letters to the family in Warsaw have been lost, it is unknown when and how he informed them of the breakup with Sand, who was adored by his sister Ludwika. His first letter touching upon the subject was addressed to Ludwika alone and written between December 26, 1847, and January 6, 1848, when it was completed, carrying at the top the notation: "One of the ancient, only begun, unburned letters."

After several pages of social and family persiflage, Chopin turned to his own problems with George, discussing them bitterly and not quite truthfully, especially where it concerned Clésinger.

"Now the mother is angrier at the son-in-law than at the daughter," Chopin said,

> though in her famous letter she wrote me that the son-in-law is not too bad, but the daughter makes him [bad]. You could think that she wanted to get rid of the daughter and me at the same time because we were inconvenient to her. . . . She will declare me as an enemy because I had taken the side of the son-in-law (whom I cannot tolerate) only because he married her daughter—a marriage I opposed the best I could. What a strange creature with all her intelligence. Insanity came upon her; she messes her own life, messes in her daughter's life, and it will end badly with the son, I predict. She would like to find, for her own excuse, something against those who wish her well, who believed her, who never did her any *grossièreté* [rudeness], and whom she cannot abide because they are mirrors of her conscience. Thus she has not written me another word, nor is she coming to Paris this winter.

And this was his version of their life together: "I do not regret having helped her suffer the most delicate eight years of her life, when her daughter grew up and the son clung to the mother; I do not regret anything I have tasted, but I regret that the daughter was . . . broken through the lack of sense and levity that can be accepted in a woman of twenty, but not in a woman of forty. . . . Madame S. can have of me only a good memory in her soul, if she ever looks back. Meanwhile, she is in the strangest paroxysm of a mother playing the role of a better and more just mother than she really is. It is a fever for which there is no remedy."

Chopin informed Ludwika that Sand's latest novel was being serialized in the *Journal des débats* and that he had heard that she was planning to write her memoirs. But, he remarked, "it is too soon for that because dear Madame S. will go through many more strange events in her life before she becomes old, many beautiful and ugly ones will happen." That was all Chopin had to say about George Sand six months after their rupture—in a letter he had not burned. But, obviously, she was still very much on his mind.

Fryderyk was quite ill during the final months of 1847. After a bout with illness in May, he enjoyed a relative recovery during the summer despite the heat of Paris. He briefly visited the Rothschilds at their Ferrières property not far from the city; it was not Nohant, but the fresh air there was good for him. Chopin kept up a busy social life and tried to go on composing during this period.

The friend he saw the most often was Delacroix, himself a social butterfly. In his *Journal*, the painter recalls visiting Chopin on the afternoon of July 1, remarking that "he was divine. . . . His trio was played for him with Fauchon, etc. Then he executed it himself and with a master's hand." Ten days later, Delacroix recounts, Chopin visited him, and was back at his studio on the morning of July 20, to read Delacroix the letter from Sand that had triggered the rupture. The painter's comment in his *Journal* was that "there is no question but that it is atrocious. The cruelty of the passions, and the impatience so long repressed, come clearly to the surface in it: and with a contrast which would be comic if the matter were not such a sad one; the author, from time to time, assumes her role as a woman and goes off into long tirades which seem like borrowings from a novel or a lecture on philosophy." Delacroix presumably shared his views with Chopin that morning to console him, if nothing else.

(Delacroix also thought little of Clésinger's sculpture, having gone to see his statue. He wrote in his *Journal:* "It is a daguerreotype in sculpture, except for the treatment of the marble, which is really very able. The proof of what I think is the weakness of the other pieces: no proportion, etc. Lack of intelligence as to the lines in the figure; one cannot see it as a whole from any angle.")

With the onset of autumn, illness returned to haunt Chopin. He wrote Grzymała in mid-September: "I am weak," and that he had trouble finding a new apartment; he had decided to move from square d'Orléans as soon as possible. He resumed giving piano lessons, but it was hard going, and Fryderyk spent most of the time reclining on a sofa as he taught his students. Writing Solange on December 14, Chopin told her that "all Paris is coughing; I am suffocating and awaiting the cholera." But determined to lead as normal an existence as he could manage, he received visits from Polish acquaintances, went on teaching, and, shortly before Christmas, invited Franchomme and his wife to dine with him. The pianist Charles Hallé recalls visiting Chopin with friends to hear the new sonata, and finding him "rather unwell: He went about the room bent like a half-opened penknife." But Fryderyk insisted on playing for them, and "having once begun, he soon became straight again, warming up as he proceeded."

In his December-January letter to Ludwika, Chopin, never wishing to worry the family, said with great understatement: "Sometimes I smell my homeopathic flasks, I give many lessons at home, and I hang on the best I can." On December 31, he wrote Solange that "I cough and I am completely absorbed in my lessons. I go out very little because it still is cold outside."

Chopin had just learned that Mendelssohn, whom he genuinely liked and admired, had died in Leipzig on November 4, at the age of thirty-eight; Fryderyk was then thirty-six. There is no record of his reaction, but he knew that Schubert had died at thirty-one. His closest personal friends—Białobłocki, Matuszyński, and Witwicki—had died very young too. Death was stalking Fryderyk.

Although he now lacked direct contact with Nohant, Chopin was nevertheless well informed by mutual friends about life there. Sand, having finished her latest novel, had plunged into *Story of My Life,* the memoirs of which he had spoken so unkindly. But George was also busy preparing Augustine's wedding to Karol de Bertholdi, a thirty-six-year-old Polish exile who taught art at a school in the town of Tulle and was a friend of Victor Borie, the young editor who seemed to have made Nohant his home and Sand his mistress.

It had not been a fertile year musically for Chopin, perhaps because he had lost his peaceful refuge, perhaps because of the inexorable progress of his illness, perhaps because the tensions with George Sand had caused him deeper depression than he admitted to family and friends.

In the course of 1847, Chopin completed three mazurkas, three waltzes, and the Sonata for cello and piano—plus the music to accompany *Melodia,* a deeply patriotic poem by Zygmunt Krasiński, one of the great exiled Polish bards.

The three mazurkas—in B major, F minor, and C-sharp minor—

form Opus 63, and they are dedicated to Laura Czosnowska, the Polish countess whom Sand had so disliked. They are not among the greatest in this genre. The waltzes of Opus 64, on the other hand, are quite memorable. The Waltz in D-flat major is remarkable for its lightness and good humor, considering Chopin's physical and mental condition at that point. But he always did the unexpected, when seen (or heard) in retrospect.

Just as curiously, Chopin dedicated this waltz to Countess Delfina Potocka, his old friend (and Krasiński's mistress), inscribing the words *"Nella Miseria"* ("In Misery") in her album. It is a line from Dante's *Inferno,* proclaiming that there is no greater pain than to remember "in misery" the happy times one had enjoyed in the past. It is intriguing to speculate whether Chopin was thinking of George Sand when he scribbled the words on the manuscript of such a happy waltz, dedicating it to a woman with whom he had probably been secretly, Platonically, and aesthetically in love for many years, given that she was so beautiful and had such a marvelous voice. The Waltz in C-sharp minor, op. 64, no. 2, was dedicated to Baroness de Rothschild. The Waltz in A-flat major, which had actually been written in 1840, was dedicated to Baroness Katarzyna Branicka. The Sonata for cello and piano, op. 65, was, of course, dedicated to Franchomme.

The three opuses had been completed before Chopin's rupture with Sand; most likely they had been started the previous year (this was certainly the case with the sonata) and finished and polished during the spring and summer of 1847. Thus, on June 30, 1847, Chopin was able to confirm in writing the sale of the mazurkas, waltzes, and the sonata to the Leipzig publishers Breitkopf & Härtel for all the world markets, except France and England (those went to the Paris publisher Brandus et Cie.) and acknowledge receipt of payment for them.

They were published in October 1847, the last of the works Chopin had personally submitted to publishers and corrected in galleys. They were also the last he ever saw in print.

Chapter 24

CHOPIN PLAYED AN ASTONISHING SELECTION of his music on Wednesday, February 16, 1848, at the Salle Pleyel on rue Rochechouart in what turned out to be his last public concert in Paris. "Extremely weak" as he was, in the words of an English music critic who was in the audience, Chopin delivered a bravura performance, presenting, in this order, a nocturne, the Barcarolle (op. 60), an étude, the Berceuse (op. 57), three movements of the Sonata in G minor (with Franchomme at the cello), several préludes and mazurkas, and a waltz. The exhausting concert, attended by the royal family and three hundred *Tout Paris* aristocrats, bankers, and businessmen, artists, and Fryderyk's personal friends, opened with a Mozart trio performed by Chopin, Franchomme, and the violinist Jean-Delphin Alard. Most of the reviews in the Paris press were ecstatic.

In a letter to Ludwika in Warsaw on February 10, Chopin wrote that his friends Pleyel, Perthuis, Léo, and Albrecht had "talked" him into agreeing to the concert. Given his detestation of public appearances, Fryderyk sounded surprisingly excited and upbeat about the approaching performance. Proudly, he informed his sister that "for a week now, there is no room [at the hall]. . . . There will be only three hundred tickets at twenty francs. I shall have the beautiful Parisian world. The King has ordered ten tickets, the Queen ten, the Duchess d'Orléans ten, Prince de Montpensier ten. They are signing up for a second [concert], which probably I shall not give because this one already bores me." He could not resist this last touch of affectation. The following day, Fryderyk wrote the family (it was unprecedented for him to write home two days in a row): "I had the grippe . . . but I am very busy with the concert on the sixteenth of this month. . . . I am astonished by the excitement, but I must play at least for my conscience because it seems to me that I play worse than previously. . . . I shall be like at home and my eyes will meet almost only familiar faces. . . . I have finally received the comforter you sent me, which is admired by people who have seen it."

On the day after the performance, Chopin told Solange in a short let-ter: "I was in bed for several days with a horrible grippe and I gave a con-cert at Pleyel's. . . . All Paris is sick." He was in bed again five days later when a revolution erupted in Paris on February 22, canceling the second concert tentatively scheduled for March, but elevating George Sand to the status of "Muse of the Revolution" and the most powerful woman in France.

The Revolution of 1848, as it became known, was "a riot that was trans-formed into a revolution," in the words of the historian Jean Tulard. "There was no plan, no organization," he wrote, explaining that the sudden explosion in the streets had resulted from an industrial, eco-nomic, and consequently "social crisis" affecting the working classes. It was not a political revolt in the sense of seeking the overthrow of a sys-tem or regime in favor of another, but a visceral uprising by impover-ished urban workers in the new industrial society against the inept and unjust role by the bourgeoisie—the middle classes of bankers and rich merchants—grown potent under the July Monarchy of King Louis-Philippe.

That the revolution came as a surprise to the reigning establishment was proof of how inept it was. On January 29, three weeks before the first riots swept Paris, Alexis de Tocqueville sounded a warning to his colleagues in a speech at the Chamber of Deputies:

It is said that there is no peril because there are no riots; it is said that inasmuch as there is no material disorder on the surface of the society, revolutions are far from us. Gentlemen, allow me to tell you that I think that you are wrong. Undoubtedly, disorder is not in the events, but it has profoundly entered the spirits. See what is happening among the work-ing classes! . . . It is true that they are not tormented by political passions to the same degree that they had been in the past, but don't you see that their passions have shifted from political to social? Don't you see that opinions and ideas are gradually spreading among them that will not merely overthrow this or that cabinet or the government itself, but the very foundations upon which society is based today?

And Gustave Flaubert, the socially conscious novelist, had one of his characters in *Sentimental Education* exclaim, "It's funny that these good people sleep peacefully! A new 1789 is in preparation! People are fed up with constitutions, charters, subtleties, lies."

Social agitation inevitably gave new life to the political opposition to the July Monarchy, and at that stage this opposition was composed of many liberal and leftist figures who were both politicians and artists in the best French tradition. And most of them were friends of George Sand—and until very recently members of her and Chopin's social circle at their Paris phalanstery and at Nohant. They included Pierre Blanc and Pierre Leroux, the ideological followers of Saint-Simon and Proudhon; politicians like the Arago brothers and Alexandre Ledru-Rollin; and a writer-politician like Lamartine, who called the uprising the "Revolution of Contempt." The mystically inclined Sand regarded herself as a Christian socialist or a communist, without making entirely clear what exactly she meant by it. Since their rupture, Chopin no longer belonged to this political scene and cared little about the political future of France—so long as he could teach for money, compose, and maintain his lifestyle.

Marx and Engels had drafted the *Communist Manifesto* late in 1847, and were taken somewhat aback when the Revolution of 1848, about which they knew nothing beforehand, erupted a few weeks after their document first appeared in print in London. Marx would later mock the French Republic born from this revolution. But in 1848, *La Réforme,* the newspaper for which Sand and Marx had both written earlier in the decade, was one of the great voices of the revolution, still publishing Sand's political pronouncements.

Though France had been remarkably stable politically since 1840, its economy had begun to falter in recent years. Indeed, the situation resembled the eve of the 1789 Revolution. Catastrophic harvests in 1845 and 1846, due mainly to droughts, had pushed up wheat and bread prices threefold. A better harvest came in 1847, and prices dropped, but workers and their families had already lost their savings and were ruined. The race to invest in the new industries had dried up the money supply (over two billion francs were invested in industrial enterprises at the end of 1847) and interest rates soared. De Tocqueville observed that the government itself had acquired the appearance of an industrial enterprise in which "all the operations are conducted from the viewpoint of profits that shareholders can earn." Then English investment capital fled home where a similar crisis was developing, and France became so short of money that the treasury could not cover the paper currency in circulation. The Maison Rothschild, the great international bank headed by Chopin's friend Baron de Rothschild, floated a 350-million-franc bond issue, but it was too late. Farm and mining production dropped sharply. Unemployment, reaching thirty-five percent of the labor force in normally prosperous Normandy, turned into a full-blown social crisis. And tales of deep corruption within the royal cabinet swept Paris.

On the morning of February 22, students and workers battled the municipal police near the Chamber of Deputies on the Left Bank and barricades went up across the city, but calm returned overnight. Around noon of February 23, mobs surged in the center of Paris, capturing much of the Montmartre area around square d'Orléans, where Chopin, in bed because of his grippe attack, could hear the rumblings of the crowd and the firing of guns without having the slightest idea of what was happening. In the evening, National Guard units, attempting to control a mob marching on the Ministry of Foreign Affairs on the boulevard des Capucins, fired on the workers. There were fifty-two dead and seventy-four wounded. At that point, the "riot turned into a revolution" as popular fury took over the capital of one million inhabitants.

On February 24 in the morning, troops fought the rioters on the barricades. Most of Paris had risen in revolt. King Louis-Philippe sought to rally the National Guard and the regular army around the Tuileries Palace, but he was greeted with shouts of *"Vive la réforme!"* He then announced his abdication to avoid more bloodshed among the French, fleeing his capital for Honfleur in Normandy and then exile in England.

Louis-Philippe had named the Duchess d'Orléans to be regent, but the Chamber of Deputies was invaded by armed crowds chanting, "No regency! . . . Republic! . . . Republic!" before it could act on her nomination. Lamartine and Ledru-Rollin rose to demand a provisional government backed by the people to avert a civil war. The deputies agreed, and revolutionary leaders moved to the city hall on the Right Bank to formalize it there. By the end of the day, the monarchy had vanished and the republic had been proclaimed. The July Monarchy had lasted nearly eighteen years. The Republican regime was headed by an amorphous collective leadership, including the extreme left and its spokesman Louis Blanc, George Sand's close friend, whose motto was "to each according to his needs." The Tuileries Palace was sacked. Delacroix painted *La Liberté guidant le peuple* ("Liberty Leading the People"), with a bare-bosom "Liberty" holding aloft the tricolor flag. George Sand, rushing to Paris from Nohant, exclaimed: "The People will reign . . . reign fraternally!"

At the square d'Orléans, Chopin did not stir from his apartment as French history was being made around him. Writing Solange on March 3, he told her that "the birth of your daughter gave me greater joy than the birth of the Republic." The baby, Solange's second, was born several days before the uprising.

Fryderyk informed her in his customary mocking manner that "during the events I was in bed. I suffered from neuralgia all week. . . . Paris is calm out of fear. All are united. All belong to the National Guard. The shops are open; there is a shortage of buyers. Foreigners with their passports are awaiting the repair of the broken railways. Clubs are beginning to be formed." In the postscript Chopin could not refrain from cutting remarks about George Sand's friends now in power. "Mallefille rules over Versailles," he commented sarcastically about the tutor whom he had replaced as George's lover. "That Louis Blanc is in the Medici Palace as chairman of the commission organizing labor is, simply, the biggest news of the day. [Armand] Barbès rules over Luxembourg Palace," Chopin concluded. (Barbès was one of the opposition politicians defended by Michel de Bourges, an earlier Sand lover, in a sedition trial in the late 1830s.)

George reached Paris on the day the Republic was proclaimed, taking up quarters at a *hôtel garni,* a furnished flat in midtown Paris. She had given up her square d'Orléans apartment the previous year, after the break with Chopin, planning to live full-time in Nohant; she could no longer afford to keep up two residences. Fryderyk, however, chose to remain at the square. He gave lessons, tried hard to compose, and took most of his meals with Grzymała or Gutmann. Charlotte Marliani, separated from her husband, had also moved away from the square, and she could no longer be depended upon as a dinner hostess for Chopin.

On Saturday, March 4, Chopin went calling on Charlotte, still a friend, at her new lodgings at 18, rue de la Ville-Évêque, below boulevard Malesherbes and quite a distance on foot from the square. He was with another friend, Edmond Combes, known by his nickname of *l'Abyssinien* because of his travels in North Africa. On their way out, Chopin and Combes ran into George Sand in the foyer of Charlotte's apartment building; she, too, was going to visit Charlotte. This was the first time Fryderyk and George had met in ten months or so; the last time was probably late in May, after Solange's wedding, when Sand came to Paris to supervise what was going to be Augustine's marriage to Rousseau. Chopin's account of this encounter appears in his letter to Solange on March 5:

> Yesterday I went to [see] Madame Marliani and, coming out, I met in the door of the foyer your mother, entering with Lambert [(Eugène) Lambert was a young painter friend of Maurice and probably Sand's latest lover]. I said good morning to your mother and asked immediately how long ago she had news from you. "A week ago," she answered me. "Didn't you have a letter yesterday or the day before yesterday?" . . . "No" . . . "In that case, I wish to inform you that you have become a grandmother; Solange has a little daughter and I am glad that I am the first to convey this news to you." I bowed and went downstairs. *L'Abyssinien* Combes was with me, and because I had forgotten to tell her that you are in good health, an important matter, especially for a mother . . . I asked Combes to go back upstairs, because I could not climb the stairs again, and he told her that you and the child are well. I was waiting for *l'Abyssinien* downstairs, and your mother came down with him, and with great interest asked about your health. I answered that you had written a few words in pencil to me the day after the child's birth, that you suffered a lot, but had forgotten all of it upon seeing your little daughter. She asked me whether your husband had been with you, and I answered that the address on the letter seemed to be in his handwriting. She also inquired about my health [and] I answered that I am well, and told the porter to open the door. I bowed and walked over to the square d'Orléans.

It was the shortest imaginable conversation, but Chopin was well informed about Sand's doings, including that she had moved away from the furnished flat. He wrote Solange: "Your mother has been here for a few days, according to what Bocage told Grzymała. She is staying with

Maurice at 8, rue Condé, near the Luxembourg [Palace]. She dines at Pinson's (the restaurant where we once went with Delatouche), and that is where she receives and that is where she told Combes to come, announcing her departure soon for Nohant. I assume that a letter from you awaits her in Nohant. She seemed healthy to me. I think that she is happy that Republican ideas had triumphed, [and] the news I imparted to her yesterday made her even happier." And he added a sarcastic postscript: "Mallefille is no longer in Versailles; he reigned for only three days!"

Sand's version of the last meeting with Chopin is contained in *Story of My Life:*

> I saw him again for an instant in March 1848. I pressed his trembling and icy hand. I wished to speak to him, he slipped away. Now it was my turn to say that he no longer loved me. I spared him this infliction, and entrusted all to the hands of Providence and the future. I was not to see him again. There were bad hearts between us. There were good ones, too, who were at loss what to do. There were frivolous ones who preferred not to meddle with such delicate matters. . . . I have been told that he had asked for me, and loved me filially up to the very end. It was thought fit to conceal this from me until then. It was also thought fit to conceal from him that I was ready to hasten to him.

(Chopin never read it: *My Life* began to be published in 1854, well after his death.)

Significantly, the two versions are not at all contradictory. Sand's statement that "I wished to speak to him, he slipped away" is corroborated by Chopin's account of their meeting. He had given her the news of Solange, replied that his health was fine, and "[I] told the porter to open the door. I bowed and walked over to the square d'Orléans." He chose not to give George a chance to engage him in a conversation that could have led to some form of reconciliation, let alone to let her "hasten to him." Sand burned all her letters to Chopin—she apparently retrieved them after his death—so there is no way of knowing whether she had ever conveyed these sentiments to him in writing. Fryderyk has never explained his behavior, but he would remain ambivalent about Sand until the end, still denouncing her in brutal terms, yet asking friends for news of her. He could never quite make up his mind about his personal life.

*   *   *

The same problem afflicted Chopin when it came to politics, depending on the geography in question. The Revolution of 1848 in France was, as he made it clear, of no interest to him. When it came to revolutions elsewhere in Europe, his passions were aroused, but not his personal involvement. George Sand wrote that when the February revolution came, "Paris became momentarily hateful to his mind, incapable of yielding to any commotion in the social form." And when he learned of new uprisings in Poland, Fryderyk made no effort, apart from epistolary rhetoric, to help even from a distance through his high-level French connections.

Sand concluded that "free to return to Poland, or certain to be tolerated there, he had preferred languishing ten (and more) years far from his family, whom he adored, to the pain of seeing his country transformed and deformed. He had fled from tyranny, as now he fled from liberty." This was classic Sand exaggeration—she obviously had no idea how Chopin might have been treated in Warsaw after the failure of the latest uprisings, which were quite minor, and she was writing long after the fact—but she made forcefully the point that his patriotism did not extend at any stage to a return to Poland. It was a thought he had never entertained after setting foot in Paris seventeen years earlier.

The French Revolution of 1848 is often regarded as part, or vanguard, of a broader European liberalizing movement known vaguely as "the Spring of the People." Revolutionary movements spread to Milan, from where Austrian forces were expelled; and Rome, from where Pope Pius IX was forced to flee when the Republic was proclaimed; to Belgium, Berlin, Vienna, and the Prussian- and Austrian-occupied regions of Poland. "National committees" were installed in Austrian-held Kraków and Lwów and in Prussian-ruled Poznań in the west. Prince Adam Czartoryski decided this time to support the patriotic conspiracies and moved from Paris to the Poznań duchy, where a liberating army was being organized.

Chopin was ecstatic. On April 4, he wrote Julian Fontana in New York that

> something will surely happen [in Poland]. Our people are assembling in Poznań. Czartoryski was the first one to go there, but only God knows how it all will happen so that there will be a Poland again. . . . As you see, it all smells of war, though we don't know where it will start. But when it

starts, all Germany will move; the Italians have already started. Milan chased away the Austrians, but they remain in the province and they will fight. France will surely help. . . . The Russian will certainly suffer sorrow when he moves against the Prussian. Peasants of Galicja have given an example to peasants in Wołyn and Podole [eastern provinces of Poland], and terrible things cannot be avoided, but in the end it will be a superb, great Poland, in one word: Poland. So, despite our impatience, let us wait until all the cards are sorted out in order not to waste pointlessly our strength that will be needed at the proper moment. This moment is near, but not today. Perhaps in a month, perhaps in a year. Everybody here is convinced that our things will be completely clarified before the autumn.

Fontana, who decided not to rush back to Europe, became acquainted in New York with Edgar Allan Poe, who was familiar with the music of Chopin, his fellow Romantic artist. In the January 3, 1846, issue of the *Broadway Journal,* of which he was one of the editors, Poe published an article in the "Fine Arts" section, mentioning that "Chapin [*sic*], the celebrated composer and pianist, has dedicated . . . several of his waltzes" to Fontana. That Chopin and Poe were perceived as having much in common is suggested in the 1896 poem "Poe-Chopin" by John B. Tabb: "O'er each the soul of Beauty flung / A shadow mingled with the breath / Of music that the Sirens sung, / Whose utterance is death." Poe, for his part, was very highly regarded in France, notably by the poet Baudelaire. Poe, who was a year older than Chopin, would die ten days before him, in 1849.

French revolutionaries seemed to share Chopin's passion for Poland, as they did in 1830, but some of their leaders attempted to use the ever-popular Polish cause as a pretext for a coup d'état against the National Assembly and the new government in power. On May 15, for example, a crowd of workers invaded the assembly chamber chanting, "Long Live Poland!" not aware that their chiefs, including Louis Blanc, had mobilized them to oust the relatively moderate Republican regime in favor of the extreme left, which had been defeated in legislative elections on May 5 (Lamartine was one of the five members of the "Executive Power Commission," the government elected by the assembly). The Goncourt brothers reported in their famous *Journal* that the leftist "Democratic clubs" took over the National Assembly to present petitions demanding independence for Poland. Barbès, they wrote, shouted from the tribune, "For Poland! France must march to the aid of all the oppressed people!"

But the attempted coup failed and the French Republican government did nothing to aid oppressed people anywhere. Even Lamartine opposed a hopeless French involvement in Poland, earning the hostility of Polish exiles, among them Chopin. Meanwhile, the Polish uprisings fizzled out. The following year, a French army seven-thousand-strong conquered Rome and liquidated the Italian Republic (the French were determined to take Rome before the Austrians did). The Spring of the People turned out to be a very short spring indeed, and even in France the Republic began to become increasingly authoritarian and intolerant of criticism and opposition.

Quite aside from the events in Poland, and even before they took shape, Chopin had concluded that postrevolutionary Paris held no immediate promise for him. Much of the aristocracy had fled, the middle classes were scared and impoverished, and no students were queuing up at the square d'Orléans for piano lessons. He had no new compositions for sale to the music publishers, who, in any case, had almost no clients. Since the rupture with George Sand, no sentimental ties kept him back in Paris. Chopin therefore agreed to go to England and Scotland for at least a half year or so, to play and compose in a different environment and, if possible, to earn some money. Given the state of his health, it may have been a foolish decision, but it opened the door for the entry into his life of a new, full-time female presence.

This was Jane Wilhelmina Stirling, Chopin's wealthy Scottish acquaintance and erstwhile pupil, six years older than he. In love with Chopin probably since the first time she heard him play in 1832—she became his student in 1843—Jane and her patience would be rewarded fifteen years later when Sand's disappearance from his side created an opening for her. Whether because she was waiting for Chopin or for other reasons, she had never married. It is most unlikely that the forty-four-year-old Jane and the thirty-eight-year-old Fryderyk became lovers—his health, if nothing else, ruled it out—when they departed Paris for London late in April, with her in charge of all the arrangements, or subsequently. In fact, they never lived together.

As George Sand had done for the previous nine years, the tall, thin

Jane now assumed the role of Chopin's protectress, nurse, and virtual mother. Stirling, the youngest of thirteen children of John Stirling, the laird of Kippendavie and lord of Kippenross House where she was born, resembled Sand "in some respects," in the words of biographer Audrey Evelyn Bone. The two women, she wrote, "were strangely similar in their masculine approach to life. . . . Both were striking women in their appearance, determined to achieve their own aims in life, and both had a knowledge of medicine, in particular cures by nature, that was in advance of their times. Their ability to care for Chopin was in itself an important factor in their relations with this genius."

Also in the same way as with George, Chopin accepted Jane's protection and love without reciprocating in any meaningful fashion—although this time he was even more dependent. In fact, Stirling's devotion failed to evoke even simple kindness on Fryderyk's part. He dismissively referred, behind their backs, to Jane and her older sister, Katherine Erskine, a widow, as "my worthy Scottish ladies." When asked by a Polish friend whether he would marry Jane, Chopin replied testily, thinking of his own condition, "She might as well marry death."

Fryderyk came back to this subject in a letter to Grzymała, observing that for marriage "there must be . . . a feeling of physical attraction." Describing Jane as "one who resembles me far too much," he said,

> how am I to kiss myself? Friendship is friendship . . . but that doesn't give anyone the right to anything else. . . . If I should fall in love with someone, who feels the same as me, I won't marry . . . because we would have nothing to eat and nowhere to live. Those who are rich must look for someone rich, and if they find someone who is poor . . . he must not be an invalid, but well groomed. One has the right to be poor alone, but together it would be the greatest misfortune. I may die in an infirmary, but I don't want to leave a wife in misery after my death. . . . You know instinctively my opinions on that. So I don't think of marrying, but of my home, my mother, and my sisters.

Highly intelligent, Jane Stirling must have understood Chopin's ways and fears, but she seemed content just to be near him and support him in every way. She helped, for example, to organize his February concert at Salle Pleyel. As Bone points out, Jane had an "intense dislike" for Sand. She writes that had Sand wished to visit Chopin after their breakup, "it would have been practically impossible when Jane Stirling was there. . . . Sand sent a friend to inquire after Chopin's health in 1849; the visitor was not even allowed inside Chopin's apartment but immediately turned away."

The notion of leaving Paris must have germinated in Chopin's mind from the moment of the February revolution. Word of it reached Warsaw rapidly because Justyna wrote her son as early as March 5, that the *Kurier* newspaper had announced that "you are giving a concert and leaving immediately afterwards, so we are guessing where: Some tell us that it is to Holland, others that it is Germany, and still others that it is [St.] Petersburg. . . . We hope that perhaps it would be to [visit] us." She added that the Jędrzejewiczes and the Barcińskis—his sisters and their husbands—were already arguing at which of their apartments Fryderyk would stay in Warsaw.

The idea of going to Poland had not crossed Chopin's mind as he contemplated his immediate future, and it was Jane Stirling who had persuaded him to travel to England. He did not seem to have alternative invitations. News that Solange's second daughter had died six days after her birth, just a few days after Fryderyk's encounter with George, did not affect his plans. He commiserated with her in a mid-March letter, sent to her father's house in Guillery, adding that "I have been told that your mother left Paris. I have not seen her since the day when I was leaving Madame Marliani. She received your letter in Nohant. She deserves compassion—it was a hard blow to her—and I do not doubt that she will do for you everything in her power."

The evening before his departure, Chopin arranged for Dr. Molin to come to the apartment to examine him and offer advice on how to take care of himself during the journey. On April 20, he left Paris for the Channel coast and England, traveling alone. It happened to be the day the army occupied the capital on orders from the Republican government to quell attempts by Louis Blanc's leftist extremists to impose by force their "socialist" program. The regime itself was moving increasingly to the right, and National Guardsmen chanted, "Down with the communists!" as they truncheoned the leftist crowd marching that day on city hall. The new disorders seemed to vindicate Chopin's decision to get away from the instability of Paris.

According to some versions, Jane Stirling had actually urged Fryderyk to move permanently to London on the grounds that it might be more comfortable and profitable for him to be in exile there rather than in Paris. Naturally, she wanted him near her as much as possible. The London *Atheneum,* for example, reported in its April 8 edition that Chopin "is expected . . . to remain in England" after his arrival. But there are no signs that he ever made such a commitment. For one thing, he kept the square d'Orléans apartment, continuing to pay the rent.

Chopin arrived in London in the late afternoon of April 20, after a short rest at Folkestone. England presented a culture shock to him, though it was his second time there, starting with the fact that he spoke not a word of English. But he found that Jane and her sister Katherine Erskine had prepared a most extraordinary welcome for him. Writing Grzymała the following day, Good Friday, Fryderyk, referring inaccurately to the sisters as "the Erskines," reported that "they had thought of everything, even of [hot] chocolate, and not only of an apartment. . . . You will not believe how good they are! Only now I notice that the stationery on which I am writing has my monogram on it, and I encountered a multitude of such small attentions."

The apartment the sisters had rented for Fryderyk was at 10, Bentinck Street, near Cavendish Square, but within a week he moved to one at 48, Dover Street, just off Piccadilly, very close to Jane and Katherine's house, paying a weekly rent of four guineas. He wrote Franchomme on May 1: "Here I am, just settled. I have at last a room—fine and large—where I shall be able to breathe and play, and the sun visits me today for the first time. I feel less suffocated this morning, but all last week I was good for nothing. . . . I haven't yet delivered my letters of introduction. I am wasting my time on nothing."

Unlike his 1837 visit to London, this time Chopin was not incognito. English publications took notice of his presence, the *Atheneum* commenting that "Mr. Chopin's visit is an event for which we most heartily thank the French Republic." The pianist Moscheles, who was in Leipzig that month, wrote Fryderyk to express his regrets over missing the latter's stay in London, but urging him to accept an invitation from his daughter and her husband. Feeling stronger, Chopin gladly joined London's social life, spending time with his Polish friends, Stanisław Egbert Koźmian and Major Karol Franciszek Szulcewski (an 1830 uprising veteran), and being received at the grandest London homes. Within days of his arrival, Chopin played at the mansion of the Duchess of Gainsborough, quite a distinction. There he performed a Mozart duet with Julius Benedict, who many years later recalled "the great pains Chopin insisted should be taken in rehearsing it, to make the rendering of it at the concert as perfect as possible." And Chopin made a point of calling on the exiled French royal family and his friend Count Perthuis, the ex-king's aide-de-camp, remembering their past kindnesses to him.

At his apartment, Fryderyk had three pianos at his disposal—an English Broadwood (sent by James Broadwood, the manufacturer, who remembered him from the visit eleven years earlier), a Pleyel, and an Erard—but, as he wrote Gutmann, "I don't know what they will be good for, because I have no time to play. I have to make and receive innumerable visits, and my days flash by like lightning. . . . I haven't had a free moment."

Chopin also heard Jenny Lind, the great Swedish opera singer, at a performance of Bellini's *La Sonnambula* at Covent Garden attended by the twenty-nine-year-old Queen Victoria; he concluded in a letter to Grzymała that both women had made "a great impression." He added that "old Wellington, who sat below the royal loge like an old monarchic dog in his doghouse," had also made an impression on him. And Fryderyk met Jenny Lind, who sent him free tickets for a loge for her next appearance "that normally cost 2½ guineas." They quickly became friends. Lind dined with him and sang polkas and Swedish songs for him at parties at friends' homes. She attended at least one of his concerts—a performance at the house of the singer Adelaide Kemble Sartoris, where he played études, nocturnes, mazurkas, two waltzes, and the Berceuse (op. 57)—and, according to a note in the *Atheneum,* "she seemed to be the most enthusiastic" in the audience.

Fryderyk thought that Lind was "charming" and had "a beautiful, clear voice," and he wrote Grzymała that although Slavs and Scandinavians had different characters, "we are closer to each other than Italians and Spaniards." Niecks observes that "the way [Lind] spoke of Chopin showed unmistakably that he made the best possible impression upon her, not only as an artist, but also as a man—she was sure of his goodness, and that he could not but have been right in the Sand affair, I mean as regards the rupture." Lind would visit Chopin in Paris the following year, shortly before his death. And Fryderyk also had the pleasure of hearing and seeing in London his old friend Pauline Viardot, who sang his songs at Covent Garden.

The most memorable highlight of Fryderyk's sojourn in London was his appearance on May 15, before Queen Victoria at Stafford House (now Lancaster House), the home of the Duchess of Sutherland, on the occasion of a family baptism. He wrote an unidentified friend in Paris that he had played "in the presence of the queen, Prince Albert, the Prussian prince, Wellington, and the entire 'Order of the Garter' society here (in a small circle of eighty persons)," and that the singers Lablache, Giovanni Mario (the Marquis of Candia), and Antonio Tamburini had also performed. Chopin reported that "Her Royal Highness said a few kind things to me"—he wrote his family that the queen spoke twice with him and Prince Albert came over to the piano—but he doubted that he would be invited to play at court, for which he had earnestly hoped, because of the official mourning for an aunt of the queen. In any event, he failed to make an impression on Victoria, who, according to Zieliński, wrote in her diary that there had been "beautiful music"; Lablache, Mario, and Tamburini "sang well"; and "some pianists played."

As in Paris, money was among Chopin's main preoccupations, while his health was again deteriorating. Jane Stirling and her sister arranged for invitations for him and looked after his comfort, but he had to earn enough himself to pay for his rented apartment and food and clothing, for his rented carriage and driver, and for his Italian manservant. His rent had gone up to ten guineas weekly. And the competition among pianists was huge in London that year with artists like Thalberg, Kalkbrenner, Osborne, and Hallé visiting there at the same time—and all striving to organize profitable concerts for themselves. Because of his reputation, Chopin was invited to play one of his concertos with the London Philharmonic Society's orchestra, which might have produced a reasonable fee. But his fear and detestation of appearing in a great hall with an orchestra made him turn down the proposal. He wrote Grzymała that he had gone there to listen to a concert and came back convinced that "there you must play Mozart, Beethoven, or Mendelssohn . . . their orchestra is like roast beef or turtle soup, strong, powerful, but that is all." Besides, there could have been only one rehearsal—which scared him.

This left performances for pay at private homes—the going rate was twenty pounds sterling for an evening—and during the spring and summer Chopin played *chez* the Duchess of Gainsborough, Mrs. Sartoris, and Lord Falmouth, among others. Some hostesses were happy to invite him to dinner and have him play afterwards, but offered no payment, often creating embarrassing situations for Fryderyk. He mentioned the Duchess of Somerset, who "is always very nice to me, and invites me to evening receptions. . . . But the duke is not generous, and they do not pay." Fryderyk recalled "the old Mrs. Rothschild, who asked me how much it would cost, and when I said 'twenty guineas,' she replied that although I play very beautifully, she would advise me to charge less because greater moderation is required during this season."

(Grzymała recounts that after his return to Paris, Chopin gave an imitation of a conversation with a London hostess who had asked him, "Mister Chopin, how much do you cost?" and when Fryderyk answered: "I take twenty-five guineas," the lady said, "Oh, but I'm just asking for a little piece." Chopin told her that it was always the same price, to which the Englishwoman exclaimed, "So you will play a lot for me?" Fryderyk assured her: "Even during two hours, if you wish.")

"I can see that they are not all that generous here and that it is hard everywhere to get money," Chopin wrote Grzymała. He also complained that the English high society was surrounded by music from morning until night to the point where "they do not care whether it is good or bad music. . . . They have here a flower exhibit with music, dinner with music, charity functions with music." Awaiting more paying invitations, Fryderyk gave a few lessons at one guinea each, the Duchess of Sutherland being one of his pupils (another lady student vanished without paying for nine lessons she took).

Chopin continued working in spite of collapsing health, fighting on. Niecks writes that when Chopin visited the Broadwood piano establishment to try the instrument on which he was to play, "he had each time to be carried up the flight of stairs which led to the piano room." He also had to be carried upstairs when he went to a recital at Hanover Square Rooms. Fryderyk wrote Grzymała on May 13 that he could not bring himself "to get up in the morning before eight o'clock . . . and after ten o'clock there are tribulations that bring no money. . . . I cannot walk nor move, so I cannot attend to my affairs, but I see that things are happening by themselves and if the season lasted six months, I would be able to earn something."

Two weeks later, Chopin wrote a friend in Paris: "I haven't become accustomed to the air in London—and life with visits, dinners, and social evenings weighs on me very much. I have been spitting blood in recent days—I treated myself only with lemons and ice cream, which helped me, as did a three-day rest I took." He told Grzymała that "every day I must go out into the world late in the evening" and "I lack the strength for such a life. If it only brought me money." On June 30, Chopin wrote Solange in Paris: "I am suffering an attack of spleen. . . . I am firing my Italian servant, a lazy liar, who knows as little English as I do." On July 10, he informed Grzymała that "I often think in the morning that I will cough my soul out. I am sad. . . . I avoid being alone in order not to think. . . . You cannot afford to be ill here very long, and I don't want to catch any fevers." He added that "I cannot finish this letter because my nerves are shot; I suffer from strange longings, and despite my resignation, I am worried about what to do with myself." And on July 17, Chopin wrote: "I can no longer know how to be sad or happy. . . . I just vegetate and wait for it to end faster."

Somehow Chopin kept afloat in London's social swirl, encountering famous personages whom he could not usually communicate with because he spoke no English, but was proud to meet. These included Thomas and Jane Carlyle, Charles Dickens, and Ralph Waldo Emerson, who lived in London at the time and with whom he must have established some sort of rapport because he later asked Fontana (who had returned to London from New York) to convey his regards to "your famous philosopher." He also met Byron's widow, Anna Isabella Milbanke, Lady Byron: "We seem to share sympathy and we talk like a goose with a piglet, she in English and I in French." Chopin must have known that Lady Byron, a mathematician and poetess, had left her husband long before his death as a result of his philandering, because he remarked in a letter home: "I understand how she must have bored Byron." Sounding like *Burke's Peerage* in Polish, Fryderyk's letter to his family in August listed every important English and Scottish aristocrat he had met—no major name was missing.

Through his Polish friends, Chopin learned of the collapse of the patriotic uprising in the Poznań region, commenting, "Oh, such grief, such grief!"—his only recorded reference to the events in Poland. He was much more outspoken, however, on the subject of the situation in France and, curiously, all his observations were couched in references to George Sand and her friends in power. He could not get her out out of his mind. Writing Grzymała on May 13, for example, Fryderyk noted that "English newspapers are not writing well about Sand . . . that she could be seen in some garden (probably Luxembourg), with Ledru-Rollin lying down and Madame S. standing next to him, carrying on a conversation." On June 2, he protested against Arago's appointment as ambassador to Prussia: "He does not speak a word of German. It would be different if he were sent to Bavaria as a friend of Lola Montès! Even Liszt would be better as a diplomat." On July 8, Chopin instructed Grzymała to write him about Sand, saying that "I know that she wrote [Pauline] Viardot, tenderly inquiring about me. . . . What a role of a just mother she must play there!" On July 17, he asked again what Solange's mother "is doing?"

Fryderyk reported on August 17 that he had heard from Viardot that Sand had gone to Tours; she did it to escape rising criticism of her radical militancy. Ledru-Rollin had made her editor of the *Bulletin de la république* in the immediate aftermath of the February revolution and, once more carried away by her enthusiasms, she urged (in *Bulletin* no. 16) the people to go to the barricades and abolish the National Assembly if voting there failed "to make social truth triumph." This was a bit much even for her best friends, particularly when she joined the mob marching on the assembly during the May 15 riots.

For his part, Chopin wondered, in a letter to Grzymała, "What was she up to?" Writing to the family in Warsaw on August 19, an immense missive dealing mainly with his London social life, he devoted several pages to attacks on Sand that bordered on the incoherent. He said that recently Sand had "foundered in mud and embarrassed many other people," and that "she is blamed for abominable proclamations that fired up a civil war." And Chopin went on: "Her other daily newspaper, which failed because it was ultra, served only to excite the shortsighted ones, and was banned although it was already dying, like the first one, from a shortage of readers. Who would have believed it just a few years ago!"

Fryderyk wrote that *La biographie contemporaine et les intrigues de George Sand,* written by Augustine Brault's father and widely circulated, complained that Sand "had demoralized his daughter, made her into a mistress for Maurice," adding that it is

the ugliest, dirtest adventure in Paris. . . . It is the good deed that she had in mind and that I opposed from the very first day of that girl's arrival. . . . She should have been left with her parents, not have her head filled with thoughts about the son who would only marry money . . . but he wanted a pretty cousin at home, and the mother placed her on the same level as Solange. She was dressed the same way, better cared for, because Maurice wanted it. . . . Thus Madame S. made a victim of that girl. Solange saw it all, so she was in the way. . . . It was uncomfortable for the mother to be with the daughter, who, unfortunately, saw everything that was happening; hence the lies, the shame, and the rest.

With the summer, the musical and social season ended in London, and Chopin gladly accepted an invitation from Jane Stirling and her friends to come to Scotland to rest and give concerts. On August 5, he traveled twelve hours by train to Edinburgh with his new servant, Daniel, an Irishman, and a representative of the Broadwood piano-manufacturing company. Fryderyk spent two days resting at Douglas Hotel and touring the city, then he was taken twelve miles to Calder House, the residence of seventy-eight-year-old Lord James Torphichen, the brother-in-law of Jane Stirling and Katherine Erskine, who were awaiting him there. It had once been the home of John Knox, the reformer of the Scottish Church. Now Chopin was firmly under the care and command of the Scottish sisters.

During the nearly three months Fryderyk spent in Scotland, he played in public in Glasgow and Edinburgh (as well as in Manchester on a brief foray there late in August) and at the magnificent homes of the sisters' relatives and friends, where he was royally received and treated. As he wrote on October 1, from Keir, the Perthshire estate of William Stirling (uncle of Jane and Katherine, and a world authority on Spanish painters), "When I have settled down in some measure, I must continue my travels, for my Scottish ladies do not allow me—to be sure with the best intentions in the world—any rest. They fetch me to introduce me to all their relations; they will at last kill me with their kindness, and I must bear it all out of pure amiability." And there was a certain relentlessness in the sisters' pursuit of Chopin as he wrote Grzymała upon his return to London in November: "My worthy Scottish ladies, whom I haven't seen for several weeks, came to see me today. I receive letters from them every day and do not reply to them, but immediately I go anywhere, they follow immediately." Their solicitude toward Fryderyk extended to the daily delivery to him of Paris newspapers while he was in Scotland, but he occasionally grew tired of the attention. He told Grzymała that "my good Scotchwomen . . . would like me to stay on to drag myself to Scottish castles, here and there, wherever I am invited. They are so good, but so boring, so help me God."

Chopin retained his sense of humor and his talent for colorful descriptions as he demonstrated in a letter from Edinburgh to Adolf Gutmann:

> Since I had news from you, I have been in Scotland, in this beautiful country of Walter Scott, with so many memories of Mary Stuart, the two Charleses, &c. I drag myself from one lord to another, from one duke to another. I find everywhere, besides extreme kindness and hospitality without limit, excellent pianos, beautiful pictures, choice libraries; there are also hunts, horses, dogs, interminable dinners, and cellars of which I avail myself less. It is impossible to form an idea of all the elaborate comfort which reigns in the English mansions. . . . Everything here has become doubly splendid, except the sun, which has done nothing more than usual. . . . Everything here furnishes matter for the imagination—a park with hundred-year-old trees, precipices, walls of the castle in ruins, endless passages with numberless old ancestors.

But Fryderyk noted in October, "Things are getting worse with me every day. I feel weaker; I cannot compose, not for want of inclination, but for physical reasons, and because I am every week in a different place. . . . I am all morning unable to do anything, and when I have dressed myself I feel again so fatigued that I must rest. After dinner, I must sit for two hours with the gentlemen, hear what they say in French, and see how much they can drink. Meanwhile I feel bored to death. I think of something totally different, and then go to the drawing room, where I require all my strength to revive, for all are anxious to hear me. Afterwards my good Daniel carries me upstairs to my bedroom, undresses me, puts me to bed, leaves the candle burning, and then I am again at liberty to sigh and dream until morning, to pass the next day just like the preceding one."

"I cannot breathe," he wrote Grzymała, "and I cannot work. I feel alone, alone, alone, although I am surrounded [by people]." And in the course of a coupé ride to visit the sisters' friends by the sea, Chopin was almost killed when the two horses spooked, the reins were torn loose, the coachman fell to the ground, and the whole vehicle crashed against a tree. The tree prevented it from tumbling down a steep precipice and his certain death, and he was able to extricate himself. "I confess," he wrote, "that I saw my last hour calmly, but the thought of smashed legs and arms scared me a lot. All I need is to be a cripple."

A pleasant surprise was finding a fellow Pole in Edinburgh, a physician named Adam Lyszczyński with whom Fryderyk spent several days toward the end of his stay in Scotland and with whom, to his immense joy, he could converse in Polish. His friend Princess Marcelina Czartoryska and her husband, Prince Aleksander, and their little son looked up Chopin during a visit to Edinburgh, then traveled to Glasgow to attend his concert, and spent a day with him at Lord Murray's nearby estate. "You have no idea how it revived me," Fryderyk told Grzymała.

On November 3, an utterly exhausted Chopin returned to London, falling gravely ill almost immediately. Major Szulcewski had found an apartment for him at 4, St. James's Street, almost next door to the palace of Lord Dudley Coutts Stuart, the president of the Friends of Poland Literary Society. It was just five minutes away from his previous digs on Dover Street, where Princess Czartoryska now resided. But Chopin reached the conclusion that there was no future for him in England—he believed, for one thing, that he was too old and tired to start learning English—and that he should go back to Paris as soon as his health improved sufficiently for travel. He was also perturbed by his belief that, to the English, "music is a profession, not art, and no one will ever call a musician an artist." He told friends that on one occasion, after his performance on the piano and a recital of Scottish songs, Lady Murray, his hostess at her great castle, had an accordion brought out and "began to play the most awful melodies." Finally, Chopin missed his Polish-speaking friends in Paris.

At this point, however, Fryderyk's principal concern was his health. He had spent eighteen days in bed suffering, he told Grzymała, from "a severe cold (with headache, difficult breathing, and all my bad symptoms)," and had to be visited daily by a homeopathic physician named Malan. Sick as he was, Chopin could not refrain from noting that the doctor "is married to a niece of Lady Gainsborough"; he was always conscious of class and social hierarchies. In any case, Dr. Malan helped him improve to the point where, on November 16, Chopin attended the charity Polish Concert and Ball at Guildhall, organized by Lord Stuart under royal patronage, and played there.

For Fryderyk, it was a poignant and pathetic affair. It was also the last time he played in public. His piano performance came after lively dancing and enthusiastic activity in the refreshment rooms, and the *Times,* without mentioning Chopin, simply reported that the concert "was much the same as on former occasions, and at its conclusion many of the company departed." A friend recalled that Fryderyk had played, among other works, two of his études from Opus 25. The scene was best described in an essay on Chopin by the music historian Francis Hueffer in *Musical Studies:* "The people, hot from dancing, who went into the room where he played, were but little in the humor to pay attention, and anxious to return to their amusement. He was in the last stage of exhaustion, and the affair resulted in disappointment. His playing at such a place was a well-intentioned mistake."

Chopin wrote that he went "home at once, after I had gone through my task" and "the whole night I could not sleep as I suffered, besides cough and asthma, from a very violent headache." To look after him in his illness, Fryderyk had Jane Stirling and her sister, who had followed him back to London, Princess Marcelina Czartoryska, and the devoted Major Szulcewski.

Readying himself for the return to Paris, Chopin asked Grzymała to find him a new apartment because his old one at the square d'Orléans was too cold during the winter. He suggested another apartment on the square, with a room for his servant, or a place in the neighborhood of the rue de la Paix or rue Royale. This train of thought triggered in Fryderyk's mind a new surge of bitterness against George Sand and all she stood for, and he vented it in a letter to Grzymała: "Why do I bother you with all this, I do not know myself; but I must think of myself and therefore I beg you to assist me. . . . I have never cursed anyone, but now I am so weary of life that I am near cursing *Lucrezia*! But she suffers, too, and suffers more because she grows daily older in her wickedness. What a pity about Soli [Solange]! Alas! Everything is going wrong in this world. Think only that Arago with the eagle on his breast now represents France!!! Louis Blanc attracts nobody's attention here."

Sounding more and more desperate, Chopin asked, "But what am I going back for? . . . Why doesn't God kill me once and for all, not slowly and in a fever of indecision? Besides, my good Scotswomen bore me again. Mrs. Erskine, a very religious Protestant, perhaps wishes to make me into a Protestant because she brought me the Bible, tells me about the soul, and marks psalms for me. . . . She always tells me that the other world is better than this one, but I know this by heart and answer with citations from Scripture, and explain that I know about it." Still practical-minded, however, Fryderyk added that "if I were healthy and could give two lessons daily, I would have enough for a decent life here—but I am weak, [and] I will eat what I have in three or at the most four months."

On November 20, Chopin wrote Dr. Malan thanking him for his care and asking for his bill. On November 21, a Tuesday, he wrote Grzymała that he would arrive on Friday at the square d'Orléans "to lie down . . . in addition to the usual things, I have neuralgia and I am swollen. . . . One more day here, and I shall go mad, not just die. My Scotswomen are so boring that God's hand must save me. They have so attached themselves [to me] that it is impossible to tear them away. Only Princess Marcelina and her family and the good Szulcewski keep me alive." Then he requested Grzymała to have fresh violets placed in the drawing room "so it would smell nicely and I could still have a little poetry returning to my home as I cross over to my bedroom where I will surely lie for a long time."

But Chopin still mustered enough strength to write a lengthy letter to Solange with advice for her husband, for which she had asked, concerning his plans to look for work as a sculptor in London or St. Petersburg, and promising letters of introduction. "Please excuse this chaotic letter," he concluded, "but I am suffering very much today."

Traveling with his friend Leonard Niedzwiecki and his servant Daniel, Chopin crossed the Channel on November 23, spent the night in Boulogne, and set foot in Paris the next day.

No sooner did Chopin reach his sickbed at the square d'Orléans than word reached him that Dr. Molin, the only physician in whom he had complete trust, had suddenly died. Fryderyk felt like a defenseless orphan. His old friends—Delacroix, Franchomme, Grzymała, the poet Cyprian Norwid, and others—hardly recognized him after the seven-month absence. Norwid described him as "an arch-delicate insect" who could be touched only with the greatest care not to damage his wings. Father Jełowicki wondered that a soul still stirred in that ravaged body. The poet Słowacki referred to him as *moribundus*.

Still, Chopin struggled on. He began sketching a mazurka and a waltz that would be his last compositions. He began giving lessons in December, but had to cease most of them—he was too weak. One evening, he dragged himself to Adam Mickiewicz's apartment to improvise on the piano for the poet though he could barely breathe.

The end of 1848 also marked, in effect, the death of the French Republic. In the December elections, Prince Charles Louis-Napoleon Bonaparte, the nephew of Napoleon Bonaparte, was elected president, defeating the leftists Ledru-Rollin and Raspail, and the moderate Lamartine. He received 5.5 million out of 7 million votes. The Second Empire with the Prince-President as Emperor Napoleon III would be established four years later in a plebiscite with an eleven-to-one margin of support.

Chopin had the satisfaction of seeing George Sand and her friends crushed politically—his bitter hatred for them had never ceased—but there was little in his own life to fill him with any hope or pleasure as he saw the new year dawn over icy, snow-covered Paris.

Chapter 25

ONLY MUSIC AND THE DEVOTION of his friends were left to sustain Chopin through the terrifying days and nights of 1849, his thirty-ninth year. Though he wrote Solange on January 30 that he had been "too ill" to have written her earlier and was forced to go back to bed "ten times a day," Fryderyk still tried to compose as best he could. He worked as well on notes for his projected piano Method manual.

It was most likely during the late winter, when he enjoyed a brief interlude of slightly improved health, that Chopin composed, at least in a preliminary form, the Mazurka in G minor and the Mazurka in F minor that were published posthumously as parts of Opus 67 and Opus 68. He may also have written at that time the Nocturne in E minor, published later in Opus 72. In any case, these are believed to have been his last works, though they were possibly begun much earlier.

His other compositions published posthumously had been completed at different times of his life, some of them even in his youth, and some were discovered long after he died in the possession of descendants of his friends and on dusty library shelves. Among them are two versions of the Waltz in E-flat, op. 18, found by the American pianist Byron Janis—one at the Château de Thoiry at Yvelines, France, in 1955, and the other at the Beinecke Library of Yale University in 1973, almost 125 years after Chopin's death. This is the famous *Grande valse brillante,* published in July 1834, but Janis believes the two versions of this waltz were composed a year apart, the first one probably in 1832. At Yale, Janis came upon not only a version of the *Grande valse brillante,* but also the Waltz in G-flat major, op. 70, no. 1, published posthumously in 1855, and most likely written in 1835. The two manuscripts were together on a library shelf. These discoveries caused a major sensation in the musical world.

Zieliński thinks that the Mazurka in F minor, op. 68, no. 4, is "unquestionably Chopin's last work," adding that "the composer did not have time to finish it and left it in the form of a very unclear and hatch-marked sketch." According to him, "at first, the manuscript was considered to be altogether illegible, and intelligible only to its author. It was deciphered with great difficulty by Franchomme, who discovered in it a work of exceptional beauty and expression." It jumped from tonality to tonality, Franchomme confessing: "I could hardly manage it." To Zieliński, it is "music in the character of a dolorous elegy, pregnant with frightening longing, *żal,* sadness, and tragic resignation." And it also represents in its chromatic chords "one of the most avant-garde phenomena in nineteenth-century music." But it was the end of Chopin's music. He wrote Grzymała in mid-June: "I have not started to play yet—I cannot compose." Delacroix, who often visited Fryderyk, wrote in his *Journal* at the end of January that "his suffering prevents him from being interested in anything, in work most of all."

And, again, the specter of death brushed close against Fryderyk. On April 3, Juliusz Słowacki, the Polish romantic poet, suddenly died in Paris; he was exactly the same age as Fryderyk. This led him, in a letter to Grzymała, to list with a touch of macabre humor the recent deaths of people he knew or knew about: "Kalkbrenner [the pianist] died, the older son of [Paul] Delaroche died in Versailles. Franchomme's excellent woman servant died. At the square d'Orléans there were no deaths, but little Étienne was mortally ill. The Scotswomen arrived this moment . . . and I told them that King Carlos Alberto died in Lisbon. . . . They suffocate me with boredom. . . . Madame Angela Catalani died of cholera."

Actually, Chopin succeeded in remaining remarkably playful and amusing notwithstanding his condition of permanent suffering. In a letter to Solange, describing his illness as well as the political unrest in Paris—it was one of his letters that skipped randomly among unrelated subjects—he explained that he was "becoming increasingly denser, which I ascribe to drinking cocoa every morning instead of my coffee. Don't ever drink cocoa yourself and dissuade your friends from it, especially those who correspond with you. In my next letter, after taking some sulphate that Dr. Simon is to give me to allow me to breathe, I shall try to write with more humor."

Chopin looked for solace in his beloved opera for the last time on Sunday, April 22, when, feeling ever so slightly better, he attended the première of Meyerbeer's *Le Prophète*. He had been too ill to attend the dress rehearsal ten days earlier, and was quite disappointed with the work and its "special effects," including artificial sunbeams produced by an electric projector, a fire on the stage, and dancers on roller skates. Even Pauline Viardot in the role of the mother did not make it more palatable to Chopin. Delacroix, who visited him later that evening, recorded in his *Journal* Fryderyk's reaction to *Le Prophète:* "His horror at that rhapsody!"

Nearly two years after their rupture, Chopin and Sand still thought a great deal about each other—though in very different ways. Fryderyk was engaged in lively correspondence with Solange—who was now spending most of her time at her father's home in Guillery, while her husband was looking for sculpting commissions in Paris—offering her encouragement and advice. Clésinger himself was frequently Chopin's guest at square d'Orléans. Whether Fryderyk went out of his way to be kind and helpful to them, despite his illness and weakness, because he genuinely liked Solange (he never really learned to like Clésinger) or to annoy Sand—or both—they were very much a matter of concern to him during his final months. Moreover Solange, who had reestablished contact with her mother, was a source of information for him about George. Notwithstanding his steady stream of invective against her, Chopin often inquired about Sand in his letters to Solange.

Chopin indulged in denunciations of George when Delacroix visited him on January 29, and the painter recalls the occasion in his *Journal*:

> In the evening, I went to see Chopin; I stayed with him until ten o'clock. The dear fellow! We talked of Mme Sand, of her strange destiny, of her mixture of virtue and of vices. It was in reference to her *Mémoires*. He told me that it would be impossible for her to write them. She has forgotten all that: She has flights of sensibility and then quickly forgets. She wept for her old friend [Louis-Maurice] Pierret, and thought no more about him. I told him that I foresaw an unhappy old age for her. He does not think so. Her conscience does not reproach her with any of the

things with which her friends reproach her. She has good health, it can stand anything. One thing alone would affect her deeply—the loss of Maurice, or his turning to the bad entirely.

As for Sand, she was anxious for news of Chopin. Learning of his return from London, she wrote Pauline Viardot to inquire about him. Viardot replied on February 15: "His health declines slowly, with passable days when he can go out in a carriage and others when he spits blood and has coughing fits that suffocate him. He does not go out anymore in the evening. However, he is able to give a few lessons and, on good days, he can be gay. Here is the exact truth. He speaks of you always with the greatest respect, and I persist in affirming that he never speaks [of you] differently." Pauline, naturally, wrote as a loyal friend of both.

But Chopin had fewer and fewer "good days." He wrote Solange on April 5: "I do not know what to do. . . . I already have my fourth doctor—they charge ten francs a visit—and they sometimes come twice a day for that, bringing me almost no relief." Jules Janin, the journalist, wrote later that Chopin "lived ten years, ten miraculous years, with his breath ready to fly away." Niecks cites another writer's remark that "in seeing Chopin so puny, thin, and pale, one thought for a long time that he was dying, and then one got accustomed to the idea that he could always live so." And pianist/composer Stephen Heller told Niecks that "Chopin was often reported to have died, so often, indeed, that people would not believe the news when he was really dead."

Delacroix, who went to visit Fryderyk on the evening of April 11, reported in his *Journal*: "I found him almost in a state of collapse, hardly breathing. At the end of a certain time, my presence restored him. He told me that boredom was his cruelest torment. I asked him whether he had not previously known that unbearable emptiness which I sometimes feel. He told me that he could always busy himself with something. As unimportant as it may be in itself, a thing one has to do fills one's time and drives away those vapors. Troubles are another matter." Chopin was still trying to put up a fight, to sound optimistic, but it was becoming excruciatingly hard.

The weekend of April 22, when Chopin went to see *Le Prophète* at the opera, may have been the last time he went out for pleasure (on April 7, he had taken the drive in the Champs-Élysées with Delacroix when they discussed music and science). From then on, his contacts with friends were confined to their visits to him—very frequent visits by very many friends, who came by to chat and make music for him. Delacroix recalls that on one evening in April, Delfina Potocka sang for Fryderyk.

By late April, Chopin entered the crisis phase. Going over his musical manuscripts, he indicated to a number of his friends—probably including Grzymała, his banker Auguste Léo, and Princess Czartoryska—that he wished the unfinished ones to be burned as unworthy and others to remain unpublished in what was left of his lifetime. It is impossible to tell to what extent, if any, his wishes were respected, given the number of his works published posthumously.

At that stage, Chopin appears to have asked his sister Ludwika to come to Paris. There is no actual record of such a request—so many of his letters to Warsaw are missing—but there is no question that it was made sometime in April. Thus, Princess Marcelina, then visiting Würzburg, had written her brother-in-law Władysław Czartoryski in Paris on May 16, asking him to call on Madame Kiseleff, the wife of the Russian ambassador, to check on the status of the application for passports for Chopin's sister and her husband. As Russian subjects, they needed Russian passports to travel and special permission to visit France. The princess wrote that she had personally applied for the documents, presumably on Fryderyk's behalf, at a meeting with Madame Kiseleff, but did not wish the matter to be mentioned to others until there was "a good result, because I would not want poor Chopin to have unnecessary mental preoccupation with it." Fryderyk must have had premonitions of an approaching end when he expressed the desire to have his sister, the closest person to him in the world, by his side.

At the end of May, heat (along with a new epidemic of cholera) invaded Paris. Chopin's physicians and friends concluded that he needed cooler and fresher air for the summer, and an apartment was found for him in the Parisian suburb of Chaillot on the Passy hills overlooking the Seine and offering a magnificent view of the city on both sides of the river. Solange had invited Fryderyk to her father's home in Guillery in the southwest of France, but a trip of such magnitude was obviously out of the question.

The monthly rental for the apartment at 74, rue Chaillot was four hundred francs, which was expensive, though it offered Chopin comfortable rooms on the second floor of a two-story house. Fryderyk, no longer able to teach and running out of money, was told that it cost only two hundred francs because rentals were cheaper in the summer; his friend Princess Natalia Obreskow secretly paid the balance. Charles Gavard, a young bookseller and a friend who spent long hours with Chopin (Daniel, the Irish servant, was Fryderyk's only live-in companion), wrote that "Rue Chaillot was then a very quiet street, where one thought one's self rather in the provinces than in the capital. A large courtyard led to Chopin's apartments on the second floor . . . with a view of Paris, which can be seen from the heights of Chaillot."

Day and night, Chopin's friends trooped to rue Chaillot to see him: the Czartoryskis; Delfina Potocka (who came from Versailles), and Jenny Lind (just in from London), both singing for Fryderyk; Gutmann, Franchomme, Norwid, Father Jełowicki, and scores of others. Delacroix, however, had commitments away from Paris; he wrote a friend on June 9: "I left Paris saddened by the [health] condition of my dear Chopin, and it was unpleasant for me to leave him in such a state." Gavard kept Fryderyk company when he was alone: "The invalid avoided everything that could make me sad, and, to shorten the hours which we passed together, generally begged me to take a book out of his library and to read to him. For the most part he chose some pages out of Voltaire's *Dictionnaire philosophique.* He valued very highly the finished form of that clear and concise language, and [such] sure judgments on questions of taste. Thus, for instance, I remember that the article on taste was one of the last I read to him."

Berlioz, who called on Chopin on rue Chaillot, recalled afterwards that visits quickly tired him and

> his weakness and his sufferings had become so great that he could no longer either play the piano or compose; even the slightest conversation fatigued him in an alarming manner. He endeavored generally to make himself understood as far as possible by signs. Hence the kind of isolation in which he wished to pass the last months of his life, an isolation which many people wrongly interpreted—some attributing it to a scornful pride, others to a melancholic temper, the one as well as the other equally foreign to the character of this charming artist.

Berlioz, of course, was being very kind and understanding.

In notes to Polish friends during June and July, Chopin excused himself for not visiting them. He told Adam Cichowski, a family friend, "I wanted to drive over to see you, but I am too weak. . . . I had even ordered the carriage, but I have no strength."

Fryderyk had written the family on June 16—his mother referred to it in a letter to him in mid-June—informing them that he was in "better health." This particular missive has disappeared, too, but it evidently followed his request to Ludwika and her husband, Kalasanty, to come to Paris, of which Justyna had to be aware. She had to know that Fryderyk was very ill. After assuring him how much she wanted to be with him "and care for you as in the past," Madame Chopin told him that God would send him friends "who will take my place." Then she wrote: "I expect that now you need some money." This indicated that she realized that he could no longer teach and lacked income: "I am sending you for now what I can afford—one thousand two hundred francs—and the good Barciński [Fryderyk's brother-in-law] will explain what else you have to do, if you find yourself in need."

The night of June 22 appears to have marked the start of the final period in Chopin's life. He wrote Grzymała on that date that "last night, I twice had a hemorrhage. But I haven't done anything about it, and now I spit less blood." A night nurse the Czartoryskis had assigned earlier that month to watch over Fryderyk, a Polish woman named Matuszewska, at once reported the hemorrhages to Hôtel Lambert, and Princess Sapieha, Czartoryski's mother-in-law, summoned her own physician, the famous Jean Cruveilhier, to rue Chaillot. The doctor apparently concluded that Chopin was in the last stage of consumption and that nothing could be done for him other than to provide medicine to relieve the suffering and as much rest as possible.

Three days later, on June 25, Chopin made a new, desperate appeal to his sister Ludwika. "My life," he wrote,

> if you can, do come. I am weak and no doctors can help me as much as you. If you lack money, borrow it; if I am better, I can earn it easily and repay the person who loaned it to you, but now I am too naked to send you [anything]. My apartment here in Chaillot is large enough to receive you even with two children. Little Ludka [Ludwika] will enjoy it from every viewpoint. Kalasanty could run around all day—there is an agriculture exhibit next door—and he would have more free time to himself, because I am weaker and I shall stay more at home with Ludwika.

My friends and people who wish me well consider that Ludwika's arrival would be the best medicine for me. . . . So try for the passport. . . . Bring with you a thimble and needles, and I shall give you handkerchiefs to monogram and stockings to make, and you will spend a few months in fresh air with the old brother and uncle. Travel now is easier. No need for much luggage. Here, we shall be able to live inexpensively. You will find dwelling and food.

If it should be too far for Kalasanty to go into town from the Champs-Élysées, he could use my square d'Orléans apartment. There are omnibuses from the square to my door here. . . . I hope that family council sends me [Ludwika]; who knows, I may accompany her back if I heal. . . . A wife always owes obedience to her husband, so one must ask the husband to bring his wife. So I am asking him very much for it, and if he reflects about it, he will know that he could not give greater joy to her and to me, and even to the children, if he brings them. . . . Send me word soon.

Chopin assured the family that the cholera epidemic had run its course, and described the view from the five windows in his apartment. He added:

You will see it when you arrive. So act quickly about the passport and the money. Write me right away. Even cypresses have their caprices: My caprice today is to see you. . . . I am of good heart because I seldom ask for much, and I would have refrained from it if I were not being pushed by all those who wish me well.

And he promised Kalasanty "a big, superb cigar: I know somebody who smokes famous cigars."

On July 4, Fryderyk penned a chatty letter to Solange, mentioning a new hemorrhage and explaining that it ruled out any possible travel on his part. And the deterioration went apace. Chopin told Grzymała on July 10: "I am weak and I have some kind of diarrhea. Yesterday, I consulted Cruveilhier, who orders me to take almost nothing, just to sit quietly. . . . I see that he considers me to be consumptive because he prescribed for me a coffee spoon of something with lichen." (Lichen was used as a homeopathic treatment for consumption.) He added: "I play less and less; I cannot write," and he planned to remain in Chaillot for another month, presumably returning to square d'Orléans afterward.

Delfina Potocka informed Chopin on July 16 that one of her noble relatives in Poland had promised to do everything possible to obtain the travel permits for Ludwika, "but the difficulties are very great in that unhappy country." Discouraged, Fryderyk told Grzymała on July 28: "I am beginning to doubt about my sister." On August 3, he informed him that "my sister still does not have a permit. . . . I breathe hard, I cough, I am sleepy, I do nothing, I don't feel like anything." And to compound matters, Solange and her husband (without money) materialized in Chaillot, looking for an apartment to rent. "What a fool he is!" Chopin exclaimed about Clésinger.

Still, he tried to be lighthearted. Asking Franchomme, in a note, to send "some of your Bordeaux," Chopin declared: "I must drink some wine today, but I have none at home. . . . Wrap the bottle and be sure to place your seal on it—because these messengers! I do not know whom you can trust with this delivery. How suspicious I have become!"

On August 9, Ludwika, Kalasanty, and their fourteen-year-old daughter, Ludka, arrived in Paris. A few days later, she wrote Marie de Rozières: "I am with my dearest Fryderyk, who suffers very much. . . . He is very tired today, and more than before suffers from insomnia and coughing fits."

Chopin moved back to his square d'Orléans apartment in the middle of August. Shortly before the move, the strange affair of "lost" thousands of francs and the "medium" who "found" the missing money unfolded before him. Reconstructed from various contemporary accounts, this is what seems to have happened, a typical Chopinesque story:

Sometime late in the winter, word had reached Jane Stirling through Franchomme and Vera de Kologrivof Rubio, a mutual friend, that Chopin had gone through all his savings, was not earning any money, and was desperate for cash. He had, in fact, asked a friend to sell his Bréguet gold watch which, he said, had cost nine hundred francs. It was Franchomme who had first raised the matter with Madame Rubio. Jane, who had taken up residence with her sister Katherine Erskine in St. Germain, on the outskirts of Paris, to be near Chopin, is said to have wrapped banknotes adding up to 25,000 francs, a tidy fortune, in a parcel addressed to the composer and had it delivered anonymously to square d'Orléans by a "trusted person" on March 8. She thought that Chopin would be embarrassed if he knew she was the source of the money. The sealed parcel was supposedly left with Madame Étienne, the concierge at the square. It was not, however, given to Chopin, according to all the versions.

On an occasion in June, when Fryderyk was already in Chaillot, in a conversation with Franchomme, he deplored his impecunious status. Franchomme reportedly replied, "But, my dear friend, you have no cause to torment yourself, you can wait for the return of your health, you have money now!" Chopin exclaimed, "But I have nothing!" According to a version published by a Mrs. A. Audley, a friend of Franchomme, to whom she attributed it, the cellist said to him, "What about the twenty-five thousand francs which were sent you lately?" Fryderyk shot back, "Twenty-five thousand francs? Where are they? Who sent it to me? I have not received a sou!"

The question naturally arose as to what had happened to the money, but the story is too convoluted to merit very detailed examination. Suffice it to say that Chopin agreed to a friend's suggestion that "Alexis," then the most famous medium and clairvoyant in Paris, be enlisted in the search for the missing banknotes. Word came back from Alexis that he needed a lock of Madame Étienne's hair or a scarf belonging to her— she was suspected of stealing the parcel—to be able to trace the money. In Chopin's own version, in a letter to Grzymała on July 28, Mrs. Erskine, Jane's sister, had been present at the séance with Alexis, and she asked Fryderyk to help obtain "something" belonging to Madame Étienne. This is Chopin's account of what followed:

> I summoned Madame Étienne under a pretext . . . and when she came, I told her that Mrs. Erskine needed my hair for a medium who heals sick people in Saint-Germain, but wanted Madame Étienne's hair to compare healthy hair with sick hair. . . . Madame Étienne then cut [a strand] of her hair at my request, wrapped it, and Mrs. Erskine took it away. . . . This morning, the "trusted man," who had carried the parcel in the first place, came here with Mrs. Erskine. "Alexis" had recognized the hair of the person to whom the packet had been originally delivered, and said that "she" had placed the sealed parcel inside a piece of furniture near her bed, and that the parcel is still with her, not lost, not returned, not unsealed. . . . The "trusted man" went directly to the square d'Orléans from here at noon, found Madame Étienne alone, and reminded her that he had delivered a packet for me. . . . She gave him the package, it was

sealed, and the 25,000 francs inside were untouched. Madame Erskine unsealed it before me. . . . What about this "medium"? This packet lost so long ago, now untouched! One's head bursts at such incidents! You can assume that I did not accept the donation.

Chopin was furious over the whole matter, not quite believing that the gift from the Scottish sisters had been lost and magically retrieved by Alexis. He wrote Grzymała that "now you can believe in magnetism! . . . There is much in this particular case—with magnetism, with lying or hallucinations by Miss S[tirling], and Madame Étienne's kindness—with which I cannot agree. It could have even been done after the fact." Fryderyk also remarked that, at first, he did not know whether to accuse Jane Stirling of "hallucinations," the "trusted man" of thievery, or to charge Madame Étienne with theft. Jane, he wrote, had visited him with "confessions" and "she answered me so stupidly [about] her sister knowing nothing about it," and "I had to tell her some truths—for example, that I would not expect such generous gifts from anybody, except perhaps the queen of England." Jane had apparently tried to make Chopin believe that the money was actually from Mrs. Erskine, not from her.

It is unclear from existing versions whether and how much Chopin had accepted from Jane in the end. Franchomme believed that he kept twelve thousand francs, but Madame Rubio (who thought the concierge had been waiting for Chopin to die to keep the packet forever) claimed that it was only one thousand francs. Others said that Fryderyk had accepted fifteen thousand francs "as a loan." Jane Stirling's discreet contributions to Chopin's financial welfare did not cease with this incident. But Fryderyk's reaction toward his benefactor, even if she "bored him to death," was stunningly ungracious. He never showed any appreciation for the sisters' interest in him. "Scornful pride," Berlioz's words notwithstanding, was part of Chopin's makeup.

On August 31, Dr. Cruveilhier, deeply concerned about Chopin's condition, summoned two colleagues, Dr. Blache and Dr. Louis, for a "consultation," to solicit "second opinions." The three physicians agreed that Fryderyk must not travel to warm climates, or anywhere, under any circumstances, but that he should move to a warmer apartment, preferably with southern exposure.

The new home selected for Chopin was a spacious, seven-room apartment on the first floor of the building at 12, place Vendôme, as fashionable an address as existed in central Paris (it had once housed the Russian embassy). His friend Thomas Albrecht, the banker, had an office in the building, and he helped in securing the apartment for Fryderyk, who moved there on September 9. From his windows, he could see not only the busy square, but also, in its center, the tall column of the Grand Army, modeled after Trajan's column and surmounted by a statue of Emperor Napoleon Bonaparte.

Although Chopin almost certainly knew that death was near, he approached the new apartment with his usual interior decorator's enthusiasm, arranging for new furniture, carpets, and curtains to be ordered. It must have given him the illusion that—of course—he would recover. And there was no more talk of money: the rent at Place Vendôme had to be extremely high (Fryderyk wrote Franchomme that it was "very dear") and the new furnishings expensive, and Chopin may have used Jane's twelve thousand (or fifteen thousand or twenty-five thousand) francs for it. Or the sisters simply and quietly paid for the rental. But Fryderyk never left the apartment: He could hardly move from room to room.

George Sand, meanwhile, learned of Ludwika's presence in Paris— from Charlotte Marliani, Marie de Rozières, or Solange—and wrote her from Nohant on September 1 that "now, through you, I shall finally have real news about Fryderyk." She said that "some people write me that he is much sicker than usual; others that he is only weak and suffering, as I have always seen him. . . . Please write me a word. . . . Memory of me has evidently been dirtied in your heart, but I think I deserve [a word] after all that I had suffered."

Dirtied or not, Sand's image must have been affected in Ludwika's mind by Fryderyk's version of the breakup—she surely heard about it from him in Paris, in addition to his letters home—and chose not to answer despite their earlier friendship. On the same day Sand had written Ludwika, she wrote Madame Grille de Beuzelin, a friend of Marie de Rozières, with whom she had been corresponding about Chopin, that "the more I become conscious of everything that had made me suffer, the less I can convince myself that he wishes any proof of my thinking about him. Ludwika will be the best judge, and she will, or not, tell him about my letter." Even with Chopin nearing death, resentments between the former lovers seemed to be mounting, more than two years after their rupture.

Tytus Woyciechowski, the oldest and most beloved of his friends, was the person whom Chopin now wished to see the most. They had not seen each other in close to twenty years—and there is no record of any correspondence between them in all these years—but their friendship was very much alive. Having evidently received word from Tytus that he expected to be in Ostend, in Belgium (this communication, too, is missing), Fryderyk wrote him on August 20:

> My dearest: Weak as I am, I am unable to move from Paris, just as you are arriving in Ostend. But I hope that God will allow you to come near me. Physicians do not allow me any travel. I am drinking waters from the Pyrenees in my room although your presence would be much more valuable than all the medicines. Yours until death. Fryderyk.

Woyciechowski had apparently agreed to come to Paris because Chopin wrote him on September 12: "I had too little time to try to obtain the permission for your visit here; I cannot go after it myself, lying in bed half the day." But, he went on,

> I have asked an influential friend to do it on my behalf. Only on Saturday will I know something for sure. I was ready to travel by train to Valenciennes, on the border, to embrace you, but I could not manage a few days ago to go to Ville d'Avraye, near Versailles, to see my goddaughter, and doctors do not allow me to leave Paris. This is why they will not let me go to a warmer climate for the winter. It is my fault that I am ill, otherwise I would somehow have found you in Belgium. Perhaps you will be able to get here. I am not enough of an egoist to demand you just for myself; being as weak as I am, you would have a few hours of boredom and disappointment, mixed with a few hours of joy and good recollections; I would prefer that the time we may spend together would be only a time of complete happiness. Yours forever. Fryderyk.

They did not see each other.

Now Chopin knew that time was running out. He again ordered the burning of his unfinished manuscripts. On October 7, while being examined in bed by a doctor, he suddenly blurted out, almost audibly, *"Maintenant, j'entre en agonie!"* ("Now, I am entering my agony").

When the doctor tried to console him, Chopin whispered, "God shows man a rare favor when He reveals to him the moment of the approach of death; this grace He shows me. Do not disturb me."

Ludwika was by Fryderyk's side day and night—her husband and daughter had to return to Warsaw—as was Adolf Gutmann. Moscheles, who paid a visit late in September, wrote in his diary: "We heard of Chopin's critical condition, made inquiries ourselves, and found all the sad news confirmed. . . . Now the days of the poor fellow are numbered, his suffering great. Sad lot!" Bohdan Zaleski, his poet friend, concluded after seeing Fryderyk: "Now he is a candidate for the next world. He is doing badly. His legs and belly are beginning to swell. He is very neglectful of religion, but perhaps God will make him realize it. He is asking for prayers and humbly listening to litany."

On October 12, Chopin had such difficulty breathing that Dr. Cruveilhier acknowledged that death could come within hours. Delfina Potocka, who had been in Nice, arrived in Paris on October 15, after being advised of the gravity of the situation. She rushed to his bedside and Gavard recounts that "Chopin exclaimed, 'God has delayed so long in calling me to Him; He wished to vouchsafe me yet the pleasure of seeing you!'" Then, Charles Gavard, the bookseller friend, writes, Fryderyk asked her to sing once more for him: "The piano was moved from the adjoining room, and the unhappy countess, mastering her sorrow and suppressing her sobs, had to force herself to sing beside the bed where her friend was exhaling his life. . . . I remember the moment when the death rattle of the departing one interrupted the Countess in the middle of the second piece." But Chopin went on struggling for nearly two more days.

There are many differing accounts of the days immediately preceding Chopin's death and of the death itself. Liszt and Karasowski, for example, wrote that Delfina sang the "Hymn to the Virgin" by Stradella and a Psalm by Benedetto Marcello; Gutmann insisted that it was a Psalm by Marcello and an air by Pergolesi; Franchomme said it was an aria from Bellini's *Beatrice di Tenda*—and nothing else. Considering that all of them were musicians (except Karasowski), it is strange that they could not agree on what they heard, or heard about. All of them were *not* present during that dramatic scene, but would not admit it. Being present at Chopin's death seemed to grant one historical and social cachet. Zieliński accepts that Delfina, accompanying herself on the piano, sang "a number of works by Italian composers, including Bellini, Stradelli and Marcella [*sic*]," and that Franchomme and Marcelina Czartoryska began to play Chopin's Sonata for cello and piano, but "had to interrupt it because the patient suffered a coughing fit and felt tired."

Sometime during that week, Chopin penned his last message with a trembling hand on a page from a notepad: "If this cough suffocates me, I beseech you to have my body opened that I not be buried alive." This was a fear Fryderyk held throughout most of his life—consciously, in hallucinations, and in dreams. His wish was granted: His heart was removed from his body and taken to Warsaw by Ludwika in an alcohol-filled glass vessel (possibly under her skirt, not to be intercepted by Russian border guards) to be placed in the Holy Cross Church near the Chopin home. The body was interred at Père Lachaise Cemetery in Paris.

On October 16, a Tuesday, Fryderyk was conscious most of the day. He issued more instructions: that all unfinished manuscripts be burned (for the third time), that his notes for the Method be given to Charles-Valentin Alkan, a musician and former square d'Orléans neighbor, and that Mozart's *Requiem* be performed at his funeral.

There are several recorded versions of Chopin's moment of death— again a great many friends claimed they were present—but it appears that those actually around his bed were Ludwika, Marcelina Czartoryska, Solange, Gutmann, Albrecht, and Father Jełowicki. Fryderyk passed away a few minutes before two o'clock in the morning of Wednesday, October 17, 1849. He was thirty-nine years and eight months old. Ludwika wrote her husband within the hour: "Oh, my dearest—*he* is no longer with us."

Chopin's attitude toward God, the Roman Catholic Church, and religion in general has been discussed since the night he died—and most particularly whether and how he had made peace with his Maker in the closing instants of his life. That he was not very observant nor religiously inclined was common knowledge among those who knew him well, but unquestionably he was a believer, often invoking God's name. With one minor exception, Fryderyk chose not to compose works that would come under the rubric of "religious music" in the accepted sense. Perhaps, being such a private person, his communion with God through his music was very private, too. It may well live on in the sonatas, the préludes, or the études. The only credible account of

Chopin before God in the final hours comes from Father Jełowicki, a close friend as well as a priest, who gave him the last rites:

Word of Chopin's approaching death reached me upon my return to Paris from Rome. At once I rushed to my childhood friend whose soul was so dear to me. We embraced, and our tears indicated to us that he was on his last legs. He was visibly deteriorating and extinguishing. . . . I reminded him about his mother [in order] to revive with her memory the faith she had taught him. "Oh," he said to me, "I understand you: I would not want to die without the Sacraments not to sadden my beloved mother, but I cannot accept them because I do not understand them anymore in your way. I would even understand the sweetness of confession flowing from confessing to a friend, but I cannot perceive confession as Sacrament. If you wish, I shall confess to you, for our friendship, but no other way." Chopin's words constricted my heart and I wept. I was sad for this good soul. I caressed [his soul] the best I could, with Our Lady, with Jesus, with the most touching images of divine mercy. Nothing worked. I offered to bring him whomever he wished as confessor. And, in the end, he told me, "If I ever wish to confess, it will be to you." This was what I feared the most, after everything he had told me.

Long months elapsed with frequent visits on my part, but with no results. But I prayed with faith that this soul would not be lost. . . . Then, at midnight, I was called by Doctor Cruveilhier, who said that he could not guarantee anything. Trembling with emotion, I stood at Chopin's doors, which, for the first time, were shut before me. But after a moment he ordered me let in, but only to shake my hand and say, "I love you very much, but do not say anything—go to sleep." The next day, I returned to Chopin's, finding him at breakfast, which he invited me [to share]. I said, "My dear friend, today is the saint's day of my [late] brother Edward. . . . On this day, give me your commitment." Chopin replied, "I shall give you whatever you wish," and I said, "Give me your soul!" He answered, "I understand you, take it," and he sat up in bed.

I dropped to my knees and I handed Chopin the crucified Jesus, placing it in both his hands. And tears burst out of his eyes. "Do you believe?" I asked. He answered: "I believe," and in a stream of tears he made his holy confession. And he accepted the Viaticum and Extreme Unction, for which he had asked himself. After a while, he ordered that the sacristan [at the church] be given twenty times as much as is generally given, and I said,

"This is too much." He replied, "Not too much because what I have accepted is beyond any price." And from that moment onward, changed by the grace of God, indeed by God, he became a different person, I would say, already a saint.

That day Chopin's agony began, lasting four days and nights. Patience, abandonment to God, and, often, joy accompanied him to his last breath. Amidst the greatest suffering, he expressed his happiness and thanked God, shouting his love for Him and his desire to be joined with Him most quickly. And he spoke of his happiness to his friends, who had come to say farewell and waited in adjoining rooms. He was running out of breath, it looked as if he were dying, even his wailing stopped, his consciousness slipped away. All became frightened and rushed into his bedroom to await, their hearts beating fast, that last moment. Then Chopin opened his eyes and, seeing all these people, asked, "What are they doing here? Why aren't they praying?" And they all went down to their knees with me as I recited the Litany to All the Saints. . . . Day and night, he almost constantly held both my hands, not wanting to let me go, and saying, "You will not abandon me in this deciding moment." And he moved close to me, as children in peril move close to their mother, and cried, "Jesus, Mary!" and kissed the cross in wonderment of faith and hope. Sometimes he spoke to those present, with the greatest tenderness, saying, "I love God and I love people! . . . It is good that I am dying. . . . My beloved sister, do not weep! Do not weep, my friends. I am happy! I feel that I am dying! . . . Pray with me!"

Father Jełowicki wrote that Chopin then turned to the physicians, who tried to keep him alive, saying, "Let me go, let me die. God has forgiven me. . . . I want to die. . . . Oh, this beautiful faculty of extending suffering. If it were in a good cause. . . . But to make me suffer and those who love me, what a beautiful faculty! . . . You are making me suffer terribly in vain. Perhaps you are wrong! But God is not wrong! He cleanses me. . . . How good God is to punish me in this world."

And, in the end, Father Jełowicki concluded, Chopin, "always elegant in his speech, wished to express his gratitude to me, did not hesitate to say, 'Without you, my friend, I would have died—like a swine.'"

Others remembered other moments. Adolf Gutmann wrote that "my loyal, dear friend died in my arms." He cut off a strand of Chopin's hair and wrapped it in paper, writing on it, "Relic." Grzymała recalled that Fryderyk's agony lasted three days and three nights after receiving the Sacraments and that "the physicians were astounded by his incredible vitality." "Smiling until the last moment," Grzymała said, Chopin "kissed Gutmann and tried to embrace Solange. . . . A few hours before his death, he asked Madame Potocka for three Bellini and Rossini melodies, which she sang weeping." Not having been present, however, Grzymała may have confused the night when Delfina enchanted Chopin for the last time with her voice.

Delacroix wrote in his *Journal* that "I learned of the death of poor Chopin. . . . What a loss! What miserable rogues fill the market place while that beautiful soul burns out!"

Pauline Viardot wrote George Sand in Nohant that "all the great ladies of Paris regarded it as their duty to faint in [Chopin's] bedroom. . . . He may have had eccentricities caused by his illness, but he was a noble human being. I am happy I knew him and that I was able to earn some of his friendship." She and Luigi Lablache were soloists in Mozart's *Requiem* at the great funeral service at the Madeleine attended by three thousand people, inside and outside, on October 30. As the casket was being carried out of the crypt, the orchestra played Chopin's own *Marche funèbre* from the Sonata in B-flat minor. The organist played two Chopin préludes.

Grzymała, who had followed Chopin's romance with George Sand from the first to the last day, had the final word on the subject: "If he had not had the misfortune of meeting G.S., who poisoned his whole being, he would have lived to be Cherubini's age." Cherubini died at eighty-two.

Frederick Niecks reports that two days before his death, Chopin told Franchomme that Sand "had said to me that I would die in no arms but hers." Gutmann recalls that Sand, or Solange on behalf of her mother, had come to place Vendôme to ask whether George might see Fryderyk, but that he had advised against it in order not to "overexcite" the patient. Perhaps Gutmann had been terribly wrong; perhaps he was acting on instructions from the savagely jealous Jane Stirling.

Chopin's charmed and unhappy life was always concealed from full sight by a mantle of privacy and mystery that was compounded by hesitation and uncertainty. He was all things to all people, first and foremost as a genius in the world of music, then as friend, lover, and even as enemy. Yet, he never seemed to be enough to himself, to give and receive love, to understand himself and others who mattered to him. An ardent Polish patriot, he died after nineteen years of self-exile, strangely unwilling to see his native land again.

Fryderyk Chopin had given so much joy and fulfillment to others through the inspiration and magnificence of his music—and taken so little for himself, always the self-deprecating figure. His terrible illness was not his only foe. Chopin died a great, sad man. And he died so very much alone.

Postlude

No sooner did Chopin die than the question arose: To whom did he belong—that is, his memory, the musical heritage?

With George Sand absent from his life for two years or so, Jane Stirling emerged as Chopin's "official widow," having managed the place Vendôme household through his final illness. Stirling's biographer Audrey Evelyn Bone reports that Jane supervised everything from the delivery of "nourishing food" to deliveries of Fryderyk's favorite Palma violets to his rooms two or three times a week. Most likely, she was paying the full rent for the apartment, or part of it (if Chopin had anything left from the twenty-five thousand francs), and many of the living expenses. Bone suggests strongly that it was on Stirling's orders that Sand was turned away from Chopin's apartment just before his death.

Jane and Ludwika were the only ones to walk immediately behind Chopin's coffin on the three-mile march from the Madeleine to the interment at Père Lachaise, followed by hundreds of the composer's friends and admirers. Delacroix, Franchomme, Pleyel, and Prince Aleksander Czartoryski were the pallbearers, and the cortège was led by the aging Prince Adam Czartoryski and Giacomo Meyerbeer. Jane and her sister were said to have provided five thousand francs to cover the expenses of the funeral. They also loaned Ludwika money to help her with the expenses of the return voyage to Warsaw—with Fryderyk's heart.

Bone writes that Jane Stirling "stayed by her broken Chopin when his charms and humor were gone and his nerves were shattered" and "by her generosity she saved Chopin from a pauper's death" (Grzymała wrote Léo that Fryderyk's financial condition at death was "zero"). Under the circumstances, Bone comments, "After Chopin's death it was Jane who considered that she alone had the right to distribute Chopin's personal effects." It is far from certain, however, that, as Bone believes, Jane "must have restored a little of Chopin's affection for her, even in his final pitiable state." As it happens, Jane was not at Fryderyk's bedside when he expired.

But she devoted the next ten years of her life, until her death in 1859, to Chopin's affairs, presumably because she believed that it was her right and obligation. When Grzymała showed Jane the first chapters of a Chopin biography he had started to write, she discouraged him from pursuing it. In Bone's words, "She soon realized that Grzymała was incapable of finishing what he had begun—he had known Chopin too well to write his life." Liszt, also working on a book on Chopin, which *was* published, wrote Jane to inquire about Fryderyk's relationship with George Sand; the reply was that Chopin's life was "pure" and he had died "like a saint."

Julian Fontana, who was a pianist and had copied many of Chopin's manuscripts, was requested by Ludwika Jędrzejewicz and Jane Stirling, upon his return from New York to Europe in 1852, to take over the task of sorting out and assembling the works Fryderyk had left behind. (Chopin trusted Fontana with his manuscripts—he described them as "spiderwebs" and "fly specks"—urging his friend in a 1841 letter, "in the name of Heaven, I beg you to respect my manuscript, don't wrinkle it, don't spot it, don't tear . . . because I have such a great feeling for my written *ennuis*."). He was given free hand in selecting the works and finding publishers, becoming, in effect, the musical-literary executor of the estate. Ludwika acted on behalf of the family and Jane was evidently accepted by them as the "official widow." Stirling's "widowhood" status was challenged by quite a few of Fryderyk's real and alleged friends, but she never budged. Without any reference to Jane, Grzymała wrote Léo three weeks after Chopin's death: "I am glad that you are honoring the composer's orders to destroy everything that was unfinished in his folders. This order does not please many of his so-called friends and publishers, but it is relevant to his good reputation."

In time, Fontana chose twenty-three piano works from different periods in Chopin's life, ranging from the first Funeral March, written in 1826, when Fryderyk was a precociously death-haunted sixteen-year-old, to the 1829 *Souvenir de Paganini*, the 1834 Fantaisie-Impromptu, the 1839 "Notre Temps" mazurka, and the final 1849 Mazurka in F minor. He assembled them in eight books, numbering them as Opus 66 to 73, and arranging for them to be published together by A. M. Schlesinger in Berlin in 1855, under the title of *Oeuvres posthumes pour le piano de Fréd. Chopin publiés sur manuscripts originaux avec autorisation de sa famille par Jules Fontana.* Fontana was subsequently severely criticized by musicologists for slapping together in one opus works from more than one genre—mazurkas, waltzes, polonaises, and nocturnes—from various stages of Chopin's life, without regard for the real sequence of their composition and thus making it impossible to trace coherently their place in the composer's creativity. In 1859, he arranged for the publication of seventeen Polish song settings by Chopin, presented together as Opus 74 and suffering the same defect, and two additional songs written in 1829–1830 (a mazurka and *czary* ["charms"]).

Twenty-eight additional Chopin works without opus numbers were published through efforts of others between 1850 and 1973. They were catalogued by Warsaw musicologist Krystyna Kobylańska and are now listed as "Kobylańska, Katalog." But the exact number of Chopin's works remains unknown. There may be new discoveries similar to Byron Janis's find of the waltz manuscript in 1973. Fryderyk, according to Niecks, had ordered that unpublished manuscripts be distributed among friends, with only unfinished fragments to be burned. There is no way of knowing what he had left behind—and what happened to whatever was. Mieczysław Tomaszewski estimates in the 1984 *Music Encyclopedia,* published in Kraków, that there are "five hundred sixty-four (Chopin) manuscripts known to us today." But this does not necessarily mean actual original works and probably includes several versions of the same composition. Chopin's musical life may not have yet run its course.

Adolf Gutmann, who was Chopin's favorite pupil, may or may not have inherited a work of music—he has never mentioned it—but the composer did leave him his notes on the proposed piano Method on which he had been working on and off for years (they are similar to notes left to Alkan). Gutmann also kept and preserved the glass from which Chopin had his last drink of water, lifted to his lips by Gutmann, moments before he died.

Among the multitude of true and self-proclaimed friends, piano pupils, fawning acquaintances, and favor-seekers who surrounded Chopin during his Paris years, Gutmann stands out with a surprisingly small group of genuinely devoted men and women who had weathered all the tough tests of Fryderyk's friendship. Among the Poles, Grzymała, Fontana (who was away when Fryderyk died), Zaleski, the Czartoryskis, Father Jełowicki, and the faraway Tytus Woyciechowski certainly qualified. So many of the old Polish friends were already dead. The true French friends were, first and foremost, Franchomme and Delacroix, then Pleyel, Léo, and Albrecht. Teofil Antoni Kwiatkowski, the painter, spent many days and nights at the place Vendôme apartment, sketching and painting the grieving friends for posterity. He was summoned the day after Chopin's death, and his gift to history is a beautiful watercolor of Fryderyk's head resting serenely on a pillow. Clésinger, hardly a friend, was called, presumably on Solange's account, to cast Chopin's death mask; he also made casts of his long hands.

Women had played a vital and fundamental role in Chopin's life. He loved, adored, venerated, worshiped, and liked them on every conceivable level—the whole gamut of sentiment, emotion, and friendship— though each in a different way. Thinking of Chopin, it is exceedingly difficult to understand, let alone define, what love meant to him—and, perhaps, it was impossible for him as well. But he attracted the most extraordinary women of his time.

Apart from his mother and sisters, his emotions toward women spanned the years of the superficial and immature infatuations with Konstancja Gładkowska and Maria Wodzińska, both highly intelligent and talented, and the adult Platonic veneration and deep friendship later for Delfina Potocka and Marcelina Czartoryska, the princess pianist, who was possibly more attuned to his art than any other contemporary musician. Pauline Viardot seems to have fallen just short of that standard.

What is to be made of George Sand? Whatever the truth underlying their relationship and however blame may be apportioned—and, historically, there is no further need to plumb it—she unquestionably was the greatest single influence on Chopin's life, one quarter of which he had spent living with her. She loved him—the man who needed to be loved—looked after him, provided him with peace crucial to concentration and composition, and surely inspired him. After all, George Sand was herself a creature of genius. So, it is irrelevant when and why and who was at fault. The préludes of Majorca, the nocturnes and polonaises of Nohant, and the mazurkas of square d'Orléans were born under her wing—and are as alive today as at the moment of conception.

Solange, about whom so much has been said and written by George and Fryderyk, never truly mattered.

Jane Stirling, the last woman in Chopin's life, belonged in her own fashion to Chopin's private world of sadness. Like Sand before her, she made it possible for him to survive longer and better against all odds.

Fryderyk Chopin gave the world a treasure in music. The world gave Chopin a treasure in human beings.

Appendix
List of the Published Works
of Fryderyk Chopin

I. WORKS PUBLISHED WITH OPUS NUMBERS
DURING THE COMPOSER'S LIFETIME

Date of Publication		*Title*
Lost		Military March (1817)
1825	Op. 1	*Premier Rondeau* in C minor
1830, about March	Op. 2	Variations in B-flat major on "Là ci darem la mano" from Mozart's *Don Giovanni*
1833	Op. 3	*Introduction and Polonaise brillante* in C major
1851	Op. 4	*Sonata* in C minor
1827?	Op. 5	*Rondeau à la Mazur* in F major
December 1832	Op. 6	*Four Mazurkas* [F-sharp minor, C-sharp minor, E major, and E-flat minor]
December 1832	Op. 7	*Five Mazurkas* [B-flat major, A minor, F minor, A-flat major, and C major]
March 1833	Op. 8	*First Trio in G minor for piano, violin, and cello*
January 1833	Op. 9	*Three Nocturnes* [B-flat minor, E-flat major, and B major]
August 1833	Op. 10	*Twelve Grandes Études* [C major, A minor, E major, C-sharp minor, G-flat major, E-flat minor, C major, F major, F minor, A-flat major, E-flat major, and C minor]
September 1833	Op. 11	*First Concerto in E minor for piano with orchestra*
November 1833	Op. 12	*Variations brillantes* in B-flat major
May 1834	Op. 13	*Grande Fantaisie in A major on Polish airs for piano with orchestra*

July 1834	Op. 14	*Krakowiak, Grand Concert Rondeau in F major for piano with orchestra*
January 1834	Op. 15	*Three Nocturnes* [F major, F-sharp major, and G minor]
March 1834	Op. 16	*Rondeau in E-flat major*
May 1834	Op. 17	*Four Mazurkas* [B-flat major, E minor, A-flat major, and A minor]
July 1834	Op. 18	*Valse brillante in E-flat major*
1834	Op. 19	*Boléro in C major*
March 1835	Op. 20	*First Scherzo in B minor*
April 1836	Op. 21	*Second Concerto in F minor for piano with orchestra*
August 1836	Op. 22	*Grande Polonaise brillante in E-flat major, preceded by Andante spianato for piano with orchestra*
June 1836	Op. 23	*Ballade in G minor*
November 1835	Op. 24	*Four Mazurkas* [G minor, C major, A-flat major, and B-flat minor]
October 1837	Op. 25	*Twelve Grandes Études* [A-flat major, F minor, F major, A minor, E minor, G-sharp minor, C-sharp minor, D-flat major, G-flat major, B minor, A minor, and C minor]
July 1836	Op. 26	*Two Polonaises* [C-sharp minor and E-flat minor]
May 1836	Op. 27	*Two Nocturnes* [C-sharp minor and D-flat major]
September 1839	Op. 28	*Twenty-four Préludes* [C major, A minor, G major, E minor, D major, B minor, A major, F-sharp minor, E major, C-sharp minor, B major, F-sharp major, E-flat major, D-flat major, B-flat minor, A-flat major, F minor, E-flat major, C minor, B-flat major, G minor, F major, and D minor]
January 1838	Op. 29	*Impromptu in A-flat major*
January 1838	Op. 30	*Four Mazurkas* [C minor, B minor, D-flat major, and C-sharp minor]
February 1838	Op. 31	*Second Scherzo in B-flat minor*
December 1837	Op. 32	*Two Nocturnes* [B major and A-flat major]
November 1838	Op. 33	*Four Mazurkas* [G-sharp minor, D major, C major, and B minor]
December 1838	Op. 34	*Three Waltzes brillantes* [A-flat major, A minor, and F major]
May 1840	Op. 35	*Sonata in B-flat minor*
May 1840	Op. 36	*Second Impromptu in F-sharp minor*
May 1840	Op. 37	*Two Nocturnes* [G minor and G major]
September 1840	Op. 38	*Second Ballade in F major*
October 1840	Op. 39	*Third Scherzo in C-sharp minor*
November 1840	Op. 40	*Two Polonaises* [A-flat major and C minor]
December 1840	Op. 41	*Four Mazurkas* [C-sharp minor, E minor, B major, and A-flat major]
July 1840	Op. 42	*Waltz in A-flat major*
[1841]	Op. 43	*Tarantella in A-flat major*
November 28, 1841	Op. 44	*Polonaise in F-sharp minor*
November 28, 1841	Op. 45	*Prélude in C-sharp minor*

January 1842	Op. 46	*Allegro de concert in A major*
January 1842	Op. 47	*Third Ballade in A-flat major*
January 1842	Op. 48	*Two Nocturnes* [C minor and F-sharp minor]
January 1842	Op. 49	*Fantaisie in F minor*
September 1842	Op. 50	*Three Mazurkas* [G major, A-flat major, and C-sharp minor]
February 1843	Op. 51	*Allegro vivace. Third Impromptu in G-flat major*
February 1843	Op. 52	*Fourth Ballade in F minor*
December 1843	Op. 53	*Polonaise in A-flat major*
December 1843	Op. 54	*Fourth Scherzo in E major*
August 1844	Op. 55	*Two Nocturnes* [F minor and E-flat major]
August 1844	Op. 56	*Three Mazurkas* [B major, C major, and C minor]
May 1845	Op. 57	*Berceuse in D-flat major*
June 1845	Op. 58	*Sonata in B minor*
[January 1846]	Op. 59	*Three Mazurkas* [A minor, A-flat major, and F-sharp minor]
December 1846	Op. 60	*Barcarolle in F-sharp major*
December 1846	Op. 61	*Polonaise-Fantaisie in A-flat major*
December 1846	Op. 62	*Two Nocturnes* [B major and E major]
September 1847	Op. 63	*Three Mazurkas* [B major, F minor, and C-sharp minor]
September 1847	Op. 64	*Three Waltzes* [D-flat major, C-sharp minor, and A-flat major]
October 1847	Op. 65	*Sonata in G minor for cello and piano*

II. WORKS PUBLISHED WITHOUT OPUS NUMBERS DURING THE COMPOSER'S LIFETIME

Date of Publication	*Title*
1833	*Grand Duo concertant in E major for cello and piano on themes from* Robert le diable
August or September 1840	*Three New Études* [F minor, A-flat major, and D-flat major]
July 25, 1841	*Variation VI* [Largo, E major] from the *Hexaméron*
February 1842	*Mazurka in A minor*

III. WORKS PUBLISHED WITH OPUS NUMBERS AFTER THE COMPOSER'S DEATH

Date of Publication		*Title*
[1835]	Op. 66	*Fantaisie-Impromptu in C-sharp minor*
	Op. 67	*Four Mazurkas* [G major (1835), G minor (1849), C major (1835), and A minor (1846)]
	Op. 68	*Four Mazurkas* [C major (1830), A minor (1827), F major (1830), and F minor (1849)]

Op. 69   *Two Waltzes* [A-flat major (1836) and B minor (1829)]
Op. 70   *Three Waltzes* [G-flat major (1835), F minor (1843), and
            D-flat major (1830)]
Op. 71   *Three Polonaises* [D minor (1827), B-flat major (1828),
            and F minor (1829)]
Op. 72   *Nocturne in E minor* (1827); *Marche funèbre in C
            minor* (1829); and *Three Écossaises* [D major, G major,
            and D-flat major (1830)]
Op. 73   *Rondeau in C major for two pianos* (1828)
Op. 74   *Seventeen Polish Songs* by Witwicki, Mickiewicz, Zaleski,
            &c., for voice with piano accompaniment

IV. WORKS PUBLISHED WITHOUT OPUS NUMBERS
AFTER THE COMPOSER'S DEATH

Date of Publication	*Title*
May 1851	*Variations in E major on a German Air* (1826)
	Mazurka in G major (1825)
	Mazurka in B-flat major (1825)
	Mazurka in D major (1829–30)
	Mazurka in D major (1832—a remodeling of the preceding mazurka)
	Mazurka in C major (1833)
	Mazurka in A minor
	Waltz in E minor
1864	*Polonaise in G-sharp minor*
1870	*Polonaise in B-flat major* (1826)
	Polonaise in G minor (1817)
1872	*Polonaise in B-flat minor* (1826)
	Waltz in E major (1829)
	Souvenir de Paganini in A major (1829)
1879	*Mazurka in G-flat major for voice*
1898	*Fugue* (1841–42)
1902	*Waltz in A-flat major* (1827)
1910	*Czary for voice and piano*
1918	*Prélude in A-flat major* (1834)
1931	*Contredanse in G-flat major* (1827)
1938	*Largo* (1837)
1938	*Nocturne in C-sharp minor* (1837)
1947	*Polonaise in B-flat major* (1817)
1947	*Polonaise in A-flat major* (1821)
1950	*Variations on* Non più mesta *from Rossini's* La Cenerentola *for flute and piano* (1824)
1955	*Waltz* ("Sostenuto") *in E-flat major*
1968	*Two Bourrées* [G minor and A major (1846); attrib.]

Bibliography

BIOGRAPHIES, MEMOIRS, LIFE, ESSAYS, LETTERS

Atwood, William G. *Fryderyk Chopin—Pianist from Warsaw.* New York: Columbia University Press, 1987.

Audley, Madame A. *Frédéric Chopin—Sa vie et ses oeuvres.* Paris: É. Plon et Cie., 1880.

Babedette, H. F. *Chopin. Essai de Critique Musicale.* Paris: Heugel et Cie., 1869.

Barraud, Henry. *Hector Berlioz.* Paris: Fayard, 1979.

Belotti, Gastone, and Wiarosław Sandelewski. *Chopin in Italia.* Warsaw: Wydawnictwo Polskiej Akademii Nauk, 1977.

Bergman-Carton, Janis. *The Woman of Ideas in French Art, 1830–1848.* New Haven: Yale University Press, 1995.

Bone, Audrey Evelyn. *Jane Wilhelmina Stirling, 1804–1859.* London: Chipstead, 1960.

Bourniquel, Camille. *Chopin.* Paris: Seuil, 1957.

Carlyle, Thomas. *The French Revolution.* New York: Modern Library, n.d.

Castelot, André. *Le Grand Siècle de Paris.* Paris: Amiot, Dumont, 1955.

Cate, Curtis. *George Sand, A Biography.* Boston: Houghton Mifflin Company, 1975.

Chainaye, Suzanne, and Denise Chainaye. *De quoi vivait Chopin?* Paris: Deux Rives, 1951.

Chamfray, Claude. *Musset-Chopin (Confrontation).* Marseilles: Éditions du Sud, 1934.

Cortot, Alfred. *Aspects de Chopin.* Paris: Éditions Albin Michel, 1960.

Czartkowski, Adam and Zofia Jeżewska. *Chopin Żywy.* Warsaw: Państwowy Instytut Wydawniczy, 1959.

Czekaj, Kazimierz. *Przewodnik Chopinowski.* Warsaw: Towarzystwo Im. Fryderyka Chopina, 1958.

Delacroix, Eugène. *Journal.* New York: Crown Publishers, 1948.

Delaigue-Moins, Sylvie. *Chopin chez George Sand à Nohant—Chronique de sept étés.* Châteauroux: Les Amis de Nohant, 1986.

Drozdowski, Marian M., and Andrzej Zahorski. *Historia Warszawy.* Warsaw: Państwowe Wydawnictwo Naukowe, 1972.

Dziębowska, Elzbieta (ed.). *Encyklopedia Muzyczna PWM.* Kraków: Polskie Wydawnictwo Muzyczne, 1984.

Dziewanowski, M. K. *Poland in the Twentieth Century.* New York: Columbia University Press, 1977.

Ehrlich, Cyril. *The Piano—A History.* New York: Clarendon Press, Oxford University Press, 1990.

Eigeldinger, Jean-Jacques. *Chopin vu par ses élèves* (3rd ed.). Boudry-Neuchâtel, Switzerland: Les Éditions de la Baconnière, 1988.

———. *Chopin, Pianist and Teacher, as Seen by His Pupils.* New York: Cambridge University Press, 1988.

———(ed.). *Frédéric Chopin—Esquisses pour une méthode de piano.* Paris: Flammarion, 1993.

Énault, Louis. *Frédéric Chopin.* Paris: Librairie Nouvelle, 1861.

Gadon, Lubomir. *Wielka Emigracja.* Paris: Księgarnia Polska w Paryżu, 1845.

Ganche, Édouard. *Souffrances de Frédéric Chopin.* Paris: Mercure de France, 1935.

Gide, André. *Notes sur Chopin.* Paris: L'Arche, Paris, 1949.

Gliński, Mateusz. *Szopen.* Warsaw: Miesięcznik "Muzyka," 1932.

Goncourt, Edmond and Jules de. *Journal: Mémoires de la vie littéraire, 1851–1896* (Vols. I, II, III). Paris: Robert Lafont, 1989.

Halecki, Oscar. *Borderlands of Western Civilization.* New York: Roland Press Company, 1952.

Hedley, Arthur. *Chopin.* London, 1947.

Herbst, Stanisław (d.). *Encyklopedia Warszawy.* Warsaw: Państwowe Wydawnictwo Naukowe, 1975.

Hoesick, Ferdynand. *Chopin—Życie i Twórczość* (Vols. I–IV). Warsaw: Polskie Wydawnictwo Muzyczne, 1967.

Hoffman, Klementyna Tańska. *Pamiętniki.* Berlin: B. Behr, 1849.

Hofstadter, Dan. *The Love Affair as a Work of Art.* New York: Farrar, Straus and Giroux, 1996.

Iwaszkiewicz, Jarosław. *Chopin.* Warsaw: Polskie Wydawnictwo Muzyczne, 1984.

Jamison, Kay Redfield. *Touched with Fire: Manic-Depressive Illness and the Artistic Temperament.* New York: The Free Press, 1994.

Jełowicki, Alexander. *Rocznik Emigracji Polskiej.* Paris: Ksiegarnia A. Jełowickiego i Spółki, 1836.

Johnson, James H. *Listening in Paris—A Cultural History.* Berkeley: University of California Press, 1995.

Jordan, David P. *Transforming Paris—The Life and Labors of Baron Haussmann.* New York: The Free Press, 1995.

Karasowski, Maurycy. *Fryderyk Chopin—Życie, Listy, Dzieła.* Warsaw: Gebethner i Wolff, 1882.

Kobylańska, Krystyna (ed.). *Korespondencja Fryderyka Chopina z George Sand i Jej Dziećmi.* Warsaw: Państwowy Instytut Wydawniczy, 1981.

———(ed.). *Korespondencja Fryderyka Chopina z Rodziną.* Warsaw: Państwowy Instytut Wydawniczy, 1972.

Król, Marcin. *Konserwatyści a Niepodległość.* Warsaw: Instytut Wydawniczy Pax, 1985.

Kurkiewicz, Władysław, et al. *Tysiąc Lat Dziejów Polski.* Ludowa Spółdzielnia, 1961.

Lenz, Wilhelm von. *Les Grands Virtuoses—Liszt, Chopin, Tausig, Henselt.* Paris: Flammarion, 1995.

Leonard, Richard Anthony. *The Stream of Music.* Garden City: Doubleday, 1952.

Liszt, Franciszek. *Chopin.* Lwów: H. Altenberg, 1924.

Majchrowski, Stefan. *Niezwykłe Postacie z Czasów Powstania Listopadowego.* Warsaw: Ludowa Spółdzielnia Wydawnicza, 1985.

Marek, George R., and Maria Gordon-Smith. *Chopin*. New York: Harper & Row, 1978.

Maurois, André. *Lélia ou la Vie de George Sand*. Paris: Hachette, 1952.

Mayzner, Tadeusz. *Chopin*. Warsaw: Polskie Wydawnictwo Muzyczne, 1959.

Michałowski, Kornel. *A Chopin Bibliography, 1849–1969*. Warsaw: Polskie Wydawnictwo Muzyczne, 1970.

Murgia, Adelaide. *Portraits of Greatness: Chopin*. New York: Elite Publishing Company, 1984.

Nicolson, Harold. *The Congress of Vienna*. New York: Viking Press, 1963.

Niecks, Frederick. *Frederic Chopin as a Man and Musician* (Vols. I, II). New York: Cooper Square Publishers, Inc., 1973.

Opieński, Henryk. *Chopin*. Lwów: H. Altenberg, 1909.

Pazdro, Michel. *Frédéric Chopin*. Paris: Gallimard, 1989.

Pereswiet-Soltan, Stanisław (ed.). *Listy Fryderyka Chopina do Jana Białobłockiego*. Warsaw: Wydawnictwo Związku Narodowego Polskiej Młodzieży, 1926.

Pernoud, Régine. *Histoire de la bourgeoisie en France—Les Temps modernes*. Paris: Éditions du Seuil, 1962.

Pourtalès, Guy de. *Frederick Chopin: A Man of Solitude*. London: Thornton Butterworth Limited, 1933.

Princet, Maurice. *Frédéric Chopin*. Paris: Réveil Économique, 1932.

Przybylski, Ryszard. *Cień Jaskółki—Esej o Myślach Chopina*. Kraków: Znak, 1995.

Rosen, Charles. *The Romantic Generation*. Cambridge: Harvard University Press, 1995.

Rubinstein, Artur. *My Young Years*. New York: Alfred A. Knopf, 1973.

Ruggieri, Eve. *Chopin—Itinéraire sentimental*. Paris: Éditions Michel Lafon, 1994.

Samson, Jim (ed.). *The Cambridge Companion to Chopin*. New York: Cambridge University Press, 1992.

Sand, George. *Correspondence* (Vols. I–VI). Paris: Calmann-Lévy, 1882–1894.

———. *Histoire de ma vie*. Paris: Michel Lévy, 1854.

———. *Lucrezia Floriani* (in *Oeuvres Complètes*). Paris: Calmann-Lévy, 1856–1897.

———. *Promenades autour d'un village*. Paris: Michel Lévy, 1866.

———. *Un hiver à Majorque*. Paris: Éditions Glénat, 1993.

Scholes, Percy A. (ed.). *The Concise Oxford Dictionary of Music*. London: Oxford University Press, 1960.

Schumann, Robert. *O Fryderyku Chopinie: Studjum*. Lwów: Gubrynowicz i Schmidt, 1876.

Śliwiński, Artur. *Powstanie Listopadowe*. Warsaw: Wydawnictwo M. Arcta, 1930.

Smoter, Jerzy Maria (ed.). *Album Chopina*. Warsaw: Polskie Wydawnictwo Muzyczne, 1975.

Solomon, Maynard. *Mozart—A Life*. New York: HarperCollins, 1995.

Stehman, Jacques. *Chopin*. Brussels: Syrinx/Éditions Messidor, 1946.

Straszewska, Maria. *Życie Literackie Wielkiej Emigracji we Francji, 1831–1840*. Warsaw: Państwowy Instytut Wydawniczy, 1971.

Sulikowski, Jerzy. *Polish Music*. Liverpool: Polish Publications Committee, 1944.

Sydow, Bronisław Edward (ed.). *Korespondencja Fryderyka Chopina* (Vols. I, II). Warsaw: Państwowy Instytut Wydawniczy, 1955.

———(Ed.). *Lettres de Chopin et de George Sand (1836–1839)*. Palma de Majorca.

Szulc, Marceli Antoni. *Fryderyk Chopin i Utwory Jego Muzyczne*. Warsaw: Polskie Wydawnictwo Muzyczne, 1986.

Thibaudet, Albert. *Histoire de la littérature française (de 1789 à nos jours)* (Vols. I, II). Paris: Éditions Stock, 1936.

Tomaszewski, Mieczysław. "Chopin." In Dziębowska, Elzbieta (ed.). *Encyklopedia Muzyczna PWM*. Kraków: Polskie Wydawnictwo Muzyczne, 1984.

Tovey, Donald Francis. *The Main Stream of Music and Other Essays.* Cleveland: World Publishing Company, 1959.

Tulard, Jean. *Les Révolutions de 1789 à 1851.* Paris: Fayard, 1985.

Valmy-Baysse, Jean. *La Curieuse Aventure des boulevards extérieurs.* Paris: Albin Michel, 1950.

Vuillermoz, Émile, and Bernard Gavoty. *Chopin Amoureux.* Paris: La Palatine, 1927.

Walker, Alan (ed.). *Franz Liszt—The Man and His Music.* New York: Taplinger Publishing Company, 1970.

Wodziński, Antoni. *Les Trois romans de Frédéric Chopin.* Paris: Calmann-Lévy, 1927.

Zamoyski, Adam. *Chopin. A Biography.* London: William Collins Sons, 1979.

Zieliński, Tadeusz A. *Chopin—Życie i Droga Twórcza.* Warsaw: Polskie Wydawnictwo Muzyczne, 1993.

ESSAYS AND DISSERTATIONS

Chopin's Health

Davila, Jean-Claude. "A Study of Chopin's Illness Through Correspondence." Doctoral dissertation (only in French), School of Medicine, University of Toulouse, 1995.

Sielużycki, Czesław. *Choroby Fryderyka Chopina, ich Patogeneza i Leczenie* (Vol. XLIV, 3/4). (Illnesses of Fryderyk Chopin, Their Pathogenesis and Treatment—Available only in Polish). Warsaw: Archiwum Historii Medycyny, 1981.

Chopiniana

Paris Guide—par Les Principaux Écrivains et Artistes de la France. Paris: Librairie Internationale, 1867.

La France et La Pologne dans leurs rélations artistiques. Paris: Bibliothèque Polonaise de Paris (André Joubin, ed.), 1939.

Chopin na Obczyźnie—Dokumenty i Pamiątki. Kraków: Polskie Wydawnictwo Muzyczne, 1965.

Chopin/Janis—The Most Dramatic Musical Discovery of the Age. (Robert O'Brien, ed.). New York: Envolve Books, 1978.

Norwid, Cyprian Kamil. Fortepian Chopina (obit by leading Polish poet, Chopin's friend). Warsaw: Fryderyk Chopin Society, 1980.

Kolekcje Chopinowskie—Catalogue of Chopin Collections Exhibit. Warsaw: Fryderyk Chopin Society, 1985.

Podróż Romantyczna Fryderyka Chopina i George Sand na Majorke—Catalogue (with documents and objects) of Chopin-Sand in Mallorca Exhibit. Warsaw: Fryderyk Chopin Society, 1990.

Polish Music Literature (1515–1990). Los Angeles: Friends of Polish Music, University of Southern California, School of Music, 1991.

Teofil Kwiatkowski, 1809–1891—Catalogue of Exhibit of Paintings by Teofil Kwiatkowski (painter of Chopin). Warsaw: Fryderyk Chopin Society, 1991.

Chopin i Liszt—Catalogue of Chopin-Liszt Exhibit. Warsaw: Fryderyk Chopin Society, 1995.

PERIODICALS

Révue musicale, special Chopin issue (including articles by Ignacy Paderewski, André Gide, Alfred Cortot, and Wanda Landowska). Paris, December 1931.

Chopin Studies—Issues 1 to 5 (1985–1995). Warsaw: Fryderyk Chopin Society.

Rocznik Chopinowski—Issues 8 to 21 (1975–1995). Warsaw: Fryderyk Chopin Society.

Annales Chopin—Issues 2 to 6 (1958–1965).Warsaw: Polskie Wydawnictwo Muzyczne.

Ruch Muzyczny, Warsaw. Issues No. 4 to 24 (1960–1995). (This is the most complete compendium of new Chopin scholarship.)

Tygodnik Emigracji Polskiej. Paris, September 7, 1835; February 1836.

Dziennik Narodowy. Paris, May 8, 1841; March 26, 1842; April 23, 1842.

Journal des débats. Paris, December 12, 1836; March 27, 1842; October 27, 1849.

La Presse. Paris, October 27, 1849; November 5, 1849.

Le National. Paris, October 18, 1849.

Gazette musicale. Paris, September 9, 1838; October 31, 1839; May 2, 1841; February 2, 1842.

France musicale. Paris, March 3, 1844.

Trzeci Maj. Paris, March 31, 1842; September 4, 1842.

Kurier Warszawski. Warsaw, May 4, 1844; July 1849.

Dziennik Polski. Poznań, October 25, 1849.

Acknowledgments

To an extraordinary extent, this book was made possible by the guidance of two distinguished music scholars who grasped from the very outset my concept of presenting Fryderyk Chopin in the context of his time and life in Paris.

Dr. Hanna Wróblewska-Straus, curator of the Fryderyk Chopin Society in Warsaw and a leading authority on Chopin and Chopiniana, was generous with her time, advice, and ideas when we first discussed the project in 1990 and again in 1995, when I became seriously committed to it. Subsequently, Dr. Wróblewska-Straus made available to me precious text materials and illustrations from the society's library and publications program. My deep gratitude goes to her and her staff, notably Tereza Lewandowska of the society's library.

Jon Newsom, head of the music division at the Library of Congress in Washington, D.C., read the manuscript chapter by chapter, as it rolled out of my typewriter (yes, typewriter), offered crucial musicological advice, saved me from committing egregious errors, and served as a patient teacher as I worked my way through Chopin's musical creation. I am most thankful to him.

In Paris, I am deeply indebted to Leszek Talko, the president of the Société Historique et Littéraire Polonaise (to which Chopin once belonged), for opening to me the resources of the société's library, a great repository of materials on Chopin's life in Paris and on Paris in the time of Chopin. Mr. Talko allowed me to work at the library long past normal hours and over weekends so that I could make full use of my time. At the library, I was advised and assisted by Ryszard Matura, Henryk M. Citko, and their associates. I wish to thank them for their patience. At the Bibliothèque Nationale of France, I received valuable guidance from Madame Ewa Talma-Davous in the music division.

In Los Angeles, Wanda Wilk, founder and honorary director of the Polish Music Reference Center at the School of Music at the University of Southern California, rendered me the vital courtesy of loaning—for much longer than she thought at first—the volumes of Chopin's Polish language correspondence and other literary materials without which my book could not have been written. My profound thanks go to Mrs. Wilk and the center.

I am grateful to the Polish Library in Washington, D.C., and its staff for locating a number of most helpful books in its collection and lending them to me for an exceedingly long time.

It should be noted that the idea of writing a Chopin biography germinated for me many years ago in conversations in New York with the distinguished American pianist Byron Janis and his wife, Maria Cooper Janis; they encouraged me to pursue my project and offered significant thoughts and suggestions.

In Washington, I had the pleasure of discussing my book in its early stages, and subsequently, with my pianist friend Eugene Istomin, one of the most respected performers of Chopin's works. He offered valuable advice as he read the manuscript.

This is my nineteenth book that my wife, Marianne, has read in early and late manuscript forms, editing, critiquing and, once more, being amazingly helpful in research, organization, and everything else it takes to have it all come together. Obrigado.

As usual, Lisa Drew, my favorite editor and publisher of Lisa Drew Books at Scribner, made it amazingly easy for me to carry out this project (our fourth together), keeping me encouraged and optimistic from chapter to chapter. Charles Naylor edited the book with extraordinary musical and literary knowledge.

And, as usual, my friend Anne Sibbald at Janklow & Nesbit Literary Agency made it all happen smoothly and happily from day one to publication date.

Index